INSIDE
MARINE ONE

FOUR U.S. PRESIDENTS, ONE PROUD MARINE, AND THE WORLD'S MOST AMAZING HELICOPTER

Colonel Ray "Frenchy" L'Heureux
with Lee Kelley

ST. MARTIN'S PRESS
NEW YORK

SEP 2 3 2014

INSIDE MARINE ONE. Copyright © 2014 by Colonel Ray L'Heureux with Lee Kelley.
All rights reserved. Printed in the United States of America. For information, address
St. Martin's Press, 175 Fifth Avenue, New York, N.Y. 10010.

429 9679

www.stmartins.com

Design by Omar Chapa

Library of Congress Cataloging-in-Publication Data

L'Heureux, Ray, 1961–
  Inside Marine One : four U.S. Presidents, one proud Marine, and the world's most
amazing helicopter / Colonel Ray "Frenchy" L'Heureux with Lee Kelley.—First
edition.
      Pages cm
  ISBN 978-1-250-04144-9 (hardcover)
  ISBN 978-1-4668-3775-1 (e-book)
  1. L'Heureux, Ray.   2. Marine One (Presidential aircraft)   3. United States. Marine
Corps—Officers—Biography.   4. Helicopter pilots—United States—Biography.
5. Presidents—Transportation—United States.   6. Presidents—United States—
Anecdotes.   I. Kelley, Lee, 1971–   II. Title.
  TL723.L45 2014
  359.9'6092—dc23
[B]

2014008046

St. Martin's Press books may be purchased for educational, business, or promotional
use. For information on bulk purchases, please contact Macmillan Corporate and
Premium Sales Department at 1-800-221-7945, extension 5442, or write specialmarkets
@macmillan.com.

First Edition: June 2014

10 9 8 7 6 5 4 3 2 1

TO MY PARENTS,

ROGER AND VIRGINIA L'HEUREUX,

AND MY CHILDREN,

RAY JR. AND DELIA

CONTENTS

INTRODUCTION

As I banked the President's helicopter to the left, I was flying only about a hundred feet above a sea of people. It was the cold and clear morning of January 20, 2009, and I was flying President George W. Bush in *Marine One*, the world's most famous helicopter. This was his "victory lap," and we were cruising over a crowd of an estimated two million people who had gathered in Washington, D.C. for President Obama's inauguration ceremony.

The view through the glass of my cockpit was better than any 3-D movie screen could ever be. It was filled with a colorful panorama of waving hands, American flags on little sticks, and smiling faces breathing puffs of frost out through their hooded winter coats and caps. The Washington Monument and the Lincoln Memorial had become more than just historical landmarks for me. I used them as reference points to maintain a good altitude and circle over the National Mall once again.

From the ground, I can only imagine what people were thinking and feeling when they turned their eyes up at *Marine One*, the President's helicopter, with UNITED STATES OF AMERICA emblazoned in white letters on each side. I swung around in a wide circle as the crowd continued to cheer and wave, and I got another spectacular view of our nation's capital draped in the traditional bright red, white, and blue bunting that is used only once every four years. At one point, I actually caught a glimpse of my own helicopter on one of the many JumboTrons set up to display the inauguration ceremonies that day.

I had been President Bush's helicopter pilot for a couple of years and I had flown him all over the planet. I had grown accustomed to carrying precious cargo. But today was different. I wasn't carrying only President Bush, the man who had been my Commander in Chief until only a few moments earlier; I was also carrying First Lady Laura Bush, their two daughters, Jenna and Barbara, Jenna's husband, Henry Hager, and their grandparents, former President George H. W. Bush and former First Lady Barbara Bush.

I knew that both former President Bushes and their families were looking down at the same sights as I was. But what were they thinking about? What did the people below us see? And what did we look like to the millions of people around the world watching us on TV? My sense of pride and patriotism swelled within me. I was both energized and humbled by the small part I was playing in this theater of living history.

I had already made a couple of laps over the crowd, trying to bide my time while Vice President Cheney made his way in a separate helicopter to Andrews Air Force Base, where he would introduce President Bush for his farewell speech to a large crowd gathered there. I was enjoying this so much that I could easily have made a hundred more laps, but this was my third lap. The boss knew how long the trip took, and I had to get my passengers to Andrews. Finally, the call came over the radio that the Vice President was almost in place.

I smiled and turned *Marine One* smoothly to the east, then made a slight turn to the right, aiming at the well-known confluence of the

Potomac and Anacostia rivers, which led into Maryland. It had been a remarkable morning, and now it was time to land President Bush one last time. As I tried to soak in every moment of the historic flight, I was still amazed that a small-town boy from New England like me could be so lucky. . . .

My name is Ray "Frenchy" L'Heureux, and I am a former Colonel in the United States Marine Corps. I received my honorable discharge in 2011, after a thirty-year career. While I had many amazing experiences, the pinnacle of my career was serving in Marine Helicopter Squadron One (HMX-1). The first and largest aviation squadron in the Marine Corps, HMX-1 employs more than seven hundred hand-selected Marines, Sailors, and civilians, including a fleet of helicopters and its complement of pilots. HMX-1 has several different missions, but the primary and most visible one is providing executive transport to the President of the United States around the clock and around the globe.

Most people are aware that *Air Force One* is the President's plane, but fewer people realize that the President also has his own helicopter support (*Marine One*). Unlike most Americans, every move the President makes is closely coordinated. In fact, the President of the United States travels in one of three ways: in his motorcade, in *Air Force One*, or in *Marine One*. *Air Force One* will take the President on long flights, but his motorcade or *Marine One* will take him on the countless shorter trips once he arrives at his destination. And since flying in a helicopter doesn't require closing down streets and impacting local traffic, over the years it has become a preferred method of travel.

The United States is the only country in the world that provides executive transport to the Commander in Chief, no matter where he travels in the world. So, whether *Air Force One* brings the President from the White House to New York City or to Europe, *Marine One* will be right there standing by when he lands.

I joined the Marine Corps during college, and then spent most of my adult life chasing and exceeding all the flying dreams and aspirations I'd had as a kid. From 1992 until 1996, I served as a young Marine Officer in HMX-1, supporting President George H. W. Bush and then President Bill Clinton, and participating in many historical operations. More recently, in 2006, I returned to HMX-1 to serve as Commanding Officer of HMX-1, assuming the duties of Presidential Helicopter Pilot for George W. Bush and then Barack Obama.

People seem to love behind-the-scenes stories of *Marine One*. I have also realized just how unique my job—my responsibility—was. Each Commanding Officer serves for only four years. I was the twenty-second out of fewer than twenty-five *Marine One* pilots in history. And since I also flew President Bush (41) and President Clinton early in my career, I may be the only Presidential Pilot in HMX-1 history to "carry" four consecutive Presidents. I am also the only Presidential Pilot to carry the last two presidents of the twentieth century and the first two of the twenty-first.

Most people see the President only through the lens of the media or news, and very few people know anything about HMX-1 or the inner workings of the green-and-white helicopter that they see landing on or taking off from the White House lawn. I'm the grateful guy who had a bird's-eye view of it all. *Marine One* has been called the world's most famous helicopter. I won't dispute that. It still astounds me to think of all the people I have flown in that aircraft. I flew four Presidents, their families, and their staffs across the United States and around the world, day and night and in every kind of weather. I've been charged with flying some of the most enigmatic and well-known leaders and personalities of our time. I've gone hiking with Pope John Paul II. I shared drinks at Normandy with WWII vets. I landed *Marine One* on the lawn of Windsor Castle, and I went mountain biking across Camp David and the ranch in Crawford with President Bush.

This is a human story, as told in human terms by an average

Marine. It is a story of a life I could not of imagined, but also one of humility, and I was privileged to have lived the story as it unfolded. I have tried to live up to the standards that were ordained for me. I think I succeeded most of the time, but not all of the time. In the end, I remain the person my parents raised me to be, and the Marine I was inspired by others to be. Always moving forward, and when knocked down, standing up the only way one can—straight and true.

Let me share my story with you. I'll take you with me on my journey through the ranks of the Marines, tell you just what it took to be selected as a member of HMX-1, how I felt when I flew those incredible machines, and how I was eventually selected as the Presidential Pilot and HMX-1 Commander. It was truly a privilege and an honor that I'd like to share with you.

Let me take you inside *Marine One.*

CHAPTER 1

A YOUNG BOY DREAMS OF FLYING

Daydreamer

I was born in Salem, Massachusetts on July 24, 1961. A couple of years before that, my parents bought a three-story, sixteen-room, old Greek Revival–style house in historic Salem, about fifteen miles north of Boston. My dad was an electrical engineer. My mom was a devoted, hardworking homemaker, and they planned to fill the place with kids. That agenda seemed to work out perfectly, because I am the third of seven siblings. My sister Yvonne and my brother Roger are older than I. My sister Marilyn was born next, followed by my three brothers, Marc, Tommy, and Paul.

The house was built in the mid-1800s, and I imagine my parents must have thought that its location and size outweighed its age and impracticality. The style resembled a miniature Parthenon—a mint-green box with white trim and a peaked roof. For a long time, my sisters shared a room, Roger and I shared a room, and the three younger brothers shared another one. As we got older, we spread out into our own spaces, but in the early years my parents consolidated all of us kids, you might say, in that big old house. From a hundred feet up, the roof with its two chimneys would have just blended in with thousands of others, jutting out from the thousands of trees standing sentinel over our storied town, best known for the witch trials held there in the late seventeenth century and a certain house with seven gables.

It was one of those houses that any kid would love to grow up in. There were so many rooms and stairwells and alcoves and they all provided endless opportunities for fort-building and hiding. I'll never forget those spots where I could hide forever—just me and my scraped knees surrounded by the look and feel of our house's beautiful old woodwork. When you walked in the front door, there was a formal staircase with a large banister that twisted up in a pattern of squared turns all the way to the top. I could stand on the first floor and look all the way up. At the back end of the house was another stairway, originally a service stairway, which rose from the kitchen to the top floor. That one was enclosed. With sixteen rooms, three bedrooms, a basement, and two stairwells, hide-and-seek was elevated to a varsity level.

Almost all my family members were musically inclined, and most of them played several instruments. While I always loved music, and while the memories of Dave Brubeck through the whole house on Saturday mornings are very dear to me, I just didn't get the musical gene. In a house full of musicians, I was the only one who didn't play an instrument or sing harmony. However, as early as the age of six or seven, I was obsessed with the idea of being a pilot. Logan Airport was due south of us, and I looked up into the sky over my neighborhood and watched countless planes going in and out of Boston.

I remember one airline that painted their planes bright yellow, and I loved to watch the big metal birds leave their contrails across the sky, imagining I was their pilot. At the time, the airline industry was growing and the wide-bodied jet was coming into fruition. McDonnell Douglas had their big DC-10, Boeing had the 747 jet, and Lockheed Martin had the L-1011. Just the sheer power and size of those aircraft fascinated me. Even though this was near the end of the Vietnam War, I wasn't really interested in high-performance aircraft yet. I was enamored with the whole commercial-airline industry and loved those big wide-bodied jets. By this time I had my own room overlooking the backyard and the walls were plastered with pictures of my heroes—pilots like Chuck Yeager and Amelia Earhart, and astronauts like Neil Armstrong and Buzz Aldrin.

Eventually, it wasn't enough to see the planes way up in the sky or on TV or even in my imagination. I wanted to get my hands on them. I would walk with my friends down to the local department store, Almy's, and check out the model airplanes made by a company called Revell. I started saving up my allowance and birthday money and even raking leaves or shoveling snow to earn money. I pretty much spent my money on model airplanes and movies. Some of the original models were pretty simple, but so much fun. I had a small mahogany school desk in my room, and I turned this into my work center. My dad gave me one of those gooseneck lamps, which stood in the corner of the desk.

If you ever made model airplanes or cars, you'll probably remember the excitement of opening the box. They always had cool photos on the lid and they always had that new-car smell when you started taking the parts out. I liked to open each box carefully and set it on its side near the edge of the desk so I always had a picture of what the plane should look like when I was done. The parts were shrink-wrapped, and I did my own inventory as I spread the parts out and read the instructions. Some of the smaller ones were mostly just an exercise in snapping parts together. They only took about ten or fifteen minutes to assemble, but I enjoyed the small parts, the precision required, and the smell of the paint.

My buddy Brad was a model-car freak and had quite a collection. Sometimes I packed up my collection in a box and transported it to Brad's house, where we would compare our craftsmanship. He showed me his model Mustangs or Barracudas, and the overall quality and precision always looked so much better than my airplanes. He knew how to use matches to create the look of exhaust and road grime on the tire wells, and he taught me that using spray paint was the way to go, especially on the larger parts.

I went through the first dozen models pretty fast and also made a lot of those simple balsa-wood glider planes. Whether it was gluing pennies to the nose to add stability or creating my own unique little rotors on the tail wings, I tried every imaginable experiment. I launched many wooden planes out my window, harassing the chickens that my dad always had in the backyard. After a while, there were a 747 and a couple of biplanes hanging at various angles from my ceiling. It was my own private aerodrome. I could soar, in my imagination, to my heart's content. While the rest of my family slept, I flew over the United States, across the Atlantic, all the way over Europe and Asia, crossing the Pacific and landing back in Salem. Here's the thing, though: I never built a helicopter. . . .

I built and built and graduated into more-complex models. I remember one day buying a DC-10 replica. I had saved some money, and I walked to Almy's department store and bought the plane. It felt like ten miles but it was probably only a few blocks. When I got home, I ran straight up to my room and got started. I opened the box and started pulling out all the parts. It was an American Airlines jet.

Over the next couple of weeks, the project became a competing priority with everything, even my homework. On the weekends, when my brothers and sisters were running around, I was in my room with my model airplane. I was late for dinner a few times, and in my household that was a capital crime. After assembling and painting every little detail, even the seats in the passenger area, I put the finishing touches on the exterior paint job with a can of spray paint in the backyard. As soon as it was dry, I carried it back up to my room and set it on my desk on its landing gear. I stood back and surveyed my work. It looked beautiful. It was kind of like the moment when Ralphie, in the movie *A Christmas Story,* finally got his Red Rider BB gun. I considered my building of that beautiful DC-10 model one of the greatest accomplishments of my life. Even then, as I looked at the completed model, I was thinking about the day when I'd get to sit in the cockpit and fly a plane just like that.

My First Time in the Sky

Probably every boy dreams of flying at one point, but very few ever have the chance to do it. One spring morning when I was twelve, I was sitting at the breakfast table with the whole family before school. It was a Monday, and as a kid that was not my favorite morning—an interruption to my weekend daydreams.

While everyone rushed to shovel food into their mouths and get out the door, my mother, a woman with blue eyes and auburn hair, smirked knowingly into her cereal for a few minutes before announcing, "Well, I won something in the church drawing yesterday, and I've decided to give it to Ray."

I stopped spooning my Lucky Charms and looked up at her. "You did?"

Smiling, she said, "Yes, and guess what?"

"What?"

"It's a free flying lesson in a real airplane!"

In the next instant I was jumping up and down, my arms wrapped around her, saying "thank you, thank you" over and over. I caught some jealous looks from my siblings at first, but I think they all understood how much flying would mean to me, and they never said a thing. It was excruciating going to school that day—all I could think about was flying.

I kept bugging my mom for every little detail about the plane all week. When Saturday finally rolled around, the whole family came along on the drive out to the Beverly, Massachusetts, Municipal Airport, which was more like an airstrip for small planes. We met the pilot instructor, a tall guy who was probably in his late twenties. He towered over me, with dark hair like mine and a serious expression that would break from time to time into a smile. Since he was the first real pilot I had ever met in person, I quickly added him to my growing list of personal heroes.

While my parents filled out some paperwork, I kept looking out the airport office windows at the little white Piper Cherokee with red stripes I'd soon be flying in. It was a tiny, single-engine plane with just enough room for a pilot, a copilot, and a little bit of cargo in the back, yet it dwarfed the model planes that covered the shelves in my room, and to me, that made it larger than life.

The pilot brought me into a small classroom in the back of the main terminal to discuss some of the safety precautions and other requirements. I wasn't expecting this part. I just wanted to fly. I couldn't stop looking around at the posters with safety messages and illustrations of aviation instruments and planes.

I was trying to pay attention, and nodding along with whatever he was saying, when suddenly he got very serious, bent down, and said, "If I tell you we have an emergency, I want you to do nothing but sit on your hands. If I have already issued you the controls, I will take them back from you. I need you to say nothing and sit on your hands." He wasn't joking.

I had never flown in a plane before, so when we walked out to the runway, it was the closest I had ever come to a real aircraft. He escorted me around the plane, which was only about twenty to twenty-five feet, and when we finally sat down in the cockpit, our shoulders were touching. I was speechless before the shiny, intricate detail of the instruments. My entire field of view was dominated by this huge instrument panel, and I could hardly see over it. These levers and dials and pedals and switches were all new to me. I wanted to click, push, pull, and press everything.

I was trying to act grown-up as the instructor gave me a brief orientation to the main controls. I kept nodding to indicate that I was paying attention, but I just wanted to fly! Then he started the engines and began to taxi toward the runway. We moved slowly. The sound of the engine roared in my ears. I kept one eye on the scene ahead of me, the runway rolling quickly below us, and the other eye on the pilot's hands. He began to pick up speed. He got faster and faster and, all at once, he lifted us off the ground! I felt that lift in my stomach. I was in the sky! I couldn't believe it. After building all those models and dreaming of being a pilot soaring over the earth, I was in the sky!

There was a set of tandem controls, typical in general-aviation airplanes. Once we were airborne, he let me handle the controls for a while and I could feel the plane respond when I pushed forward or pulled back or otherwise manipulated the controls, causing the plane to climb, dive, or roll. I could feel how sensitive the controls were to my touch. The pilot gave me some pointers, and I think I was a fast learner, but my strongest memory of that day was the view. For the next hour, we flew over our little town.

He pointed out certain landmarks and neighborhoods I barely recognized, and then we flew over my house, my school, and my friends' houses. From that altitude, my town looked like one of those towns you see under a Christmas tree with a toy train circling it. Even the Beverly Airport looked tiny from that elevation. At takeoff, the airport runway looked enormous. It was the biggest runway I'd ever seen. From that altitude, it was just a gray strip of asphalt carved into a field of green.

After maybe half an hour, the pilot took back the controls, and I sat wide-eyed as we drew closer to the runway. We got lower and lower. I was a little afraid, but I knew the pilot was in control. My family, below, slowly got larger, pointing up and clapping for me, my little brother Tommy jumping up and down. I felt like a hero. The pilot landed gently. I noticed the way he put the brakes on and stopped the plane exactly where he wanted. His control was incredible. After that day there was no doubt what I wanted to do with my life; I was hooked on flying. I wanted to be a pilot, just like that guy.

That was one day I'll never forget. As I got older, making model airplanes gradually was replaced, as it is with a lot of boys, by thinking a lot about girls. What can I say? It happens. I was starting to date and hanging out more with my friends, but one thing never changed: my dream of becoming a pilot. It only became stronger and stayed with me no matter what girl I met or friend I made. That day at the Beverly Municipal Airport gave me my goal in life.

A College with Wings

Life rolled on and I grew up, pretty much like any other guy. Between my sophomore and junior years of high school, my family moved to New Hampshire. I always had a job and was working as a dishwasher at the time, and I was almost sixteen. Seeing a way to use my dishwashing skills to hang out with friends and meet girls, I had signed up to work as part of the kitchen staff at a girls' summer camp. I mean, how great was that? A job *and* girls! I went there right after school let out that year. When the camp was over, my family picked me up and we drove to the new house in New Hampshire. All my boxes had been stuffed into my new room. I went off to the camp from Salem, Massachusetts and came back to a new neighborhood, a new high school, and a new city in New Hampshire.

I got a job as a waiter in one of the local restaurants, started dating a bit more seriously, and moved toward my final year of high school. And I still had no doubt about what I wanted to be. My dad wanted me to go to Boston College, but I had other plans. Even though there were more-inexpensive colleges nearby, such as the University of New Hampshire, I had my eyes on a private school called Nathaniel Hawthorne, which had a flight program. The idea of joining the military didn't even cross my mind.

I had been drooling over the college brochure, which featured scenic photos of the campus in the fall, and the DC-3 aircraft that was the workhorse of their flight program. When the school started advertising an open house for prospective students, my parents really didn't want to go, so I persuaded a couple of my buddies to go with me. We drove up for the open house and received a quick tour of the campus, which was very green and appealing to me. Before long we made our way to the small airport that was actually part of the school. I loved to see the pilots' lounge, to smell the fuel out on the runway, to see the little hangars and maintenance sheds all over, and especially to see the old DC-3 aircraft painted in the school colors with the Hawthorne College logo emblazoned on both sides.

I couldn't have been more excited when it was time for the flight. I knew that the DC-3 was the one of the original transport planes and had been used pretty extensively in WW II (when it was called a C-47, or Sky Train). I was impatient to fly. We received a short safety briefing and then approached the aircraft. It was a "tail dragger," so the tail sat low and the cockpit high. When we boarded, the plane was angled back, so we had to walk up a slight incline to find our seats. I got to see the cockpit briefly, but this wasn't another flying lesson just yet. This was a joy ride, and my buddies and I sat in the back with other kids, some of whom had their parents with them.

It was about a thirty-minute ride over the campus, and over the mountains of southern New Hampshire. They were trying to give the parents the best possible ride because they were also trying to "sell" the school and its flight program.

As I walked off the plane and talked to the pilot some more, I thought, *This is where I want to be.* Before we left that day, I made sure I had a handful of school information that included the application. Picturing myself as a student in this aviation program brought my dream of becoming a pilot to life.

My application was accepted, and when I graduated from high school in 1979, I packed up my stuff and eagerly relocated to the college campus. I bought an old Ford Maverick from my buddy Darren for $150, and it didn't even have a heater. I didn't care, as long as the car could make the one-hour drive between college and home.

Moving into the dorms was exciting, and before long I landed a job as a waiter near the school. I could still see my girlfriend on the weekends. I knew (and my parents reminded me) that this was an expensive proposition. First of all, it was a private school with high tuition. But more important, the flight program came with additional expenses that I wasn't sure how I was going to afford. My parents and my grandmother agreed to help out as much as they could. I also worked as much as possible, applied for every grant I could find, and maxed out the available student loans. Somehow, I patched together enough money to get started. I was an Aeronautical Science major who was officially earning his pilot's license.

I was required to enroll in the same academic core curriculum as any other major, but I also had to take courses like aeronautical science, transportation economics, and meteorology. In my young mind, these were the kinds of things pilots had to know,. At one point, I spent literally my last penny to buy a pair of aviation sunglasses. I thought I was pretty cool, all things considered.

My classmates and I were also indoctrinated into the pilot program. I met the flight instructors and set up my curriculum. Although each student went through the same training, they didn't necessarily go through it at the same pace. This was partly because some people struggle to learn different aspects of flying more than others do. But mostly it was a financial issue. Getting into the cockpit and up in the air was obviously a key part of the program, and you could actually fly as much as you wanted (within reason). But here was the catch: you had to maintain at least five hundred dollars in your flight account, and this was used to cover the one-hundred-dollars-per-hour cost for fuel, maintenance, and instructional flying.

As a waiter I was making a little over a dollar an hour plus tips and my flight account got drained very quickly. I didn't always have the money to replenish it. It didn't take me long to realize that I was going to school mostly with people whose families could afford to fund their educations. I remember using one of the pay phones in the training area one day, and a kid next to me said into the phone, "Hey, Dad, I need you to deposit another four thousand dollars into my flight account, okay?" I couldn't help but eavesdrop, and when the kid said "thanks," I was astounded to realize that his dad must have said "sure." My parents would have done the same thing if they could, no doubt in my mind, but they just couldn't. So, although I was keeping up with the classwork and overall syllabus, my limited flight account was keeping me on the ground way too much, and slowing down the best part of the program—flying!

Eventually, the cost of my tuition, books, and flight-program expenses became too much, and left me with a crucial choice: opt into a cheaper degree and give up the dream of flying or find another way to pay for college. I had six brothers and sisters, and I didn't want to place any additional burden on my parents, who had always been so supportive. I dropped out of the flight program and changed my major to Aviation Management. I wasn't depressed about it. I maintained a positive outlook, but I was disappointed with the realization that I wasn't going to be able to finish college, and take the necessary steps to finish pilot training all at the same time.

I needed a new plan.

CHAPTER 2

FROM BRAVO COMPANY TO HMX-1

Boot Camp, USMC Reserves, and College

Even though I grew up daydreaming about being a pilot, I really didn't know much about all those heroic pilots dropping Marines into combat zones under enemy fire. They were fighting overseas, defending us, and for me it was a world away. It was the Vietnam War era, a tough time for the military. Many people were unfortunately turning away from the armed forces.

Shortly after I dropped out of the flight program, something shifted. I had vaguely noticed Marine Corps recruiting pamphlets around campus, but I was already in flight school so I didn't pay them much attention. In fact, I had probably walked countless times past the small table in the cafeteria where the Marine recruiter hung out. Suddenly I was much more cognizant of the recruiting pamphlets, especially the ones about Marine Aviation. I noticed that some of the pamphlets were all about becoming a Marine pilot. There was also a video presentation on a continuous loop showing the various Marine aircraft. The videos were kind of corny and predictable, but I still liked them. Jets making sharp turns and leaving contrails across the sky. The afterburners lighting up as the aircraft took off into a fiery sunset. I think there might even have been a couple of helicopters in the video.

One day, instead of entering the cafeteria and just walking past the table, I stopped by. The Marine sitting there stood up, looked me right in the eye, and put his hand out. I shook his hand, and he introduced himself and asked my name. From that moment forward he called me by my first name.

"Are you in the flight program, Ray?"

"Well, I was, but I had to drop out because I couldn't afford the expenses." He caught me off guard, and I said too much too soon. I think I saw a little glimmer in his eye, and I think he knew he had me.

He immediately launched into an explanation of the Marine Corps aviation history, and told me that by joining the Marines I would have a chance to become a Marine pilot. The Marines would train me and pay for everything. I knew the rumors about recruiters, and while he was a nice guy who answered all my questions, I also knew that he was probably trying to meet a quota. Still, I had to admit that his uniform looked pretty sharp, and he seemed to have his stuff together.

I didn't want to rush into anything, but before I knew it I was filling out forms, we were playing phone tag, and then I took the initial evaluations to see if I met the basic requirements. The process had begun, and then it seemed almost inevitable. I also learned that you had to be an officer to become a pilot, and at that point I was only halfway toward my degree. The recruiter convinced me that it would be a good idea just to enlist as an infantryman first, to set the foundation for my career, and then I could decide about becoming an officer in a couple of years.

So that's exactly what I did. I became the first person in my family to join the military, and spent the next couple of years serving as an infantryman in the Marine Corps Reserves. But first, between my freshman and sophomore year of college, I had to go to boot camp at Parris Island, South Carolina.

In the Marine Corps, boot camp lasts twelve weeks—pretty much the entire summer break. To a certain degree, boot camp is like a factory that takes young men and women from all walks of life and transforms them into Marines. The training is broken up into three phases. There is a great deal of classroom instruction, but it's mostly hands-on training in the field. Marching and learning all the accurate drills is a major element of the disciplined environment, and you learn everything from marksmanship, to hand-to-hand combat, to tactical infantry maneuvers over and over again. The concepts of "team," "esprit de corps," and "brotherhood" are reinforced. I'm sure that to some degree, every Marine has similar experiences in boot camp. But we all end up seeing it differently depending on our state of mind, our physical abilities, and all those personal challenges we carry with us.

On the rainy day I headed off to boot camp in 1980, there was no fanfare, just me telling my wife and family goodbye at the Manchester Municipal Airport in New Hampshire. I could tell that my parents were proud, though Mom was anxious. I think they were nervous because they knew less about the Marine Corps than I did—and that wasn't much. I found myself sitting on plastic airport chairs with two other kids from the area. We swapped stories and proved just how little we knew. This was a completely new adventure for me. I had never even flown in a commercial aircraft.

As I boarded and found my seat, I admired the sheer size of this big Conair twin-engine plane. I did a quick mental assessment, comparing the gigantic airplane to the scale of my model airplanes. I surmised that the aircraft had probably been built in the fifties or sixties. The first leg of the flight was to LaGuardia International Airport in New York, and I had a seat just aft of the wing, giving me a clear view of all the aircraft's control movements. I took in every moment of the takeoff and landing and listened to the landing gear retract into the belly like talons under the body of a bird. When we touched down, we bounded and then touched down again, and I heard and felt the brakes. We switched planes and then flew into Savannah, Georgia. And that's where I got my first reality check.

I yawned and walked out of the terminal, stopping to hit the bathroom like any other traveler. I was still oblivious, just walking with my fellow recruits, wearing jeans and absorbing my surroundings. I had never even been away from home. And then we turned a corner and I saw a gaggle of other kids that looked just like me, anxious and unaware. It was a very diverse crowd, and as I walked up, a Marine approached and asked my name. I told him, then handed over the official orders my recruiter had told me to carry. The Marine checked me off a list with his pencil and directed me where to sit. I quickly realized that they were marshaling recruits from all over the country to move us to Parris Island together.

And then, right there in the middle of that crowd, something started happening. From somewhere, a domineering energy started to assert itself over the group. Loud, even angry voices were being raised and I thought, *What is going on here?* And, for the first time, I saw the famous Marine drill instructors. These were men who looked hardened; they were physically fit and steely-eyed and wore big wide-brim hats and perfectly starched uniforms. And they were not being kind. They seemed genuinely pissed that we were using up good oxygen. They were staring people down, intimidating us, playing the power game to see how we would react. My first thought was, *Jeez, we're civilians. We're in a public place. They can't treat us like that.* Boy, was I wrong. . . .

They were yelling at people to stay seated, and directing them exactly where to sit. Hundreds of us sat Indian-style in rows. As I looked around and nodded at the kids near me, and as I instinctively kept my head down and just kept quiet until I understood what was expected of me, I realized that I was now in the system. I still had on my jeans and sneakers, but I was definitely being treated like a recruit.

After a few hours it was time to load the buses. So far, I had been yelled at only a little, and I hadn't done anything except look around. That was all about to change. A dozen drill sergeants moved us through the crowd like ushers from Hell, herding and jostling us into the bus. "Get up and get on my bus." The ride from Savannah to Parris Island, in Beaufort, South Carolina, took about an hour, and there were about fifty kids on my bus. The bus was quiet and tense. You could have cut the tension with a knife, it was so thick. There were also a couple of drill instructors sitting up in the front row. Even they were being quiet, but I guessed correctly that it wouldn't last.

Everyone's eyes and ears perked up when we stopped at a guard gate briefly before driving into Parris Island. Everyone sat up straight. I remember looking down as we passed and seeing Marines standing guard who looked young like me. *That's my future,* I thought. Even though it was dark, I could see the old World War II–style building I had seen in movies, the linear landscaping and architecture that symbolize military bases. I saw the perfectly manicured training fields, and the trees everywhere, and I knew I had entered a whole new world.

When you first get off the bus at Parris Island, before you're even assigned to the company that you'll train with, you are inducted into the Marine Corps through a receiving barracks. This is the initial place they take you for basic medical evaluations, to assign you gear and uniforms, and to have you fill out tons of paperwork. When we pulled up to the receiving barracks, we were all looking out the bus windows, and I was getting a little nervous. You know that feeling you get that something very bad is about to happen? Well, that's the feeling I had. The bus rolled to a slow stop. The drill sergeants in the front of the bus stood up, turned around, and began screaming. More drill sergeants boarded the bus, and then all joined together in an angry chorus of demands and insults: "Are you stupid?"; "Can you hear me?"; "Do you know your right foot from your left?"; "Do you think this is a joke?"; "Do you want your mommy?"

There were hundreds of yellow footprints painted in formation right there on the street. They looked like the soles of two boots spread a few inches apart and facing outward at a forty-five-degree angle. The drill instructors were pissed off and impatient. They wanted us to keep our bags off the ground and move in an orderly manner. It felt more like complete chaos, and I quickly realized that even if you do exactly what you're told, it's still wrong. Nobody was going to be right. None of us knew a damn thing. We were screwed up and they took every opportunity to point out just how much.

I stood on the yellow footprints and tried to stare straight ahead as they were yelling at us to do. But this caused a dilemma because many of the drill instructors were also yelling at people, "Don't look at me. Look straight ahead." This didn't work when they stood right in front of you and stared in your face. All I could hear after a while were the various drill instructors yelling over one another, because us recruits were saying very little except "sir, yes sir," or whatever they told us to say.

I had been told what to do by teachers and parents and bosses lots of times. I could take direction. But it was never this kind of aggressive, demeaning, apparently blind fury. I knew (or hoped I did) that they wouldn't hurt me physically, so I just did exactly what I was told. I tried to blend in, but sometimes I looked up and made eye contact, and got yelled at. It was almost like I'd just gotten caught in the line of some drill instructor's fire. Just hours earlier, I had been back in New Hampshire. A college kid. Now, I was a Marine recruit standing at attention in a place I didn't know, being yelled at by drill instructors who could snap me in two, if they wanted to. I was scared shitless.

Eventually, we were broken down into groups and assigned to a squad bay in the receiving barracks. In what would become three months of learning a new culture and vocabulary, I soon learned that a bed was a "rack." When we began the process of filling out paperwork, everyone had to sit down and write a short letter home. It was a form letter, and basically said, "Hi, Mom and Dad. I've arrived. I'm okay. Don't call me. I'll call you." Within a day, my head was shaved and I looked like everyone else. Individuality was discouraged. All my civilian belongings had been taken until after graduation, and I was issued a sea-bag that contained my new wardrobe—camouflage utility uniforms and PT clothes.

Next, they assigned me to Delta Company, Platoon 2028, 2nd Recruit Training Battalion. When I went to sleep in my strange and jarring new environment, surrounded by unknowns, the shady breezeways and cozy library of Nathaniel Hawthorne College seemed very far away.

To put it simply, boot camp is designed to break you down, mentally and physically, and then use that clean slate to build you back up as a Marine. I did pretty well with the mental part of boot camp. Inside, it took some getting used to. Part of you wants to scream back and then another part doesn't dare to blink an eye. With so many people and personalities, there were lots of different reactions. Some kids seemed to have it together and just took it in stride. Other kids, even some who thought they were tough, just wilted under the gaze of the drill instructors, and broke down in tears.

Whether we were drilling for hours on end until everyone's heels clicked at the same exact time, or whether we were being forced on a twelve-mile hump with packs on sandy and treacherous trails, I just gritted my teeth and pushed on. One night in the first week, I was one of a row of those kids we've all seen in movies standing at attention at the foot of their racks at 3:00 A.M. while the drill instructors screamed because the floor wasn't shiny enough. My name wasn't so easy to spell or pronounce, and I actually think it saved me from being called out so much in the beginning.

Nevertheless, the drill instructors were masters at the art of sensing and exploiting any weakness, any individuality. I mostly stayed out of trouble, and out of the way, and learned to compartmentalize my feelings when a grown man was standing with his nose inches from mine, breathing his lunch in my face, and screaming at me as if I had personally offended his mother. As I was forced to do countless push-ups, sit-ups, leg squats, or other exercises until I reached muscle failure, I don't remember ever crying. But I do remember being angry, being scared, wanting to rebel, and feeling frustrated as I was constantly punished and corrected, even for someone else's mistake. More than once, I thought to myself, *Holy shit. Did I make a big mistake? These guys are nuts. What in the hell am I doing here?*

As I got better at controlling my emotions and showing only a blank mask of obedience to the drill instructors, I was able to see through the immediate intensity and focus on the larger lessons I was being taught: Follow orders. Pay attention to details. Don't try to be an individual. Do what's best for the overall organization. Look out for your brothers in arms. Another thing that was ingrained in us from day one was diversity and acceptance. It didn't matter where someone was from or what they looked like. The drill instructors made it crystal clear that there were only two kinds of Marines: light green Marines and dark green Marines. Period.

The Vietnam War had just ended and most of the drill instructors had Vietnam campaign ribbons on their uniforms. These were battle-hardened Marines, fresh from the conflict in Southeast Asia, and now they were focusing every ounce of their energy and attention on making sure we could follow in their footsteps. Or else. They had been trained to instill in us the Marine ethos, a mental and physical toughness that would drive us to overcome any obstacle put in our way.

Everyone knew that they really weren't supposed to hit us, but the drill instructors were covering for one another. They certainly wouldn't hesitate to slap or punch someone in the gut. At one point in the training we learned close combat with "Pugil sticks." Imagine long sticks with fairly hard pads on each end, like a giant Q-tip. We had to stand in the center of the group and face off against one another, or compete against other squads and platoons. My platoon actually won the Pugil stick competition, and one of the drill instructors started carrying a Pugil stick around with him everywhere. Many times while we were standing in formation being yelled at for something, this particular drill sergeant would walk down the line looking for any reason to instill discipline. When he was displeased with something about how you looked or sounded, he would just pop you in the head with the end of the Pugil stick. I watched him do this a few times through my peripheral vision, and felt lucky when he passed me without hitting me in the face.

As a kid and in high school, I had never been more than generally interested in sports or exercise. I certainly played sports as a kid, and I was pretty good when I applied myself. During high school I was more busy partying with my friends and dating than worrying about any kind of fitness. Likewise, I didn't pursue any sports in college. Sure, I hit the gym a little bit here and there, but it wasn't a big focus of my life at all. I would say I was in average shape when I arrived at boot camp. Very early on, we had to do an inventory physical fitness test, or PFT. The test consisted of pull-ups, a three-mile run, and sit-ups. Of course, everyone was comparing their performance and competing. A lot of people couldn't pass even the most basic physical requirements, while some kids scored the maximum of 300 on their first physical fitness test. I fell somewhere in the middle.

During this period I was eating like a madman, drinking huge volumes of water, absorbing so much training, sweating off body fat I didn't know I had, and running more than I ever thought possible. I was getting whipped into the best shape of my life in a relatively short period of time, and I noticed. I was getting faster on each run, and I liked it. Over the course of boot camp, I progressed physically from somewhere in the middle to much closer to the high end. Boot camp is truly where my lifelong love of fitness and running took root, and led me to compete in many triathlons later in life.

By design, most people go through an internal shift at around week nine or ten. By that point, you have been there long enough that you are immersed, mentally and physically. You like the way you feel, the growing strength and energy, and you take pride in reducing the frequency with which you screw up. It definitely happened to me. In that little microcosm of 2nd Battalion on Parris Island in 1980, I did take pride when my platoon did the right thing. It felt good when we looked sharp and made our turns and stops in unison. It felt so good to triumph over the other groups in competition. It felt good to run faster and harder and longer. I was becoming a Marine.

During the first few weeks, I noticed groups that had arrived before us. They looked different because they had been working hard, and it showed. They also looked different because they were allowed to "blouse" their trousers. This meant that instead of their trousers just hanging loosely near the bottoms of their boots, which made them look generally sloppy, they put these little blousing bands inside the bottoms of their trousers. Now their trousers seemed to stop around the top of the boot. This was how Marines should look, and we did not.

As we neared the final month of boot camp, we were told to carry our blousing bands in our pockets. We weren't deserving enough to use them yet, of course, but we at least could hope. After dragging it out over and over and really building it up, we finally performed one single task very well. The drill instructor was pleased. Finally, he gave us the order to "blouse boots!" From that point on, we were the cool guys. We were the ones that the new recruits looked up to.

The biggest physical and mental challenge of the entire three months, again by design, was a simulated war exercise that took place at Elliot Beach (we called it "EB"). It was like a big final exam in which you were pushed and tested in everything you had learned mentally, physically, and tactically. It was a big deal, and failing in that exercise could easily get you sent home. It wasn't supposed to test just our personal mettle; this was about coming together as a team. I made it through, and I learned even more about myself and the power of teamwork. We completed that exercise and marched back to the barracks, and we knew that the rest of our time was going to be smooth sailing—admin, paperwork, and getting ready for graduation. I stood with a deep sense of accomplishment and pride at the Emblem Ceremony, where we were all presented with the infamous Eagle, Globe and Anchor emblem that personifies the Marine Corps.

I was in the best shape of my life, I felt like after that I could handle just about anything, and I definitely shared that perverse pride that comes with completing boot camp. I had never been so proud of anything as that moment at graduation when they addressed us as Marines for the first time in twelve long weeks. About seventy-five of us had started, and about fifty-five of us had earned the title of United States Marine.

When I returned to New Hampshire to continue my college studies, I was still Ray L'Heureux, but—even though I thought I hadn't—I had changed: I felt stronger and more confident in almost every aspect of my life, and I enjoyed being a new Marine. I was assigned to Bravo Company, 25th Marines, a Marine Reserve detachment in Manchester, New Hampshire. I trained with them one weekend a month while I finished my degree. I also began seriously to think about the idea of becoming an officer and a Marine pilot. Along with all the other big steps I was taking at the time, I took one more: I got married. And then it happened: during my junior year of college, Dianna and I had our first child, Ray Jr., in July 1982. Besides being a new Marine, I was now also a proud dad and I said to myself, "Go for it!"

That's all it took. I began to coordinate with the Officer's Selection office in Manchester. Eventually, I secured a guaranteed aviation spot, which meant a new set of contracts. I would no longer be a Marine Reservist. Now I was going to be an officer candidate who would enter active duty after graduating from college. If I made it through OCS and all the flight training, I would "owe" the Marine Corps six years of service in exchange for my training.

Officer Candidate School and Early Flight Training

I graduated from Nathaniel Hawthorne College in May 1983, with a Bachelor's Degree in Aviation Management. My daughter Delia was born that day, and then I shipped back out to Marine Base Quantico. It was time for OCS, which included ten weeks of officer training completely focused on developing Marine officers. At boot camp, the PT went from easier to more difficult. At OCS, we did PT all the time. It was intense and some of the grueling obstacle courses defined the word *grueling*.

We also spent a lot of time in the classroom. We learned foundational leadership skills, core principles, tactics, and Marine Corps history we would need to someday lead Marines. Most important, we were placed in varying leadership roles in the platoon and rigorously evaluated and coached on our performance. Again, poor performance could get you sent home.

Ten weeks passed, and I graduated near the top of my class at OCS. I was a 2nd Lieutenant—a Marine officer—and I left Quantico even more determined to become a Marine aviator. Just a couple of months later, I was right back at Quantico for The Basic School. This course was required for all new Marine officers and was my last obstacle before starting flight school! In my mind, The Basic School was a natural extension of OCS, and it further developed the skills I would need to lead and mentor Marines.

In the spring of 1984, I moved to Pensacola, Florida, the cradle of Marine Corps aviation, and finally entered the Aviation Indoctrination Program at the Naval Air Station there. This is where all Navy, Marine Corps, Coast Guard, and even some international pilots begin their flight training. We initially rented a home just a few miles from base and lived there for the next two years.

I started the training with around twenty other people, but it's a very dynamic, challenging, and competitive process. Approximately 50 percent of the class didn't graduate. And there were plenty of ways to wash out of the training: you could have been psychologically unfit to fly or unable to handle the physical demands. People are held back or kicked out for poor performance, medical issues, or any number of other reasons. So, you get ahead of some of your buddies, or get behind them, but you pretty much see many of the same faces throughout your two years there. Additionally, there are always classes that started ahead of you and new classes beginning. I was just one of maybe a thousand faces somewhere inside that big, complex training cycle.

Here's the real killer: everyone knew that if you didn't graduate from flight school, you got "grounded" but still had to finish your active-duty commitment. I knew there was nothing wrong with being part of the ground forces, but that wasn't my goal. Compared to college, boot camp, OCS, and The Basic School, for me this was the most exciting. I probably never wanted anything so badly. My attitude was that I had made the choice to be there, I had taken on the commitment, so I might as well pour my heart and soul into the training.

The training was set up in a "crawl-walk-run" style of syllabus that is very common in the military. This meant I learned one small step at a time, but each new step built on the last. We started with six weeks in a classroom before even touching an aircraft, including courses like Basic Engineering, Meteorology, and Aerodynamics. I was so excited that the information learned in the classroom could be parlayed into the cockpit, and I was intent on being a great student. The thought of flying kept me on the books.

Being a Marine meant working with a dynamic and ever-changing cast of characters that inspired me, taught me, and made me laugh, while a few of them become lifelong friends. I forged a relationship with Steve Paquette during this period. He is one of those people. Steve is from Chippewa Falls, Wisconsin. He's the kind of person everyone wants to be around, and he has an infectious laugh.

Steve and I, and other buddies we met along the way, would study together and test each other's knowledge. Once we completed the rigorous academic portion of the training, we moved to nearby Whiting Field, Florida, to begin the actual flight training. Since I was married, I lived in base housing with my wife and two young kids. First up, I was introduced to the T-34 Charlie, a turbo-charged aircraft that the Navy used as a basic flight-training plane. It's about the same size as the Piper Cherokee I had taken my first lesson in as a kid, but the T-34 could fly circles around that little commercial aircraft. It was a two-seater with a jet engine, so it was "acrobatic." Part of the training included doing loops, rolls, half loops, split S's, and a slew of other stunts. I thought, *All right, this is way cooler than the Piper Cherokee I started learning to fly back in college!*

I started spending more and more time in the air around the Florida coast, learning to fly and maneuver as they led us through yet another crawl-walk-run syllabus. I was also learning all the safety and emergency procedures. Water-survival training was one of the more intense parts of this phase. The first step was to go through "drown proofing," which included several mental and physical tests, like swimming a mile and treading water with twenty-five pounds of full flight gear on, including my Nomex flight suit, steel-toed boots, gloves, a survival vest, and a heavy helmet.

The biggest challenge that everyone talked about was "The Dunker." Imagine a mock cockpit with no doors, and then imagine being seated in that pretend cockpit with all your seatbelts and safety straps secured and buckled tightly, and then being blindfolded. Now imagine that cockpit dropping into and sinking to the bottom of an Olympic-size swimming pool. The Dunker was one of the most feared courses in the school, designed to simulate crashing in water and escaping a sinking aircraft. Before any Marine could fly, he had to dunk.

On the day of the test, some people pretended to be very excited. Others were obviously scared to death. I had already watched a couple of classmates freak out under the water, so when it was my turn, I tried my best to keep my cool. I had paid attention in the briefing and I knew that the key was to stay calm and follow procedures. I climbed in and an instructor secured all my safety belts and then blindfolded me. He explained that my goal was to "release your safety harness, climb out of the cockpit, and swim to the surface." I nodded, taking lots of deep breaths while I still could.

And then it was time. After a short countdown, the cockpit slid backward and crashed through the surface of the water, flipping end-over-end as it sank to the bottom. I was completely disoriented as the cockpit filled with water, the stinging scent of chlorine filling my nose. I managed to gulp a large breath of air just before the little cabin filled up completely. I felt lucky. Some of my classmates hadn't gotten that breath in time, and it cost them.

Following the training precisely, I unstrapped myself and, using my right hand, located the right side of the cockpit. I tripped the release lever and worked my way out and into the open water. Remembering a trick my instructor had taught me, I blew bubbles to get my bearings, trying to remain calm and not give in to the instinct to start swimming frantically until I knew which way was up. Agonizing seconds went by as I let a few precious air bubbles escape and waited for them to slide across my face, in whichever direction the surface was. Finally I got my bearings, and burst to the surface as fast as I could. I heard my classmates cheering when my head appeared above the water. I had passed The Dunker, but I hoped never to have to use those skills in real life.

It was exhilarating to fly the T-34 and learn all the various aspects of being a Marine pilot, but halfway through the program, we all had to start the process of "selecting" which type of aircraft we wanted to fly: helicopters or jets. I wasn't very clear or even concerned at that point about which type of aircraft I would be trained to fly. I was just happy to be there at all.

I knew that if I got selected for jets, I would have to move to Texas, or one of the Navy's other jet-training bases, since there was no jet training in Pensacola. At the time, the F-18, the sleek Marine fighter seen in movies like *Independence Day* and *Behind Enemy Lines,* was a brand-new aircraft, and most of my buddies wanted to fly those. For some reason, I really had no desire to fly jets. Maybe because they weren't the huge birds floating across the sky of my boyhood memories back in Salem. And although I had never been in a helicopter, I was intrigued by the precision required to control rotary-wing aircraft.

Similarly, we had to decide on which bases we would like to be stationed. I could also arrange my selections based on "coast," so the choices were East, West, or Hawaii. Finally, I could place a stronger emphasis on location than aircraft. This was like saying, "If I get stationed in the place I choose, then I don't care what aircraft I fly, helicopter or jet. Duty location is more important to me than choice of aircraft." Finally, I could place the emphasis on a type of aircraft over location, and they would try to find you a position somewhere flying that particular aircraft.

This was yet another competitive selection process, based on your performance throughout the training. Steve and I turned in our top three choices, selecting either Hueys, Cobras, or CH-46s or CH-53s. At the young age of twenty-four I knew I wanted two things: to explore a different coast and to fly something very different from what I was accustomed to. I had never been to Hawaii, so I basically said, "I'll fly anything you throw at me as long as I get to live in Hawaii." In fact, at that point in my life I had never been west of the Mississippi. But I also knew that whatever my preference, my assignment would ultimately come down to the needs of the Marine Corps.

I was selected to fly helicopters, but nothing was guaranteed. As always, there was another hurdle to overcome. I still had to complete my helicopter training at the Navy Helicopter Training Squadron on the other side of Whiting Field. I received an entirely different set of gear, and then checked into Training Squadron HT-18. For the next six months, the same type of rigor applied, including extensive classroom instruction and then lots of time in the cockpit.

We started off with three weeks of ground school, attending classes on helicopter aerodynamics, engineering, FAA regulations, and safety procedures. Since we were already pilots, this was more-specialized training. The stakes seemed to be higher and the academic regimen even more intense. Class standing was directly related to selection and assignments, so failing a test could actually get you bounced from the course.

As we moved closer to getting in the air, we used a "static cockpit trainer" to become familiar with being inside a cockpit. In these standalone cockpits, I learned all the basic switchology and emergency procedures, in preparation for the real thing. Just as I had learned in the T-34, and just as every pilot in virtually every aircraft did, the cockpit procedures revolved around a series of detailed checklists. There are checklists covering pre-flight, start-up, engine shutdown, post-flight, and more. And each one has a series of "challenge-response" steps, in which one person reads off the commands and the other performs the correction action and replies with the appropriate response. In a typical flight, the pilot and copilot have this verbal exchange, but there in the training helicopter, the instructor was reading off the commands and watching my every move.

Not unlike the classroom-testing portion of the course, if you did not perform to standard, you received what we called a "down." Otherwise known as a failure. To get a "down" on two flights, or on two written tests for that matter, you had to stand before a board that would assess whether or not you had what it took to continue. Cockpit procedures are a major, integral part of flight training, and everyone knew it. I had posters on the wall of my office that showed all the switches, buttons, and gauges in the cockpit. I spent many hours studying those posters and memorizing every little word on the checklists.

But learning cockpit procedures in my room and applying them in the actual cockpit trainer with the instructor watching were two different things. When he called them out, it better be obvious that I knew what to do and what to say. I'd better not be "hunting" for switches, or I'd most definitely receive a "down." I had a flawless training record so far, and I wasn't about to mess that up.

"Fuel selector valve."

"Open."

"Auxiliary power unit."

"Start."

"Sequencing flashing lights."

"Flash."

The next step was the simulator, called the Cockpit Procedures Trainer (CPT). The simulator did not involve any motion, but it did help me to get even more familiar with the overall feel and functions of a helicopter cockpit.

Finally, it was time. We trained on the Bell Jet Ranger, which is a very common, small helicopter still in use today by many local TV news stations. Not unlike the static trainer, sitting in the cockpit felt like sitting in a bubble-shaped greenhouse. There were some major differences between this and the T-34 I had learned to fly prior to helicopter training. First of all, the T-34 was a small plane that sat on wheels. The Bell Jet Ranger was a small helicopter that sat on skids. The T-34 had a tandem cockpit, meaning that the instructor pilot was always in a seat right behind me. But in the Bell Jet Ranger, I sat right next to my instructor pilot.

After some additional training on start-up and shutdown procedures, safety, and troubleshooting, we began to cycle through our actual helicopter flight training broken up into a series of familiarization flights we called FAMs. When it was my turn for FAM, the instructor pilot and I climbed into the helicopter and he took the controls. I was serious and attentive, but inside I was thinking, *This is so incredibly cool. Let's get up in the air!*

The instructor started up the bird and began to do an "air taxi" from the parking area to the runway. As soon as he lifted the skids just a few feet off the ground, I experienced a very new feeling. This was nothing like picking up speed down the runway and then using momentum to take off. Instead, we were hovering right above the ground and still moving forward. I watched his hands and feet and tried to follow his movements in relation to the simulator training.

Once we made it to the runway and he called over the radio for the proper clearances, he began to lift directly up into the air and fly us over to the large grassy area where all the helicopter flight training took place. There were dozens of helicopter-landing pads below us, and he landed on one of them. The first time I performed all the start-up procedures in a real helicopter was intense. As the instructor called off the various commands from the checklist, the helicopter actually re-

sponded. I had to focus my mental energies and hand–eye coordination, because the smell of jet fuel, the sound and feel of the engines
starting, and various lights coming on threatened to break my concen-
tration.

One of the very first and most fundamental skills a helicopter pilot
must learn is the art of hovering. Since a helicopter lifts straight off the
ground, you take off and land by hovering, and it is a central part of
flying helicopters in general. Hovering is a very difficult thing to teach
and a very difficult thing to do, but I would learn out on those fields.
There are three main functions. First, there is the "stick" right in front
of you and between your legs. This is called the "cyclic," and it controls
the angle of the rotor blades. Then there is the stick in your left hand,
called the "collective," which controls the pitch of the rotor blades. By
pulling on the collective, you lift the aircraft up into the sky. Finally,
there are the rudder pedals, which turn the nose of the aircraft and
change the angle of the tail rotor. I had to learn to perform all three of
these functions at the same exact time, seamlessly. The cyclic is the
hardest part to master, because there is a natural tendency to "control
the stick." When this happens, you aren't hovering, you are just all over
the place.

The instructor used several key techniques to teach me. First, he
took us up to about 25 feet, turned the helicopter, and told me to "ride
the controls" with him. This meant that he was flying the aircraft, but
I could feel what he was doing. I then rode the controls as he landed
and took off a few more times. Next, he had me work the pedals only,
while he did everything else. He carefully "guarded the controls," in
case I screwed up, and instructed me to turn the pedals while in midair
to see how it felt. It was time for me to lift off. I was very unsteady, but
I did it.

The hand–eye coordination required to hover was unlike anything
I had experienced in a cockpit before. To a passenger, it could feel like

the aircraft might succumb to gravity and drop out of the sky at any moment, like floating on an invisible cushion of air. But to the pilot, the act (and art) of hovering actually had physical sensations associated with it. With the pressure of the stick in my hand, the pedal under my foot, I could actually "feel the hover." In other words, the physics and mechanics of hovering actually gave me "feedback" through the controls, and it felt wonderful as I started to "get it."

One of the most popular T-shirts in the gift shop on base made light of the long-standing (and usually good-mannered) polarity between jet pilots and helicopter pilots. The shirt read, TO FLY IS HEAVEN . . . TO HOVER IS DIVINE. After learning how to do both, I couldn't have agreed with the joke more. Over the next week or so, during the FAM stage, I had gotten pretty good at lifting off and was hovering steadily on my own. That's when the real growth began, and each time I flew I got smoother and more confident.

We moved into the next level of training, which was called "pattern work." Part of the field had large, square patterns painted on the ground, and I had to "slide" the helicopter down each side of the square, following the lines precisely and making sharp turns at the ninety-degree angles. Over time, my instructor pilot integrated all the instrumentation, so that I was eventually flying totally on my own. And after a few months of that, I was learning to control the helicopter in more tactical movements, such as following the terrain and flying "near as possible" or NAP of the earth. I had already learned how to fly the T-34 and made successful solo flights. Now I had learned to start, take off, maneuver, hover, and land an entirely different kind of aircraft with new aerodynamic principles. This was a huge rite of passage and brought me one step closer to the fleet. I felt larger than life, and probably walked with just a bit more swagger. I know that a lot of my buddies shared the feeling.

I knew that part of the training involved a cross-country flight like

I had done in the T-34. I was excited when the time approached, because I knew I would get to work on my long-range navigational planning. On top of that, I had heard how fun it was to fly down to Key West and back, with some downtime in between. My partner in the cross-country flight was my buddy Ron Colyer. The instructor did the flying, and Ron and I did all the navigation.

It took us the better part of the day to get to Key West, as we had to traverse the entire Florida Panhandle and make a couple of fuel stops. We flew between 1,000 and 2,000 feet over the land, until we hit the Atlantic coast. At that point, we turned south and dropped our altitude to about 200 feet. I was amazed as we flew over Palm Beach, looking down at all the mansions, swimmers, surfers, and beachgoers. As far as I could see, there was powder-white sand to my right and aquamarine water to my left.

When we landed at Naval Air Station Key West, we buttoned up the aircraft and headed over to the officer's quarters. We each changed into civilian clothing, picked up a rental car, and headed out for some dinner and drinks. After idolizing the flight instructor for so long, it was a treat to be able to hang out with him. And since the only kind of unit I had ever been in was a training unit, this experience gave me a small taste of what it would be like to hang out with my fellow pilots after the work was done.

Three years after graduating from college, and after about eight months of intensive flight training, I became a fully instrument-rated solo pilot, with some pretty decent skills. I earned my Marine Corps aviator wings on May 16, 1986. I felt like a kid all over again on graduation day as I stood in formation and scanned the crowd for my family. My wife and kids were there, along with my father-in-law and sister-in-law. My brother Roger had even driven in to show his support.

My recruiter had been right about one thing: I didn't have to worry about keeping my "flight account" full anymore. I also didn't have to work after class to pay for the training. Now, the training had become my job, and I loved every minute of it. I had achieved and even exceeded my childhood dreams of becoming a pilot, and I was a Marine!

Now that I had earned my wings and the initial training was finally over, the clock officially began on my six-year active duty commitment. There were no slots available in Hawaii at the time, but both Steve and I got one of our wishes, and we were assigned to the same unit flying massive CH-53 helicopters in California. I relocated my family to California, totally energized about starting my very first assignment in the Marine Corps.

Air Station Tustin—My First Active Duty Assignment

My first active duty assignment was at Air Station Tustin, California. The original name of the base was Tustin, LTA, an old WW II "Lighter than Air" (LTA) base. There are actually still two blimp hangars standing from WW II, and they are some of the largest freestanding wooden structures in the country.

The CH-53 was a huge helicopter that could carry up to forty-two combat-equipped Marines, with six titanium rotor blades that weighed four hundred pounds each. This was a big and loud aircraft that you could hear coming from a long way off. Flying this war machine always entailed a mix of adrenaline, brute force, the strong smell of jet fuel, and the pure joy of handling two 4,000-horsepower jet engines. As expected, I had to go through even more training just to be able to fly the CH-53.

Once we were certified to fly, Steve and I were assigned to HMH-363, also known as the Red Lions, a moniker the unit earned during Vietnam. Since its inception, the Marine Corps helicopter community has designated its aircraft in a few ways, depending on the sizes and capabilities. Among others, there is the Helicopter, Marine Heavy

(HMH); the Helicopter, Medium Light (HML—also called Hueys); and the Helicopter, Marine Attack (HMA—also called Cobras). These classifications are also sometimes used to name organizations, such as HMH-363, the Red Lions, or HMX-1 (originally called Marine Helicopter Experimental Squadron One).

As anyone who has ever been in the military can tell you, there is a major difference between a training environment and your actual duty station. Even if you stay for only a year or so, and even if you have to go through six more months of advanced helicopter training right when you get there, you don't feel like a transient anymore.

I met Scott "Bayou" Minaldi and Craig "Spanky" Clement during my time in Tustin, and they both became lifelong friends as well. Bayou was a tall, dark ladies' man from Louisiana; a slick southern gentleman who was one of the best pilots I've ever met. Spanky was a blond-haired, blue-eyed Catholic from Virginia with a great sense of humor. He could fix anything you put in front of him, from engines to houses.

Growing up in New England, the beach had never been a big part of my experience. It was always too cold. But California was my new home, and I fell in love with it immediately. I really had the best of both worlds. Even in the line of duty, I was flying over the coast during training, enthralled by the seemingly endless horizon and the land jutting out into the water. On weekends we would get together and explore coves and beaches, trails and mountains on foot or on bike, and during the week we might fly a massive helicopter over the very same spots. I began to appreciate the fact that I got to see things in a way that many people never will. From boats to surfers, to the rooftops and trees in the area, I saw it all through the magical lens of the helicopter's cockpit.

It was also there at Tustin that I met two people who would become my greatest mentors and supporters throughout my career: my commanding officers, Lieutenant Colonel Richard "Willie" Willard and Lieutenant Colonel Ned Paulson. Steve and I never hit it off with the first CO, as he didn't pay us much attention. When Willie took over, he became the first CO who saw my potential and personally mentored me. He was known in the community as "Mr. 53" because he knew the CH-53 aircraft so well. He was technically brilliant and extremely serious about teaching us to fly in combat, but he also knew how to kick back in the Officer's Club. To put it simply, Willie was legendary in the community, and larger than life. He's probably the best 53 pilot I ever flew with. You couldn't help but respect his presence, his rank, his leadership, and his technical expertise, but more than that, he treated us as human beings. He created an environment based on high performance standards, but one in which you could also make and learn from mistakes.

Not only did I see something in Willie, he saw something in me. Shortly after I became an Aircraft Commander, he did one of my check rides. As I became a bit more seasoned, he assigned me as the Naval Air Training and Operating Procedures Standardization (NATOPS) Officer. This was an important role in virtually every Navy, Coast Guard, or Marine squadron. Not only that, but this was a position usually reserved for more-senior Captains, since the NATOPS Officer rode with the CO and performed check rides on other pilots. Nevertheless, Willie felt that I was the right person for the job. Willie mentored Steve as well, and Steve would sometimes tease me for being the teacher's pet, but I didn't mind.

Again, this didn't feel like training anymore, although we still participated in lots of training missions. Now I was a member of an organization that had a proud history, and that felt like an extension of my family. We went to countless barbecues and social events, and the kids were just getting old enough to start school. Like every married Marine, I tried to balance work with family. When Willie finally retired and we found out we were going to get a new Commander, we were all a bit disheartened. But as it turned out, we were so lucky to get Ned. He was Greek and had huge brown eyes that could look right through you. He also had a loud voice and a personality that could fill up a room with its intensity. He took me under his wing as well, and one of his greatest strengths was putting the right people in the right jobs. Once he put you in a position, he gave you his absolute trust to do your job, and the resources and support you needed to be successful.

Ned was always protective of his Marines. I once accompanied Ned to a high-level meeting with a full bird Colonel, and the Colonel was trying to micromanage what he wanted Ned to do. I think my mouth must have been open for a few seconds when Ned said, "With all due respect, sir, keep your fucking hands off my squadron." That's how seriously Ned took his job. I worked extremely hard to meet and exceed the Commander's guidance, and played just as hard when time allowed. This was the period in my life when I became really active in the local culture of endurance competitions, which involved a combination of swimming, running, and biking.

Between 1986 and 1988, I was promoted to Captain and went on three overseas deployments in Thailand, the Philippines and Japan, and Korea. I had already flown and traveled more than I ever would have imagined just a few short years earlier. There was no war going on at the time, but we still called this a deployment. Due to a national security agreement with Japan, virtually any Marine stationed in the Pacific was going to spend some time in Japan. At the time, we still had two large military bases in the area. On the first deployment, I had never been out of the country, so this was like going on an international field trip with my fraternity brothers—but with the ultimate toys!

While there, we flew in three major multinational training exercises. Although the CH-53 was a workhorse, it was also prone to maintenance issues back then. This knowledge made it very interesting to fly with nine or ten other CH-53s from Okinawa to the island of Luzon for training. Once we left Okinawa, we didn't see land again for eight hours. We had safety procedures for crash landings in the water, and I had never forgotten The Dunker training back in flight school, but none of us wanted to land in the water unless there was no other option. So there was a running joke during the trips that if a warning light started going off in the cockpit, just stick a piece of gum over it, because there was nothing you could do about it.

Luckily, we all made it in one piece, and then we stopped to refuel in a slick little operation called Rapid Group Refueling (RGR). We landed in a remote area on the island of Batan. Basically, a huge C-130 full of fuel lands in this remote area—the Marine Corps' traveling gas station. We would land nearby, hook up the hoses, and get fueled up again for the next leg. We took off and flew a while longer, until we hit the northern coast of Luzon. Then we followed the coast all the way to Subic Bay, north of Manila.

Steve and I shared a dorm-style room right across the street from the Officer's Club, which we frequented whenever we had some downtime. In those moments, after flying a CH-53 all day, and bellying up to the bar for a few drinks, we would smile with the knowledge that we were living the dream. We were copiloting these complex tactical aircraft in what felt like a very exotic setting, and even though we were separated from our families, we were also having fun.

We also made the kinds of memories that probably seemed funny only to us. One Friday night, I was sound asleep after an evening of drinking and socializing and a long week at work. Steve stumbled into the room at three in the morning. I squinted up at him, and he said, "Holy crap, my wife just went to the hospital. I'm going down to get a flight home right now."

This was some big news he had obviously been expecting, but the reality of it seemed to have him stunned. For some reason, the smallest detail has always stuck with me. We had just gone to the commissary and stocked up on food few days earlier, and just before Steve walked out of the room to fly across the ocean to meet his new baby, he seemed to recall this important fact.

He turned back and said, "Frenchy, eat my food," and then left.

When I returned from that first deployment a few months later, I felt pretty salty, pretty accomplished. I was an international traveler, after all! At a certain point, I had the option to leave the Marine Corps, and many of my buddies did exactly that. But the excitement and fulfillment I got during those deployments cemented my decision to stay in. More than ever, the Marine Corps felt like a brotherhood, and I couldn't have been more content.

Ronald Reagan Landing

In the spring of 1988, I had an experience that would change my life—and the course of my career—forever. President Ronald Reagan landed at Air Station Tustin on his way to a fund-raiser in Newport, California.

Steve and I were eager faces in the crowd as seemingly everyone on base stood behind a rope line to watch the squadron arrive. At that time, the Marine Corps was still governed by Cold War policies, so military bases were almost completely off-limits to civilian visitors. It was a purely military crowd gathered at the airstrip, and we had come out in droves to watch the President land.

I had heard of HMX-1, the Presidential Helicopter Squadron One, and the *Marine One* helicopter itself. When I was in OCS at Quantico, where *Marine One* is headquartered, I sometimes saw the white-top helicopters flying in formation to and from the base, but I was too preoccupied with getting through my training to give it much thought.

But now I was witnessing the President's squadron firsthand. First, a couple of sleek helicopters with their tops painted white took turns landing, and some media personnel climbed out. Finally, the very last white-top came in, the one designated *Marine One*. It was obvious that the President was on board from the roar of the cheering crowd around me. At that point in my career, I had worked only with large cargo-type helicopters like the CH-53. I had never seen *Marine One* up close, and I was struck by the nimble movements of the helicopters in formation that seemed almost like an aerial ballet. I was a goner, completely captivated by the choreography of the aircraft hovering and landing in perfect synchronicity.

The President climbed out of the helicopter, waved, and left with his entourage in a motorcade of black limousines. I kept my eyes on the pilots, wearing their dress uniforms with blue pants and khaki shirts, as they milled around their helicopters, apparently waiting for the President to return. They looked so poised and professional, and I knew I was watching the very best of the best. That's when I knew that I wanted to join whatever club they were in.

The week after *Marine One*'s visit, I began to research HMX-1 and inquire about what it took to join the squadron. I learned from a buddy that the group of helicopters used to support the President on any given mission was called the "lift package," and that every single lift was a little different. They landed in a carefully orchestrated formation, specifically planned based on location, weather, wind, and who was on board. I also learned that the Commander of the lift was in charge of making sure that nothing was too predictable and that nobody on the ground could tell which helicopter carried the President, right up until he climbed out. Some call this "the shell game," referring to the old magic trick.

Applying for HMX-1

I wanted to know everything. One of my senior officers in the Red Lions, Major Lee Dial, had been in HMX-1 a few years previously, and was always regaling us with stories of his days in the squadron, carrying President Reagan around the world. I was one of the few pilots who would stick around in the pilots' ready room and listen, enamored with the idea of flying the President.

I did my own research as well, and it wasn't too hard to find the history of HMX-1. The squadron was commissioned on December 1, 1947, at Quantico. The original intent of the Marine Corps' first-ever helicopter squadron was to create an organization focused on developing ways to use helicopters in combat. Within about a year, the squadron conducted the first ship-to-shore helicopter lift in military history. Among numerous other things, HMX-1 developed tactics and techniques that were used very effectively in Vietnam. The pilot fired 2.36-inch rockets that were mounted on the sides of the helicopter and also delivered aerial bombs from up to 8,000 feet.

Throughout the 1950s, the Marines in HMX-1 continued to assess and refine helicopter tactics. The CH-37 and the UH-34 were used extensively during the late 1950s and early 1960s. In September 1957, President Dwight D. Eisenhower was vacationing in Newport, Rhode Island, and flew in a UH-34 back to *Air Force One*. That was the first time a President of the United States had ever flown in a Marine Corps helicopter. President Eisenhower liked the convenience and speed of helicopter travel for short trips, and since then, HMX-1 has provided Executive Support to the President.

As the Executive Support mission evolved, the Marine Corps worked with Sikorsky Aircraft to adopt a special model of the UH-34, called the VH-34. The VH model was equipped with a VIP passenger interior, more-advanced instrumentation, and emergency flotation devices. After a few more iterations, the aircraft was designated the VH-3, an executive version of the Navy's SH-3. The VH-3 was equipped with special soundproofing features, air-conditioning, and even-more-advanced navigational and communications equipment. All in all, the VH-3 provided increased overall safety, reliability, speed, and range. In fact, the style and functionality of the aircraft was so perfect for the mission that it is still in use today.

Since 1947, HMX-1 has supported eleven Presidents and their staffs in more than thirty-three countries, averaging ten thousand flight hours each year. All this has been done in close coordination with Sikorsky. In fact, at one point, an engineer named Harry Asbury noticed that some commercial airlines were painting the tops of their aircraft white to reduce the temperature of the interiors. Rumor has it that the paint upset the pilots and maintenance crews, since it created a lot of extra work and didn't even have a significant impact on the temperature in the cabin. Nevertheless, the "white tops" have persisted, becoming the trademark of *Marine One* for more than five decades.

"White tops," as we call them, are the iconic VH-3 and VH-60 model helicopters authorized to fly the President, the Vice President, the Secretary of Defense, the Chief of Naval Operations, and the Commandant of the Marine Corps. There is no other country, even when they come to the United States, that brings their own helicopter assets. But wherever our Commander in Chief needs to fly, and every time he lands in *Air Force One*, his helicopter is always waiting. The only time a white top is actually referred to as *Marine One* is when the President is on board. With a record free of a single mishap incident, HMX-1 and the white tops have gained a sterling reputation as a truly world-class aviation squadron.

In 1988, I was scheduled to attend a special school called the Weapons and Tactics Instructors Course (WTI), in Yuma, Arizona, to which less than 3 percent of all military aviators are accepted. WTI is an environment not unlike the movie *Top Gun*, except with helicopter pilots, and it took everything I had learned so far to stay ahead of the curve at this level.

Pilots are always given nicknames or radio call signs that everyone tends to use instead of their real names. Every pilot has a different story about how he got his call sign. During this particular course, if you didn't have a call sign—or if the instructors didn't like the one you had—you got a new one. One day I was sitting in a room with other pilots preparing for a flight briefing, and my instructor, a Captain named Jordan Yankov, started asking each of us about our call signs. He took one look at my nametag and said, "No one's ever going to be able to spell that name or pronounce it, so we're just going to call you Frenchy."

Up until that point, I had been given a couple of call signs, like Lash and Rain Man. But none of them had lasted. I wasn't that big of a fan of "Frenchy," but from then on it stuck. Over the years, there were a couple of times when people tried to change my call sign to reflect my passion for fitness and competing in triathlons, but I refused to change it. Jordan had died in an aircraft crash not too long after giving me my call sign, and I kept it in his honor. To this day, there are people I've known for years who don't even know my first name.

Typically, pilots in the Red Lions would do only a couple of overseas deployments in a three- or four-year tour. I had already been to the Western Pacific region on two deployments, which included duty in Okinawa, Japan, and Korea. But when I returned from the WTI course, my commanding officer, Lieutenant Colonel Ned Paulson, asked if I would stick around and do a third deployment. This time it would be Japan and the Philippines, and I happily agreed. Steve had recently been assigned to the Red Lions' higher headquarters, Aircraft Group 16, and had made the decision to leave the Marines at some point to pursue a civilian career. He was right there with me on my first two tours. He had also gotten married while we were stationed in California, and our families spent a lot of time together. It felt strange to deploy without him.

I continued to become a better pilot and became more and more obsessed with the possibility of joining HMX-1. A couple of years after seeing President Reagan land on base, Major Dial was mentoring me through the application process. I had to describe all my training and assignments in detail. I also had to demonstrate through my flight logs that I had flown at least fifteen hundred hours. There were physical and medical requirements as well. I even had to show that I was eligible for a Top Secret clearance. I was advised that a lack of requirements in any of these areas could knock me out of the running, but I felt that I had a pretty good chance. I had received strong performance evaluations in each course, and each year since joining the Red Lions. I was still a young Captain, but I had already gained a great deal of experience.

As if all that wasn't enough, I also needed letters of recommendation, including at least one from someone within HMX-1. The message here was that HMX-1 wanted someone "in the know" to vouch for you, or at least state that they thought you had the potential to thrive at HMX-1. Maybe because he knew how much I wanted the job, Major Dial's recommendation was one of the first that I received. My good friend Marc Hohle had recently left California and entered HMX-1, so I reached out to him and he wrote me a letter as well. I turned in my application packet for HMX-1 in 1991, just before heading out for my third deployment.

I went to Asia, where I worked and flew in the Philippines, in the South China Sea, away from my family, during my last year in the Red Lions.

While I was overseas, Saddam Hussein crossed the border into Kuwait, and the Marine Corps went to war along with the rest of the U.S. military. Operation Desert Shield and then Operation Desert Storm had officially begun, and because of the Marine Corps' stop-loss policy, Steve was deployed to Kuwait for about six months. When he got home, he left the Marines and embarked on a new career in government, but we never lost touch.

I spent the whole war in Japan, and during that time I received news about my HMX-1 application. Command had reviewed it, and I had been selected only as an alternate, which meant that I would not have the opportunity to join HMX-1 for that training year. For me, it was a personal failure. Even though Major Dial and others assured me that it was nothing personal and that I would surely be accepted the next year, it took me a couple of weeks to shake that feeling of failure. It helped when my boss called some of his contacts at HMX-1 and found out that I had been named as an alternate only because I was deployed at the time. They recommended that I apply again the following year, and I learned that alternates are usually a sure thing on their second application.

By 1992 I was already back in the United States and halfway through yet another specialized course—the Amphibious Warfare School (AWS). It was during this school that I was finally accepted into HMX-1. After almost four years of learning all I could about the squadron, submitting two applications, and completing several overseas assignments, I was going to be a pilot in the Presidential Helicopter Squadron! Now we knew we would be in the area for at least five years, so we built a home in nearby Fredericksburg, Virginia.

Spanky got accepted into HMX-1 at the same time, and Bayou would follow us a year later. This was it, and I knew I'd be flying with the best of the best, and in some of the most advanced aircraft in the world.

CHAPTER 3

MY FIRST TOUR

The Big Leagues. The varsity team. I can't believe I'm finally here! These were the thoughts and feelings floating around in my head in the first minutes, hours, and days after arriving at HMX-1 in late May 1992. I rolled up to the main gate of the air facility, deep inside Marine Corps Base Quantico, where a young Marine MP checked my ID, asked the purpose of my visit, and then saluted as I drove off. I knew this was the beginning of a four-year journey unlike anything I had experienced thus far. The Authorization of Deadly Force signs I passed driving to the main HMX HQ building confirmed that. After another vehicle checkpoint, I entered the main compound of HMX-1, that storied organization I had been dreaming about for years now.

I had spent time on Quantico and seen some of the secure areas, but I never had the proper clearances to enter this particular part of the base. I was also accustomed to squadrons that could house their entire staff and aircraft in a single hangar, but this place was huge. It was more of a campus than a hangar.

My buddy Spanky arrived around the same time that day, and we met up and began the week-long process of checking in. First, we went to the Operations Department to hand off our log books and check in with the Operations Duty Officer. This guy was a Captain just like us. And he had a bad attitude. Now, Spanky is not the kind of guy you mouth off to. So, when this Captain did, Spanky asked him very matter-of-factly whether or not he would like a knuckle sandwich.

Spanky looked at me and said, "Great, we've been here less than five minutes and we're going to get into a bar fight!" Both guys stood down, and we continued on to our next stop.

In the Red Lions, I had become a bit of a self-proclaimed expert on HMX-1 history, absorbing all that I could for several years. For example, I knew that this was the largest aviation squadron in the Marine Corps, with a workforce of seven hundred Marines. The pilots, various technicians, and maintenance experts were hand-selected from all over the Marine Corps—they were the best of the best at what they did. But just as a photograph rarely does an ocean sunset justice, my research didn't even come close to preparing me for what this felt like.

We were at the pinnacle of Marine helicopter aviation, and to our fresh eyes it seemed as if half of the workforce was out and about. It was noisy and fast-paced. There were Presidential Seals painted on various signs and I craned my neck to watch as several green-side aircraft and CH-53s flew in pattern above us. A sculptor looks at a block of clay and sees a form hiding inside. As a pilot, I saw the sights and sounds of this exhilarating environment, and saw how I could be part of the history of HMX-1.

One of our next stops was Marine Corps Supply at the other end of the airfield. The young Marine we encountered called the room to attention. I looked behind us to determine what senior officer was sneaking in behind us and then realized, *Holy shit . . . he called the room to attention for us!* We were definitely not in California anymore. The Gunnery Sergeant sitting behind a desk asked us who we were, and then went into a back room to get our supplies.

We had been required to turn in almost all of our gear back at our last commands. We still had some flight suits, but the Sergeant handed over new ones, saying we would need clean ones. I thought that mine were already clean, but apparently they meant *really* clean. My old flight suits had certainly been washed, but it had been so long since I was issued a new one that the hydraulic-fluid stains on mine blended into one color.

We also received a pair of LOX boots. I had no idea what these were at first, or why we were being issued these boots that went only to ankle height and had no laces. We would find out later. For now we just stuffed them into the bag. One thing I had kept from the Red Lions was my flight helmet. Now I had to turn it in for a new one. My helmet had become sort of a friend over the years. I had personally "taped" it up over the years with designs from my old squadron and remembrances from various deployments. I asked why we had to turn in our helmets, and the Gunny stated evenly, "They need to be retaped with the HMX-1 scheme." I reluctantly placed my old friend on the counter.

We were also told to make sure we had a serviceable set of Dress Blue trousers and Service Charlie shirts, which would serve as our official uniform only when flying the white tops on a Presidential lift. This was cool. I was in a whole different league.

We then received four new Squadron patches: one with the HMX-1 insignia, another that was a hybrid of the Presidential Seal and the words "United States Marine Corps Executive Flight Detachment," one with the Presidential Seal, and one with the Vice Presidential Seal. The Gunny informed us that the Presidential and VP patches were for our leather flight jackets, which we would wear during cold-weather lifts. More than any other part of the check-in process, getting these distinctive patches was the most humbling. Who knew how many missions I would wear them on, and who would be in my helicopter? In my own

way, I think I knew what a brand-new NFL quarterback must feel
like when he is first handed his team's helmet.

We left the supply room and brought our bounty back to our vehicle, securing it all in the trunk. Spanky and I couldn't believe that the
Supply Officer was actually handing us all this gear, instead of telling
us he had nothing left and to make do with the ratty old gear we had—
which often happened in the fleet. We had some other in-processing to
do that day, and I also couldn't wait to get down to the hangars and
check out the aircraft. We had both seen the airfield before, since we
had spent time on Quantico during OCS.

It was still a new experience to get inside the wire and to walk right
up to the white tops. The shiny green paint jobs stood out, as did the
HMX-1 markings, a far cry from the dirty, hydraulic-fluid stained paint
jobs of most fleet aircraft. Along with the white tops (the VH-3 Sea
King and VH-60 White Hawk), the HMX-1 fleet includes large cargo
helicopters like CH-46s and CH-53s. These platforms participate on
Presidential missions but carry only the press, staff, Secret Service, and
other supporting personnel.

Over the next couple of days, we checked into other areas of the
squadron such as Operations, and met some of our peers as they
came on board. We also met the Commanding Officer, Colonel Ed
Langston.

On Monday morning, we went into the ready room at 0800. The ready
room is the nucleus of daily pilot life, and the heartbeat of HMX-1 operations. Some of the strategic and long-term planning might be done
outside that room, but this is where pilots received their daily flight
briefs and where All Officer's Meetings (AOMs) were held every morning. In the "normal" fleet, those meetings happened only once a week.
It was a fairly plain room with dozens of seats and a big briefing area
up front. The most striking things were the pictures on the walls of all

the Presidents boarding and coming off HMX helicopters through history.

There was a certain familiarity that is common to all ready rooms in the Marine Corps helicopter community, since the subject matter was helicopters and missions and associated logistics. But the subject matter of the missions was completely new, and that feeling of newness far outweighed my sense of familiarity.

In that first AOM, I was struck by how many pilots across all platforms were there from around the country. I soon realized that our contractors from Sikorsky and Boeing attended these AOMs, along with our Ground Officers, MPs, Supply Officers, the Adjutant, and others. The room was packed with at least fifty people, and half of the HMX-1 pilots were out on missions. Suddenly someone near the back of the room yelled, "Attention on deck!"

We all stopped talking and stood up at the position of attention. Colonel Langston walked in, followed by the Executive Officer, Colonel Mel Demars (who had already been selected to "fleet up" to be the next Commanding Officer). They both walked from the back to the front of the room, and as they did, Colonel Langston said in a very kind voice, "Please be seated." His demeanor was unexpected and very professional. We all sat down. After the Operations Duty Officer conducted the business for that morning's meeting, the CO stood up and faced us from behind a lectern that had the Presidential Seal on it. At the end of his remarks, he said, "We have two new pilots joining us today. Captain Ray 'Frenchy' L'Heureux and Captain Craig 'Spanky' Clement." Each year a new freshman class of pilots came aboard, and we were the latest two of our class to check in. At this introduction, all the other pilots yelled in unison, "Stand up!" We did. The moment we were on our feet, they yelled even louder, "Sit down!" The CO was smiling, and we sat back down, red faced. We were the rookies for the time being, and we knew it.

The CO said, "Welcome," and then it was business as usual. Operations weren't going to slow down or stop until we felt comfortable and understood everything going on. We would just need to catch up and keep up. President Bush 41 had been in office since 1988 and in 1992 was just entering the full swing of campaign mode. The CO said he wouldn't be around that afternoon because he had a meeting at the White House. The President was going out of town for a few days and spending the coming weekend at Camp David. I knew it shouldn't have surprised me, but sitting there hearing that kind of thing blew me away. I had never had anything to do with such high-profile missions back at the Red Lions.

The CO then outlined several current and pending missions, using a whiteboard and some graphics. I felt honored to be working alongside friends from Tustin, like Marc Hohle and Spanky. I even ran into a couple of guys who had been my flight instructors back in Pensacola. The Marine Corps is founded on pride in excellence and esprit de corps, and I had experienced my share of both. But not quite like this. We worked all day, and then on many nights we could actually see the results of our work in the media and in the news. Everyone at HMX-1 seemed to be aware of just how special their jobs were, and everyone seemed extremely proud to be part of this organization. It was contagious. The common denominator was that everyone knew we had a flawless record of achievement, and no one wanted to be the first one in history to change that record.

I had of course read and heard about HMX-1's different missions, but as I settled into the unit, I began to really see how the organization was arrayed. Operationally speaking, there was not only one mission but three, and each one was complex and unique.

The first came from Operational Test and Evaluation (OT&E) and was the reason for the *X* in *HMX*. Back in the early days, when the squadron was formed to develop new helicopter tactics born out of the advent of rotary-wing aircraft and the requirement for that capability in the Korean Conflict, the *X* had stood for *Experimental.* The mission had evolved into the area of testing and evaluation of helicopter systems for use across the Marine Corps. Up until 2011, HMX-1 flew the Operational Test and Evaluation for all rotary-wing aircraft in the inventory. We also tested associated systems such as night-vision goggles, laser eye protection, electronic-warfare equipment, and other flight-physiology-related equipment.

The second mission came directly from the Commandant of the Marine Corps, to the Deputy Chief of Staff for Aviation, to HMX-1. Within this chain of command, we provided helicopter support for various Department of Defense missions, including tactical troop lifts in support of OCS, The Basic School, and Infantry Officer's School. We used the CH-46E Sea Knights, CH-53D Sea Stallions, and CH-53E Super Stallions for these missions.

The most high-profile and unusual mission came directly from the White House—the Executive Transport mission. This was a global mission, meaning that the full contingent of an HMX-1 lift package would be there waiting no matter where the President landed in *Air Force One.* Since President Bush was in campaign mode, the flight schedule was extremely complex and kinetic. We didn't just fly in with a single helicopter. We brought a full lift package wherever we went, and that included a good number of folks for each event site, three or four helicopters, security, maintenance support, and a host of other technicians and communications personnel. Making this seamless involved extremely complex and overlapping logistics and advance planning, as the entire lift package had to be packed up and configured to load onto massive Air Force cargo planes.

From the perspective of the pilots, HMX-1 is set up like a college: you start out as a "freshman" and work your way up to a "senior" during your four-year tour of duty. From the pilots to the crew chiefs, to the maintenance and support personnel, everyone seemed to be at the top of their game. And since you had to be a top gun even to be considered for HMX-1, the pilots jokingly referred to the whole process as going from "hero to zero." For the first year or so, pilots typically serve as Helicopter Aircraft Commander for support aircraft and as copilot for those aircraft during actual Presidential lifts. For the second year, they complete the proper training to become copilots on *Marine One*, which is the whole reason most pilots wanted to join HMX-1 in the first place.

For the last two years of the tour, pilots pretty much end up in one of three categories, each one smaller than the last. The first category is the majority of pilots who are assigned to a supporting role, doing test and evaluation or training missions.

The next category is a little smaller, and fewer than ten of seventy pilots are selected to serve as White House Liaison Officers (WHLOs), which we pronounced "Weelos." This was an important and coveted role because, as the name implied, WHLOs coordinated directly with the White House Communications Office, the Secret Service, the HMX-1 Commander, and numerous other agencies and individuals involved in planning and preparation of the President's movements. Seemingly every one of these entities had its own advance personnel, and the whole group traveled together. The WHLOs were perhaps the most critical component to this overall team, since they arrived in advance, set everything up, and handled the complex logistics of *Marine One*.

The smallest group of pilots in HMX-1 were the four individuals selected by the Commander to fly the President in his absence, or when the logistics of travel made it impossible to keep pace with *Air Force One* around the globe, or simply to fly the other white tops during each Presidential lift. I had to work my way up through these stages just like everyone else.

I was still current in the CH-53, and I began flying again within just a couple of weeks of arriving at the squadron. During this period I also hit my six-year commitment to the Marine Corps, and I didn't consider getting out for even one minute. Some of my peers across the Marine Corps aviation community got out at that point and went into the commercial-aviation industry. Arguably, they could have a lot more personal freedom and make a lot more money on the outside, but I don't recall anyone in HMX-1 getting out for that reason. Yes, I was a freshman, a young Captain, a "zero" finding my way in the juggernaut of a squadron that was HMX-1. But I was also entrusted to fly VIPs in some of the nation's most famous and visible helicopters.

Flying Bush 41

It wasn't long before I began participating in the ongoing support of the President's campaign trail. I wasn't qualified to actually fly President Bush yet, but I flew all over the country with him on support missions. My first full Presidential lift happened a few months into my tour, flying President Bush from the airport in Detroit to a few locations in the area to speak with workers in the automotive industry.

Our squadron arrived in Detroit a couple of days early to rehearse the lift. The stakes are high when the President is on board, and with numerous helicopters taking off and landing in a specific formation, there is no room for error. I understood the mission and knew all the tactics, so I thought I was ready to go on the morning of the lift. I was sitting in the cockpit as the Aircraft Commander of Night Hawk 3, one of four helicopters assigned to the lift package for that day. My big CH-53 would carry members of the President's staff, the press, and the Secret Service.

We were positioned right on the runway, and there were members of the Secret Service, White House staff, and other security all around. I was wearing my official Presidential lift flight suit for the first time. I had almost two thousand flying hours by then, and years of training.

None of that helped me to be any less nervous. I was sweating under my flight jacket despite the morning cold.

I could see the crowd out behind the rope line, not unlike the one I stood behind just a few years before in California. Now here I was walking around freely inside the secure area. I might have been only a pilot on one of the support aircraft on my first Presidential lift, but I was finally in "the club," and that was good enough for me. I talked to some of the other pilots and the Secret Service personnel, but we had to keep our conversations to a minimum. I needed to stay close to the aircraft since we were already in position, waiting for *Air Force One* to arrive.

We monitored several communication channels, the radio crackling with chatter from secure and nonsecure communications, control towers, my Mission Commander (who happened to be the new HMX-1 Commander, Colonel Mel Demars), and the Secret Service. After about a half hour, we got the call on the radio from the WHLO: "Man up . . . *Air Force One* is thirty minutes out."

I climbed back into the cockpit and performed last-minute checks and procedures. I started up the engines, waited for all the other aircraft to get their engines on line, then participated in a quick systems check. *Marine One* then initiated another radio check, and I did not want to miss that one or screw it up in any way. I glanced over at *Marine One*. I could not even fathom the kind of pressure it took to command a flight like that, and what it was like for him to fly with the President of the United States sitting in the back of his aircraft, and perhaps conducting business as the Chief Executive of the United States.

As I watched this gleaming blue-and-white symbol of our country come into view and then touch down, I tried to remind myself, *He's the boss, he's done this dozens of times, he's got this.*

In my imagination, *Air Force One* was a sleek executive jet, not this massive 747 airliner that was now barreling right toward us. The exhaust from the engines made optical illusions in the air around them. This modified 747 was specifically missionized to transport the President of the United States. From talking to other pilots who had toured the aircraft, I knew that *Air Force One* contained a specially outfitted conference room, sleeping quarters, and state-of-the-art communications and security equipment. I would learn later that President Bush 41 was the first President to use this particular aircraft. President Reagan used an older 707, which is now forever parked at the Reagan library.

The jumbo jet kept getting closer and bigger, and I thought that my CH-53 helicopter must look like a metallic bug on the runway. My heart was pumping and my hands were clammy. It was all I could do not to point like a kid pointing at a big yellow jet flying across the sky and say, *Whoa. Look at that!* Once again I tried to play it cool behind my sunglasses while the boy inside me who built that 747 model was going crazy.

For a minute there I thought there had been a mistake, and that they were going to run right over us. Instead, *Air Force One* taxied and rolled to a smooth stop. The wheels were on a predetermined "T" on the ground, which had been precisely measured and marked off by the *Air Force One* advance team. I knew exactly where that spot was, because I had walked out to it and conducted a mental and visual measurement in my head. I had been shocked by how close it seemed to our aircraft. When it finally stopped, security rolled the stairs up to the plane and got to work in a flurry of activity. Then the door opened, and I watched the President step out, wave, walk down the stairs, and greet the staff members, Secret Service personnel, and automotive-industry executives gathered at the bottom.

This was the first time I had seen the President in person. My co-pilot and I just sat there staring fixedly through the cockpit windows, watching the President make his way to Colonel Demars's helicopter. I wouldn't be surprised if our mouths were open. After a couple of minutes, the President and his entourage climbed aboard *Marine One*. Meanwhile, our own passengers climbed on board as well. I had a detailed list of those names approved to be on the flight, and security was extremely tight. I checked the list carefully and ensured everyone was properly buckled in. We usually had seating for twenty-four passengers, but some of the seats were used to hold cameras and other equipment on this flight.

Mary Matalin, a popular news personality, walked on and the whole thing became slightly surreal. Once the President boarded *Marine One*, my Commanding Officer took off. I was still getting our passengers seated and buckled in, so there were a few intense moments as I tried to complete the task, unnecessarily hurrying the ever-competent crew chief in the back. I was nervous, and as soon as I possibly could, I got the rotors turning so I would be ready to take off with the rest of the lift package.

Colonel Demars was all business, and some of us young officers tried to give him a wide berth. It was cold that morning, and I was supposed to be carrying a backup heater and a battery pack in my aircraft that would support the white tops. He knew I didn't have the heater because his crew chief had noticed it in the hangar and grabbed it before we lifted off.

His deep voice came over the radio, "Night Hawk 3, is the auxiliary heating unit on your aircraft?" I froze. Just total radio silence for a few seconds. I looked over at my crew chief in terror. I knew that everyone on the radio was imagining me squirming in my seat, which was pretty accurate.

My crew chief just looked at me with wide eyes and shook his head.

I gulped and prepared to press the Transmit button. The boss was waiting, and I had to say something.

Before I could, the radio crackled again, and Colonel Demars said in a monotone, "The answer would be no."

This became a running joke (they were laughing at me, not with me) for virtually the rest of my time in the squadron.

The sting of being called out over the radio subsided a little when we lifted off. Because *Marine One* took off ahead of us, and my flight needed to land first to get our passengers in place, we increased our speed and passed the President's helicopter, keeping up the shell game as we wove through the Detroit skyscrapers at 200 feet. I had never flown like this before. This was just as amazing as flying over the beach any day. At one point, I saw my own helicopter's reflection on the side of a building and took a quick second to think, *Wow, that is so crazy!* This kind of airspace is normally highly restricted, and loud military aircraft don't typically zoom around the skies of an urban city.

When we arrived at the Ford Motor Company, we landed in the parking lot to a cheering crowd, with camera lights flashing all around us. The President stepped out of *Marine One*, waved at the throngs of people beyond the rope perimeter, and strode into the factory. Sometimes the pilots in a Presidential lift actually get to attend the event, but not this one. We milled around the helicopters, checking all the equipment and waiting for word that the President would be back. That's when we became the celebrities. I was almost embarrassed when people from the local fire and police departments approached us to take pictures with them, and soon the camera flashes were aimed at us. Members of HMX-1 get used to that kind of thing after a while, but it was a new experience for me.

Appointments like this are precisely timed, and we monitored the play-by-play report of the event and its timeline over the radio. Thirty minutes prior to the President's arrival back at the airfield, we would have all aircraft manned with engines running. Finally, the WHLO got the call through his earpiece and relayed to us, "They're wrapping it up. The motorcade is ten minutes out."

We received a similar radio call from the Secret Service at the five-minute mark. We all climbed back into our cockpits with engines running, ready to go. The President and all the other passengers came out of the building and climbed back into the aircraft, and we flew back to the airport. *Marine One* landed last, taxied right up to the nose of *Air Force One*, and discharged the President.

While my passengers were filing out of the helicopter, I had a front-row seat as *Air Force One* turned, accelerated down the runway, then lifted off and flew out of sight. Once it was safely airborne, and the "ramp freeze" was lifted, we taxied to our own "bed down" area on the airport. Next, crews came out to help with cleaning the aircraft and to tow them back into the hangar. We debriefed the flight, then went back to the hotel and changed clothes. *Mission complete!*

Though it still felt like one, the experience had been more exciting than any daydream. I couldn't quite believe that this was now my job. When I got back to the hotel, I immediately called my wife, then my parents, then Steve, and probably a few others. I probably sounded like a kid, "Did you see me on TV?" Of course they hadn't, but the exhilaration of that relatively short lift had left me with a strong desire to turn around and do it all again.

Walleyball? With the President?

Later in 1992, I got to meet President Bush 41 up close. We flew the President and First Lady to Camp David—my first official trip to the Presidential retreat that sits 2,300 feet above sea level in the beautiful wooded hill country of Maryland. Because Camp David is run by the Navy, when the First Family is not there it's quite like any other military installation—except for the fact that it sits beneath a dome of highly prohibited airspace.

I had been to the camp a couple of times in a training capacity, but now the Boss was on the lift and the pressure and excitement grew exponentially. By helicopter, the trip from the White House lasts about forty-five minutes, and is fairly technical and challenging. This was a mountainous area, and it was difficult to spot the landing zone cut out from the dense trees until we were fairly close. It was beautiful to fly in so low over the trees in the morning sun, but I kept my mind focused on the task at hand.

Not unlike the approach to the White House lawn, the small clearing in the trees below did not seem large enough to land the lift package. But of course it was. We finally landed and shut down the engines. The landing zone was actually a large grassy area that doubled as a skeet-shooting and driving range when the First Family was in residence. It was obvious that Camp David had been readied for the First Family's arrival—flags flying in the wind, with Marines and Sailors standing at attention or saluting in their crisp dress uniforms. The President, the First Lady, and a few of their grandchildren climbed out of *Marine One* and into the prestaged golf carts waiting for them at the top of the landing zone. We watched them drive off and then began to do final checks and preparations to button up the aircraft before they were towed to the hangar. No matter what, care and maintenance of the aircraft was always a top priority.

Pilots are considered guests at Camp David, since they have to stay there as long as the President is there and must be ready to leave on a moment's notice. We were technically on duty all weekend. Camp David is officially known as Naval Support Facility Thurmont. It was originally designed as a camp for military officers and their families; then President Franklin Delano Roosevelt turned it into his Presidential retreat and named it Shangri-La. President Eisenhower later changed the name to Camp David, after his grandson. The place is meticulously maintained all year and kept lush and green, with wide open spaces and shaded trails connecting the buildings where camp employees work and live. Not surprisingly, Camp David is well equipped.

You can find anything there that one would expect at a military facility: barracks for the Marines and Sailors, guest cottages, dining halls, even a gym and small movie theater.

We put the aircraft in the hangar and then received a quick briefing about the weekend plans and schedule. My buddy Mike Manzer, another copilot, drove me over to the pilots' cabins in a golf cart. It was called Walnut, and it was furnished like a hotel, with two bedrooms, TVs, and a private bathroom.

That evening, the military aide called Mike and said, "Hey, the Boss wants to play walleyball, and he wants to play with the Marines. Be down at Wye Oak gym at 1600."

He stopped by my cabin and gave me the news.

" 'Walleyball'?" I asked.

"Yeah, it's volleyball, but on a racquetball court. And the President is damn good at it."

A short golf-cart ride later, I was standing in a racquetball court with a net running the width of it. The courts were inside the gym, which was a beautiful facility housing basketball courts, a swimming pool, a sauna, and a weight room. It was designed by Arnold Schwarzenegger when he served as Bush 41's Chairman of the President's Council on Physical Fitness and Sports. As I stood there with other pilots, the military aide, and a couple of the ubiquitous Secret Service guys, President Bush walked onto the court smiling and said, "Hey, fellas, how you doing?" He was wearing a T-shirt, shorts, and tennis shoes. It was the first time I had ever seen him out of a suit.

I managed to say, "Great, sir."

He was tall and athletic, smiling as he shook our hands. Being that close to the President of the United States for the first time—and knowing that I was about to compete against him—was a little intimidating. Once we started, though, we became just a bunch of guys playing a game.

This was my first time playing walleyball, and being a pretty competitive person, I decided to do my best, but there was no way I was going to spike the President! Alex Gierber, one of the copilots playing that day, was a huge Argentinean guy who probably stood six feet tall and weighed 250 pounds. He was playing right up on the net, directly across from President Bush. The game was moving fast, and I could tell that Alex had the same concerns that I had. He'd had a couple of opportunities to really smash the ball, but he was holding back.

Then the President grabbed up the ball and said, "Hold up. Hold up, guys." He looked Alex square in the eyes and grinned. "Look, son, if you're not going to play the game, I can get somebody in here that will." It was like he was saying, *Don't you go easy on me. I can take it.*

Alex is one of those people you have to tell only once. And sure enough, within the next couple of volleys, he stuffed the President pretty good. The President's glasses were hanging askew and he lost his balance a bit. Everyone froze, especially on our side of the net. A second later I could hear the Secret Service guys chuckling.

President Bush stood up, straightened his glasses, looked at Alex again, and said, "Now that's what I'm talking about." The game picked up again, and eventually the President said, "Okay, that's it for me. Thanks for the fun and the exercise and I'll catch you later," while wiping the sweat off his forehead with a towel. I managed to stay cool until the President headed back to his cabin.

I made some excited phone calls to family and friends when I got back to my cabin that night. I spent the rest of the weekend reading, working out, and eating at the chow hall. On Saturday night it was nearing dusk and I was playing horseshoes outside the cabins with a couple of the other pilots. As the sun dropped behind the mountain and it really started getting dark, we were starting to finish up our game.

Barbara Bush was walking nearby with her grandchildren, whom they had brought on the trip. As she passed within about twenty feet of us, she looked in our direction and said, "Who is that over there bangin' up George's shoes?"

We laughed and said, "Ma'am, it's just us, the Marines."

She said, "Okay then, before one more horseshoe gets thrown, it's getting cold out and you all better put on jackets."

We all said, "Yes, ma'am, of course," and we knew the game was over. It was getting too dark anyway. I still don't know for sure if that was her subtle way of telling us to stop banging horseshoes or if she was actually concerned that we were going to get cold. On Sunday evening we flew the First Family back to D.C., and I was once again blown away by the types of things I did in a day's work at HMX-1. The First Family always treated us wonderfully up there at Camp David, and everywhere else for that matter.

These were some of the best years of my life. I was participating in the most unusual and exciting missions, and learning so much. We lived in Fredericksburg, Virginia, and Ray Jr. and Delia were around nine and ten during this period. While I worked fifty to sixty hours a week, and traveled quite often, my wife handled everything at home. Thanks to her, the kids were doing great and thriving in school, soccer, band, and other activities. Steve was busy in his new career, but we kept in close contact. He even spent a couple of weekends at our house when he was in the area, and I had the opportunity to show him around HMX-1 a bit.

On "normal" weekends, when enough of us "locals" were in town, we would plan family barbecues, birthday parties, dinners—any excuse to get together and have some fun. Spanky bought a home in southern Stafford, Virginia, and I remember thinking it was the biggest house I'd ever seen for a single guy. Spanky has that MacGyver gene, and he can fix anything. He did a lot of the work on the house himself, including the planning and construction of a hot tub and a bar on the back deck. His house became the nexus of our social activities. The bar became affectionately known as the Beach Bongo Belly Up Bar, and it even featured a thatched roof. About a year after Spanky and I arrived, Bayou finally showed up and took his usual place in our ongoing professional and personal adventures.

President Bush Departs and President Clinton Comes on Board

President Bush and his family treated all of us like gold, and we supported them proudly. It was as if our intimate connection with the President made him not only our boss but almost a father figure. During the Presidential elections of November 1992, the country really was polarized by the differences between President Bush 41 and Presidential candidate Bill Clinton (not unlike the polarity we would experience later with Bush 43 and Obama), but we all assumed President Bush 41 would win the election.

Instead, we woke up to learn that we were going to serve a forty-second President, Bill Clinton. I had been in HMX-1 for only about a year, but the overwhelming feeling was that of a favorite coach being replaced. Over the next few months we were in state of transition and preparation for the incoming administration.

In January 1993, we had to say farewell to President Bush. As chance would have it, I was off duty and not required to fly during President Clinton's Inauguration Ceremony. Instead, I watched on a TV at Quantico as my Commanding Officer at the time (Colonel Ed Langston) flew President Bush on a victory lap over the National Mall. I knew that while the Colonel's relationship with the President was kept purely on a professional level, he had a deep respect for his boss. I could only imagine how he felt giving his Commander in Chief one last ride to honor and thank him.

Although we maintained the highest professionalism during the transition from Bush 41 to Clinton, it was a major adjustment both operationally and emotionally. It was during this time that I really began to appreciate how apolitical being a White House pilot was. It didn't matter if you agreed personally with a President's political standing or policies. He was the Commander in Chief, and you had to provide the same world-class support at all times.

Still somewhat of a new guy, I just did my job and watched the chaos of the transition unfold. Bush 41 was very punctual and always had a detailed calendar of events. As a result, the squadron had become accustomed to an orderly, well-thought-out travel plan. Naturally, with an entirely new (and very young) staff replacing an experienced one, things were not nearly as organized or predictable.

I remember one story that makes the point real: The first time HMX-1 flew President Clinton, nobody on his staff briefed him on the protocol for saluting as he boarded *Marine One*. There is always a Marine standing at the base of the stairs of *Marine One*, and he salutes the Commander in Chief. Of course, the President is supposed to salute the Marine back and then put his arm down. For some reason, he just boarded the aircraft without saluting. This created some confusion for the Marine and a generally awkward moment. Since this was Clinton's first time in *Marine One*, there was a lot of press coverage and the moment was captured on TV. The media ate it up, and it became a major topic of discussion for a while there. Half of the media outlets stated how shameful and disrespectful it was, and the other half said it was a simple mistake, while correspondents and military advisers chimed in on the issue.

Internally, we figured he simply hadn't been briefed. He had never been in the military and was not familiar with our customs and courtesies. No big deal. Over time, that little incident blew over and it did not happen again. Operations settled into a smoother rhythm, and I served as a Presidential copilot flying President Clinton all over the planet. The Clintons didn't own a home anywhere, so when they were away from the White House they were either at Camp David or with friends. For example, I flew them to Martha's Vineyard once, to spend a weekend with Warren Buffett. Because of my job in HMX-1, I often accompanied them on these trips and came to see that the Clintons were extremely kind and grateful toward the military, not unlike President Bush 41 and his family.

Over the course of my career, I would land on the White House lawn countless times, and it was almost always in the Sea King. I'll never forget the first time, which was during a Presidential lift not long after Clinton's inauguration. The First Lady's father had passed away, so the President was returning from the memorial services that had been held in Arkansas. Due to weather concerns, on the way out he had gone from the White House to Andrews AFB in his motorcade. *Marine One* was scheduled to pick him up at Andrews and bring him home this evening.

I had recently completed my saturation training, and Colonel Langston had selected me as his copilot for this lift. I had already been part of a few lifts, and even commanded support aircraft, but now I was going to copilot *Marine One* itself, with the President on board! I had also flown past the White House a number of times, but had never taken that right turn toward the South Lawn. This was going to be another brand-new experience, but one that I had already played out in my mind many times.

Everyone was well aware that because the copilot was in the left seat, the same side of the aircraft as the air stair, the copilot usually showed up in all the official photographs. In fact, pilots teased one another about this phenomenon, and sometimes made a point to stare at the White House after landing. When it worked out and we found the shot later on one of the media sites, we passed it around the ready room and jokingly called it the Geek of the Day photo. This was going to be a night landing, so there wouldn't be those kinds of photos, and I certainly wouldn't be the Geek of the Day.

Earlier in the day, we took the aircraft up for a test flight, and to burn off some fuel so that conditions were just perfect when we picked up the President. Now it was go time. It was a breezy evening when I walked out to the flight line with Colonel Langston, both of us wearing our formal lift uniform and leather flight jackets. We climbed aboard and began preparing the aircraft for our mission, following every step precisely. We started the engines, called the control tower, and received clearance for the flight.

The trip from Anacostia to Andrews AFB takes only a few minutes, but there is an invisible maze of restricted airspace that you cannot see using the natural landmarks in the area. We landed at Andrews just in time, and waited for *Air Force One* to arrive with the President. Within minutes, *Air Force One* landed, the President boarded *Marine One*, and we received clearance to lift off once more.

We gained altitude and turned toward the nearby Potomac River. Easing up to 200 feet, we turned to the northwest and followed the river. I immediately noticed that there was no moon, but a number of stars were out. The Potomac was nothing more than a dark line threading between two black horizons, its glassy surface reflecting the lights of the structures near its banks. The sunlight that usually lit the cockpit had now been replaced by the ambient light of the backlit controls. I had to call upon my training in an entirely different way to monitor and manipulate the panel of green and yellow indicator lights and gauges floating between me and the night sky. This was more intense than any video game. This was true point-of-view game play, virtual reality that included all five senses.

As copilot, I had a great deal of responsibility, such as making radio calls, overall navigation, choreographing the other aircraft in the lift, and giving the pilot all the visual cues he needed throughout the flight. There's a specific spot on the Potomac where you can turn right in between the two prohibited areas, one being over the White House, the other being over the Naval Observatory where the Vice President lives.

When we approached the right spot, I called the National Tower: "*Marine One*. Three minutes out."

The tower knew what I meant, and granted us permission.

We neared the Washington Monument, adorned in its nightly gown of white light. I again called for clearance as Colonel Langston put the monument on our right and started our final approach to the South Lawn. I knew that I was flying low over streets and suburbs, but at that moment it was a constellation of lights below that challenged me to stay focused on the most important lights of all—the ones straight ahead. The White House looked like a miniature version of itself all glowing with soft white light. The South Lawn was not lit, but I could see the vague shape of the fountain, as small as a toy in the darkness below us.

Our landing lights broadened our visibility as we moved closer, exposing the details I needed to guide Colonel Langston in. I was humbled by the Colonel's finesse as he flew us into what seemed like a black hole. I helped him to stay clear of the trees on the left. Finally, I could clearly see the three six-foot-long red disks that we needed to land on. The disks were used to ensure the same landing spot each time, and to protect the manicured lawn.

Colonel Langston's pedal turned the aircraft to the left, while turning the nose to the right, as if he were squeezing into a tight parking space. Now the White House was on our left. The pilot can only see directly in front of him, so I had a much better view of the disks by looking out to the left of the cockpit. I knew that if we put the front-left landing gear on the center of the front-left disk, and if Colonel Langston kept the aircraft straight, then all three landing gears should be right on target.

As we hovered ten feet off the ground, then five, I gave him instructions: "A little forward. A little left. You're good." Not surprisingly, he had deftly maneuvered the Sea King in between those dark and protective trees and made a perfect landing. Trying to control my oscillating sense of accomplishment and complete childish glee, I realized how very few people would ever get the chance to land on this spot of earth.

Making the moment even more memorable, President Clinton came up into the cockpit before climbing off the aircraft. He thanked us for the flight, and I turned sideways in my seat so that I could see him better. Knowing that our passengers had just attended the memorial services, Colonel Langston looked him right in the eye and said, "Sir, all of the Marines of HMX-1 are very sorry for your loss." He remained in the cockpit for about five minutes, and in the night outside the aircraft, I could see the Secret Service getting a little antsy.

I knew that life in Washington, D.C. went on below us. Couples were perhaps finishing up a late dinner after a long day at work, while parents tucked in their kids or watched TV. My family was nearby in Fredericksburg, doing the same. And as they did, we lifted off and headed back to Anacostia, talking about the President's kind words in the cockpit.

Besides my heightened sense of awareness (and nervousness), I was acutely aware of how Colonel Langston handled himself. I knew that he had recently flown President Bush on his victory lap, after serving as his pilot for several years. With about six months to go in his tenure as CO, he had just flown a new President for the first time. I couldn't have predicted it then, but years later I would find myself in the same situation as Colonel Langston, when I flew President Obama for the very first time.

A couple of weeks later, I had my first daytime landing on the

White House lawn. This time I was copilot for one of the Command
Pilots, Major Jay Anderson, and we were going to pick up the President and fly him to Delaware. In some ways, the day landing was much
like the nighttime landing. Same time frame, same control of the aircraft, same goal. In another sense, it was an utterly different sensory
experience.

After lifting off just as I had with Colonel Langston, the Washington Monument loomed in the distance. I had stood at its base with my
family when we first moved to the area, shielding our eyes from the
sun and looking up toward the top. At over 500 feet tall, the monument
now towered over our helicopter as we came in at 200 feet. Jay made
precise adjustments to maintain a very specific distance from the monument. Once again I called on the radio to receive final clearance to
approach the White House and land on the South Lawn. This was far
away from those grassy fields in Pensacola where I first learned how to
hover.

If I could snap a mental picture and freeze-frame it for a just a
moment, this is what I would have seen: to my left, treetops and houses
spanning out for miles. To my right, the Washington Monument and
the Potomac, and a sea of trees beyond that. Below me, busy city
streets and intersections. People were driving and walking around,
some looking up at the helicopter that might or might not be carrying
their President. And straight ahead, the White House itself, more
white and vivid than any photograph I had ever seen. More gleaming
and patriotic than I had even expected. But I did not stop to enjoy the
view. I just scanned and processed all those sights. I remained alert
and present.

The South Lawn looked tiny, blocked in by large trees, and the
fountain seemed to be placed right up against the building. I marveled
that Colonel Langston had made it look so easy, even in darkness.
There seemed not to be enough room to fit our helicopter in there, but

as we moved in closer, my depth perception moved right along with me. The grass was startlingly green and the trees seemed way too close, but I realized that there was ample room for a very precise maneuver. I couldn't help but remind myself that all the trees towering over the South Lawn, flailing their branches and leaves in the wind, had been planted by former Presidents.

Seeing the White House from this angle had me a little nervous. Thought after thought bounced around in my brain as I used my training to be the best copilot I possibly could be. I guided the pilot in for a precise landing, and this time the press was there in full force. I found myself looking toward the White House as the President came out and walked to the helicopter, and I wondered if someone was snapping my picture. We flew the President to the event in Delaware and then flew him back home. Put it down in the book: it was yet another great day to be part of HMX-1.

President Clinton used Camp David as a retreat the least of all the Presidents I flew. Still, I did take him and Mrs. Clinton to Camp David a couple of times. One day, we picked them up at the White House, and as always, the First Lady said good morning as she climbed the stairs while holding Chelsea's hand. Once we landed them on camp and settled into the cabins, the military aide called and said we had been invited to join the First Family in the theater. The film happened to be *Starship Troopers*, which is about a futuristic Marine unit.

I sat right behind the Clintons with another pilot, and as the film began, the President turned around and asked if we wanted any popcorn. The President asked *us* if we wanted popcorn.

"Sure thing, sir."

At one point in the movie, the Marines were firing these fictitious weapons called Morita MK 1s, which seemed to work pretty well on humans but weren't working all that well on the arachnids. The President turned around and said, "How would you guys like some of those?" then chuckled.

I was hoping he meant the guns and not the spiders. "Ha-ha . . . uh . . . yes, sir," we both mumbled. I mostly sat there mesmerized, my eyes drifting down from the screen to the three heads in front of me. I was watching a movie about a futuristic battle against alien bugs where the humans were fighting for survival with guns that didn't seem to be working all that well on the bugs, while the President of the United States and his family were sitting right in front of me and we were all eating popcorn.

This was no regular night at the local Cineplex.

With Pope John Paul II in the Passenger Seat

While I was becoming accustomed to flying precious cargo and had now been a Presidential copilot for some time, nothing prepared me to fly Pope John Paul II in 1993. He was in the United States for World Youth Day in Denver, Colorado, and I felt like I had won the lottery when I was selected as the copilot for the mission. HMX-1 doesn't usually fly anyone except the President and his staff outside the D.C. Beltway—except the Pope. I spoke to Bayou and Spanky the day before the lift, and they teased me about being the lucky one to get selected. Lucky or not, I was just happy to have the opportunity.

My family is very, very Catholic. To them, carrying the Pope held a lot more water than carrying the President. My grandmother was a blue-blooded Bostonian Catholic, and in her opinion the Pope could do no wrong. She even said, "The heck with Clinton. You're flying the Pope, I can die now."

As usual, we showed up early to coordinate the landing site, security, and the multitude of other concerns. Not only were we supporting the Pope's visit, but President Clinton was also coming to Denver to meet with the Pope, so HMX-1 had a very strong presence in the area. In the days preceding the Pope's visit, there was a palpable electricity in the air. There were police, security personnel, people from the Catholic Diocese, Cardinals, and Bishops getting everything ready. We went out to dinner in town in the evenings, and there were peddlers everywhere selling Pope-related memorabilia like the poetically named Pope Scopes, which were like little plastic periscopes you could use to see the Pope from within the massive crowd.

When the Pope actually arrived, we were positioned at Stapleton International Airport, and I watched this huge Alitalia Airlines jet land and taxi up to us. It's one thing to see the President walking down the steps of *Air Force One* toward you, but this was a completely different kind of feeling. This went beyond professional and entered into the personal. This was the Pope, and when he climbed on board, I felt his powerful presence. I remember feeling like, *This is probably as close to God as I'm ever going to get.* There were a few days before World Youth Day, and the Pope didn't motorcade anywhere. Since the President was not on board, and the Pope was considered a head of state, the call sign for the day was "State One." We flew in State One to schoolyards, monasteries, and parks, and each time there was a swarm of security, Vatican personnel, and onlookers.

When the day of the event arrived, we flew the Pope right over the rim of Mile High Stadium before landing in a secure location. I had to imagine that there was a security blanket over the entire state of Colorado, and every radar in the world probably had a pinpoint location on where we were. After all, we were carrying the leader of one of the largest faiths in the world. As we flew up over the lip of the stadium, one of the other aircraft had already gone ahead of us, and I heard the crowd going wild. We cleared the rim and I saw the largest crowd I had ever flown over at that point in my life.

There was a sea of people in the stands and on the field who had

descended on Denver for the event. I had never even landed a President
in a crowd this big. Tens of thousands of people stood and cheered in
pockets of color, representing their countries by wearing uniforms that
matched their flags. Throngs of Nuns, Bishops, and security personal
swarmed among them. The other helicopters carrying the Vatican staff
landed first, so they could get into position. We finally landed and the
Pope got off and into the Popemobile, a modified vehicle that looked like
a high-end golf cart encased in bulletproof glass.

You never know if you'll be invited into an event, and most of the
time we weren't. But we were invited into this one, so, after securing
the aircraft, I walked through the crowd with my buddy Mike Sparr,
who is one of the funniest people I've ever met in my life. We found a
spot right at the base of the huge statue of a bronco, and we had a
pretty decent view overlooking the stage. I noticed that Mike had little
vials of water in all his pockets, which he hoped to get blessed by the
Pope.

I said, "You better hope you don't fall down. You'll look like you
pissed your pants."

He said, "Don't worry about me. I have a hundred bucks' worth of
lottery tickets right here," as he patted his left breast pocket. "If it's going to happen, it's going to happen now."

When the Pope took the stage, we could barely see him amid the
sea of Pope Scopes. The energy of the place was palpable, and I was
inspired to have the honor of watching and hearing the Pope speak
that day. Thirty minutes before the event ended, the WHLO alerted us
to prep the aircraft. We quickly made our way back to the landing
zone. When the event was over and the Pope made his way back to the
aircraft, he presented two young Marines with a pair of blessed rosary
beads and papal coins. They were grateful to say the least. We lifted off
from Mile High Stadium and flew the Pope to a couple more events
that day, including a meeting with President Clinton.

The next day, we flew him to a Catholic retreat called Saint Malo's, way up in the Rocky Mountains. The plan was that he would relax there for the weekend before his last event on Sunday. We jokingly called the event "Popestock" because there were supposed to be half a million people at a place called Cherry Creek Park for Sunday Mass.

The weekend retreat was not one of those trips where we fly the VIP or person to the destination and then fly away. The staff wanted us there so that if anything happened, we could get the Pope out of there quickly. The place was empty that weekend except for the Pope, close Vatican staff, Secret Service, the resort staff, and us HMX-1 personnel. We all got to meet the Pope, and he gave us rosary beads. When we met, I shook his hand, and he asked me a few questions. When I answered his questions, he usually smiled and said, "I bless your families."

He also decided to go on a hike at one point and invited us to join him. When I showed up at the appointed time and place for the hike, the Pope was still wearing his garments, but instead of the typical headgear he was wearing a white driver's cap, the same kind that the cartoon character Andy Capp used to wear. He reminded me of my grandfather.

When we flew the Pope to Cherry Creek Park for Sunday Mass, I quickly added that day to the growing list of my most memorable experiences. We got a call from the Vatican staff, saying that they wanted to put a video guy in the back of the aircraft and record the Pope as we circled the park before landing. The video of the Pope waving down at the crowd would be instantly transmitted to the JumboTrons set up on both sides of the stage. We had never done that before but got approval to do it for the Pope. As usual, we landed in a predetermined spot behind the stage, and then the Pope got out and climbed into a Winnebago. When he emerged, he was dressed in his vestments for celebrating Mass, and I had another opportunity to interact with him. All the pilots were standing in a kind of receiving line with other people who had been allowed backstage.

Right next to me was a little girl in a wheelchair with her mother. I could tell that the little girl had a severe case of muscular dystrophy, and there were several other ill children beside them. As the Pope made his way down the line, looking everyone in the eye and shaking their hands and speaking a few words of blessing, the little girl's mother had tears streaming down her face. I was overcome by emotion myself, as I could only imagine the challenges this woman had overcome and how meaningful it must have been for her to be in the presence of the Pope. The Pope said a few words to me, and I was again enthralled by his energy, and then he got down on one knee in front of the crippled girl as her mother sobbed.

He took the little girl's hands into his and bowed his head. The mother was sobbing hysterically now, clearly overcome with hope and releasing all the pain she'd built up. He then stood up, took the little girl's face in his hands, and then took the mother's hands, and blessed them both. Her display of raw emotion had just about everyone crying, even us tough Marines.

He got up onto the stage and delivered a wonderful Mass, and I heard the massive crowd just going nuts. During the Mass, his words were being translated into different languages. Once the event was over, we flew him back to the airport for his flight back to Rome. But before he boarded his plane, he was scheduled to meet with Vice President Al Gore. From our perspective, Vice President Gore was always very stoic and rarely had anything to say to us. Since he didn't display much congeniality with us, we never really formed a bond with him. He certainly never asked or offered to take pictures with us.

But apparently this day was different. As the pilots were taking a photograph with members of the Denver Police Department, the Pope came over to thank us one last time and to get in the picture. To our surprise, Vice President Gore came over and joined the photo. In my humble opinion, he would never have done that if the Pope had not been there.

The Pope boarded his aircraft, and the events in Colorado were complete. We were all very pleased with our performance in supporting the Pope and the President and how unusual the whole experience had been. I got back to the hotel room and immediately called my parents and grandmother to tell them all the details I knew they were expecting. When I told them about the Pope blessing the little girl backstage, and the speech at World Youth Day, and the hike up at Saint Malo's, they were proud of me, a member of the Marine Corps who flew with the Pope.

White House Liaison Officer (1995–1996)

Before long my second year was almost finished, and it was time for another phase within HMX-1. Although I did perform well, at the time there were a lot of other qualified pilots who had more seniority than I had. I was still a Captain, and there was an abundance of qualified Majors. I knew that the math just wasn't working in my favor, and resigned myself to the fact that I could still fly the Vice President and still copilot a Presidential lift, but I was not going to be one of the four command pilots serving right under the HMX-1 Commander. I was okay with that, because more than anything, I wanted to be one of the eight pilots selected as a WHLO. It's one of the most unusual jobs in HMX-1 and in the Marine Corps in general. I also knew that as a WHLO, in certain situations I would represent and make decisions on behalf of the HMX-1 Commander in the field. I felt like I was up for that challenge, and saw it as an opportunity.

I was selected, and I spent the last two years of my tour as a WHLO. During that time, I traveled to several countries, and sometimes literally at the last moment. My flight time dropped because I was always on the road, but when I was in town, the operations section made sure I got time in the cockpit. More than anything, being a WHLO made me an expert in HMX-1 planning and logistics, and it was by far the most responsibility I had ever had or dreamed of having.

My mentor and friend Willie Willard (former CO of the Red Lions) was working at Naval Air Systems Command and living in Springfield, Virginia. Every couple of months he invited us up for a Sunday barbecue. I was up for promotion to Major, and the small ceremony would take place on December 1, 1995. Promotion or "pinning" ceremonies are among many traditions in the Marine Corps. Usually my Commanding Officer would promote me, but you always had the option of requesting that someone else stand in at the ceremony. I asked Colonel Demars if he would be okay with Willie promoting me, and he said, "Absolutely."

I then asked Willie if he would promote me, and he readily agreed. Willie is one of those great orators who can speak off-the-cuff, while injecting hilarious anecdotes and fun into his speeches. Again, it was a very small ceremony, with my family and a couple of my buddies. Willie made a few remarks and a few jokes as my expense, then placed my new rank on my uniform. It was another of countless proud moments for me.

I am always shocked when I see myself, as a member of HMX-1, through my family's eyes. I was still just the same old Ray, but when my family saw me in the line of duty, I realized on an even more profound level just how incredible my job was. During the midterm elections of 1995, President Clinton was traveling to Manchester, Nashua, and some other areas near my hometown. One of those stops was Franklin, New Hampshire, which was only about thirty miles from my parents' home.

Steve "Cujo" Cusomano was with me, as I was training him on WHLO activities, and we were in a local hotel for the event. Following standard procedure, we arrived a couple of days early to start coordinating the trip. One night we drove down to my parents' house for dinner, then went out for a few drinks with my brothers. As a WHLO, we always checked out the restaurants and businesses in the local area, but this was different. This was my old stomping ground. I showed Cujo where I had gone to school and one of the restaurants where I had worked, and we ended up at a new microbrewery that seemed to pop up amid a string of nationwide microbreweries. We sampled some of the local brew, relaxed, and listened to the live band. My brother Roger, a musician through and through, pulled out his harmonica and started jamming with the band. I had seen him do this so many times I'd lost count, but Cujo thought it was simply amazing. Instead of going back to our hotel, I crashed in my parents' spare bedroom and Cujo crashed on the couch.

The next morning we had to get out to the airfield early and coordinate the lift package with law enforcement and the Secret Service. We had to blend in, so we were wearing suits and ties, not our Marine uniforms. Once we got down to the site, we secured the rope line, and my wife, parents and in-laws were there among the crowd of faces, not unlike the time Steve and I first saw President Reagan land back in Tustin. But now I was the suited Marine moving around and making arrangements within the secure area of the airfield. I talked to the Secret Service guys, coordinated with the aircraft on the radio, and when the *Marine One* lift package finally came into view and approached us, I choreographed the landing perfectly. This was the first time my family had seen me working in person like this, and I'd be lying if I said I didn't steal a look or two over at them, and that I didn't enjoy the immense look of pride in their eyes. After the President landed, another rare opportunity made the day even more memorable.

Just because *Marine One* happens to be in your hometown, and just because you happen to be a WHLO, that doesn't mean you're guaranteed to have your family meet the President. In fact, it's highly unlikely. Well, it was one of my lucky days. As the President made his way to the rope line to shake hands and meet with the locals, I asked the military aide over the radio if he thought the President might want to take a picture with the family of one of his HMX-1 WHLOs.

The aide spoke to the President, then came back on the radio and said yes, that would be fine. He then asked me where they were standing, and told me to head over in that direction. I made my way to the rope line and stood next to my family before the President got there. The President walked up to us, with his Secret Service guys all around, said "Hi, Major," and then kindly offered to take the picture. I said, "Thank you, sir," after the camera went off and he began to move down the rope line. My mother-in-law was a big Clinton fan, so she was completely enamored. In real time, the moment lasted only a few seconds, but in the memory of my family, the moment will go on forever.

The Fiftieth Anniversary of D-day

In 1994, I was one of the WHLOs assigned to the advance team during President Clinton's visit to Normandy, France, for the fiftieth anniversary of D-day. I arrived early to coordinate all the logistics, landing zones, schedules, and security surrounding *Marine One*'s support of the President. I had never been to France at that point, and since joining HMX-1 it was my first time traveling overseas as a member of the advance team.

I had been in Europe for seventeen days when the President arrived. His trip began in Naples and included Rome and Paris before ending in Normandy. After a few days of traveling around just hundreds of feet above the European countryside, we arrived in Calais, which is a little seaside town next to Normandy.

The city was completely electrified with activity, and there were WW II veterans all over the place. On my downtime, I walked the streets, just taking in the scene and talking to some of the local townspeople. It didn't take me long to realize that the people living in the region remembered what had happened. They never forgot the fact that the United States and its allies had liberated France. It was a very important part of their history, and for the fiftieth anniversary, many homes proudly flew American and French flags side by side.

One day I was out with some other Marines on the advance team, some Secret Service guys, some Air Force guys, and a couple of White House staffers. There were little cafés and pubs all over the place, and they were all teeming with patrons. While having a drink inside one, we struck up a conversation with some old retired Army guys. One of them in particular was very talkative, and I was humbled and amazed by the fact that they had actually landed on those beaches in 1944, and survived, and now here they were back in Normandy fifty years later to remember the occasion.

I said, "Sir, can I buy you a beer?"

He started laughing at me and said, "Son, you start that, and you're going to have to buy this whole event a beer and you can't do that. So tell you what, let me buy you a beer instead."

I was stumped. These guys had stormed the beaches of Normandy, and now they were thanking us for our service and buying us a beer!

Later during the trip, my Commanding Officer flew President Clinton to the American cemetery that overlooks Omaha Beach. It's located in Colleville-sur-Mer, and almost 9,400 people are buried there. Since the cemetery is actually U.S. Park territory, we are the only helicopters that can land our head of state ceremonially right there at the cemetery.

As I watched President Clinton speak to the crowd on that cloudy day in June, I was moved by the history of what had happened in that place, the survivors standing all around me, the dead buried row on row. That I was part of it all made me even more proud to be an American than I usually am.

•   •   •

I stayed busy, spending time at home when I was in town, coordinating Presidential lifts all over the country, and making several overseas trips as well. Although the Clintons definitely treated the Marines of HMX-1 very well, sometimes we were still reminded of how great President Bush's organized schedule had been. In early 1996, I was in Rhode Island planning a lift, and I received a call from HQ.

"Frenchy, you're the last guy available. The President just added Cairo to his Israeli trip, and you need to go there. Now."

"Right now?" I said. "When will the President arrive?"

"If you leave now, you might have about ten to twelve hours before the lift package arrives," he said.

Now I knew this was serious. Usually, I would have days or even weeks to coordinate a trip. I was already way behind the power curve. I packed up my suitcase and went straight down to the airport, where my reservation was waiting for me. This had all happened so quickly, I had no idea who was going to meet me there. After the first leg of the trip, I had to switch to an Egyptair plane at the Frankfurt, Germany, airport. I finally landed at Cairo International Airport, and it was a bit of a culture shock. I had never been to Egypt, and I had some mental images of what I was expecting, but I wasn't prepared at all for what awaited me. As I wove my way through the massive crowd, smells surrounded me that I had never noticed in an airport before. There were goats and chickens running around the airport. I kept my eye out and finally found what I was looking for: a local Egyptian with a sign that read U.S. EMBASSY. We identified each other, then I went with him out to the Embassy van. The van was armored and had bulletproof glass. Rhode Island was far behind me now.

Driving to the hotel, I noticed how densely populated the poverty-stricken streets were. The air was brown, the ground was brown. Everything was dirty, dusty, and brown. I hadn't slept much on the ten-hour international flights, so when I got into my room I checked in with the squadron and then grabbed a two-hour nap. Next, I went into the control room we had set up. It was nice to see some familiar faces—the Secret Service, the military aide, the White House staff—but everyone was trying to pull together a last-minute plan.

I needed to know exactly when the squadron would arrive, so that I would know how long I had to find hangar space for the aircraft. I found out that we had eight hours, and it wasn't lost on me that Colonel Demars was on the flight as well. Against all odds, I worked with my counterparts and local authorities to secure some hangar space. Once the squadron arrived in a massive C-5 cargo plane, I coordinated to have all the helicopters secured in a nearby hangar. Over the next two days, we had time to rehearse the mission and even ended up with one day of downtime before the President arrived. This was my first time in the Middle East, and I wanted to see as much as I could. The night before, I had asked one of the Secret Service guys what he thought about my doing an early-morning run through the city. He advised me that based on the predominant religion and culture in the area, running around with my PT uniform probably wasn't the most respectful thing to do. I had to agree. Instead, I worked out in the hotel gym, then spent the day meandering through packed alleys, walkways, and shops, marveling at the diverse culture and the colorful wares for sale. The way people dressed, the languages they spoke, the smells of exotic cooking—it was all so new to me, and, as I said, the city was more densely populated than any I had ever visited before. People seemed to live and work and shop shoulder-to-shoulder.

I bought some papyrus art paper for my family and, on a recommendation from a buddy, some Egyptian cotton shirts. Later in the afternoon, I met up with other members of the squadron for a tour we had scheduled at the famous Cairo Museum. I felt like I had wandered into another time as we strolled past the King Tut exhibit and the House of Mummies.

The mission to Egypt was a total success, and once I got the squadron back on their C-5, I had one final day left in Cairo to wrap things up. On the long flight home, I took it all in and imagined the President flying back to the United States on *Air Force One*, and the HMX-1 crew in the back of a C-5 with the white tops and all our equipment. I had just completed a major international mission that honed my rapid-planning skills to an even finer point—and I felt a deep sense of accomplishment.

CHAPTER 4

SEA KINGS AND WHITE HAWKS

None of the incredible experiences I was having at HMX-1 would have been possible if I had not passed all the certifications and levels of training that accompanied my four-year tour. Shortly after flying the CH-53 support helicopter on that first Presidential lift to Detroit, I had to attend the ground school for the VH-3 (Sea King) and VH-60 (White Hawk) helicopters. These are the classic white tops I had daydreamed about for so long.

The ground schools were run right there at Quantico by Sikorsky Aircraft Corporation, and included two weeks of in-depth classroom instruction. Just by virtue of the fact that I had been selected for HMX-1, it was assumed that I was already an experienced aviator. In a typical aviation squadron, new pilots check into their squadrons with about two hundred hours, which is all instructional flight time. At HMX-1, even the newest freshman pilot showed up with at least fifteen hundred flying hours—the minimum requirement. Consequently, the combined flight hours in any HMX-1 cockpit were significantly higher than average, and therefore you always ended up with what we called a "seasoned cockpit."

doors on each side of the cockpit. The primary entry for passengers is a set of double doors that swing outward with the two VIP seats facing each other as you look into the cabin. Unlike the Sea King, the main cabin in the White Hawk is separated from the cockpit by a wall. The cutting-edge cockpit features digital gauges and numerous classified navigational and communications technologies. The interior is once again plush, with seating and accommodations for up to eleven passengers.

The White Hawk is slightly smaller than the Sea King, making it easily transportable and ideal for overseas missions. The rotor blades can be quickly folded backward over the fuselage. The aircraft can then be loaded into a single cargo plane such as a C-17, including the crew and the entire contingent of support personnel and equipment. Within just a few hours of landing, it can then be totally configured and ready to fly.

White House Hack

The next step was saturation training, which required me to spend six weeks living in a facility near Reagan National Airport, and training on a four-day-on, two-day-off schedule. During this highly classified training, I learned all the intricacies, idiosyncrasies, methodologies, tactics, and principles of transporting the President of the United States.

With saturation training complete, the next rite of passage was to become qualified as a Helicopter Aircraft Commander (HAC) in the VH-3 and the VH-60, otherwise known as "White House HAC" training. This regimented training was tried and true, and planned well in advance, as I was still working and participating on various missions. I completed my White House hack training just before the flight with the Pope. I now had the authority to sign for the aircraft and play a more key role as the primary pilot on a Presidential lift. I was fully qualified to fly as primary pilot for any passenger in the world—except the President himself.

I also had to become qualified as a White House copilot. As was the case in any FAA or aviation certification or evaluation, all the training culminated in a final evaluation flight called a "check ride." Before long, I was designated as a certified Presidential copilot by the Secret Service and the White House. I could now serve as the copilot of an aircraft crew that carried the President, Vice President, or any number of VIP passengers, to include visiting heads of state.

I once read that Igor Sikorsky built his first helicopter at the age of nineteen, using sketches by Leonardo da Vinci. Today, Igor Sikorsky is a legend, his creations proudly transport the President of the United States, and each lift is a testament to Igor's incredible sense of style and engineering. His magnificent machines could defy gravity, and were loyal as a dog if you treated them right. After spending more than a thousand hours in the air flying his Sea Kings and White Hawks, I am forever grateful to Igor. The man was a genius.

Leaving HMX-1: Hail and Farewell

My four years at HMX-1, so rich with excitement and challenge, flew by at the speed of light. A month or so before I left, I received my new orders. My next assignment was Operations Officer at HMH-463, a Marine Heavy Helicopter squadron headquartered at Marine Corps Air Station Kaneohe Bay, Hawaii. I would be flying CH-53s again.

Leaving was bittersweet, but I had been out of the "fleet" for four years, and I knew that this tour could not last forever. In a way, I also couldn't wait to move to Hawaii, to get back into the CH-53 and join the boys in doing what I was trained to do. We were a military family, and we knew the drill. We sold the house and prepared for yet another move.

One of the greatest perks of working at HMX-1 is that whenever someone leaves the White House Military Unit, they get a photo with the President. I showed up at the White House in my Dress Blues for the occasion and was escorted to the Oval Office. Although I had seen tried to follow the mission from afar. Now I was going down to see what the city looked like a year later. I was very intrigued because, aside from driving through the area and layovers at the airport, I had never actually spent time in New Orleans. Also I had flown only a couple of times since leaving the Ugly Angels, and I was excited to get back into the cockpit.

The trip leader was Major Garret Hoffman, and we were going to fly four aircraft from D.C. to Louisiana (two VH-60s and two CH-53s). I was going to fly one of the CH-53s in the lift package. I'm sure it was an unusual experience for Major Hoffman and the other pilots to have a full bird Colonel, and their next CO, flying a supporting aircraft. My goal was simply to learn, observe, and see the squadron in action.

We left early on an August morning and arrived around dinner-time. The flight took us through various types of airspace and over several states. As we came into the northern part of New Orleans over Lake Pontchartrain, I could still see the remnants of a long bridge that had been swept away. Soon, we were flying right over the city, making wide-sweeping turns to set up for the landing to the south, and I could tell that something had gone horribly wrong there. In some areas it looked like the storm had hit the day before: devastation, trash, abandoned neighborhoods, and countless blue tarps on still-unrepaired roofs.

I looked down and thought, *Holy crap, this place looks like a war zone.*

We finally bedded down at a Naval Air Station in Belle Chasse, which is a few miles south of New Orleans proper. Before we descended for landing, I saw in the distance the seemingly endless marshes. From studying my map, I knew that this vast geographical area was where the Mississippi River transforms and washes out into the marshes that dominate the southern tip of Louisiana.

We then drove rental cars to our hotel, just blocks from the French Quarter. The hotel was fine, and I couldn't tell whether it had been affected by the storm. We had an early morning, but we did go out for dinner, then explored the area just a bit. Really, besides a few spots that seemed abandoned and washed out, the entire French Quarter felt pretty much like I had expected it to—a party atmosphere full of music and fun-loving people.

One of my favorite rituals is to take a run around a city in the early morning, especially if I've never been there before. I almost always get the bird's-eye view of a place, but my morning runs give me a chance to get the lay of the land in another way. So, a few hours before work began the next morning, I went for a run around downtown New Orleans. I ran a few blocks to the river, then turned left and followed it for a couple of miles. I made my way in toward the French Quarter, and passed Jackson Square and the Saint Louis Cathedral. As I ran through the humid and historic streets, I couldn't help but admire the stunning architecture. Deep in the heart of the French Quarter there was little evidence of a hurricane or flood.

I may have been too distracted by the sights and sounds. As I approached Bourbon Street and looked left and right, I saw a car slowing down at the intersection. I also saw that I had the green light and right-of-way on my side. I slowed down but kept running and began to cross the street. I then noticed on my near left that the car wasn't slowing down after all. I actually had to jump onto the hood so that the bumper didn't hit me. I rolled off the hood and hit the ground. The car didn't stop. I stood up slowly and did a self-inspection. Nothing was broken, and I was okay, but I did have road rash on both arms and legs.

A man nearby had been cleaning the street when I got hit, and he had seen the whole thing. He asked if I was okay. I looked down again. My scrapes were red and bleeding a bit, but not too bad. "Yeah, I'm fine, thanks." I said, then decided to finish my run. "Welcome to New Orleans."

A few hours later, we were doing rehearsals, coordinating with the

WHLOs, and just getting everything prepped for the two days of lifts. It was refreshing for me to see the amount of professionalism demonstrated by everyone involved. The squadron had integrated some new technology since my first tour, but overall the rhythm and process were the same. On the first day, we flew the President to the Ninth Ward, one of the areas most affected by the flooding. As we landed in a field, I saw President Bush from a distance, and I wondered what it was like for Major Hoffman. We also flew him to visit a school that had been rebuilt since the flooding. Out there on the edges of New Orleans, some progress could certainly be seen, but then again there was still a great deal of trash and seemingly abandoned neighborhoods.

The press was there all along, of course, capturing everything. The next day, we picked up Haley Barbour, the Governor of Mississippi, and flew over the state's coastline. New Orleans had taken all the headlines, because of the flooding and state-leadership issues. Many people don't realize that the Gulf Coast of Mississippi took a direct hit. Although this area was not as large as New Orleans, it did appear that much more work had been completed there. I flew over the large concrete slabs that had once held casinos and resort hotels. There were construction cranes everywhere, and the sense that progress was being made.

We got the President back to *Air Force One*, and from my vantage point in the cockpit of my CH-53, not far behind *Marine One*, I saw him climb the airplane's stairwell and step inside. For the first of many times, I then watched him take off in the huge jet, until it was only a tiny airplane fading into the distance.

Meeting George W. Bush

During this period, I also took several trips back to Camp David. I had not been there since the days of Bush 41 and Clinton, and I soon found out why I wasn't hearing much talk about Camp David. Apparently, the current Camp Commander had created a culture of separation. He encouraged all military personnel to stay "out of sight, out of mind" whenever the President and his family were in residence at the camp. I was surprised and a bit disappointed to hear this, because I remembered how much it meant to us when we interacted with President Bush 41.

On this particular visit, I had just landed with another pilot, Major Jim Toth. It was around 5:00 P.M., and we were traveling down a paved path on our way to the lodging area when Jim abruptly pulled the golf cart off the path and into the woods.

"What are you doing, Jim?"

"Sir, the President is right in front of our cabin," he said, as if I should understand his actions based on this statement. I didn't.

"So, why did we pull into the woods?"

"Oh, we were told not to bother the President when he's on Camp."

"Why would we bother him? He'll think we don't like him. Pull on up, Jim."

He looked at me cautiously, as if to say, *You're the boss,* but he did as I'd asked.

As we pulled up, President Bush, wearing jeans and a windbreaker jacket, was trying to coerce into the golf cart the black Scottish terrier we had all seen on the White House lawn. "Come on, Barney, come on," he said.

We parked right beside his golf cart, and I respectfully said, "Good evening, sir. Do you need any help?" I was smiling politely because we both knew he didn't really need my help with the little dog.

The President looked at us and said, "How are you doing tonight, fellas? No, I think I've got it under control." Then he laughed and said, "Can't you see he's ferocious?"

We shared in the joke and wished him a great night. He returned the gesture and didn't seem the least bit bothered by our presence. I had a feeling that I would spend many weekends at Camp David, and that night I made another mental note: the culture at Camp David would be changed.

A Day in the Life

In June 2007, we held a formal change-of-command ceremony out on the flight line, and Colonel O'Donnell said his goodbyes. When it was my turn to speak, I mentioned just how privileged I felt, and thanked Drew for all his help and guidance in preparing me for this huge responsibility.

The clock had officially started ticking, and I began settling in to my tour as Commander. One of the first things I did was move into my new office. Located in the heart of HMX-1 HQ, it was a small room with wood-paneled walls. Photographs of former HMX-1 Commanders and the last few U.S. Presidents lined the walls.

My desk sat on one side, with a small wooden table and two chairs positioned in front. On my desk was my computer, along with secure and nonsecure telephones. It was bigger, but—in an odd way—it wasn't much different from the desk on which I had built model airplanes when I was a boy. Beside those I placed some photos of my family, and there were framed posters of several aircraft on the wall behind my desk. On the other side of my desk, in customary fashion, were two flags in a metal stand that allowed the long wooden poles to crisscross. One was the American flag, and the other was the official Marine Corps Standard, or the squadron colors. It was just another office, but now it was my office. On the table across from my desk stood a replica of a Night Hawk helicopter, forever frozen at an angle in midflight. It could have hung from my bedroom ceiling when I was a boy.

In so many ways, I was still the boy who couldn't wait to get home and open the box of his new model airplane, but here I was, the head of HMX-1. It was both empowering and daunting to be in charge of such a large and talented workforce. I had learned a lot as Commander of the Ugly Angels, but this was a new kind of challenge. I now had a great number of aircraft and four entirely different models under my command. There was the VH-3 Sea King, the VH-60 White Hawk, the CH-43, and the CH-53E.

I also had eight hundred "employees," including Marines, Sailors, and "civilian Marines." Among them, I had what were considered some of the top helicopter pilots in the Marine Corps and hundreds of support personnel specializing in maintenance, communications, security, and safety, to name a few. The ranks of my diverse workforce ranged from Lance Corporals (E3) to Lieutenant Colonels (O5), and there were various ages and educational and cultural backgrounds represented. My immediate staff was comprised of the normal complement of field grade officers, an extremely seasoned and competent group.

My perspective had changed, too. I was no longer a young boy or the recruit at boot camp or that young Captain or Major serving as a copilot. I was now going to be the Presidential Helicopter Pilot, with ultimate responsibility for the success or failure of all of HMX-1's complex operations. All of HMX-1's diverse training, operational testing, and executive support missions fell under my scope of responsibility, and I was accountable to three different chains of command. We provided testing and evaluation of helicopter systems for use across the Marine Corps and helicopter support for various Department of Defense training missions.

Most important of all, though, was the Executive Support mission: I would be flying the President, his family, his staff, and a multitude of other dignitaries and government officials all over the world. Most aviation organizations have a specific Area of Responsibility (AOR), but because of the Executive Support mission, our AOR spanned the entire planet.

Quite often, after a twenty-five-year career, the Commander of an aviation squadron does exactly that—command; he or she does not necessarily fly very much. But HMX-1 was different, since the Commander of HMX-1 had the billet description of "Presidential Helicopter Pilot." I was considered one of the old men by that point, but I still got to fly almost daily, just like the young pilots. And although I orchestrated HMX-1's global missions through my talented staff, at the end of the day, the organization's fifty years of operational perfection were mine to mar.

My days and weeks were filled with a combination of complex planning, flying, and leading young and old Marines, always instilling growth and introducing a human element to the job as well. I also strove to mentor my staff to new heights of professionalism by fostering an environment of continual learning and development. The ready room was our professional and social nucleus, as in any squadron. It was a modest room with rows of chairs, and a large podium and counter up front where the Operations Duty Officer sat. Behind that was the "grease board," which was again so prevalent in any aviation ready room. Back in the day, this would have been a clear Plexiglas surface that we wrote on with grease pencils. Modern technology has since transformed it into a large flat-screen monitor with a digital version of the flight schedule, but we still called it a grease board.

Each morning, we held an All Officer's Meeting (AOM) in the ready room to get everyone on the same page. On any given day, there were twenty to forty pilots and copilots in the room, along with other administrative and support personnel to include our civilian contractors and technical representatives. It was not as simple as a landing on the White House lawn or on a school yard in New Jersey. The safety and security of the President and our pilots were always the top priorities. There are countless other decisions, preplanning, and actions that had to take place for everything to run seamlessly. Still, anything could change at any moment, so my staff had to be flexible and dynamic in the face of those possibilities.

Assimilating my higher-level guidance from my boss and the White House Military Office, I synchronized HMX-1's activities to be as efficient as possible. Under my guidance, the Operations Department developed a daily and monthly flight schedule to ensure that each trip, lift, and mission had the right talent and mix of capabilities to meet the particular mission set.

When there were multiple missions taking place at once, I needed a few other pilots to act on my behalf. I hand-selected four command pilots based on maturity and capacity to make decisions when things were not going as planned. The command pilots had to undergo some additional training to be qualified to fly *Marine One*, and then I did a final check ride with each one. One of those pilots was Major Jennifer Grieves, who was the first female *Marine One* pilot in history. When she joined the squadron in 2005, she became only the second female to do so. In May 2008, I selected her as one of my command pilots. On July 16, 2009, Jennifer led the first all-female *Marine One* crew when they picked up President Obama on the White House lawn.

We were Marines, and we knew how to follow orders. That's how the chain of command was supposed to work. In order to carry out my orders, and to provide direction to the workforce, I made daily decisions internal to HMX-1 operations. I also sometimes made decisions that directly affected the President himself. I had an enormous responsibility when I had the President in the air. For those few minutes or hours, his life was in my hands, quite literally. That responsibility alone could be quite daunting. The Secret Service was integral to mission planning and security, but at some point they had to relinquish a level of control until I landed the Boss safely at his destination.

As a helicopter pilot, I was very cognizant of the impacts of weather on aviation operations. Safety is always a critical planning factor, but in combat training you were not dealing with VIPs, so you learned to deal with highly adverse weather situations. Being the Commander of HMX-1 took weather considerations to an entirely new level, as I was not going to put the President in the air if there was any kind of weather risk. I now had access to the country's most advanced meteorological reports and analyses, which I used to make critical decisions on whether or not to fly. These kinds of decisions were some of the most agonizing because we ran a zero-fail mission. My decisions had to be precise and every possible course of action and effect had to be taken into account. Plus, let's face it, nobody wants to say no to the President, and nobody wants the embarrassment (and possible disciplinary action) of making the wrong call.

I was mandated by White House standard operations procedures to make a weather call at a certain point in time, which was but one small decision point in the larger, complex, and nonstop scheduling and coordination effort. For example, thunderstorms often roll across the property in Crawford, Texas. There were times that the Secret Service asked me for the weather call, and procedure made the decision more frustrating. My boss was all about following strict protocol, and I agreed. I knew how a deviation from policy or process could cause a domino effect of issues at multiple levels. It wasn't worth the risk. Still, I remember standing there in Texas looking up at the sky and talking to the Secret Service guys.

I told them I had been watching the radar and that I knew we'd be clear in two hours, when the President was scheduled to leave the ranch. But at that exact moment in time, when they needed a decision so that they could coordinate (or not) a motorcade and get local law enforcement involved in blocking off roads, I simply couldn't approve the lift. On the other hand, I could use the informaiton at hand to approve the lift, but if the weather didn't clear up as predicted, then the Secret Service would have to scramble to put together the motorcade, and I would be the squeaky wheel in an otherwise well-oiled machine. Worst of all would have been if the weather was actually bad and I made the decision to fly the President, and put him in danger. Luckily, this never happened during my tenure. It was always better to be safe than sorry, period.

During one of the many weekends at Camp David, I was standing on the porch of my cabin Sunday morning, eyeing the weather. It didn't look good. Camp David was socked in with thick fog. I could fly in the rain as long as I had visibility. I knew that appearances could be misleading, so my copilot called the Camp David weather office for the official meteorological reports. I quickly realized that if things went my way, I would have a safe window of opportunity to get the First Family off the mountain and back to the White House. But if things went another way, I would not have visibility, and would not be able to fly.

Safety was my most important deciding factor, but I was also aware of the domino effect my decision could have. If I decided that we could not fly, then the Secret Service, Camp David personnel, and local law enforcement would all have to work together to plan and secure the route for the President's motorcade. This would not be so uncommon, but then again it was an inconvenience for the local communities, and took a lot more time and energy than just flying him home in his helicopter. In my opinion, a day like that was probably one of the reasons *Marine One* became such a preferred method of travel.

I called the military aide and told him about my concerns.

"They're just about to head off to church. Should I tell them we have to go?" he asked.

"No, not yet. I think the weather is going to break in about an hour, but then there is another band of nasty weather coming our way. As soon as the weather breaks, I will be sitting on the landing zone and I'll call you with a five-minute warning."

I packed up my stuff, drove over to the hangar, and positioned the aircraft at the landing zone. I kept in close contact with the weather folks, and then it was time. I had maybe twenty minutes to get him off the mountain and out of the weather. It was going to be a bumpy ride, perhaps, but I was willing to accept that and knew that I could fly safely.

I called the military aide and said, "If the President wants to fly, it's now or never."

He then told the President, "Colonel L'Heureux says if we want to get off this mountain by helicopter, we have to leave now."

The President was a pilot himself, and he understood. The vast majority of the flying we did with him on board was done by what is called "visual flight rules" or VFR. This basically means that you're flying in clear weather, and you can see where you're going, so you manually control the aircraft. When the weather doesn't allow for enough visibility, you fly under "instrument flight rules" or IFR. This means that the air traffic control (ATC) folks guide you through certain airspace on a predetermined flight path. And since you really can't see where you're going, you rely on the ATC's deeper visibility of the entire airspace, and their ability to guide you using the technology and instrumentation on board. It's not autopilot. We're still flying the helicopter, but navigation and other things are determined by the ATC.

My least favorite thing about flying the President in IFR was that if something happened to the aircraft, or there was any type of emergency at all, I would not have the capability to land. I wouldn't be able to see the ground below me. Instead, I would have to declare an emergency in flight, which would initiate another ATC protocol for those types of situations. Finally, in an IFR scenario, the whole lift package didn't fly in our normal formation, using "eyes on" to orchestrate our aerial maneuvers. Instead, each aircraft was being vectored and guided to our destination by the ATC system.

As I checked the helicopter and positioned it on the landing zone, I coordinated with ATC for IFR support and airspace priority. I felt

Flight student, freshman year, Nathaniel Hawthorne College, Antrim, New Hampshire, 1979.

On stage, third from right, top row: Winging class, Whiting Field, Florida, May 1986.

2nd Lieutenant L'Heureux, flight school, 1985.

Instructor Ensign Walt Rossi, flight school, Pensacola, Florida.

Left to right: Captain Rich Hall, 1st Lieutenant L'Heureux, 1st Lieutenant Alex Gierber, 1st Lieutenant Steve Paquette, Republic of Korea, 1987.

The dreaded and feared "helo-dunker," Pensacola, Florida.

My father and me at Ray Jr.'s commencement.

Commanding Officer, HMH 363, Lieutenant Colonel "Willy" Willard, 1988.

Commissioning my son at Virginia Military Institute commencement, May 2004.

With my father and son.

Emotional tribute, outgoing change of command, HMH 362 Ugly Angels, 2004.

Presenting the President with his one-of-a-kind Marine One mountain biking helmet, 2009.

After an especially bloody ride, 2008.

Taking a break while building the biking trail on Prairie Chapel Ranch in Crawford, Texas, 2008.

President Bush exits the aircraft.

Meeting Pope John Paul II, World Youth Day, Denver, Colorado, 1994.

Pope John Paul II exiting Marine One, New York City, 1996.

Marine One crew during President Bush's visit to Windsor Castle, 2008.

President Obama bids farewell to former President Bush, Inauguration Day, January 2009.

Marine One lifting off from the South Lawn.

pretty good about the conditions. I had spoken to the White House, and I knew the weather was clear there. Within a matter of minutes, the First Family approached the helicopter, their golf cart dripping rain off the sides of the plastic roof. Then it was all umbrellas and walking lightly through the wet grass and up the stairs. My crew chief stood beside the stairs, as usual, and saluted as our passengers boarded. They quickly shook out umbrellas, removed their raincoats, and took their seats. Then the President stepped into the cockpit, slapped me on the shoulder, and said, "Let's get out of here, Frenchman!"

I lifted off seemingly right into a massive cloud. I could see the size and shape of the cloud bank in my mind. In close coordination with ATC, I followed the flight path and eventually rose above the clouds. Once they set me on the final approach to Ronald Reagan Washington National Airport, I canceled IFR and proceeded visually. Within forty minutes, we landed safely on the South Lawn, where the sky was sunny and clear. I had made the right call.

In 2007, I had the unlikely opportunity to serve with Bayou and Spanky again. As part of HMX-1's Operational Testing and Evaluation role in the Marine Corps, we were fielding a new Presidential helicopter. I decided to assign a team of five officers to work with the White House, Lockheed Martin, and other agencies to coordinate the project. I knew firsthand how uncommon it was for anyone to come back to HMX-1, unless he came back as Commander.

Then again, anything was possible, and I knew that Bayou and Spanky had the kind of institutional knowledge and technical expertise we needed. I thought about this issue long and hard, and even discussed it with Willie. Eventually I approached my boss, the Marine Corps Deputy Commandant for Aviation, and proposed that we reassign Bayou and Spanky back to HMX-1 as part of this special team. I knew they were both nearing retirement and looking for assignments back in

Virginia, so it would be a win-win for everyone. My boss approved the decision, and Bayou and Spanky joined me back on our old stomping grounds. It would be the last assignment in both of their careers, and they loved it.

My First Ride with Peloton One

The Marine Corps is like many other organizations in at least one way: word gets around quickly. By the time the new guy comes on board, especially the new boss, everyone knows everything about him. Now I was the new boss, and I learned later that I was known as the forty-something *Marine One* pilot who loved competing and who could apparently outrun most people in the squadron.

As the new Presidential Pilot, I stayed connected to the President, his staff, and his operations schedule through his five military aides (one each for the Army, Air Force, Navy, Marines, and Coast Guard). I quickly began to form strong relationships with each of the aides.

The first time I flew President Bush to Camp David, I was waiting on the South Lawn of the White House with the engines running. He would be coming out the doors at any moment. The Air Force military aide was standing in the cabin of *Marine One*, chatting with me and my copilot. I asked him about these rumors that the boss was into mountain biking.

"The President used to run a lot. But a couple of years ago his knees got pretty bad and the doctor told him to lay off the running. Now it seems like he brings his bike wherever he goes," the aide said. "In fact, we'll be biking forty-five minutes after we land today. We call it bike ops."

"Wow, really? I ride triathlon-style bikes when I compete, but I've never tried mountain biking," I said.

"Well, the Boss is in really great shape. He goes all out," he said.

I watched the President approach the aircraft and salute my crew chief, who was standing outside near the steps. The military aide moved to his seat. I listened and watched for the crew chief to board the aircraft, then secure the steps. That was my cue. I called for clearance over the radio, and lifted off.

It was a sunny afternoon with low winds, and I was pleased that the flight was so smooth. When we landed at Camp David, the President came up to the cockpit, slapped me on the shoulder, and said, "Thanks a lot, fellas." Then he climbed into his golf cart and drove to his cabin.

I was still taking care of post-flight procedures—going through my checklists and making sure the aircraft was tucked away nicely in the hangar—when I saw a group of mountain bikers moving quickly through the trees. *Goes all out . . .* I thought.

A couple of hours later, I was settled into my cabin, and I received a call from the Air Force aide. He must have spoken to the President about our conversation on the South Lawn. He said, "Hey, the Boss invited you to join us for bike ops tomorrow morning."

I said, "Awesome. Thanks!"

"Okay, be in front of the President's cabin at eleven A.M.," he said.

Some of the rumors about me were true. I was passionate about physical fitness, and I felt that I was in pretty decent shape. Marines are supposed to be tough, and the Marine Corps obviously promotes fitness, but senior officers are sometimes seen as slower or less fit than the younger folks. As a seasoned Colonel, I took pride in leading by example. I fell asleep imagining a nice ride through the back country on Camp David, maybe even getting in some good cardio before hitting the gym later in the day.

The next morning I was up early and ready to go. Someone had already put a couple of "mountain bikes" in front of the guest cottages for the pilots to get around camp, each with a helmet hanging off it. I didn't know it yet, but there is a big difference between real mountain bikes and the knockoffs some people call mountain bikes. These loaners had very basic components, they were pretty heavy, and they had little or no suspension—not exactly what you want when flying down mountain trails at high rates of speed. Innocently, I just picked one at random.

I wore my Marine physical-training uniform, which consists of running shoes, a pair of small, nylon running shorts Marines refer to as "silkies," and a green T-shirt. I hopped on my bike and pedaled over to the President's cabin. By that point in my career, I had met dozens of famous people, interacted with Presidents and their families and staffs, and even gone hiking with Pope John Paul II. I was not one to get "starstruck." But the thought of going mountain biking with a President was totally unexpected and, I had to admit, just really cool.

When I pulled up to the cabin, I exchanged good-mornings with the dozen or so people already waiting for the President to come out. There were a couple of Secret Service guys, several other people I knew who worked on camp, and some of the President's friends from back in Texas. It was a stunningly sunny June day, and everyone was cheerful and friendly.

I like to think that I am an intuitive guy, and I realized pretty quickly that I stood out from the rest of the group. No one else had a loaner bike like mine. Theirs seemed bigger, newer. They were all geared up with specialized biking equipment, and there I was in my running gear. They had on special shoes that clipped into their pedals. They all had on spandex shorts, gloves, and CamelBak hydration systems. It was a bit like showing up to a Ferrari convention in a Volkswagen bus. Everyone was kind enough to resist blatant mockery, but I guessed by their shared looks that I seemed pretty ridiculous showing up to a serious ride in just my silkies.

Pretty soon, President Bush came out of the cabin with a bounce in his step, all geared up and full of energy. He smiled and said, "Good morning, fellas. Great day for a ride!" He was wearing full mountain-biking gear, including a mouthpiece, helmet, a blue shirt made of a kind of Gore-Tex mesh specifically designed for biking, shorts, and sunglasses. His iPod earplugs were hanging down over his shoulder. He just looked like one of the guys.

He noticed me and said, "Colonel?"

"Yes, sir?"

"You must be Frenchy."

Obviously, the military aide had told him my call sign. I said, "Yes, sir, I am."

"Welcome. Glad to have you on the ride. Have you done this before?"

"No, sir, I have not."

It was only a nanosecond, only a beat, but I saw the knowing smile in his eyes that would make a lot more sense later. Then he nonchalantly started describing the plans for the morning.

"Okay, first we're going to warm up a bit around camp, just to get our heart rates going. We'll do some speed trials on a technical single track and then hit some unimproved trails on the other side of the mountain too."

He was using a lot of biking jargon, and I basically had no idea what he was talking about. I just kept nodding my head and saying, "Yes, sir. Roger that, sir."

Finally, he put in his mouth guard and started leading us toward the trails. I still couldn't believe I was mountain biking with the President. Within twenty minutes, that feeling of exuberance was gone and I realized I was in way over my head.

I was already sweating, and my silky running shorts had turned into an evil saw between my thighs. The "technical single track" that the President had so calmly explained was actually a challenging course of rocks, logs, bumps, and hills. There is no nice way to say it: my bike was a piece of shit.

I soon learned why everyone else's feet were clipped into their pedals.

When they approached a bump or log, they simply pulled the front tire up, bent their legs, and let the bike's suspension system do its magic. But seemingly every time I went over an obstacle, my feet came off the pedals or the chain came off. Then the opposite pedal would spin around and hit me in the shin.

My pedals were made of metal, with sharp spikes for traction, and before long I was sweating and bleeding profusely from my legs. At times, I had to get off the bike and carry it over logs or other obstacles. Nobody stopped. Nobody slowed down. The President didn't even look back. It was almost noon, and it was growing hotter by the minute. Unlike the other riders, I had come unprepared, and had no CamelBak or water bottle.

My body could get me through a lot, but this was a new experience. A new skill set. Muscle memory that simply did not exist. As my frustration and fatigue grew, I thought to myself, *Okay, this really sucks. In fact, it really hurts.*

My pride also kicked in. I had been invited to ride with the President. I was a United States Marine, for God's sake, and I couldn't keep up on a bike? I was not going to be the guy who dropped out. I silently swore that I would die on that trail before I let that happen.

I kept pushing on, trying to keep up, and cursing my bike. At one point I hit a log while going downhill, and I flew headfirst over the handlebars and into the brush. Someone said, "You okay, Colonel?" as he flew by.

I didn't want any help. I didn't want the attention, so I said, "I'm fine, fine." I stood up, checked for broken bones, and climbed back onto that sorry excuse for a bike. I checked my watch and saw that it had been almost two hours of nonstop hard-core mountain biking.

I was bloody, hot, dehydrated, and pissed off at being so unprepared. I was not having fun. I was in survival mode. There is a saying in the military that some physical challenges are 5 percent body and 95 percent heart. I was clearly working on the 95 percent by this point, relying on my stamina to overcome my lack of skill. Somehow I was keeping up, but just barely.

Eventually, we came to a flat area at the bottom of a long downhill ride. I was painfully aware that Camp David rested on the top of a mountain, so the more we rode downhill, the farther we would have to climb back up.

There was a moment when my front tire was parallel with the President's back tire. He looked over his left shoulder at me and asked, "Well, Frenchman, what do you think?"

Of course, I wasn't going to give him an inch. I was not going to admit that I was being dogged. I said, "So far, so good, sir."

He said, "Okay good, good. We have to climb this mountain, so we're gonna hit this little single track and take it straight up. It's going to work your quads a little bit."

I looked up. I couldn't see the top of the hill. If a President had ever understated something, this had to be it. *Work your quads a little bit, huh?*

I said, "Sounds good, sir."

Although they all had the right gear and precious water, they seemed to be reaching their physical limits by this point. I was thinking that the agony of climbing this hill would be a huge improvement to the last couple of hours. If I could just keep my feet on the pedals, and the chain didn't come off, I could make it. This ride would end.

I switched into low gear, leaned forward, put my head down, and started pumping. Everyone was breathing hard, and my heart was beating in my ears. The next thing I knew, I started passing some of the other riders. A couple of Secret Service guys just got off their bikes and started walking them up the massive hill.

When we got maybe three-quarters of the way up the hill, it was only the President and I. I just kept pedaling from moment to moment, trying to keep up with him.

He looked back at me. He was breathing hard and pumping those pedals as he asked, "Frenchman, are you sweating yet?"

This was not a good time for me to talk. I wasn't just sweating, I was bleeding and battered. I had been irritated for hours. Now I was mad at the hill and mad at the stupid bike and mad at myself. I was beyond physical exhaustion, in a lot of pain, dehydrated, and a little delirious.

Of course, I didn't think about all that at the time. Instead, I just said, "Fuck yeah, I'm sweating!" I don't know if the President heard my exact words, because he always rode with an iPod. I saw him chuckle just a bit with that familiar raising of his shoulders, though. We both kept pressing onward and upward. Even in my state, I realized instantly what I had just said. I thought, *Oh my god. Oh my god. I just dropped the F-bomb on the President. I'm done. I'm toast.* I was mad at myself once again for the lapse in judgment.

The President and I finally reached the top of the hill, and we both were heaving to catch our breath. He looked at me while he took a long drink of what must have been delicious water. He noticed that I didn't have any and offered me some of his.

"Frenchman! You did okay," he said. We stood there for a while next to our bikes while everyone else was catching up. He didn't say anything about my comment, so I assumed that either he hadn't heard me or he didn't care.

Within a few minutes, we were pedaling on the paved road that led back to the cabins. All of the mountain bike rides began and ended in front of the President's cabin. I was elated that the ride was over. I had made it. As we milled around a bit, talking about the ride and taking off our gear, the President offered to take a photo with me.

In biking jargon, a peloton is simply a group of riders. Apparently, the President's mountain biking group came to be known as Peloton One. If it was your first ride, you got a pair of biking socks that said PELOTON ONE on them and took a photo with the President.

We posed for a quick picture near the trees in front of his cabin.

The President looked at me and said, "Frenchman, you did really well for having a piece-of-shit bike."

I laughed and said, "Yes, sir."

"You're going to need a better bike," he said. Then he looked over at his aide and added, "Let's make sure that next time the Frenchman has a better bike."

He looked back at me. "All right, Frenchman, you need to get some shoes and gear, and the guys will work on getting you a better bike."

I couldn't believe he was already talking about the next ride. Maybe he hadn't heard me after all.

After a few comments to the other riders in the group, he said, "Okay, fellas, good ride. I'll see you later," and he went back into his cabin.

Now that the excitement was over, the pain really hit me. I was happy and amazed that I'd just had the opportunity to ride bikes with the President, but I was also assessing the damage.

I had gashes up and down both legs. I had whip marks across my arms from branches. I had blisters on my hands. My inner thighs were beyond raw. I skipped the gym that weekend.

When I got back to my cabin and into the shower, everything stung. But as always, I couldn't wait to call everyone and share this latest adventure. Before going to bed, I spent more than an hour telling the story a couple of times. The next morning, my entire body was stiff, and I couldn't lift my legs without pain. For about the next week, back at Quantico, I borrowed my wife's car to drive to work because it hurt to climb up into my Jeep. I smelled like rash cream and Bengay for days.

I would learn later that President Bush loved his Marines, and he also loved to test people on their first ride with Peloton One. I also found out that this had been the first time he had invited his pilot on a ride, and that most rides were not nearly as long.

I never dared to ask him if he had heard my F-bomb as we climbed that final hill. The military aide told me that when the President heard his new pilot had a reputation for being physically fit, his expressed intent that morning was to dog me. I'd say he succeeded. All I knew was that there was more to this man than met the eye, and he would never call me "Frenchy" again. I had officially become "the Frenchman."

CHAPTER 6

GETTING TO KNOW THE PRESIDENT

Crawford, Texas

When I tell people some of the stories from my time as a Presidential Pilot, the conversation often turns to politics. I don't mind discussing politics with my friends, but many people are surprised when I tell them that politics had absolutely nothing to do with my job. The President's politics were completely irrelevant to HMX-1, aside from the fact that his very job was political, and that job defined our schedule. Our mission was to provide executive-lift support for the President and his staff, wherever they wanted to go, and regardless of why.

First and foremost, being a Presidential Pilot was my job, and I was accountable to the White House Military Office for performing in that role. Aside from that, I would say it was much more personal than political. This is because, for some reason, the President gave me the opportunity to join him as part of Peloton One, his mountain biking club. Mountain biking seemed to be his favorite pastime, his favorite form of exercise, and I guessed it was probably therapeutic as well.

Obviously, the life of the President is fast paced and very demanding. And even though my role as HMX-1 Commander was also demanding, my primary role was to accompany and support the President wherever he went, as much as possible and as needed. Since the President used Camp David as the Presidential retreat it was meant to be, I found myself using it in the same way: as a refuge of relative quiet amid a chaotic job and schedule. Those weekends spent at camp are some of my most memorable.

The same thing applied to the ranch in Crawford, Texas. The First Family lived in the White House for most of the year, but they spent many weekends and each August on their ranch in Crawford. That was home, and the President was even more relaxed and in his element there. Just like Camp David, I became a regular visitor to the ranch, and rode bikes there with the President many times.

Sometimes I had to pass—I mean, I was working when I was there; but whenever I could, I was all in for the rides. I was still competing in triathlons, and this mountain biking also gave me a chance to work out. Riding with the President was never just a relaxing pedal through the back country. He was really good, and this was hard-charging, advanced riding. Just as with HMX-1 itself, there was no room for incompetence in Peloton One. If you couldn't keep up, you probably wouldn't be invited back.

As time went on, I always shared the mountain biking stories with my staff and everyone at HMX-1, and included them as much as possible. The President was also very friendly and generous about it, always taking pictures with any new riders. Even as Marines in the largest aviation squadron in the Corps, we still had a certain amount of downtime. This was not a bad way to spend some of it. I didn't let it go to my head, but my workforce was well aware that their boss was getting to ride with President Bush. I'm pretty sure they thought this was cool. I know I did.

Every single move the President made, including every bike ride, was carefully tracked by the Secret Service and on certain radio frequencies. The details of who went on the rides were also transparent, and my name was mentioned more and more as my life synced with the President's schedule. Even my leadership was aware of these activities. I was at a meeting in the White House one afternoon, and my boss, a two-star Admiral, looked at me with a grin and said, "How is the President, Frenchman," using the nickname the President had given me.

The first time I actually flew the Boss to Crawford, I had visited the ranch only briefly while still transitioning into my role as Commander. I didn't know much about the ranch at all, except that the family called it home. We flew down a lift package to a civilian aviation facility in Waco, Texas, a couple of days before the President arrived. The squadron members always stayed in a hotel in Waco. We also had a small facility on the ranch itself, with a small hangar, a double-wide trailer, and a helicopter-landing pad. Marines assigned to Crawford worked in shifts. There was always going to be some downtime, and we had an arrangement with Baylor University to use their gym, but I'm also pretty sure some of my Marines took full advantage of the local dating possibilities. . . .

One day *Air Force One* landed at the base, and I was waiting in *Marine One*. The President and the First Lady climbed aboard, and I flew them to the small helipad on the ranch. I then flew over the countryside back to Waco and put the helicopter away for the night. The military aide called later to tell me that I had been invited to ride bikes on the ranch the following morning.

The drive from Waco to Crawford is about forty-five minutes and takes you through rural Texas farmland. With a mountain bike in the back of my rental truck, I showed my credentials at the main gate. I then parked near the HMX-1 trailer and rode my bike through several other Secret Service checkpoints that led to the compound where the President actually resides.

The mountain biking bug finally bit me, as I'm sure the President knew it would. I was pumped to see what kinds of trails he had on the ranch. I thought it couldn't be that bad. It was flat, right? The last time I was this wrong, I was misjudging the Marine drill sergeants at Parris Island. There is a flagpole near his home, and this is where I was told to link up. When I rode up, a few people were already there, including some Secret Service guys, some local friends from the area, and the military aide. Two of the ranch hands were also riding this morning. I was introduced, and found out later that the President called them "the Dirken boys." They were good riders.

Everyone was geared up, stretching out, and it was already turning out to be a hot August day. My CamelBak would serve me well. The President emerged from his house right on time, in a great mood as always. He greeted his friends, and said, "Hey, meet the Frenchman!" The President was ready to ride, and in a matter of minutes he had put on his gloves, his helmet, and his iPod, and he led the pack. We spent about fifteen to twenty minutes warming up on a flat area of the ranch, and I again thought this was going to be a lot easier than Camp David.

Little did I know that there was a large canyon on the ranch. If you were to look at the ranch from a satellite view, it would appear as if someone had taken a huge cleaver and dug out a five- or six-mile stretch of land. We dropped down into this canyon, and the riding suddenly became much more technical and challenging. Everyone was working hard to keep up with the President as he flew over the washboard trails, maneuvering his bike over hills and rocks.

After some time, we stopped at what looked like a trailhead. Everyone drank some water. I then joined the President, the Dirken boys, and the Secret Service guys as we left the bikes in place and started hiking on a crude and unimproved trail. I noticed some wooden markers nearby, and some engineering flags. The President explained to me that he had invited members of the International Mountain Biking Association to ride on the ranch, and that they had helped him map out this two-mile trail. It was clear that the President intended to build the trail eventually, but right then it didn't look much like a trail. It was just a beautiful, overgrown canyon.

Over the next couple of years, the President strove to turn his vision into reality. There were people working on the trail when he wasn't in Texas, but when he was there, he did not shy away from the work himself. And believe me, it was hard work. There was a trail marked out, but for it to take shape, countless trees had to be cut down, boulders dug out, ground smoothed out.

I still had not forgotten how Marines avoided the President on Camp David when I returned as Commander. I also had not forgotten how much we appreciated interacting with President Bush 41 and President Clinton. I saw the trail as a potential way to make some positive changes to the culture I had inherited at HMX-1. I knew I was usually going to be in Waco when the President was at the ranch, so after one of my first rides there, I asked, "Do you need any help, sir? I might be able to round up a few volunteers."

He said, "Well, we can definitely use all the help we can get." He then looked right at me and said, "Frenchman, make sure they are volunteers only," putting emphasis on the word *volunteers.*

"Roger that, sir." I knew what he meant. I was the Commander, but he did not want me to order my Marines to come out and help on their personal time. I would never have done such a thing.

If I had gone back to Waco and told my Gunny, *Hey, I need some volunteers to go and do backbreaking, heavy-lifting work in the field in the hot sun,* you would have seen Marines scurrying into the woodwork. This was an unusual situation, so instead I said, "Gunny, the Boss needs some help with some trail-building on the ranch and he's open to volunteers." I then looked at him in the serious way the President had looked at me, because this was not a joke. "This needs to be one hundred percent volunteer only. All I can tell you is that they will work their asses off, and if they haven't already, they will probably get to meet the President. I've volunteered to help out tomorrow, and I'll take up to ten volunteers."

Once word got out, it seemed as if everyone in Waco that weekend wanted to help. I could have easily taken more, but I stuck with ten Marines. I then told my Gunny that the uniform would be jeans and work clothes. The next morning, I met my volunteers in the parking lot and gave them a quick briefing. I thanked them for volunteering, and explained that they might meet some high-level leadership, and just to address anyone they were introduced to as "sir" or "ma'am."

We drove to the ranch in rental cars and then climbed into the backs of pickup trucks and moved to the trailhead. The President was already there waiting, along with his National Security Advisor, some White House staff members, and the Dirkin brothers. The President was wearing jeans, a T-shirt, boots, and a baseball cap.

In his usual animated fashion, he smiled and said, "Holy cow! Here's the Marines. Hi, fellas, how are you?" He shook their hands and introduced everyone. He then addressed me directly: "Frenchman. These Marines are all volunteers, right?"

"Absolutely, sir," I said, as my Marines nodded in assent.

"Well then, thanks for coming out. Let's get to work." We all grabbed tools out of a nearby pickup and followed the President and his guests down the trail. I could hear chainsaws and sledgehammers up ahead.

The work crew developed a certain rhythm, almost like the way railroad workers would have laid tracks back in the day. There was a team out in front doing clearing, cutting through trees with chainsaws, digging up rocks with shovels or breaking them up with sledgehammers. The next team in line worked on flattening and leveling the ground with hoes and rakes. Yet another team or two would come behind to fill in any areas needed to ensure that the trail was wide enough, and just to make final touches. At times, progress was incredibly slow, and we would all get stuck on one spot for hours at a time. The President always led the way on the front team, and almost always preferred to do so with a chainsaw.

Eventually, the sun began to set, so we all walked off the trail, dusty and tired. We had worked hard, and the President thanked us as we loaded all the tools into the bed of his pickup. We took a group photo near the pickups. He was so kind and appreciative to the kids, and they got to see a side of him that they never would have seen otherwise. I could tell that my Marines were thrilled to be hanging out with the President, and I could only imagine how much fun they would have sharing the photo with their families and friends. The President was grinning from ear to ear when he drove away in his truck. I'm quite sure this had been a new experience for him, too.

I helped out many more times, and before long, trail building got rolled up into my open invitation to ride bikes. If I was in the area, I would coordinate through the military aide and bring volunteers if possible. Word spread quickly around HMX-1, and many Marines seemed to appreciate the opportunity to do something very different on their downtime. I also made it clear that the President did not expect our help, but that he certainly appreciated it. All who volunteered confirmed this, sharing their own personal experiences from the ranch. Considering Major Jim Toth's reaction to seeing President Bush on Camp David, we had already come a long way in creating a more inclusive culture between the President and the squadron that supported him.

President Bush often caused those around him to laugh out loud. During one of our bike rides not long after that day, my CamelBak had pulled my shirt up, and the President noticed a small tattoo I have on my lower back. He asked, "Frenchman, what is that on your back?" I quoted Jimmy Buffet and said, "Sir, that's a permanent reminder of a temporary feeling." I further explained that I'd gotten the tattoo during the early years of my ongoing infatuation with the Hawaiian surf and triathlon cultures. From that point on, when I brought some of my Marines on a bike ride or to help with the trail, after introducing them to the President, he would say something like "Has your Colonel showed you the tattoo on his ass?"

I'll never forget a time at the ranch when his humor was unintentional. On this particular day I had brought perhaps a dozen of my Marines, all of whom had volunteered as usual. In this extremely sweaty and tough trail work, the President was leading the front team. He was working the chainsaw and overseeing a section of the trail that had just been cleared of trees and rocks. As was very common in the course of a typical "work day," he yelled over the sounds of our laboring, "I need the hoes. Get my hoes up here."

As chance would have it, two of my female Marines had volunteered that day, and yes, they were working the hoes. Hearing the President's voice, they quickly ran up to the front of the crew and stopped short when they reached him. There was an awkward silence as the President, my two Marines, and everyone else realized what he had just said. After a brief pause, the whole group busted out laughing. It was such a human moment, and so endearing to watch the look on the President's face when he realized what he had said. No one was offended. Nothing needed to be said or explained, because we all knew that the comment was completely unintentional. He just needed the hoes up there to get the trail cleared!

On a couple of occasions, I actually spent a few minutes alone with the President, or as alone as one can get with the Secret Service close by. I was invited to ride on the ranch one day, and went through all the checkpoints, making my way to the flagpole. I was expecting to see a group of people, as usual, but I was the only one there besides two Secret Service guys.

The President came out in a jovial mood, all geared up, and said, "Okay, Frenchman, are you ready?"

"Yes, sir!'

As we took off, the Secret Service guys kept up with us, but at a distance. It was clear that they weren't necessarily along for the thrill of riding this day—they were just trying to keep up with the Boss and his helicopter pilot. We stopped every so often to drink water and just take in the view. There wasn't much conversation, as we were both out of breath and both wearing iPods.

At one point, I watched his back tire slip in the dirt and he almost crashed. It reminded me of an icy ride on Camp David one winter morning. The President's tires had slipped on the ice, and I watched him slam into the ground, all tangled up in his bike. The Secret Service was immediately at his side, but he just stood up, shook it off, and finished the ride.

He didn't crash this time, but the moment and the memory once again threw me into nostalgia. As I pedaled up a hill, trying to keep up, I thought to myself, *The whole world is going about its business, and someone may be thinking, "What is the President of the United States doing right now?" I can tell you what he's doing—he's riding bikes on his ranch with a bucket-head Marine Colonel!*

We made another stop and the military aide caught up to us in a four-wheeler. He handed the President a cold bottle of Gatorade. The President proceeded to chug about half of it down, then handed me the bottle and said, "Frenchman, you want some Gatorade?"

I thanked him, took a few gulps, and handed it back. He didn't think anything of it at the time, and neither did I. For a moment, we weren't President and Colonel—we were just two dudes out on a ride.

•   •   •

On another day, months later, the trail was nearing completion. I had volunteered to help out, and was busy breaking up a boulder. I happened to be separated from the rest of the group when I noticed the President walking toward me on the trail.

As he approached, I said, "Hey, Boss, what's going on?"

He said, "Just surveying our work. Hey, take a walk with me, will you?"

I put down the sledgehammer and followed him up the trail. I could hear voices and the sounds of the work crew around a bend. We walked about fifty feet farther up the trail. On one particular turn, one of two things needed to happen. We could cut down some large trees, but that would mean extensive excavation and backfill work. Or the trail could go underneath a rocky ledge, which would mean a lot of digging to ensure there was enough clearance.

We just stood there examining our options and discussing the best ways to complete that segment of the trail. Eric Draper was the White House photographer at the time, and, like the characters from the movie *Men in Black*, he seemed to show up everywhere. He came walking down the trail and, upon seeing us standing there, snapped a candid shot. To this day, it's one of my favorite photos of all time. By the time President Bush left office, we were riding the completed trail. He did an interview with Sean Hannity after his presidency, and they were walking on the mountain biking trail we helped to build.

Perhaps the most vivid memory that demonstrates our mutual respect and friendship happened back at Camp David. The Peloton was killing the trails one day, completely in the groove. Toward the end of the ride, we were going down a steep single track, and my handlebars clipped a branch. I had wiped out before, so I knew what to expect. I hit the front brake too hard and went head over heels down this hill.

I did a somersault in the air, twisting to avoid landing on my back. I came down hard on my side and slid a few feet in rock and gravel. I immediately checked for broken bones, and when I found none, I got up and checked out my bike. It was fine. I had a good case of road rash, with several abrasions on my right arm, leg, and thigh bleeding freely. I hopped back on my bike and kept riding.

When we stopped, everyone was cooling down, discussing the ride, and the President was only a few feet away. He saw the blood dripping from my arm and leg and said, "Holy shit, Frenchman! Are you bleeding again?"

I said that it was nothing, then he said, "Damn, Frenchman, that looks bad, but it's also the best wound we've ever had at camp. We've got to get a picture."

A few moments later, the Camp David photographer came over. President Bush bent over to get a closer look at my leg, and said something to make me laugh. The photographer snapped the picture right at that moment. As I turned my head to say something to one of the other riders, I felt something and looked down.

The President had poured some of his drinking water on my leg and was cleaning my wound up with his bare hand. I was quite taken aback, because where I came from, only a dear friend would do something like that without hesitation. This man was my Commander in Chief, and the President of the United States, and he was worried about me? This lasted for a few seconds, until a Camp David nurse walked over to assess the damage.

When we departed Camp David that Sunday afternoon, the President handed me a copy of the photo. Normally, he would sign photos with something like "Ride on."

This time, he quoted something I had said jokingly to him on a previous ride. The handwriting on the photo said, "Frenchman, if you're not bleeding, you're not riding."

In California with the Terminator

I supported the President on a trip to California in January 2008 for a fund-raiser and a meeting with state leadership. There would be multiple lifts over the course of two days, as we were stopping at various locations in Orange County.

On one of these days, California's governor, Arnold Schwarzenegger, would fly with us from Torrance to Brentwood for the fund-raiser. During preparation for this trip, I realized that the President and I had another thing in common: we liked to have a little fun.

For the past decade or so, it had become standard practice to pack our aircraft up into a large cargo plane and fly them to our destination. In the past, it was more common to fly the lift package across the country. Many of my pilots had never done this. In order to ensure that my Marines still maintained those skill sets, and to provide them with a new challenge, I decided that we would actually fly across the country to California with a full complement of five helicopters (including two white tops).

The basic route of flight was from northern Virginia to Barksdale Air Force Base in Louisiana, on to Tucson, Arizona, and then into California. We conformed to FAA rules near any cities, but over the rural areas we flew at 200 feet, which is a very interesting way to see the country. I'm sure this was the first time the people in those towns saw white tops flying over their land.

Since it was January, the weather got pretty rough a few times as we traveled through some major ice storms in Louisiana and Texas. We were forced to land in Texas and spend the night there until the weather broke. Ice actually cracked one of the windshields, so we had to plan for repairs. All along, I was closely watching the clock and calculating whether we could make it to California in time. I even called back to my Operations Department and had them coordinate a backup lift package just in case. Finally, we pushed through and made it to

Tucson, Arizona and then on to California just a couple of days before the event.

It had been an adventurous trip for me and my copilots, and more than once I questioned whether I had made the right call to fly all the way there. The President did not realize the unforeseen challenges we had overcome to get *Marine One* in place, and when he landed in *Air Force One*, we were right there waiting as usual.

Once the event began, and Governor Schwarzenegger climbed on board *Marine One*, he was nice enough to come up into the cockpit and say hello. As I turned around to shake the governor's hand, President Bush's face popped up over one of the governor's massive shoulders with a delighted smile, and said, "Look, Frenchman, it's the Terminator!" The governor just laughed it off. He probably heard that joke a lot, but I'm willing to bet that he had never heard it from his President.

The White House

I was settling in to the high-intensity job of leading HMX-1. I was getting to know my staff, fostering strong relationships with stakeholders in the Secret Service, the White House, and numerous other agencies. I had flown the President on a number of missions. In a very unexpected manner, I had been given an opportunity to show the President my character, and to see him outside the cockpit and on the trail.

I was having the time of my life, and the White House began to take on a whole new level of familiarity. On any given morning, while people commuted into D.C., I drove into Anacostia before sunrise because I had to pick up the President at the White House. Usually I took the helicopter out to burn off a bit of fuel and perform a final systems check. This was probably one of my favorite times of the day, especially in the winter. As I walked out to the flight line in the predawn darkness with my hot mug of coffee, and the aircraft was already warmed up for me, the air was so crisp. I would take off smoothly and start heading up the Potomac. And then there would be a moment when the sun became visible on the horizon. I would make a buttonhook turn to the right, take us up to about 1000 feet, and then do a 180-degree turn. This positioned me at the top of Sixteenth Street, which ends at the front door of the White House. The Potomac looked like a ribbon of light when the sun hit the water.

Now I would fly directly toward the White House as the city woke up below me. Everything looked so vivid as I sat in my warm cockpit with the knowledge that I and my crew were certainly the only people flying in that airspace. I had my office, and I had my home, but at work, the cockpit was my home. I loved the feel of the cushions of the pilot seat, the resistance of the pedals. I monitored the way all systems worked together under my touch, and reveled once again as this great machine obediently followed my commands.

What had been a few lights quickly became a flowing river of red brake lights on I-95. That was their morning commute, and this was mine. All was right in the world somehow during those surreal early-morning flights. Favorite place to work? Check!

After the test ride, I would fly back to the base, grab another cup of coffee, and change into my lift uniform. By the time I came back to pick up the President, the city had risen. At least a few people usually stood outside the White House grounds, waving and taking pictures as I passed by. Once I entered the grounds, there was often another group waiting near the landing zone, this time made up of the media. I was confident in my ability to fly the President safely, but it was a strange feeling for this old CH-53 pilot to have so many eyes and cameras always pointed at my helicopter.

If something were to go wrong, it would be on the national news in a matter of minutes. It was time to focus. Put aside the crazy fact that the President was about to board, and that you might be able to watch your takeoff on the news that night. The President boarded, and it was time to fly him out of there and link up with the rest of the helicopters in the lift package. I may choose to be in front of the other aircraft, in the middle, or in the back. Only we would know which one carried the President. It was always a good feeling to pick him up and execute another successful mission.

I lost count of how many times I landed him on the South Lawn after a long day. Usually this meant that he landed at Andrews Air Force base at night, so I would pre-position *Marine One* an hour before *Air Force One* was set to land.

I knew exactly when that was, but it never got old seeing and hearing the massive plane land and then scream toward me. In the light, I could see the classic blue-and-white paint. Under cover of darkness, the plane's bulk was lined with running lights, and I could see the profiles of Colonel Mark Tillman and his copilot up in the illuminated cockpit. The President then climbed down the steps and walked over to his helicopter, his air taxi. I would then make a short flight back to the White House to bring him home.

Americans seem to have a certain curiosity about the White House, and—before I was Commander of HMX-1—I was one of them. This had been the formal home of every American President since Thomas Jefferson. As HMX-1 Commander, I was an integral part of the decision-making process in the White House Military Office for everything that pertained to helicopter aviation support for the White House. To accomplish this, I became part of a very small percentage of people who get inside access to the White House.

My White House boss was the Director of the White House Military Office, and his office was located in the East Wing. The East Wing is pretty much reserved for all the Protocol folks, the First Lady's offices, and the White House Military Office. My boss required all his subordinate Commanders to come in for a weekly meeting, which was usually held in a conference room in the White House basement. Attending these weekly meetings would be my counterparts in the White House Military Office: the Commander of Camp David, the Commander of the Presidential Aircraft Group, the Commander of the White House Communications Agency, and the Commander of the White House Mess.

On occasion, I was also invited to the White House for formal and social events, such as when someone left the White House staff or the Secret Service. Whether I was there for a meeting or an event like this, I had the right credentials to gain almost unfettered access. Because of my unique role in the President's schedule, I also knew most of the senior Secret Service personnel who oversaw White House security.

I arrived early for meetings, making my way through security, then walking the entire length of the White House to the West Wing, and the old Executive Office Building. There is a cafeteria there, and I typically stopped by for a cup of coffee. Next, I walked through the halls again until I reached the East Wing, and my boss's office. It never got old and I never took it for granted.

Inside, I always felt a certain giddiness that came from being in the most powerful office building on the planet, and being allowed to walk within the storied walls of so much American history. I always remembered taking my parents on the White House tour, and taking the photo with President Clinton in the Oval Office.

On several levels, my second tour in HMX-1 often created a sense of coming full circle. I had gone from young pilot to more seasoned pilot. From Presidential copilot to Presidential Pilot. From freshman to Commander. By 2008, Ray Jr. had been deployed to Iraq twice, during some heavy fighting in Fallujah, and was now assigned to Parris Island as part of the training organization for new recruits.

In a very "full circle" experience, he asked me if I could promote him to Captain. As a CO, the opportunity and privilege to promote Marines to their next rank occurs on the first of each month. It is a highlight for any CO to shake a Marine's hand and say "atta boy" or "atta girl" in front of the entire unit in formation. I always enjoyed participating in these time-honored milestones, and I was thrilled to be able to promote my son. The idea of promoting one's son in front of his peers and leadership not only evokes pride in the traditional Marine Corps sense, but it brings up a deep sense of parental pride. We made the drive down to Parris Island and promoted him in a short ceremony.

As I stood in front of Ray in the position of attention, eyeball to eyeball, and while the promotion order was being read, a sense of emotion came over me that almost dropped me to my knees. There I was, some twenty-eight years after his birth, looking at my mirror image. Same uniform, same name tape, same blood, same profession. Here was my son, walking in my footsteps, but that's where the similarities ended, in a sense.

I was also looking into the eyes of a young Marine who had already seen so much in his short career. You see, my son volunteered during this nation's time of need, willing to serve during a very tenuous time in our history. This was his generation's war, and they will be the new "greatest generation." My son had entered the very exclusive club of the less than 1 percent of the country's population who serve . . . and serve he did. Ray served two tours in Iraq and one in Afghanistan, and saw friends and Marines he served with die in combat.

In my almost thirty years of service, I never once had to bear witness to a shot fired in anger, but my son had been in harm's way right out of the chute. So, in that seemingly endless moment as I stared into his eyes—through the lens of pride, angst, admiration, and love—I also knew that I was staring into the eyes of a Marine Corps Officer who had earned the right to wear the rank of Captain. There are no words to adequately convey the amount of pride that I had at that very moment, and that I still carry with me to this day.

While we were there, we also took the opportunity to look around a bit. There were certainly new structures and buildings after all those years, but so much of it looked hauntingly the same. It was nostalgic to be standing there, especially when Ray Jr. shared funny and crazy stories with me about the drill instructors and the recruits. He said, "Dad, we actually have a new group coming in tomorrow. Do you want to watch?"

I said that I would love to, and I knew that these kinds of visits from other officers were allowed. Then again, I didn't want to cause any trouble with his chain of command. He got permission and I agreed to just watch and stay out of the way. The next morning, I showed up early and watched as hundreds of recruits from all over the country came out of the barracks and began to assemble for first formation. They all stood at attention on the same yellow footprints in front of the same recruit barracks where I had nervously stood one spring day back in 1980.

I silently looked at this young Marine Officer and reveled at the fact that he was my son. Not only that, but he was a Captain and a Platoon Commander at the very same recruit depot where I had begun my career. I was now at the end of my career, and he was at the beginning of his. Yet, he had already been part of a young man's war, and had seen so very much during his time in the Marine Corps. When I snapped back from nostalgia to the present moment, it struck me again just how far I had come.

Wounded Warriors

As a Marine and career military man, I had always been fascinated with the man who was President, especially the way he took up his role of Commander in Chief. Now I had a front-row seat. Years before I became his pilot, I watched President Bush talk to the first responders in New York City after 9/11. I watched him address the nation each year in the State of the Union address. I knew that the war in Iraq was a hot political issue that had polarized the nation.

I had many friends serving in Operations Iraqi Freedom and Enduring Freedom, many of them from the Red Lions and Ugly Angels. In 2008, I took the President to visit some of the wounded warriors. Every other trip he took was a highly orchestrated event in terms of logistics, security, and all the other necessary coordination. There was always press involved, tight security, and very clear start and end times.

Taking the President to visit wounded warriors in military hospitals was different from anything I had done up to that point. For instance, no press was invited, and the President wasn't his usual jovial self. He was much more somber. Also, there was no specific time of departure on this type of trip. It simply ended when he was done visiting with injured military personnel and their families.

The first trip was to a military hospital in Bethesda, Maryland. The trip lasted about four hours, and the President visited with more than a dozen injured service members. He presented them with Purple Hearts, thanked them for their service, and spoke with their families. While he was inside, I waited near the aircraft with the other pilots. Here was the President, pinning Purple Hearts on these injured kids and talking to parents. Although we weren't currently serving in a combat-operations role, we were part of the larger U.S. military machine. We knew it could be any of us in there, and we spoke proudly about the fact that the Commander in Chief was in there visiting our brothers and sisters in arms.

I finally saw the President's limousine making its way back to the helicopter, and I was expecting a very solemn President climbing the stairs, shaking his head, exhaling heavily, just taking his seat and riding back home. To my absolute amazement, when the limousine stopped just beside *Marine One*, the President climbed out with a huge smile on his face. He bounded up the aircraft stairs, ran into the cockpit, smacked me on the shoulder, and said, "Frenchman, it's a good day to be a Marine!"

I did not dare ask the President how he felt about all of it, but I had my own ideas. I heard firsthand accounts about some of the visits. I knew that he had sincerely asked the injured service members, "Is there anything I can do for you?" Many of them had replied, "Yes, sir. Get me back to my unit!"

Even though the country was against the war efforts in the Middle East and the mainstream media would not let up, I believe the President found strength and inspiration in the very people who were fighting in the wars he had sent them into. I took him on many more trips to visit wounded warriors, most of them to Walter Reed Medical Center.

On another visit, the White House press was allowed to go along. I remember seeing the footage on the news, but I had a different perspective than most. I had dropped him off that day and seen his mood. I had been there when he came out. I figured it was as close to being in the room as one could get without being in the Secret Service. I couldn't help but wonder what it must have been like for him to walk in there and face the reality of those horrific injuries, seeing the great loss and anger in the parents' eyes.

From what I could see, he never let the experiences affect him in a negative way. He actually seemed inspired after the visits, as if he was fueled by their sacrifice, commitment, and professionalism. I could only imagine that he dealt with it in his own private space, with his own family and loved ones.

I had interacted with President Bush 41 and President Clinton a few times during my first tour. When I became President George W. Bush's pilot, I expected the same type of interaction. I couldn't claim to understand exactly why it had happened, but for some reason, I was the first pilot the President had invited on the trails. And after that first ride with Peloton One, it almost seemed that I was expected to participate in the rides.

I wasn't going to ask him, *Mr. President, why do I get to ride bikes with you?* I just assumed that since I could keep up, and since my job required me to be wherever he was anyway, he decided to invite me. Regardless of why he did it, I appreciated the opportunities and the memories. Through the media, one gets a certain sense of the President, which is of course colored by any number of personal and political beliefs. I saw the President through that perspective just like anyone else, watching him address the nation and speak on TV.

I also knew firsthand where he was going, and why, and got to witness his overall demeanor as he climbed on and off *Marine One.*

Even so, I didn't get to sit around and have coffee and discuss world politics with the President. We didn't interact on that kind of level. I was his pilot. He was my boss. There was a certain protocol and professionalism, a line in the sand that I would never have crossed. Then again, within the context of our respective roles, we spent a significant amount of time together either in the air or on the trail. In countless moments, I was just one among a gaggle of riders, elated after a hard and fast ride, sweating and laughing as we drank water from CamelBaks. No job titles. No politics. Just a few people speeding through the woods on high-tech mountain bikes.

It was through that lens—the way he pushed himself physically, the way he jokes, the way he shook it off after crashing on his bike—that I gained a different sense of the President's character. In my book, these kinds of moments are some of the most meaningful in life, and there is a certain unspoken camaraderie that didn't even need to be discussed. Both as my Commander in Chief and as a mountain biking buddy, I came to respect President Bush as a deeply kind, hilarious, and driven human being.

CHAPTER 7

During my first tour, I was a player in the complex chess game that HMX-1 operations represented. My role was perhaps that of a bishop or a rook. As CO, I was still a player, but I could see the whole chessboard on an entirely different and more strategic level. Not only did I have an entire HQ at Quantico, but we also maintained a secure facility at Anacostia. A lift package, ready to rock, and a contingent of my workforce rotated through Anacostia to keep the facility secure and operating 24/7/365.

Quantico is the heart of HMX-1's planning and helicopter maintenance, but Anacostia is where all planning becomes reality—where a mission briefed in the ready room becomes the sound of a helicopter starting, a pilot's hand on the stick, hovering above the airfield before gliding through the air en route to the White House or another locale.

Keeping the fleet flying was more than simply ensuring that the helicopters themselves were impeccably maintained. This was more like leading a highly complex orchestra with a thousand instruments, planning factors, and tasks to consider. I was the conductor of this structured symphony, this well-oiled machine that had not stopped running in more than fifty years. And although we made every effort to develop comprehensive and overlapping plans, and contingency plans, and emergency plans, world events actually dictated what the President might want to do, or when and where he might want to go—and therefore those events directly affected our daily operations.

We had some of the best of the best among our ranks, and the pursuit of excellence was viewed as standard operating procedure. I had a great staff and workforce that I would literally trust with my life. None of our success would have been possible without them. In fact, without the talented and dedicated people who showed up at Quantico and Anacostia every single day, HMX-1 would just be a really cool museum.

Still, the burden of responsibility fell on me. If there was any problem whatsoever with coordinating the President's helicopter support, or if *Marine One* ever failed to be in its preplanned location at exactly the right moment, or, God forbid, we ever had a flying accident or mishap, I would have to answer for it. Since I could not do everything or be everywhere at once, I had to trust my personnel implicitly. And I did.

Part of what made this kind of trust possible were the recurring, intensive efforts we made to recruit, hire, train, and retain the right people. All military units have what is called a Table of Organization (TOA), which lays out exactly how many and what types of positions are needed to run properly. In most Marine aviation squadrons, the staffing goal is 80 percent of the TOA. HMX-1 is one of fewer than five organizations that is authorized and required to maintain 100 percent staffing at all times.

I had personnel at virtually every level of the chain of command, including young kids who had enlisted right out of high school, seasoned pilots, and operations specialists. I had combat veterans and people from various locations and walks of life. Although we spanned the full range of organizational structure, experience, and functional areas—such as planning, operations, administration, security, communications, finance, training, recruiting, and more—I had to continuously focus my diverse workforce on shared goals. Every summer, a good percentage of the workforce got transferred when their four-year tour was up, so recruiting and training were perpetual planning factors.

As a result, one of the most important aspects of my annual schedule was traveling across the country with my internal recruiting team to various training facilities in search of talent. Of course, we did not expect to waltz in and grab all the best talent, but we made our best efforts to develop relationships and get as many as we could. My recruiting team included the maintenance chief, several senior enlisted members, a psychologist, and others.

The psychologist who helped us played a key role in identifying the right people. She also did recruiting for the Marine units that operated the White House ceremonial drill teams, and for a platoon of Marines that provided security at Camp David. It made perfect sense for her to help us, since those organizations had similar concerns as HMX-1. Think about it: the people we recruited would be working in a highly unusual environment, dealing with national assets and sometimes standing within feet of the President and other leaders. In that sense alone, it was similar to hiring a member of the Secret Service. They needed to have a certain type of psychological makeup for this kind of work, and we made sure to screen everyone thoroughly.

Even if we found a perfect candidate, we could never hire him if he failed the background checks for any reason. Typical Top Secret security investigations go back fifteen years into an individual's life. Our security clearances investigated the individual's entire lifetime. So even if a person thinks he got something expunged from his records, he is actually still judged by his past decisions and choices. Clearly, this stringent process leveled the playing field and shortened the list of potential candidates significantly. At the end of the day, we succeeded at maintaining a full-strength workforce in this dynamic environment, and the individual personnel were assigned to various organizational areas depending on their particular training and skill sets.

For example, on the pilot side of the house, my predecessor was leaving, and a couple of other *Marine One* pilots were nearing the end of their tours. I needed to start thinking about whom I was going to select as my backup *Marine One* pilots. We all had type-A personalities, and everyone wanted to be what only four people could ultimately become. I needed people who not only could fly but who could make split-second decisions even when chaos ensued. As I assessed my workforce and all the incredible talent surrounding me, my sights fell on Major Scotty Volkert. I knew him from Hawaii, and at the time he was assigned to HMX-1's Operational Testing and Evaluation mission. I wanted to make him my Operations Officer and one of my *Marine One* pilots. I knew he was a brilliant pilot with a good head on his shoulders.

I sat him down and told him about my plan for him. I would be increasing his workload, increasing his stress, and he would be away from home significantly more in his new role. After discussing the change with his family, he accepted the offer and became a member of my core team. This was one of the best decisions I ever made. Scotty was well respected and extremely meticulous in his planning and coordination. He is now a Lieutenant Colonel assigned to the White House Military Office's Airlift Operations Division, the organization that tasks *Marine One* and *Air Force One*.

Likewise, among the many personnel decisions and amazing people I worked with, one individual stands out as perhaps my best decision on the maintenance side of the house. I hand-selected Sergeant Harrison Kish to serve as the primary *Marine One* crew chief, and he never disappointed me once. In fact, he took support to a whole new level and did his job right 100 percent of the time. Sergeant Kish was a highly successful crew chief and participated on the vast majority of my Presidential lifts. Like many of his peers, he served honorably and then decided to leave the Marine Corps and go to college.

Planning and Operations

Planning is always central to military operations, with a constant flexibility to tweak the plan when conditions change (which they inevitably will). This was never more true than in HMX-1. The entire globe was our area of responsibility, current events informed our plans, and we did not have the luxury of shutting down the airfield or taking an operational pause. Ever. In my previous command back in Hawaii, there were a couple of times when I initiated a "safety stand-down." We didn't fly for about a week and instead focused on safety and other areas of concern.

This was a great leadership-and-training tool, but it was never an option at HMX-1. When the President was ready to go, my aircraft would be there and my crew chief would be standing like a statue beside the air stair, ready to salute. Period. I could make the decision not to fly the President if I felt he would be in danger, but that was rare. Normally, if the airfield at Anacostia was iced over, we simply had to integrate snowplows into the plan at the right time.

With such complex and intense mission sets, my operations planners were constantly thinking ahead to identify and mitigate risk. Under my direction, they developed and enforced strict processes and procedures to overcome human error and complacency. We did not get second chances. If anyone cut a corner or failed to follow procedure, especially if it caused some problem or safety issue, he or she was very likely to be fired and reassigned.

Another way to minimize risk is good old-fashioned military discipline. Every member of the workforce knew the rules and regulations, and of course they were strictly enforced by me and my subordinate leaders. But I also understand the ideology of teenagers. I had a standing order that I wanted to speak personally with every new member of the squadron. Sometimes this was one or more new personnel every week. My First Sergeant would sometimes wait until we had fifteen or twenty and then plan a time for me to meet with them all at once. My goal was to show them that I would be compassionate and understanding, and to express my pride at having them under my command.

I also wanted to give them a reality check. They were still kids, but they had to be absolutely devoted to the mission. I needed to make sure they understood the ramifications that simple life choices could have on their careers. Any infraction could be cause for dismissal.

I would often stand in front of them and ask, "By a show of hands, how many of you are under the age of twenty-one?" Most would raise their hands.

Next, I asked, "Okay, how many of you with your hands up have ever had a drink?" When, inevitably, only a couple of hands stayed up, I said, "Now you're lying," in a joking manner. They got the point. I went on to explain that when I grew up, eighteen was the legal drinking age, and that I didn't necessarily make the rules but I had to enforce them. I talked to them about the national importance of our mission and how critical every single person was to attaining that mission.

"You will work your ass off, and you will love it, and your parents will be proud," I would say, "but if you make a bad decision, or get caught drinking underage, you're gone. And it will follow you for your whole career in the Marine Corps." I certainly dealt with disciplinary issues at HMX-1, but not nearly as many as I had seen in previous assignments.

Because of the nature of our mission, security was a major planning factor and ongoing consideration. In previous assignments, there was always a contingent of security personnel, depending on the type of mission or operation. In my former command, my Marines often provided security support in a range of combat scenarios. At HMX-1, I had the largest MP company in the entire Marine Corps, comprised of more than one hundred personnel and dozens of canines. This highly professional group maintained 24/7/365 security of our HQ area, Anacostia, and also the lift package anytime it was on a mission. Just to make sure we had the place locked down tight, we sometimes got "visited" by certain White House assets to test our security and vulnerability.

The Cage

Never once in history has *Marine One* suffered a mishap, and this kind of record is almost unheard of in the military-aviation community, not to mention the private-aviation community. We can thank every member of the HMX-1 workforce for that. But perhaps we should give the biggest thanks to the mechanics, quality-control crews, and other aircraft experts. That corps of support personnel kept operations running while my pilots controlled the helicopters in the air. We always relied on the fact that the aircraft were always ready to go. And the hundreds of personnel that made up HMX-1's highly robust maintenance effort gave us that peace of mind.

There was no room for shortcuts when it came to maintenance, and any instance of malpractice would be another cause for dismissal. To mitigate this, we constantly refined the procedures, processes, and standards we used to ensure world-class maintenance. So, the most visible and famous helicopters in the world are also the most well maintained. HMX-1's rigorous standards of maintenance surpassed that of virtually any other helicopter on the planet. Why? We hold ourselves to a much higher maintenance standard than most aviation organizations. We fly the President.

We had an aggressive and perpetual inspection process that diminished complacency and sharpened preparedness and preventive maintenance to a finer point. Another "secret" is that each aircraft is flown for a very specific and limited period of time. Every single part is then refurbished and checked, essentially resulting in having a brand-new aircraft at all times that is in a state of 100 percent maintenance and repair.

In any helicopter, there are static components (the piece of metal that makes up the rotor blade), and dynamic components (moving or spinning parts like a transmission or rotor head, or other hydraulics). All these parts have a service life that lets the maintenance folks know specifically when a part needs to be replaced or overhauled. An encyclopedic amount of documentation tracks a given part's time on the aircraft. Let's say that a dynamic component happens to have a service life of five hundred hours. In HMX-1, we cut that number in half, replacing or servicing the part twice as often as is required in a normal squadron.

The vital importance of maintenance can be seen in the fact that most of my workforce fell into that category. When the young mechanics, hydraulics specialists, and communications and systems specialists came to HMX-1 from one of the Marine Corps training facilities, we also put them through our own internal training. This was a graduated process in which they spent a year or more working on the green-side aircraft before ever touching a white top. During this period, they learned how we did things, grew accustomed to the rhythm, and proved that they were ready to work on the white tops.

I also had seasoned maintenance leaders and quality assurance (QA) personnel. QA in this context is all about personal safety, aircraft safety, mechanical inspection, and maintenance-program auditing. In other words, QA provided ongoing supervision and oversight to all maintenance efforts, adding another layer of accountability and helping to ensure that the squadron is running the way that it is supposed to. Finally, the maintenance leadership is always assessing the workforce closely to determine which individuals will be assigned to which air-craft or shop, and which would be trusted to work in the highest and most classified level of HMX-1 maintenance: the Cage.

Physically, the Cage is a couple of hangars where HMX-1 mainte-nance takes place, and where the white tops are kept and maintained in pristine condition. Everyone who works in the Cage needs a Top Secret clearance, or else he is escorted by armed guards. Despite these points of distinction, in many ways the Cage is just like any other main-tenance operation. It is HMX-1's primary maintenance-management facility, and on any given day there might be a couple of hundred people working inside. It is the heartbeat of the maintenance effort for the executive fleet of aircraft.

As might be expected, the Cage is full of mechanics in work-soiled coveralls, aviator glasses, and steel-toe safety boots, with greasy hands from working in the tight, oily confines of the helicopter engines. One would also find the pungent smells of hydraulic fluid, oil, and cleaning solvent. The sounds of people talking and various power tools and avi-onics equipment fill the air. Sometimes I would come in from a mis-sion at night and walk through the hangar, talking to Marines on the night shift. There was a different vibe at these times, probably since maintenance was slow and there were fewer leaders on shift. I think the Marines on the night shift appreciated the time, and they would often have their music playing.

Although these were world-class maintenance personnel working on some of the most important and visible aircraft in the world, back then, we were stuffed into a hangar that was old and inadequate. They have since moved the Cage to a state-of-the-art facility, but back then, we were using the same hangars we had been using since the 1940s. It reminded me that the Marine Corps could adapt and overcome, doing so much with so little.

The *Marine One* Crew

With the plans perfectly dovetailed across every functional area, and when the moment came to fly the President where he wanted to go, I had to move the white noise of pressure and accountability into the proverbial backseat. I needed to be hyper-focused on the stick in my hand, the geography below, the weather, the architecture all around me, and on the singular goal of transporting the President safely to his destination. During those magical moments, I was just a pilot once again, and my "workforce" was distilled down to three: my copilot, my crew chief, and I.

The pilots and copilots certainly walked around the aircraft to do a visual inspection, and of course we were intimately familiar with the cockpit, but even we were discouraged from climbing on top of the aircraft and doing detailed inspections. This goes back to what I said about having complete trust in the processes and the people. When it came to maintaining the aircraft, we pilots and copilots respectfully stayed out of the way of the smart folks. Speaking of smart folks, no discussion about *Marine One*—or its ongoing inspection, maintenance, and upkeep—would be complete without mentioning the crew chief.

If the pilot and the copilot are the "brain" that keeps the aircraft flying, then the crew chief is the heart. And the *Marine One* crew chief is a little different from most crew chiefs. He's often considered the most photographed Marine in the world. In another sense, HMX-1 crew chiefs also served as the "face" of *Marine One*, since every time the President approached *Marine One*, and a camera shutter caught the moment, there was the crew chief standing like a statue beside the air stair. Not only do the crew chiefs take center stage in the images of *Marine One* that the world sees in photographs and videos, but they play an important role in ensuring that the helicopters are properly cared for and maintained.

This process begins when the potential crew chief completes boot camp and begins specialty training. There are four different schools required to become a CH-46 or CH-53 crew chief in the Marines, including three months of mechanic's training and six months of crew chief and flight training. After all that, a new crew chief can be selected for HMX-1, and then it's time for more training. Although there are variations to this scenario, a new crew chief might go through the following steps: first, he spends a year or two working on the green-side aircraft, learning about HMX-1 operations, and waiting for his Top Secret clearance to be complete. Once he gets the clearance, he may be selected to work on white tops, but typically only for Vice Presidential lifts and heads of state. Eventually, a crew chief may or may not be selected as a *Marine One* crew chief. At any given time, there are only four crew chiefs for each white-top model, and there is a constant turnover. Every few months, a new crew chief replaces an existing one, so there is always a "new guy" in learning mode, and a senior crew chief who mentors the others.

Not unlike my having to fulfill certain requirements before even being considered as HMX-1 CO, a *Marine One* crew chief must meet certain requirements. For example, an individual must complete the training to become a Collateral Duty Inspector (CDI). In the capacity of a CDI, the crew chief assists the QA personnel in inspecting maintenance efforts. They also had to meet certain standards on the physical fitness test and have a certain number of flight hours and Vice Presidential lifts. On top of all that, a crew chief had to be "voted on" by the peers in his respective maintenance shop.

Not only do the crew chiefs participate in any pre-flight rehearsals and preparation, but they play an important role during actual flight as well. The crew chief sits in the cockpit, between and a little behind the pilot and copilot seats. Among other things, the crew chief is constantly monitoring gauges, managing various internal and external lighting systems, the auxillary power unit, and the landing gears. Once *Marine One* lands, let's say on the White House lawn, the crew chief is already out of his seat and ready to spring into action.

The door that opens into the air stair on the VH-3 is quite heavy and must be lowered using only one rope, but the crew chiefs are well practiced in making it look smooth and easy. The door goes down and the crew chief catches it with his right hand and then sets it down gently on the lawn. The second the door is down, the crew chief starts walking ceremonially down the steps. Most Marines do drill only when they are back at their units. The *Marine One* crew chief performs highly ceremonial drill on every lift, and sometimes in front of the whole world (through the media). When he gets to the bottom of the steps, he takes eight steps out, pivots left, takes another eight steps, and another left. If it's a VH-3 on the lift, the crew chief opens the back door as well (where any other passengers will board). He then marches back the way he came to position himself right beneath the copilot's window and next to the air stair.

He may stand there for five minutes or an hour, and whether it's 10 below or a sweltering 110 degrees, the crew chief will stand there like a guard at Buckingham Palace, moving only after saluting the President as he boards. Approximately ten seconds after the President boards, the crew chief makes his way to the back door, then gets visual confirmation from the Secret Service that the President is securely on board. After getting the thumbs-up, he closes the back door and then walks back up the main steps and pulls the door closed behind him. Once the aircraft takes off, the crew chief is once again in his rightful place in the cockpit. Although the crew is a mere ten feet from the President and his guests, the only interaction happens either right before or after landing.

After landing back at Anacostia following a lift, and after the pilot and copilot turn over control of the aircraft, the crew chief still has a lot of work to do. Whether the lift lasted thirty minutes or all day, the crew chief (and possibly some of his fellow crew chiefs on shift) immediately performs a thorough aircraft inspection, cleaning, and preparation that could easily last three hours or much longer. Technically this process could be viewed as both pre- and post-flight procedures, since another lift could be planned at any moment, and this process was ongoing between all lifts. In other words, immediately following every lift, the aircraft had to be prepared for another one.

The inspection process involves a checklist with hundreds of entries and requires the crew chiefs to "touch" every part of the aircraft, inside and out. They check for visible damage, corrosion, breakage, and the service limitations on numerous parts on the engine, rotor head, tail, tiller head, the belly, and the interior. During the comprehensive inspections, the entire aircraft is also cleaned. The outside is washed and shined to maintain its high gloss. Cleaning the inside is treated with the same care. The cockpit windows are washed, the entire interior is vacuumed, and the seats and walls are cleaned with furniture polish. Snacks and beverages are replenished, according to the President's tastes. The crew chiefs even make sure the framed photos on the walls are straight, and that the seat belts are always positioned in the same way.

After all the cleaning and inspections are done, the crew chief finishes the associated paperwork. If any maintenance issues are identified during the inspection, the crew chief initiates a maintenance request and then physically assists in performing the maintenance. For instance, let's say a rotor blade needed to be changed out. The crew chief would help to change out the blade, then go back out for in-flight balance testing. Then they land, and QA tests the new blade again. If everything checks out with maintenance and QA, the crew chief might be able to go off shift for the day. But many times, they spent entire days testing, inspecting, retesting, and reinspecting to get a correct balance and measure on a replaced part. As if that wasn't enough, the crew chiefs have to be constantly prepared to present the most professional appearance, while providing the pilots with any pertinent follow-up information. Like I said, every single person in HMX-1 played an important role in overall operations, and the crew chief was at the very center of successful Presidential lifts.

Whether it's security, maintaining a trained and engaged workforce, ongoing planning and change management, personnel discipline, QA, or maintenance issues—there was simply no room for incompetence in HMX-1. Ultimately, I feel that I succeeded in forming and leading the right workforce, and we did not have any mishaps under my watch. I kept the fleet flying, as it were, and if HMX-1 continues to operate with enough vigilance and synergy, it should have another fifty years of operational excellence.

CHAPTER 8

FLYING THE COMMANDER IN CHIEF
AROUND THE GLOBE

Europe

Whether I was leapfrogging helicopters, equipment, and personnel on cargo planes and trains to ensure the right placement at the right time, or moving the entire lift package overseas, or simply flying *Marine One* in formation at a few hundred feet above countless American cities, it never got old. Despite the high pressure and immense responsibility that came with the job, the time away from home, and the seemingly endless amount of work that needed to be done in order to keep HMX-1 running, I never burned out, or looked forward to the end of my tour. If allowed, I would have gladly done a third tour.

As CO, I had the opportunity to travel all over the world with HMX-1. Sometimes I had to send one of my hand-selected *Marine One* pilots in my place, but I was on most of the trips. One of my favorite trips was flying the President all over Europe. He was going to meet with Angela Dorothea Merkel, the German Chancellor. After a few stops in Berlin, Poland, and the Ukraine, he would travel to London and meet with the Queen of England at Windsor Castle.

As usual, I collaborated with my Operations Department to develop the plan. Although VH-60s were much easier to transport overseas in cargo planes, this was a highly political and publicized trip, so I decided to bring VH-3s. I actually sent out three separate and complete lift packages, each comprised of all the right equipment and personnel. Two of the lift packages included VH-60s, which would support the President at the locations between Berlin and London. I would lead the primary lift package with the VH-3s, flying the President around Berlin, handing him off to *Air Force One* for the other short stops, and then flying the lift package to meet up with him in London.

Breaking down and configuring the VH-3s to fit into C-17s was a major undertaking from a logistical and maintenance perspective, and it was also a perishable skill since we didn't do it very often. I had a lot of experience within the Maintenance Department at that time, but there were also a number of personnel who had not yet taken VH-3s overseas. I was planning on doing the same thing for the D-day Sixty-fifth Anniversary event that I knew we would support with President Obama, and this mission was going to be a great training opportunity as well. It took an intensive maintenance effort to make the VH-3s fit into the C-17s. First of all, we used a crane to remove the entire white-top portion of the helicopter, which includes the engines and transmission. The WHLO would have to coordinate for similar cranes on the receiving end. The aircraft was still too tall to tow into the C-17. Next, the maintenance personnel had to install a different set of tires (we called them the training wheels) to shorten the height. Even after this, the VH-3 barely fit.

Once the helicopters were secured inside the C-17, we climbed up the back ramp and chose our spots on the cargo seating lining both sides of the aircraft. Our helicopters were right there in the middle of the massive space. We knew there was a lot of work ahead of us, and that we would probably get to see parts of a country we had not seen before. Once we rolled down the runway at Quantico, and pointed the nose of the aircraft to the east, there was a sense of calm before the storm. The flight across the Atlantic took six or seven hours, and once we reached altitude, everyone spread out

Since we traveled in the back of Air Force cargo planes a lot, everyone had a "C-17 kit," which usually contained creature comforts like a sleeping mat, snacks, books, movies, and anything else they wanted in there. The pilots switched to the red interior lights used in darkness, which create a soft and surreal ambience that just lulls you to sleep. And it's an unusual brand of C-17 sleep, where your pillow is gliding 30,000 feet above the ocean. People could be seen lying around on sleeping mats, watching movies on laptops, reading, and of course, sleeping.

I always changed into sweatpants for the flight, and relaxed on my sleeping mat as the massive bird flew silently over the dark waters below. It was a pretty nice way to travel, actually. Everyone knew when touchdown was getting close, so we packed up and prepared to get back to work. When that back ramp opened, everyone snapped into action to get the helicopters reconfigured.

According to our stringent maintenance and QA policies and procedures, certain things have to occur anytime the VH-3 is "deconstructed" to that level. Once the VH-3s are put back together under the close care of our maintenance and QA personnel, I had to fly it for ten hours before putting the President on the aircraft. Some of those hours would be burned off during a functional test flight, which is mandatory every time a dynamic component is removed. More of the ten hours would be burned off during rehearsals. But inevitably, I had to spend a couple of hours just flying around the countryside, doing our particular form of sightseeing. I wasn't complaining.

I had never been to Berlin before, so during rehearsals it was compelling to fly around the large industrial city, surrounded by vast countryside. While burning off the remaining ten hours, I even flew right over the place where the Berlin Wall once stood. When going overseas, we often don't pack up the green sides, or supporting aircraft. Instead, we coordinate with other U.S. military units nearby for support. In this case, a U.S. Army Black Hawk unit attached several helicopters and pilots to us all the way from Berlin to London. Although they were highly professional, HMX-1 is unlike any other organization. To overcome their lack of training in HMX-1 operations, I put one of my pilots and crew chiefs in each of the attached aircraft. The WHLO had done a great job in coordinating everything, and the rehearsals went off without a hitch as well.

At the appointed time, *Air Force One* landed and the President and the Chancellor climbed on board my aircraft. It was obvious from their body language that they were great friends. Among other stops, I flew them to their equivalent of our Camp David, called the Strauss. We landed next to a massive, regal building that looked like an old German villa with walls of soft, light pink, as if it had been built out of quartz. This main building and surrounding structures dotted a dense, old forest. Landing in a new place was always spectacular, and this day was especially exciting. The architecture, the trees, and just the whole affairs-of-state aura surrounding the event . . .

This was our head of state being hosted by another head of state, and as we flew across the countryside, we saw people lined up below to watch the green-and-white helicopters with the American flag and Presidential Seal on them. Although I was focused on the mission, in a sense we were putting on an international airshow in the German Chancellor's own backyard. The next day, I took the President back to *Air Force One*, and he headed out for the smaller trips that my other lift packages would support.

As I prepared to fly my own lift package across Germany and into London, I received daily and sometimes hourly updates about the status of the other lift packages. In the map of my mind, I could visualize all my assets operating across Europe. My route of travel would take me across Germany and the Netherlands, then over a corner of Denmark, into France, and then over the English Channel into London. I would fly us at a few hundred feet and at our normal cruising speed of 131 miles per hour.

A few hours in, we ran into some bad weather, and I had to make a decision to make an unscheduled stop in Europe, without clearance. I found a small airfield in the Netherlands, and we landed the entire lift package there. As soon as we got on the ground, I met with the airfield customs officials and called the White House Military Office. The right calls and coordination took place, and before long the weather cleared. We were all fueled up and ready to go.

The last leg of the trip was the most exciting for me. I had never been to that part of Europe before, and as an avid student of World War II, the vision in my mind was of a huge expanse of geography. I was amazed by how relatively small the area was. Conversely, the flight made me think about just how big our country is. In comparison, it would take me approximately three days (with the last day being pretty short) to fly from Washington, D.C. to California. Flying from Berlin to London took only the better part of one day.

More than anything else, my crew and I could not wait to see what the World War II pilots saw when they knew they had made it home safely—the White Cliffs of Dover. As we approached the English Channel, flying from the west coast of France toward the east coast of England, I saw the cliffs myself. I had flown the President over water before—off both coasts of the United States—but for the next twenty minutes I was almost rendered speechless as I flew *Marine One* across the Channel. I wasn't really speechless, because I was communicating with the air traffic controllers as I reached the far bank and flew up the river toward our destination—a military airfield north of London proper. Below me, I saw all those iconic buildings, including Tower Bridge, Big Ben, and Buckingham Palace.

Once we landed in London, I began the preparation and coordination for several full-scale rehearsals. I had to work with the English security organizations, including security around the Royal Family, their military police, and their civilian police. Everything had to be perfect. A couple of days later, and after rehearsal landings at Windsor Castle, the President arrived. I was sitting on the runway at Heathrow International Airport, watching *Air Force One* barrel toward me. That first day, I flew the President to his temporary residence.

On the second day of his visit, I flew the President to Windsor Castle for tea and lunch with the Queen. The flight took approximately the same length of time as it took me to fly from the White House to Camp David (about forty minutes). I flew right over little hamlets and old churches dotting the landscape beneath us. This did not look or feel anything like the United States, especially when I saw what I thought were fairly large castles and medieval estates. I was sure I wasn't in the United States any longer when I saw the size of Windsor Castle, a five-hundred-person estate that is actually the largest occupied castle in Europe.

When we landed, the Secret Service had a motorcade waiting to transport the President to his meeting with the Queen. While President Bush sipped tea with the Queen, I remained with the aircraft on the lawn, going over the communications channels, checking in with my pilots and our liaisons from the Secret Service, and mentally rehearsing the order of takeoff.

He returned exactly two hours later and was smiling as he walked from the motorcade to *Marine One*. He stopped in the cockpit for a moment, slapped me on the back reassuringly as we started to take off, and said, "Frenchman, try not to hit the castle."

I flew the President back to *Air Force One* and watched him take off. Another mission complete.

North America

Flying a helicopter, even in HMX-1, could never be assumed to be 100 percent safe. Parts can fail. Natural disasters can occur. Helicopters can crash. Of course, none of these things had ever happened at HMX-1, and I did not plan on them happening under my watch, but they could.

Obviously, President Bush was certainly a desirable target for many terrorist groups. Although we took precautions (and all of them are highly classified), flying *Marine One* could be considered dangerous in its own way.

And while *Marine One* was certainly not a first responder by any means, it was still the President's preferred method of travel. This meant that when natural disasters or national emergencies occurred, he wanted us to get him there fast. Really, all of HMX-1 operations required rapid planning and a high operations tempo, but national situations kicked it up a notch.

In August 2007, a bridge collapsed on I-35 near Minneapolis and St. Paul, Minnesota, killing a dozen people and injuring more than a hundred. I didn't know any of this right away because I was in the auditorium at Quantico when it happened. Although we couldn't do "real" safety stand-downs as I had at the Ugly Angels, even HMX-1 was mandated to do some kind of safety stand-down. To the degree possible, I had assembled some of the workforce for one day of safety briefings.

During a break, I received a call from my Operations Officer.

"Sir, a bridge collapsed in Minnesota. It's not good. We just got the call from the White House, the President wants to be there tomorrow."

I had to get a package of aircraft out there that same night. When the group returned from the break, I alerted them to the situation and said, "Okay, here's what we're going to do. We need a lift package in Minneapolis tonight for a lift tomorrow. Anyone that is needed to make that happen, you know who you are. Go, now. The rest of you, we'll finish the briefings."

A few dozen folks made their way out, and I looked at the rest of them and said, "This exemplifies why we are here today. The mission never stops, but we can still pause and discuss safety when we can."

I got back to Quantico just an hour or two later, met up with my crew, packed up, and flew the entire lift package to Minneapolis. The President was going to meet with state officials, then he wanted to fly to and land right near the bridge and see the destruction for himself.

I brought two VH-60s and three CH-53s, as I knew there would be a lot of press. All the support personnel and gear would travel by C-130 and meet us there. After a five-hour flight across the nation's heartland, flying over the Shenandoah and Ohio valleys, and making two quick fuel stops, we landed at an Air National Guard base that was part of the Minneapolis–Saint Paul airport.

I immediately linked up with my WHLO, and spoke with the White House press personnel, who wanted to get a shot of the President flying over the bridge in *Marine One*. I coordinated to have the photographer in one of my support aircraft. I then told the pilot of that aircraft that when the time came for the shot, he could just direct me over our internal radio frequency.

That night, I watched the news coverage of the collapsed bridge, which was now close by. I felt so bad for the families affected. This was one of those somber missions. The next morning, *Air Force One* landed at the airfield, and the President climbed aboard my aircraft.

I lifted off and headed straight to the bridge. Coordinating everything over the various communication channels, I took him in at just a couple of hundred feet. The images from the news the night before were now vivid below me. This was an active emergency scene. Some of the victims had still not been accounted for. The bridge, which normally spanned the Mississippi River, was now submerged in the water. I could see huge blocks of concrete, rebar or some other kinds of exposed metal, cars and trucks in the water, and a school bus caught up against one railing. Rescue boats were nearby. There was an intact bridge right next to the collapsed one, creating a disturbing before-and-after rendering.

I circled the scene several times to let the President get a good look. I was a pilot first and foremost, using all my experience to provide the safest flight possible for the President. I was also aware that the whole world was watching through the lens of the media. I also spoke with one of my pilots about the photograph. We got that taken care of, and I headed over to the predetermined landing zone on the bank of the river.

My WHLO had coordinated for us to land in a field right near the bridge. The choreography of this particular landing was tricky, because the CH-53s (Night Hawks 3 and 4) were carrying the press, and they had to land before the President. Typically, we would all touch down in the same landing zone, but this one was not large enough. In a highly synchronized set of maneuvers, the two CH-53s landed and their passengers disembarked. I then brought the President in and shut the aircraft down, and it quickly became a secure area.

The President toured the site with officials and spoke with some of the rescue workers. Because we were already inside the secure area, we were allowed to walk right up to the precipice of the collapsed bridge. It was a frightening view from that vantage point, and the area of the bridge that was once over land now looked like some concrete ramp ready to launch vehicles into the water. We tracked the President's movements and were ready to take off when he returned to *Marine One.*

Later that night, I was back in my hotel room, watching HMX-1 in action on the evening news. When the President was safely back in *Air Force One* the next day, and I was flying into the sun back to Quantico, I felt a great sense of accomplishment. We had made the whole thing work, but it had taken a lot of people jumping through hoops. This had been an unscheduled, rapid-planning trip, and we had operated outside of normal operating procedures with the landing zone. I was proud of us. The President wanted to react to an emerging situation, and we had made it seamless for him. Not too many aviation units in the world could have pulled that one off.

During my tenure, we performed several other similar missions, such as when tornadoes hit the Midwest, and the California wildfires. In each case, we worked together as a massive organization focused on a shared goal. The President was exactly where he wanted to be—showing his support to those affected by the disasters—exactly when he wanted to be there. On a personal level, I felt deeply for those people, and saw firsthand what the swath of destruction of a major tornado looked like from 200 feet. I remember how odd it seemed that it was such a clear and beautiful day, but just days before we arrived, Mother Nature had scoured the earth.

In between these kinds of lifts, there were also numerous planned lifts. Most of these were a perfect combination of hard work and fun. We prepared in the way that only HMX-1 could, and then carried out our mission. If we had a little downtime, some destinations were more fun than others. New York City was a favorite destination for everyone in the squadron. I had made the trip dozens of times, and in 2008 I flew the President there for the United Nations convention. International allies, foreign dignitaries, and military and government officials would be descending on the city from around the globe, adding an unusual flavor to the overall mission.

We planned out the mission specifics back at Quantico, including contingency plans and pilot and crew selection. We would fly the lift package from Quantico to JFK International Airport, in Queens. There, we would link up with *Air Force One* and then transport the President to Manhattan. As chance would have it, the National Geographic Channel was filming a show called *Onboard Marine One*, and parts of this trip were featured in the show. So, along with all the normal planning factors, we actually integrated National Geographic camera crews and other personnel into our plans.

We arrived a few days early and began rehearsals. Peter Schnall, the National Geographic producer, asked if we could get some aerial shots. I happily agreed and took him up for a flight over Central Park. We took off from JFK and made our way across the city. There was a lot more helicopter traffic in and around Manhattan than usual. It is always a treat to fly smoothly between the buildings of New York City, getting a glimpse of the swimming pools, gardens, and even tennis courts on top of some of them. There's also something really special about flying over Central Park, that green expanse that breaks up the otherwise dominant architecture of the massive city. Peter got the footage he wanted, which I enjoyed later when the show was aired.

On the morning of the convention, I gathered everyone around me in a large, open hangar at JFK. There were about seventy pilots and support personnel in flight suits, standing in a semicircle. I gave one final safety briefing, then said, "Nobody can do it better than us. Let's get it done. And yes, we are in Manhattan, so enjoy yourselves. Any questions?"

I knew that one of my white tops had picked up the President at the White House that morning at the designated time and transported him to Andrews, where he boarded *Air Force One* for the trip to New York City. Like clockwork, we climbed into our aircraft to wait for the President's arrival. Once on board, I flew him to the Wall Street heliport, which is a narrow strip of concrete jutting out into the East River.

I called for clearance from air traffic control, then dropped down and flew in at a low altitude, heading west right along the shore. Coney Island was below us, teeming with people all over the boardwalk. Some of them waved as we flew overhead. Roller coasters and other amusement park rides look very different from the air. We hit the tip of Coney Island, turned right, and flew right between the left and right stanchions of the Verrazano-Narrows Bridge, which connects Staten Island and Brooklyn.

Now I aimed the formation toward the tip of Manhattan, with the Statue of Liberty to the left and Governor's Island on the right. Approaching that iconic skyline from the south, the first thing I always noticed was the absence of the World Trade Center. During my first tour the towers had still been standing. We came in for the final approach to the Wall Street heliport. I had sent my WHLO team in to carefully designate where each helicopter would land. They were wearing suits (business casual) rather than their Marine uniforms, so as not to draw attention. I could see them below us, blending in with the Secret Service, the U.S. Coast Guard, local law enforcement, and other security personnel awaiting our arrival.

This landing could be tricky. If the winds were coming from the north, it was not too bad, much like landing on a ship. If the winds were out of the south, though, then I would have to head toward the Brooklyn Bridge, do a 180-degree turn, and fly right over the top of the other helicopters before landing. Luckily, the winds were coming in from the north on this particular morning.

I directed the other aircraft to land first, then took *Marine One* in for the final descent. The heliport was packed with people and aircraft, but I had landed in tight spaces before. When we were safely on the heliport, the President was whisked away in his motorcade under incredibly tight security. He was actually there for the whole weekend, and the next day we flew him to a school yard in New Jersey for a local event. As always, when the mission came to an end, we linked up with *Air Force One*, then made our way home and began preparing for the next mission.

The Boss Says Goodbye

In late 2008, President Bush was approaching the end of his second and last term. I knew firsthand how much he appreciated his military, and HMX-1. Still, he certainly wasn't expected to do anything special to let us know that. As he had so many times since I had met him, he surprised me.

In his last months in office, President Bush made an unprecedented trip to our hangar at Quantico to express his gratitude personally. No other President in history had ever visited Quantico to thank the members of HMX-1.

The President's visit to Quantico was a very big deal for us. The same kind of security measures were executed on that base regarding his arrival and transporting actions. The morning of his visit, the hangars had been prepared, and the Secret Service had carried out their usual checks and sweeps. I told my entire workforce to be in the hangar at the right time.

Meanwhile, I picked up the President for one of the very last times on the White House lawn. This mission was different. I was picking him up at his home, and on that day I felt like I was bringing him to my home-away-from-home. Imagine getting to bring the President of the United States home for a visit.

Right on time, he walked out of the South Portico and boarded *Marine One*. He came up into the cockpit and said, "Frenchman, how you doing today?"

"I'm doing great, sir."

"I guess you know the way we're going, right?"

I laughed. "Yes, sir, I got it."

I flew him first to the FBI Academy at Quantico, where he addressed the graduating class. I then flew him five minutes across Quantico to the HMX-1 compound. Normally I would be out on the landing strip, but on this day I landed right in front of the hangar filled with my beloved Marines. Another difference this day was that, while I usually stayed put in the cockpit until the President had exited the aircraft, this time I got off the aircraft, too, which felt kind of strange.

It was one of those really cold days, and the hangar doors were shut to keep the heat it. There were some members of the media just outside the hangar, but they knew the President was just saying goodbye, so they weren't actually part of the event. As we approached, someone cracked the hangar doors about two feet wide so that we could walk through the opening.

Inside, more than eight hundred pilots, mechanics, and administrative, communications, logistics, and other personnel were arrayed in a large semicircle. When I walked in with the President, the group immediately exploded into a loud roar of applause and yelling. Goose bumps jumped up on my neck, because I did not anticipate this kind of reception. It was like a rock star had just entered the premises. I could see it in their eyes. They were utterly motivated by the sight of their Commander in Chief and their own Commanding Officer.

As we made our way to the small stage and podium that had been set up, my Sergeant Major commented to me that this was an inappropriate reception. "Sir," he said, "this is their Commander in Chief. They should be standing at attention." I said, "Nah, not today, Sergeant Major. He loves it."

The media tried to rush the hangar to capture this spirited reception, but the Secret Service kept them at bay outside. President Bush and I walked up onto the stage together, and I looked out at my workforce. Their faces were beaming. These were the people who enabled HMX-1 to fulfill its mission on a daily basis, and without them none of it would have been possible. I saw Bayou and Spanky out in the crowd, clapping almost as hard for me as for the Commander in Chief.

As I waited a few minutes for the screaming and cheering to simmer down, I realized that this was the only time in my life I would ever have the chance to introduce the President of the United States. I walked up to the microphone and said, "Good morning, HMX-1." More cheering.

I then looked directly at the President and said, "It's an honor to have your here, sir. It's not lost on me that this is the first time any President has ever entered this hangar, even though it's been standing since Harry Truman was in office." This got a few laughs from the crowd and a smile from the President. I then turned to the crowd and said, "He obviously needs no introduction from me, but I am proud and honored to introduce our Commander in Chief."

There was even more roaring applause as the President came forward and gave a short and moving speech. His words were very heartfelt, as he thanked us sincerely for all that we had done for him and his family. He thanked us for our service and dedication and for serving our country in uniform. He made some comments about how many lifts we had done during his presidency and said that he understood and appreciated the constant and hard work that went on behind the scenes.

It felt like my role as Commander of HMX-1 and my friendship with the President joined on that stage, as I stood next to my boss and friend with my Marines watching. After his speech we presented him with a few tokens of our appreciation. First, we presented him with the glass from the very window of *Marine One* that he had looked out of so many times. What thoughts had he cast through that glass?

We had mounted the glass on a nice plaque and had engraved on it FAIR WINDS AND FOLLOWING SEAS. This was a common phrase used in Marine hail-and-farewell ceremonies, and had been passed down through history as a nautical phrase of good luck for the person heading out on his new "voyage." The squadron logo also adorned the plaque.

Next, we presented him with a tail rotor blade from *Marine One*. Our paint shop had finished the blade with a high-gloss paint, making it look like the white tops themselves. That was mounted on a plaque as well. Even though he appreciated the gifts, as I knew he would, I wanted to do something even more personalized and special.

In the weeks preceding the event, I had come up with the idea of designing a *Marine One* bicycle helmet. I bought a nice helmet and asked Lance Corporal Meekins to paint it in the *Marine One* theme. He was a very talented and artistic young man, and I knew he could do it justice. He accepted the challenge, taped everything up, and then painted it perfectly in several layers. The end product was gorgeous, and absolutely unique.

The President was thanking us for the other gifts when I said, "We have something else for you, Boss." I then had Lance Corporal Meekins come forward and present President Bush with the helmet. The smile on the President's face while I explained the images on the helmet said it all—he loved it.

I honestly thought that once he made his remarks, he would do an about-face, and we would head back out of the hangar and get him back to the White House. Instead, he spent an hour taking photos and shaking hands with as many people as he could. This caused an even bigger frenzy, because collectively we were all so grateful for his show of gratitude.

I was kind of following him around, just soaking it all in, when he suggested that we take a group picture. The White House photographer stood on a work stand and took the shot of the entire squadron in a semicircle, with the President right in the middle. Of course, there was a point in time when I had to get back into the aircraft and start it up for the flight back to the White House. I coordinated this with the military aide, and was in my pilot seat when the President walked out to *Marine One*.

He leaned into the cockpit again and said, "Frenchman, thank you so much for that. That was great. That was just awesome." I flew the aircraft back up the Potomac to the White House lawn, and my crew and I were still reeling from the energy in the hangar. We dropped him off and headed back to Quantico once more.

I was beyond appreciative that the President had recognized my Marines like that. It made what they do every day even more real for them. I was giddy by the time I got back to the HQ, and my Sergeant Major looked at me and said, "Sir, I have to tell you. You shined today."

The next time I flew the President to Camp David was one of the last visits, and one of the last excursions for Peloton One. We met up in the morning and, sure enough, he was wearing the helmet.

Everyone noticed it and commented on how cool it was. The President was just looking at me, beaming, and saying proudly without a beat, "Yep! This is my *Marine One* helmet. It's my new favorite helmet."

It was a fairly typical and strenuous ride, and afterward we were cooling down in front of the President's cabin.

He looked at me innocently and said, "Frenchman, I love the helmet so much, but I need a size bigger."

"Roger that, sir." I smiled as I rode away, because the President obviously thought we had a gift shop at the squadron. We hadn't told him how much we had put into it, and he didn't realize that it was one-of-a-kind. I wasn't going to tell him. I took the helmet back to Lance Corporal Meekins, and he agreed to do another one, no problem.

What is it that is so enthralling about serving a President in such a direct, personal way? First of all, the immense pride and sense of privilege that comes with serving the President cannot be understated. The access to the most powerful man on the planet and the daunting responsibility of my role were not lost on me, either. But it wasn't just the "star quality," because I had become accustomed to interacting with famous or powerful people long ago. So what was it? Why did Corporal Meekins smile, nod, and so diligently create another helmet? Why did I savor my work for the President like no other job before or since? Why did we all work so hard to support him?

Maybe it was the access to the inner circle of the highest levels of our government. You can watch movies with a White House theme, watch the news, even watch reruns of *The West Wing* and marvel at what it must be like. But living it day to day for a couple of years gave me an education and an opportunity that will stick with me for life. I felt so lucky every time I entered the White House with the credentials I had, because of the job I had. From the first to the last time I went into the White House—walking alone from the East Wing to the West Wing, looking at portraits and photographs, the plates displayed in the China Room, the murals in the Diplomatic Reception Room, nodding in recognition to staff members and Secret Service members, or just pausing at the Rose Garden as I walked down the West Wing Colonnade—I never lost the "holy shit!" feeling that I was part of a small minority of Americans who had the privilege to do and see these things.

On another level, maybe it was the unique flying role. In the aircraft, the sense of privilege and responsibility took on a whole new dimension. For a few moments in time, I was charged with the safety and security of the President of the United States. Every time I strapped that aircraft on and sat at the ready, waiting for the President to climb aboard, I uttered the small but extremely relevant "Alan Shepard prayer" that all pilots learn and have uttered many times: "Please, Lord . . . do not let me fuck this up." And on yet another level, there was a sense of privilege and exclusivity that came with spending weeks on Camp David. Although it was my job to be there, we were still treated as guests of the President at a little green patch on the planet that feels like paradise. Whether I was mountain biking, sitting in the chow hall, or hanging out in my cabin, I knew that "paradise" was surrounded by an intensely secured airspace, which we called the "doughnut of death" for those who would try to penetrate it without approval.

Or maybe the magic was in the faces of friends, family, and the public, when they heard about my job. I could always read the wow factor in their faces, especially when meeting someone for the first time. I think all these different aspects of flying the President coalesced into an unforgettable and very fulfilling experience. I always tried to find the right balance of humility, while believing at a very deep and personal level that I seriously had the coolest job in the world.

Inauguration Day 2009

The buildup to the January 2009 Inauguration began weeks in advance. As commander of HMX-1, I had sole responsibility for orchestrating helicopter support for the event, which included rehearsals and extensive coordination with the White House staff, the Inauguration Committee, the Secret Service, and dozens of other military and civilian contacts.

By the Friday before the Inauguration, the squadron, support, and security were all in place. Since President Bush and his family spent that last weekend at Camp David, that's where I spent the weekend as well. It was pretty cold when we took our final ride the Sunday morning before the inauguration, and we didn't get to talk much in what the President called a "balmy twenty degrees."

I returned the President and his family to the White House on Sunday evening and flew back to my headquarters at Quantico. I lived only a few miles from base, and falling asleep that night was a challenge to say the least. I jumped out of bed early on the morning of the Inauguration, already running through the day's procedures in my head while I was brushing my teeth. It was going to be a day of rich American history and tradition, and I had a front-row seat. I wanted to make sure that I gave President Bush a real send-off. I had so much admiration for the man, and I just wanted to do my small part to be supportive during what must have been a very emotional morning.

While the past and future Presidents of the United States and their families were no doubt waking and stirring about with nervous excitement and anticipation, my crew and I warmed up *Marine One* and took it for a spin around Washington, D.C. The horizon was nothing more than a thin sliver of light just starting to burn away the deep blue sheet of the sky. I looked out at the city lights in every direction and took the aircraft slow and low over the city.

It was maybe 5:30 A.M., but the city was not asleep. The National Mall was all lit up, and people were already camping out even though the Inauguration Ceremony would not begin until noon. I had to be in place at the Capitol by 7:00 A.M., so I headed back to base to make my final preparations. We realized that the heater unit was malfunctioning, and of course that would not do. So, in the hours before the Presidential Inauguration, we switched white tops. Of course we had plans for this type of contingency, and we had other white tops ready, for the most part. Still, it's not the type of thing you want to do on a morning like that.

I did a final briefing before we headed back downtown. Every single *Marine One* mission was treated with the utmost importance, and our job was the same no matter who the President or what the event. Still, the gravity of the day was not lost on any of us as I gave a detailed mission briefing about our flights, security, and other planning, made all the more complex by the events of the day and the size of the crowd.

By the time I took off again to position *Marine One* for the Inauguration Ceremony, D.C. was absolutely brimming with activity. On the morning of a Presidential Inauguration, it is traditional for the outgoing President and the First Lady to host the incoming President and new First Lady. While the Bush family was hosting the Obama family in the White House, probably having coffee or a light breakfast, I flew over D.C. toward the Capitol, sipping my own cup of coffee from the machine in my office.

The streets were clogged with traffic, and even more people were pouring into the National Mall. I flew over the Lincoln Memorial and landed very close to the Capitol steps—something that can happen only during an Inauguration. People were cheering and waving as cameras flashed. The Capitol was decorated in patriotic colors and the glowing interior lights were framed by the crisp blue sky.

I had hand-selected a team of four that morning: myself; my co-pilot, Captain Chris Roy; my crew chief, Sergeant Harrison Kish; and one of my security Marines, Sergeant Jordan Hardy, who was already at the Capitol to keep the landing site secure. We walked up the steps and into the Capitol with almost five hours until we took off again for the final flight to Andrews Air Force Base. But with all the activity behind the scenes, those hours went by like minutes.

I was obviously focused on the operational side of things. *Marine One* had been providing Presidents with impeccable support for more than fifty years, and I had every intention of carrying on that tradition today. But I was also immersed in the personal and historical side of the event. I walked out to the same rotunda where past Presidents had stood, and where our future President would be standing in just a few hours. I looked out at the Mall and got yet another incredible perspective of the enormous crowd that had swelled even more since my pre-dawn flight.

Just downstairs from the rotunda, an executive office had been designated for those of us behind the scenes. I grabbed another cup of coffee and watched the media coverage of the event on a TV nearby. Watching the news, I knew those cameras were just outside the building, pointed right at us. I spent the next few hours talking to colleagues and associates, going out to warm up the helicopter every hour or so, and generally trying to stay out of the way. The press was poised, so even my warming up the engines became something to report. Each time I went back into the building and sat down, I saw on the news what I looked like from everyone else's perspective. I knew that my parents were watching with pride.

Eventually, dignitaries like Congressmen, Senators, Justices, family members, and other VIPs began to arrive and be seated for the event. I monitored the radio to track the President's movements. It was reflex. It was my job to know where he was, to know where he wanted to go, and then to take action to get him there. On TV, I saw the Obamas climbing into a motorcade for the trip from the White House to the Capitol. Next, I saw the Bushes, and I knew that it wouldn't be long until it was go time.

When the actual Inauguration of our forty-fourth President finally began, I was glued to the TV just like anyone else. The only difference was that I was right behind those walls. As President Obama finished his speech, I looked at my crew and said, "Okay, boys, giddy up."

When we walked out to the aircraft this time, the crowd started roaring. They had gotten as close as possible to the Capitol without entering the secure area, and were taking thousands of photos. I walked up the steps, took a look around the cabin, and climbed into the warm cockpit. Sergeant Kish was out there, standing at attention in the bitter cold.

As I sat there waiting for the Bush family to board, I had yet another great perspective. I had been part of so many military and Presidential speeches and ceremonies, but nothing as important and steeped in tradition as this. The stairs of the Capitol were lined with military personnel in dress uniforms when three iconic couples in long winter coats came into view and began to descend: the Bushes, the Obamas, and the Bidens. They all stopped at the bottom of the stairs and exchanged pleasantries.

Around this time, President Bush 41 and Barbara Bush approached the steps. It was clear that he was struggling as his wife helped him up the stairs. He had aged a lot since we played walleyball all those years ago.

Once inside, he put his hand on my shoulder, smiled, and said, "It's tough getting old," then laughed and took his seat.

Jenna and Barbara Bush and Jenna's husband boarded the aircraft next. I turned and greeted them as they did, and I could sense their energy and excitement. Finally, the man who had been the President of the United States until just a few moments earlier made his way toward my aircraft. Laura Bush entered first, as the President turned and waved to the crowd and to the Obama and Biden families, who were waving from the Capitol steps.

I had also gotten to know Laura quite well during all my time at Camp David and the Crawford ranch. True to her days as a teacher and a true southern lady, Laura looked at me with that warm and friendly smile she always had. "Good morning," she said.

"Good morning, ma'am."

She made her way back to sit down with her family. I had the stomach butterflies when President Bush finally boarded *Marine One*. I'm not sure what I was expecting, but as he came up to the cockpit to greet us, he looked more exuberant and content than I had ever seen him before. He grinned as he put his hand on my shoulder and said, "Frenchman, let's go."

"Roger that, Boss." The engines had been running, and now I started to spin the rotors. Outside, the crowd went wild.

It was an exercise in personal discipline to remain focused on the task at hand in the excitement of the moment, as I lifted gently off the east side of the Capitol and began a very slow circle over the frenzied chaos below.

Even though my job description didn't change from President to President, I still felt a sense of loss that morning. I had ridden mountain bikes with President Bush so many times I had lost count, and I had gotten to know him so much more than I ever would have imagined. I had flown him to locations all over North America, South

America, Europe, and Asia, but the grand adventure was coming to an end today. He was moving on, and I would be retiring soon.

The night before, I had written him a note:

Sir, it has been my honor and privilege being your helicopter pilot for the last couple of years. I've enjoyed every moment of serving you, and riding with you . . . you will always be MY President.
Semper Fi,
The Frenchman

I placed the note on the President's seat before the flight, but I didn't know if he would read it right then or tuck it into his jacket pocket for later. As I circled the crowd for the second time, one of the aides called me on the helicopter's internal radio system and said, "Colonel L'Heureux, he just read your note. He seems really moved by it."

That was the first time the White House photographer had ever flown in my aircraft, but his timing couldn't have been better that morning. I found out later that as the President looked down at the Capitol and the massive crowd below him with my note in his hand, the photographer snapped a picture.

I had been in so many historical flights, but I doubt that more eyes were ever on me than at that moment. Every President is supposed to get a final flight in *Marine One*, but President Clinton's had been canceled due to inclement weather. The last time this historical "victory lap" had taken place had been sixteen years ago. I had been a young Captain watching my Commander fly President Bush 41. Today, I was the Commander, and I was flying both generations.

Vice President Cheney was in a wheelchair that day and traveling in a separate aircraft to Andrews Air Force Base. He had to arrive before us, because he was supposed to introduce the President. It was traditional to fly around the Mall, but I was also buying time.

I called over the radio to get a status update: "This is *Marine One.* Any word on the location of the Vice President?"

"Roger, still en route."

He still wasn't there. *Slower, Frenchy, slower.*

I was starting to worry. I was on my third lap over the crowd, but you don't just keep flying the President and his family around without good reason. I made another radio call and learned that the Vice President was finally getting close. I turned to the east and flew away from the crowd and toward Andrews Air Force Base. After only a couple of minutes, I landed right at the nose of *Air Force One* and shut down the rotors. Usually, I would remain in the cockpit until the First Family left the aircraft, then climb down and start the post-flight procedures. This was the last time the Boss would be leaving my aircraft, and the emotion of the moment was upon me. I wanted to remember it.

I got out of my seat and stood inside the aircraft near the top of the stairs. I exchanged hugs with everyone on board, until only Laura and President Bush remained. Laura came up first, wearing a large black coat. She gave me perhaps the warmest smile I have ever received, and then we hugged and she said, "Thank you for taking such good care of my family these years."

"My pleasure, ma'am."

As she went down the stairs, President Bush approached me with his own warm and knowing smile. I tried to come up with something poignant to say, as all the memories we'd shared over the past few years flashed by in my head. I think he could tell I was struggling with the words.

He just walked right up to me and gave me a big hug. I hugged him back. He said, simply, "I'm going to miss you."

"I'm going to miss you, too," I said, and he walked off *Marine One* for the last time. As he descended the steps, he was greeted by yet another crowd.

I walked over to *Air Force One* and climbed the steps. I greeted the security guard and walked up to the cockpit to talk with Colonel Mark Tillman, my counterpart and the pilot of *Air Force One*. I knew that the day was a big deal for him, too, because he was retiring from the Air Force right around the same time as President Bush left office. After talking with Mark about what it felt like to fly President Bush for the last time, I went into the hangar where the President's speech was about to begin.

I was surrounded by hundreds of people I had come to know so well over the past couple of years. When the speech ended, there was security and a rope line to contain the crowd. I was milling around near the hangar doors, talking to some colleagues, when the President and his family made their way to the steps of the 747.

Throngs of people were trying to get their attention, and in their typical way they stopped to talk to most of them. They shook hands and exchanged hugs with all the well-wishers, and I just stood there smiling broadly. I had already said my goodbyes, and my crew had done an amazing job at the Inauguration. It was another touching moment, and I was proud of President Bush.

At that moment, the President caught my eye. He walked right over to me before boarding the plane. While the crowd watched and cheered, he just smiled at me again, then put his hand on top of my head and tousled my hair, like a dad congratulating his son after a good game. I caught a couple of bemused looks from people standing close-by.

They climbed the stairs, waved, and boarded the aircraft. The plane began to taxi down the runway. As it took off and headed south and west toward Crawford, Texas, I felt the weight of the day leave me.

A few weeks later, I received a letter in the mail dated just before the Inauguration, on White House letterhead. It reads:

> *A Prime Minister, a NATO head, ambassadors, cabinet secretaries, and a mayor.*
> *A general, chopper pilots, Camp David chargers, military vets, mil aides, and doctors.*
> *Family, White House family, campaign vets, Fellows, agents, advance dudes, photo dogs, and a State Department "chick."*
> *Pro racers, bike fitters, bike builders, trail builders, and a noted author.*
> *Bike company owners, entrepreneurs, executives, and a head coach.*
> *Amputees, Olympians, 24 hour racers, reporters, radio talkers, and a mailman.*
> *E Pluribus Unum—out of many = Peloton One.*
> *Thanks for the memories,*
> *George Bush*

Along with the letter was another pair of biking socks, but this time they had the Presidential Seal with PELOTON ONE around it, and below that: PELOTON ONE—FINAL EDITION. I still had an important job to do, and I could only hope that my new boss would be as gracious, kind, and warm as this one had been. I soon met President Obama, and my final chapter with HMX-1 began.

Meeting the Obamas

The day after the Inauguration, I had a meeting at the White House to meet my new boss (Louis Caldera, the Director of the White House Military Office). He had served as Secretary of the Army under President Clinton, and he wanted to meet with all the Directors and Commanding Officers under his scope of responsibility.

I arrived early so that I had time to walk through the White House for a few minutes. I grabbed a cup of coffee, then stopped by to chat with the Director of the Secret Service, who had become a friend of mine. I then made my way back through the West Wing and ran into Colonel Tillman. His replacement, and my new counterpart, Colonel Scott Turner, was also there.

We talked for a few moments, right near the stairs where the Situation Room and the entrance to the Press Room are located. We were preparing to walk back to the East Wing when I saw the Secret Service guys coming through. I knew by their body language that the President was very close by. We just kind of backed up to the wall to make way, and President Obama and Vice President Biden came around the corner. They both seemed in high spirits as they introduced themselves to people. Then suddenly they were heading right at us. We were all wearing suits that morning, which we always did unless it was a designated uniform day or we had a lift.

When National Geographic had filmed President Obama on *Air Force One*, Scott was the pilot. Obama looked at Scott with a friendly smile and said, "I know you."

Scott said, "Yes, sir, you do."

The President then extended his hand to me and said, "Hi, how are you doing? Barack Obama."

"I'm doing fine, sir. I'm your helicopter pilot, and I've got one up on Scott here . . . I'm actually a Marine."

Scott laughed at the jab, and Obama seemed to get it, too. "You know what? I can't wait to fly with you. I've never been in a helicopter before."

I looked him right in the eye, nodded, and said, "Sir, it was nice to meet you. And congratulations."

He said, "Thank you very much."

Biden was right behind him, observing all this, and then he shook our hands and said, "Good to meet you fellows."

And that was the first time I actually met my new Commander in Chief.

His first opportunity to fly came just a couple of weeks later. This was a significant event, and everyone wanted to be part of the first Presidential lift. Sergeant Williams and Sergeant Kish were my two senior crew chiefs, and they had flipped a coin to decide who would fly the Inauguration and who would fly this lift. Sergeant Kish had done the Inauguration, so now it was Sergeant Williams on the crew this morning.

We were only going to fly the President from the White House to marry up with *Air Force One* at Andrews, but it was a good chance for me to observe how the new administration played with others. Not unlike the transfer of power from President Bush 41 to President Clinton, HMX-1 was adjusting again to a new boss.

Because of my experiences during the transition from Bush 41 to Clinton, I assigned my staff to gather certain information. For instance, we sent in a request to Obama's staff about his family's preferences for snacks and beverages on *Marine One*. The staff was incredulous that we were asking this kind of stuff, because the President and First Lady were not yet accustomed to flying in an aircraft that catered to their wishes. They pretty much just asked for healthy snacks, juice and water, so we stocked the cabin with those items.

Not only did we reconfigure *Marine One* to suit the new President, but I remembered all too well the hubbub in the media when President Clinton had failed to salute the crew chief on his first *Marine One* flight. I knew that President Obama had no military experience, so I doubted that he would be familiar with our traditions and ceremonies.

I called my boss and said, "Sir, I'm willing to bet that nobody on the staff has thought to mention the protocol for saluting my crew chief. We don't want the whole world to see him botch it."

My boss agreed that it was a good idea, and said he would bring the issue up to the new staff. I later spoke about the issue to the military aide prior to the flight. He said, "Trust me, Frenchy, all five of us mil aides sat the boss down and gave him our guidance on how to board the aircraft properly. He's got it."

I was relieved to hear it, and glad to avoid another awkward moment and subsequent media blitz. We landed on the White House lawn exactly five minutes before the designated pickup time. I shut down the rotors, kept the engines running, and Sergeant Williams positioned the air stairs and waited for the President's arrival. Perfect timing.

Twenty minutes passed. I wasn't going to make judgment calls, but President Bush's staff was the most synchronized I had ever seen, and perhaps I had gotten spoiled by their consistent punctuality. President Clinton's staff had sometimes kept us waiting like this, but I just chalked it up to this being the first lift, and the new administration getting into a good rhythm.

As always, I had a backup aircraft positioned in the air nearby, just in case I need them. Due to fuel concerns, I eventually called the pilot on the radio and told him, "Night Hawk Two, head back to base and stand by. I will let you know when I'm airborne."

The President came out twenty-five minutes after we landed, and the cameras went crazy. There were also hundreds of people on the rope line, cheering and snapping their own pictures. I watched out the cockpit window as he approached the stairs.

Sergeant Williams threw his hand up in a snappy salute, and the President returned it perfectly. The military aide had also briefed him that he didn't need to talk to the Marine or anything like that, but he decided otherwise. After the salute, the President walked right up to Sergeant Williams and extended his hand. "How you doing? I'm President Obama."

I could only imagine what was going through Sergeant Williams's head as he stood there frozen in time for a moment. Dozens of cameras caught the moment, and Sergeant Williams had that surprised look in his eyes, as if to say, *Are you actually talking to me?*

I watched as he moved his hand from the salute position to shake the President's hand and exchange a few words. Next, the President climbed aboard and leaned into the cockpit. He shook my hand and my copilot's, and thanked us jokingly in advance for a smooth ride. He then went into the cabin and took his seat, and I imagined what it must be like to occupy the Presidential seat for the first time.

A few seconds later, Sergeant Williams entered the cockpit and sat down. He put on his headset, looked at me in distress, and said, "Sir, I am so sorry. I didn't know what to do. He just started talking to me."

Williams thought he was in trouble with me because he had broken the position of attention to shake the President's hand.

I looked at him and said, "Sergeant Williams, the President of the United States put his hand out and started talking to you. You did exactly what you were supposed to do. Forget about it. No big deal at all."

We brought the President over to Andrews, where he thanked us again before boarding *Air Force One*. Before I even got back to Anacostia, I was getting calls from the military aide: "Who was that Marine? Why was the President talking to him?"

I had to call my boss and explain to him what had happened, and why Sergeant Williams had broken protocol. The next day, of course, all this was televised. It provided a great newsreel, portraying President Obama taking time out to talk to a Marine as he was boarding *Marine One*. This kind of thing had not happened in a decade, so Sergeant Williams was the focus of a good deal of teasing, I'm sure, but everyone knew that he had done exactly the right thing.

•   •   •

Not long after that first lift, I flew the Obama family to Camp David for the first time. Again, this was a place I was intimately familiar with, so it was fascinating to imagine how the First Family would like it.

I was on the White House lawn at the right time, and out comes the President, the First Lady, her mother, and their two daughters. I knew who would be on the lift, so I had picked up a couple of HMX-1 models that were all the rage in our HMX-1 gift shop.

I had placed notes on all the seats, and for the girls, the notes were tucked under the helicopters. The note to the President and First Lady simply said, "Welcome aboard *Marine One*. We are looking forward to serving you. Colonel Frenchy L'Heureux."

The notes for the girls said, "Welcome, Malia and Sasha. We are happy to have you aboard. Colonel Frenchy L'Heureux."

When the family boarded, the President leaned in and said hello in his congenial manner. Mrs. Obama then stopped by the cockpit as well, and said, "Oh my gosh. This is my first helicopter ride. I am so excited!"

When I landed at Camp David, Mrs. Obama again stopped by and said, "Thank you so much for the toys, they are absolutely wonderful. The flight was beautiful, I just loved it."

She also had each of the girls come into the cockpit and say thank you, which was very sweet.

That weekend, there was no Peloton One. I did challenge some of the guys to a friendly game of walleyball, and some of them were later invited to play basketball with the President. I don't have an ounce of talent on the basketball court, so I passed on that one. This was going to be one of my last visits to Camp David, and I felt quite nostalgic as I tried to soak it all in. I was already training the next HMX-1 CO by this time, and over the next few months I began to let my other *Marine One* pilots handle more lifts as I prepared for my next assignment.

The Sixty-fifth Anniversary of D-day

My last mission with HMX-1 was one of the most historically significant events of my life. This time, I flew President Obama during the
sixty-fifth anniversary of D-day in Normandy. The last time I was here,
I had flown President Clinton as the WHLO for the fiftieth anniversary
of the event. I don't think very many Marines got a chance to do this
once, let alone twice. Now I was the CO, and would actually land the
President right at the cemetery. They did an "anniversary" every five
years or so, and this was probably one of the last ones in which any
WW II vets would still be alive.

Sergeant Kish was my crew chief on this trip, and just like the trip
to Germany and London, we broke down the VH-3s to fit them in the
back of a C-17. In the day preceding the event, we had to again fly the
ten hours after reassembling the VH-3s. First, we flew over the countryside a bit, then I took the crew up and down the coast, looking down at
places like Deauville, Caille, Isigny-sur-Mer, Red Beach, Gold Beach,
and Omaha Beach.

I was still stunned by what had happened on those beaches below
us. We could still see obstacles in the water, big craters in the ground,
and the gun emplacements in Pointe du Hoc. On the day of the ceremony, we landed *Marine One* and Night Hawk Two right there in
Colleville at the Normandy American Cemetary and Memorial, where
our war dead are buried. All of the other visiting heads of state had
to land in a field down below and then ride in a motorcade up to the
cemetery. But this is U.S. sovereign soil, so all eyes and cameras were
on us when we landed.

The President left the aircraft and participated in a summit with
other world leaders. Next, there was a long ceremony with lots of
speakers. We had free access to the area, so we walked around and
took in the sights. Steven Spielberg and Tom Hanks, the guys who
brought us *Saving Private Ryan*, were in the crowd.

After the day's events, we flew the President back to the airfield and began preparing for the journey home. We were good at this, and everything was smooth and synchronized. Now we broke down the VH-3s again and walked up the back ramp of the C-17.

For most of the guys, it was just another ride home. But it was especially poignant for me, since I knew it would be my last. I spent some time in quiet reflection, looking around me and thinking about everything I had been privileged to do with this outstanding organization.

CHAPTER 9

MARINE ONE, OUT

I had flown the Obama family around the United States, to Camp David, and to France, watching them settle into their new lives. Now it was my turn to say goodbye. Six months into President Obama's tenure, I handed over the reins of my beloved HMX-1 to the next Commander. Colonel Jerry Glavy would become the twenty-third HMX-1 Commander.

My change-of-command ceremony took place on June 19, 2009. This was the height of HMX-1 ceremony and tradition, and there were more than five hundred people in attendance. We were actually on the flight line at Quantico, which had been closed down for the event. Distinguished guests were seated under a special tent in the middle of it all. I watched with everyone else as the white tops came in, smooth and shining in the bright afternoon sun. Most of the HMX-1 workforce was standing in a traditional formation, and with the white tops prestaged among them, they became part of a gorgeous and powerful panorama of machines and Marines.

After several people from the squadron made some remarks, after my wife and the new HMX-1 Commander's wife were presented with bouquets of roses, and after the band and Color Guard performed several songs and movements, the event narrator read a letter from President Bush and another from President Obama. Finally, I was introduced.

I walked up to the predetermined spot and turned around to face the crowd. I had done so many things and met so many interesting characters along the way, and here were many of them, smiling back at me, waiting to hear what I would say. Talk about full circle. Standing there before my mentors, family, and friends, with the white tops and all my Marines in formation behind me, everything felt just right. I could still remember that flying lesson as a kid.

I took a breath and gave my speech, which I had thought about in the days and weeks before, but which I chose to do without notes, and from the heart. My parents were there, and their pride was palpable. They had supported me so much. And from seeing Camp David and *Marine One* and Crawford and everything else vicariously through my excited phone calls and visits home, to visiting the Oval Office and attending military ceremonies like this one, my parents had enjoyed a front-row seat to the incredible career they made possible.

During the speech I thanked Dianna for her strength and love and support, and mentioned my kids, Delia and Ray Jr., who were sitting right next to her. I shared with the guests how my "kids" were now a lawyer and a Marine Officer, and how I couldn't have been more proud. Steve, Bayou, and Spanky were there, and I smiled over at them when I mentioned all the people who had shared this incredible journey with me. I thanked a lot of other people, congratulated Colonel Glavy, and made special mention of my mentors. Ned and Willie were sitting right there among them.

But most of all, I spoke about how much I loved the dedicated people standing behind me in formation. I ended with a quote from Ronald Reagan: "We got something pretty good. We made it a little better. We're leaving it in good hands. Overall, not bad."

I had two more assignments and posts after HMX-1, working with some of the finest men and women you can imagine. My predecessor at HMX-1 once said, "We are not a bunch of special Marines do an average mission. We are a bunch of average Marines doing a very special mission." I could not have agreed more. Knowing that nothing could ever top my incredible experiences as CO of HMX-1, I decided to end my career in the Marine Corps in 2011, after three decades of service.

Looking Back

In the five decades that HMX-1 has been transporting the President of the United States, I was the twenty-second Commanding Officer. One hundred years from now, I'll be one of the faces looking out from a nice frame in the HMX-1 hallway or museum. Because of the timing of my tours, I straddled two administrations each time and experienced the transition of power. I also got to fly the last two Presidents of the twentieth century and the first two of the twenty-first. Likewise, I flew the first Presidential Inauguration and victory lap of the twenty-first century. My parents, family, friends, and thousands of fellow Marines were right there with me the whole time. Since my family lived near Quantico during my HMX-1 tours, there were even a couple of times when I got to fly *Marine One* over my house, and look down at my own kids waving. Wow.

I was the first person in my family to join the Marine Corps, and the military. When I joined, I had no idea where it would take me. What began as a young college student's plan to become a pilot became a thirty-year adventure, and the greatest honor of my life. The Marine Corps gave me the opportunity to travel to numerous countries and multiple continents, and to see most of it from the cockpit of a helicopter. I can't say enough about all the incredible men and women I worked with there, and in all of my positions.

I was assigned to Hawaii for much of my career, which led to my decision to live here after leaving the Marines. I am now serving as the Assistant Superintendent of the Office of School Facilities and Support Services for the Hawaii Department of Education, in which both of my children finished their high school educations. While we have a very different mission, the complexity of my job is not much different than that of HMX-1. I've been trained and expected to create results in dynamic working conditions, and those skill sets still apply to my work today. Instead of helicopters and Marines and world leaders, I now interact with educators, school leadership, and state-government officials to manage the security and operations of hundreds of facilities.

While I was in the Marine Corps, I never looked back. I was too engaged in the work I was doing to focus on the past. As I write this, I've been out for a couple of years, and I can reflect with hindsight on all the lessons the Marine Corps taught me. Perhaps the most fundamental lessons I learned in thirty years are that leadership is a contact sport and that you must be willing to get your hands dirty. In the leadership positions I was selected for, I could not be afraid to make decisions. But, as with any human behavior, be it personal or professional, sometimes you make a decision and wish you had a do-over. In the Marines, you don't get many do-overs. You just take full responsibility for your actions, take accountability for the entire team, and continuously learn and grow from mistakes and successes alike.

I remember the feeling when I first took over HMX-1. It was the pinnacle of my career, and I knew it, and all I had to rely on with regard to handling that level of responsibility and the scope of that job was my experience as the Commanding Officer of HMH-362 (the Ugly Angels). During that role, I had been a very hands-on Commanding Officer, engaging with the workforce at every level of the squadron. Ultimately, I was able to hone the workforce into a dynamic and cohesive unit with a shared vision. The patches we wore on our flight suits became emblems of our deep sense of collective pride and devotion to the organization and to one another.

I was told that I would not be able to lead HMX-1 in the same way. It was just too big, and there were too many moving parts. After a career of learning as much as I could from my former Commanders and mentors, and then from my own Command experience, I disagreed. One of the things I learned as CO of HMH-362 was that I had a gift for learning and being able to recall a Marine's name. This may not seem like much, or be viewed as important to the casual observer. But to that young Marine, that Lance Corporal walking across the hangar deck, it means something. He might feel like he is so far down on the totem pole that his presence in the squadron is unremarkable. Then, the "boss" addresses him by his earned rank and name, recalls his home state, and initiates a conversation about his work in the squadron, and that young Marine realizes that his CO knows exactly who he is and is actually *thanking* him for his efforts!

HMX-1 was seven times the size of HMH-362, but I made it a point to learn the name and personal information of every single member of the unit. Among many other forms of leadership, this helped me to propel HMX-1's overall morale and esprit de corps through the roof. For example, as in any job or task I was given, I always strove to do the right thing, to put Marines first and mission second. Such a culture breeds success. Of course, HMX-1 was a bit more kinetic than most organizations, and the mission so visible that it really did consume most daily interactions and decision making. There was no room for human or mechanical incompetence, and every facet of operations had to be flawless. I was awestruck by the professionalism and dedication of the men and women who made it all possible.

I served in amazing organizations with incredible people, and HMX-1 is the most professional, most beloved organization of them all. I don't know what would've happened if somehow I had botched a landing, put the President in danger, or, God forbid, crashed *Marine*

One. I like to think that my Marines, and the incredible support system of HMX-1, would have understood that these things do happen. But deep down where it really counts, I put more pressure on myself than anyone else ever could.

Another one of my most cherished memories and experiences, and the opportunity of a lifetime, was the relationship I was able to have with President Bush. Even though my job required me to take a very nonpolitical approach to the President, whoever he may be, I still got to see the personal side of President Bush. In between all the missions, logistics, and planning, I rode bikes with him and helped with the trail at Crawford. And in doing so, I couldn't help but begin to see him as a regular guy. Of course, I did not forget that the regular guy was also the President of the United States, but I still marveled at the privilege of getting to know him on that level. I never once took it for granted, and I was giddy as a kid about every bike ride or conversation that took place.

I have kept in touch with President Bush, exchanging Christmas cards each year. In April 2013, I received an invitation to the dedication ceremony for the George W. Bush Presidential Library and Museum. When Presidents Bush 41, Bush 43, Clinton, and Carter stood on the stage with their wives, I was sitting in the audience, and realized that I had flown almost everyone up there.

At the prededication dinner the night before the ceremony, the President was just as I remembered him—a man with the energy of a teenager, a comic's sense of humor and timing, and a serious set of lungs and legs that could propel him on the trails with speed and stamina. Despite having one of the most intense jobs in the world, and dealing with a plethora of national issues, I always found President Bush down-to-earth, kind, and selfless. I feel very lucky to have served as his pilot and to call him a friend. He even told me that the invitation to come back to ride the trail at Crawford still stands.

•   •   •

So many things have changed, but some remain the same. I still see Marine helicopters flying around Hawaii all the time. I still run on the beaches and compete in local triathlons. I still scan the horizon for weather on my drive into the office, as if I were going to fly the Boss that day. I also have nine helicopter models that sit on a shelf in my office now. When I was a kid, those models hanging from the ceiling of my bedroom represented a hopeful career in aviation. The ones that sit before me now are daily reminders of the wonderful career I've had.

Someone once wrote, "Every man's memory is his own private literature." I don't think I could possibly be more grateful or humbled by my own collection.

ACKNOWLEDGMENTS

There are so many people I could thank, because without them these stories, these memories, and this book would not have been possible. I would like to thank all of the Marines, Sailors, and civilians I have served with, and those still serving. There are personalities with names like Paco, Quarters, Spanky, Bayou, Skippy, and Cajun—aviators all. And those venerable and salty Crew Chiefs—if not for them, I am quite sure I would never have become the pilot and leader I was entrusted to be. In dark nights and choppy seas, tight landing zones and unstable suspended loads . . . they did the real work.

I would also like to thank some of my mentors, including Lieutenant Colonel Richard "Willie" Willard, Lieutenant Colonel Ned Paulson, Admiral Tom Fargo, and Lieutenant General Keith Stalder. You are all incredible patriots, mentors, and friends.

Finally, I would like to personally thank President George W. Bush for introducing me to the thrill of mountain biking, and for the unforgettable rides. As the President once said to me after a particularly brutal day on the trails: "If you're not bleeding, you're not riding!"

INDEX

Dead Heading

Dead Heading

CATHERINE AIRD

Allison & Busby Limited
12 Fitzroy Mews
London W1T 6DW
www.allisonandbusby.com

First published in Great Britain by Allison & Busby in 2013.

A CIP catalogue record for this book is available from
the British Library.

First Edition

ISBN 978-0-7490-1388-2

Typeset in 11/16 pt Sabon by
Allison & Busby Ltd.

The paper used for this Allison & Busby publication
has been produced from trees that have been legally sourced
from well-managed and credibly certified forests.

Printed and bound by
CPI Group (UK) Ltd, Croydon, CR0 4YY

For Torrin Wojtunik Macmillan
With love

CHAPTER ONE

'I don't believe it,' spluttered Jack Haines, the colour in his face draining away. 'All dead, you say?'

'Every last one, boss,' announced Russell Aqueel, his foreman. 'Well, all of them in number one and number two houses – the two farthest ones – anyway.'

'Good grief.' Jack Haines leant forward in his office chair and sank his head between his hands on his desk. He was a burly man and the chair creaked under his weight.

'The other greenhouses seem all right,' offered Mandy Lamb, the firm's secretary, automatically pushing a cup of coffee along the desk in front of him.

'They are. I've had a good look at the rest to be quite sure,' said Russell, a short, stocky man. He sniffed. 'First thing I did. Naturally.'

'But the young orchids and the special orders?' his employer asked tightly, lifting his head to look at the man.

'All dead,' said Russ. 'Every flaming one.'

'A flame would have been a help,' remarked Mandy Lamb detachedly, 'seeing as how it was the cold that killed them.'

'There was a frost last night . . .' began Russ.

'I do know that,' snapped Haines, his facial colour rapidly changing from grey to a rising red. 'You don't have to tell me. I've got a thermometer alarm by my bed, remember.' He stopped suddenly and said softly in quite a different tone of voice, 'Except that it didn't go off last night, did it?'

'I wouldn't know about that, would I?' said the foreman truculently.

'Go on, Russ,' said Jack Haines evenly. 'Tell me exactly what's happened.'

'When I came in this morning, first thing, both those greenhouse doors were wide open.' The man scowled at his employer. 'And before you ask, no, it wasn't me.'

'I didn't think it would have been, Russ,' said Jack Haines pacifically. 'So calm down.'

'But who on earth would do an awful thing like that?' demanded Mandy Lamb.

'Only someone malicious or careless, Russ,' said Haines bleakly.

'It could well ruin us, boss,' said the foreman. 'And where's the gain in that?'

'I wouldn't begin to know,' said Jack Haines tonelessly, although he thought he had a good idea.

Mandy Lamb shrugged her shoulders and said, 'On the other hand, anyone could forget to shut a couple of doors.'

Both men stared at her.

'Never,' said the foreman robustly.

'Not at a plant nursery,' sighed Jack Haines. 'It could kill the lot at this time of the year.'

'It has killed the lot,' pointed out the foreman soberly. 'Well, everything in those two houses, anyway.'

'What about all those plants Anthony Berra had in there for the admiral's garden?' put in Mandy Lamb suddenly. Waldo Catterick, an old sailor, was a favourite of hers.

'They're goners all right,' said the foreman. 'So is most of the stuff for Benedict Feakins, but not all of it though. He mostly wanted shrubs anyway, thank goodness, and they're still alive, being hardy. And Miss Osgathorp's special orchids were in the packing shed so they're safe enough.' He hesitated and then went on in more muted tones, 'But not Anthony Berra's other plants – the ones for the Lingards at the Grange. They're all goners too.'

Jack Haines groaned aloud.

'Dead as doornails, the lot,' said Russ. 'And there sure were plenty of them.'

'Who locked up?' demanded Haines suddenly.

'I did,' said Russ, adding with great emphasis, 'and I really did, Jack. Honest. Everywhere. The main gate was locked as usual when I got here this morning.'

'So someone got in somewhere else,' concluded Jack Haines.

'They sure did,' said the foreman instantly.

'But who?'

'Search me, boss, but I can tell you where. They came

through the fence that backs on to the field sure enough. You know, just where the compost heap backs up there. If you ask me . . .'

'I am asking you, Russ,' said Haines pointedly.

'It was a bolt croppers' job on the fence. That or wire cutters. Something like that anyway.'

Jack Haines pushed his coffee mug away and snapped into action. 'That makes it a matter for the police. Right, Russ, you go over to the Berebury Garden Centre, pronto, and then on to the Leanaig boys' place and see what you can pick up in the way of replacements before word of this gets out and their prices go up. So watch what you say to them all – especially Bob Steele at the garden centre. Oh, and call in at Staple St James Nurseries too. They may have something.'

'I'm on my way,' nodded the foreman.

'Sling me that phone, Mandy,' ordered Haines, 'and I'll get on to the police this minute. Well, what is it?' he said to Russ, who had paused at the office door, his hand on the handle. 'What are you waiting for?'

'Shall I call in at Capstan Purlieu Plants while I'm about it,' asked the man, 'and collect some replacement orchids?'

'Certainly not,' snapped Haines, his colour starting to rise again. 'Just get going. Now.'

Benedict Feakins was sitting with his wife at their dining-room table, lingering over a late breakfast that had included a couple of pain-killing tablets. He was going through his post whilst Mary Feakins was toying with a piece of dry toast. She had been doing this for some time.

10

After a few moments Benedict lifted his head from opening yet another bill to survey the garden through the window. While anyone else who was looking at it would only see a large patch of nondescript ground, loosely dug over and edged by some dispirited rhododendrons, what he saw in his mind's eye were banks of well-established flowering shrubs with an under-planting of hardy perennials, dotted about with something spectacular in the way of palms.

'I'll need a really good mulch to give everything a proper start,' he said.

'Benedict,' exploded Mary Feakins, 'how could you talk about mulch when I feel so sick!'

Benedict Feakins, who was unaware that he had spoken aloud, was instantly apologetic. 'Dearest, I'm so sorry.'

'And what I said – had you been listening – was that we need some more fuel for the boiler. It drinks oil.'

'So soon?' He brought his mind back to reality with an effort.

'Hot water doesn't grow on trees,' she said.

The pair hadn't been married long enough for him to find this remark anything but charmingly original. 'Very true.'

'It was all very well in your father's day,' she said, 'but we don't seem to have as much money as he had to run the place.'

'We haven't,' he said simply. 'Is it urgent? I mean, could it wait a few days until I've sorted things out a bit?' He waved at the little pile of post on the table. 'There are a couple of big bills in this lot.'

'Do you want your son to freeze to death?'

Benedict Feakins winced. The son in question had yet to be born but his welfare was already a priority in the household. He was all apologies. 'I'll get on to the bank,' he promised, 'and ask them what they can do about beefing up our overdraft. Don't forget we've got to go into Berebury today anyway to sign some papers for Simon Puckle.'

Simon Puckle was a partner in the firm of Puckle, Puckle and Nunnery, Solicitors and Commissioners for Oaths.

Mary Feakins, her morning sickness temporarily forgotten, gave a luxurious stretch and said, 'And then everything out here at Pelling will be really and truly ours?'

'It will, although,' he added conscientiously, 'naturally I didn't want Dad to die just so that we could inherit the place.'

'Of course not,' she responded swiftly, 'but he was ill and unhappy. He was never the same after your mother died, you know.'

'I don't suppose I would be if you were to die before me,' said Benedict fondly.

'Nonsense,' said Mary Feakins, her eyes sparkling mischievously. 'If I did, I bet you'd be married again within the year.'

'What,' he started up again, grimaced with pain and fell back in his chair, 'and let someone else look after young Benedict? Never!' He gripped the arms of the chair and this time moved with extreme caution as he tried to rise. 'I'm sorry but you'll have to do the driving into Berebury today. My back's still too painful.'

'What did you expect if you will dig up ground like

you did . . .' Mary Feakins' own attitude to pain in other people had started to change as her pregnancy advanced. 'You're not used to that sort of work and Anthony Berra seems to be.'

'We can't afford a professional garden designer. You know that's why I had to cancel his coming here to give the garden a proper grounding. But I really need to get those shrubs in soon,' he said earnestly, 'and I didn't know that digging was going to do my back in, did I?'

'You might have guessed.' She reached for another piece of dry toast. 'So how do you suppose with your bad back that you're going to be able to put these precious shrubs in the ground when you do get them?'

'I'll manage somehow,' he said through gritted teeth as another spasm of pain shot through his frame.

'You could always cancel that plant order for the front garden just like you put Anthony Berra off,' she suggested, not meeting his eye. 'They're going to cost an absolute bomb.'

'Then we'd miss a whole season of growth,' he said, waving a hand towards the window.

'I would have thought you could put a packet of seeds in instead. Some annuals there would look pretty.'

He shook his head. 'That would be no good in the long run. You'd only have to look at all this desolation for another winter.' He added another letter to the little pile on the table. 'We can't have that. Besides,' he smiled, 'you'll want somewhere nice outside to sit with young Benedict in his pram.'

'It was a pity your father was so keen on his cacti and nothing else in the garden,' she responded obliquely, 'and then you wouldn't have had to do all that work in the first place.'

'It'll look lovely this year as well next, I promise,' he said, blowing her a kiss.

'At least you don't take after him,' said his wife.

Benedict Feakins' head shot up. 'What do you mean?' he demanded hotly.

'In specialising in cacti like he did, that's all.' She shuddered. 'Nasty-looking things.'

'Prickly too,' said Benedict ambiguously. 'Mother didn't like them either but they gave Dad something to do and kept him happy enough after she died and that's what mattered.'

'He didn't really like gardening, did he?' she said, scanning the untended ground outside the window. 'Proper gardening, I mean, like you do. He liked fiddling around with little bits of things that looked as if they should have stayed in the desert where they belong.'

Benedict Feakins gave this some thought. 'I suppose not. Dad wasn't keen on the garden even before his hip got bad, but afterwards, of course, when he couldn't get about so easily the cacti were ideal. He must have spent hours in the greenhouse with them.'

Mary Feakins shivered. 'They give me the willies. Can we get rid of them before . . . before . . .'

'Before Benedict the Third arrives . . .' he finished the sentence for her, smiling. 'Of course we can. I might even get Jack Haines to take them in part-exchange.'

'That would be good.'

'I know what,' he said, 'we'll call in at the nursery on our way into Berebury and ask him.'

Mary Feakins changed tack suddenly. 'I suppose,' she admitted, 'you do need to be getting on with planting those shrubs anyway now. If you can manage it. But do be careful. You don't want the office saying you've got a self-inflicted injury like they do with sunburn.'

'The shrubs can't wait beyond the end of March,' he said. 'Ideally some of them should have gone in the ground last October . . .'

'But we weren't here in October, were we?' She looked round with pleasure at their dining room. 'We were making out in a grotty basement flat in Luston.'

Benedict Feakins acknowledged this with a quick jerk of his head. 'You were making out, Mary. I'm not sure that I was.' He looked out at the garden again in wonder. 'And now we've got all this.'

'You weren't expecting your father to die quite so soon, that's all.' She waved a hand in a gesture that took in the neat double-fronted Edwardian house. 'All this would have come to you one day anyway. You know that.'

'True, but you must admit that it couldn't have come at a better time.'

'For all three of us,' she said with manifest satisfaction. She got up from the table. 'Now, we really should be getting going . . .'

CHAPTER TWO

'Ah, there you are, Sloan.' Somehow Police Superintendent Leeyes was always able to make his subordinates feel that they had kept him waiting even when they hadn't done anything of the sort. It was, they felt, a gift. 'Two jobs for you this morning. Both out the same way, which saves time.'

'Sir?' He knew it would not be Sloan's time that the superintendent was saving but money. Police finances were as much under pressure as everyone else's these days and Sloan knew that saving his time never figured anyway.

'Both out Pelling way but not connected.' Superintendent Leeyes waved a message sheet in his hand. 'A missing person and trouble at a nursery.'

Detective Inspector Sloan groaned. Small children always spelt trouble, big time and all the time.

'A plant nursery, Sloan.'

He relaxed. That sounded better. Until the superintendent explained, that is.

'Surely that's hardly a crime, sir, leaving doors open,' protested Detective Inspector Sloan. He was the head of the tiny Criminal Investigation Department of 'F' Division of the County of Calleshire Police Force at Berebury and thought he knew the law as well as the next man. 'Not yet, anyway,' Sloan went on cautiously, since these days all governments seemed to be hell-bent on making more and more activities illegal.

Besides which, the detective inspector reminded himself hastily, this was the time of the year for his annual appraisal and it wouldn't do to put a foot wrong just now.

Superintendent Leeyes said, 'The owner thinks it is, Sloan. In fact, he's absolutely sure a criminal act is involved. Says he can prove it. And he's hopping mad about it.'

'Of course I quite understand how he must feel,' said Sloan untruthfully, subconsciously noting that the superintendent had used the word owner rather than householder, 'but even so . . . just an open door, I think you said . . .'

'Two doors opened and left open, to be precise,' said the superintendent, waving a message sheet in his hand, 'and a fence damaged.'

'Even so . . .' repeated Sloan, realising as soon as he'd said it that he should have been more circumspect. It didn't do to upset his superior officer at appraisal time. Although greenhouse doors left open with or without guilty intent – even fences broken with undoubted guilty intent – wouldn't usually warrant the attention of a detective inspector, Sloan decided against pointing this out. 'And the missing person?'

'Old party not back from her hols,' said Leeyes. 'Gone walkabout, I expect.'

'Has she done it before?' asked Sloan. 'What do the family say?'

'She hasn't got any family. Lives alone,' said Leeyes, turning over the message sheet. 'It's a neighbour who's been in touch and no, she hasn't done it before.'

Detective Inspector Sloan sighed but said nothing.

'Even so . . .' harrumphed Leeyes, noting the sigh, 'I want you out there soonest.'

Sloan's unusual reticence was because there was something sinister pending at the Berebury Police Station as part of the appraisal element of his PDD – otherwise known as a 'Personal Development Discussion'. This was to be held with his superior officer quite soon. He hadn't been told exactly when it would be yet but it wouldn't do to jeopardise the interview by an unguarded response about a quite possibly disorientated old lady.

'Because,' went on the superintendent, the message flimsy still clasped in his hand, 'the owner of the nursery would seem to have had very good reasons for sending for us for something like that. And since as you know we're well under establishment these days . . .'

Sloan privately decided that they'd better be very good reasons indeed or he himself would want to know why. Since technically all law-breaking in the market town of Berebury and its environs, excepting traffic violations, eventually landed on his desk, he automatically took out his notebook. 'Just two open doors, did you say, sir, and a hole in a fence?'

'That's all that he seems to be complaining about. So far anyway,' trumpeted the superintendent. 'He said he'd tell us more when we got there.'

At this Sloan sighed again, his superior officer being given to using the royal 'We' only when he had no intention of doing any of the work himself.

'Right, sir,' he said without enthusiasm. 'I'll get out there straightaway.' The distinction between open and closed doors as far as crime was concerned was one beloved by insurance companies but disliked by those whose duty it was to frame charges – 'breaking and entering' was only one of them – when doors had been closed. Doors left open were quite a different ball game when it came to insurers and policemen alike.

'Two open doors and a broken fence so far,' repeated Leeyes, ever the pessimist. 'I'm told the man seemed a bit guarded on the phone.'

Sloan cleared his throat and in carefully neutral tones asked his superior officer if the police had any further information about either case. There were other – and indisputably really criminal – cases on his own desk awaiting his attention that were – would seem to be, anyway, he added a silent caveat of his own – more urgent than open doors and elderly ladies on the loose.

'Was there, for instance, anything stolen at the nursery, sir?' he enquired.

'No, Sloan, nothing at all.' The superintendent gave the message sheet another wave. 'It would appear from information received that theft would not seem to have been what whoever left the doors open had in mind since nothing would appear to have been taken.' He sniffed. 'What exactly was the object of the exercise is presumably too soon to say.'

'I'd better have some names,' said Sloan, taking a pencil out of his pocket and suppressing any references to gross carelessness that sprang to his mind. 'And their addresses, sir, please.'

'The missing person is an Enid Maude Osgathorp of Canonry Cottage, Church Street, Pelling,' said Leeyes. 'And man is Haines – a Jack Haines.'

'Jack Haines? Not the nurseryman?' Sloan's pencil stayed poised in his hand above his notebook.

'That's him. At Pelling too.' Leeyes, an urban man if ever there was one, sniffed. 'Back of beyond.'

'Ah.' Detective Inspector Christopher Dennis Sloan, who was known as 'Seedy' to his family and friends, had lived in the small market town of Berebury all his life. In his spare time he was a keen gardener and thus knew most of the nurseries for miles around. This one was out in the far reaches of the Calleshire countryside.

'None other. Proprietor of that big outfit on the Calleford road there.'

'What sort of doors?' asked Sloan, his attention now thoroughly engaged. This was different. Jack Haines was a nurseryman on a substantial scale, well known to professional and amateur gardeners alike and not above, when in a mellow frame of mind, dispensing his expertise to both. 'I mean doors to where exactly?'

'Greenhouses, Sloan.'

'Ah, I understand now.' Any gardener knew that that was something quite different too. 'Right, sir. I've got that. Greenhouse doors at the nursery.'

'Left open overnight, or,' Leeyes added ominously, 'deliberately opened during the hours of darkness.'

'I understand.' Sloan nodded, tacitly agreeing that this was different too. There was another distinction, as well, one between criminal activity that took place in the hours of darkness as opposed to in daylight – a distinction that went back to what was engagingly known as 'time out of mind' – but was still important in law.

'When no one was supposed to be there anyway,' amplified Leeyes, adding the automatic caveat, policeman that he was, 'or so the owner says.'

'I see, sir.' Because Sloan was an off-duty gardener himself he was beginning to be aware where this might be leading. 'And, of course, there was quite a frost last night . . .' He knew this because he'd only just pruned his own floribunda roses and when he had woken in the morning he had seen the hoary ground. He had hoped, then, that he hadn't done it too late in the season and wondered, as he did every year, whether he should have done the job in the autumn instead. Horticultural opinion was divided but 'the later the pruning the bigger the bush' was something on which everyone was agreed.

'There was. A really heavy one, too, for early March.' Superintendent Leeyes grunted and consulted the message sheet again. 'He says that Russell Aqueel – he's their foreman out there – came on as usual this morning at seven o'clock and found one entire greenhouse full of baby orchids and another one of young other plants killed off.'

'Not good, sir,' agreed Sloan. Nothing might have been stolen but even so there was undoubtedly loss involved. Heavy loss, certainly: crime, as well, if there had been a break-in. It was too soon to say. 'Were the doors usually locked? Or, rather, had they been locked last night?'

'You don't lock greenhouses,' said the superintendent irritably.

Detective Inspector Sloan forbore to say that you did if they contained valuable plants. He said instead, 'I'd heard that Jack had some young orchids that he's been growing out there. He's a bit of a specialist in them. Are they all right?'

'No, they're not,' Leeyes came back quickly. 'And judging from his present state of mind I should think he's pretty well lost the lot.'

'That's bad,' said Sloan. 'They must have been worth a packet.' He looked up and asked, 'Is Jack Haines talking about malice aforethought?'

'Jack Haines,' came back the superintendent impressively, 'is talking about sabotage. You'd better get out there and see him, pronto. And you can take that dim-witted constable, Crosby, with you. We may be short-staffed but I still don't want him here all day upsetting the civilian staff.'

'No, sir, of course not,' Sloan hastily agreed with this sentiment. Both men knew without saying that the superintendent was referring to Mrs Mabel Murgatroyd, the civilian staff supervisor, a lady of a certain age who took the view that uniformed policemen were an illiterate bunch who got in the way of the important work of the clerical staff.

When told about it, Detective Constable Crosby viewed the prospect of a journey far out into the hinterland with evident pleasure. Detective Inspector Sloan locked the seat belt of the police car into place with markedly less enthusiasm.

'There is no hurry, Crosby,' he said as the car took off at speed. 'The missing person hasn't been seen for three weeks and wilted plants don't run away. We'll go to the nursery first while any evidence that there might be there is still fresh.'

'Nobody dead, then?' said the constable.

'Not yet,' said Sloan dryly, averting his eyes from a near miss with a refuse lorry, all public service vehicles being anathema to the constable. 'It would seem that the only things that are dead to date are plant cuttings and I would like to keep it that way, please.'

It was something on his wish list he was destined to remember for a long time.

'That you, Anthony?' Jack Haines had reluctantly picked up the telephone to ring one of his professional customers and he wasn't enjoying the conversation.

'It is,' a throaty voice came down the telephone in reply.

'It doesn't sound like you.'

'Well, it is,' insisted the voice testily. 'I'm a bit chesty, that's all.'

'It's Jack Haines from the nursery here.' Haines groaned inwardly. The last thing he wanted was an Anthony Berra under the weather and in a low mood. 'I've got a bit of bad news for you, I'm afraid.'

'Tell me.' Anthony Berra was a thrusting young landscape designer beginning to be very popular with the landed gentry of the county of Calleshire and starting to be quite an important user of the nursery too.

'You're not going to like it.' Haines swallowed uneasily while he waited for the man to finish coughing. Although still with his name to make in the landscape design world, Anthony Berra was nothing if not business-like and rather formal into the bargain.

'How bad?' asked Berra shortly when he had recovered his breath.

'Bad.' Jack Haines told him about all the damaged plants in the greenhouses.

'Good God, man, you don't mean to say that I've lost the lot?'

Gloomily, the nurseryman admitted that the majority of the plants ordered by Berra for his client, Admiral Catterick, and all of those being grown for the Lingards at the Grange were now either dead or dying. 'And some of those for Benedict Feakins too.'

Anthony Berra took a deep breath and said frostily, 'I don't know what I'm going to say to the Lingards, Jack, if I can't get their Mediterranean garden fixed in time for their garden party in June. It was part of their contract with me that it would be.'

'I've been ringing round everywhere trying get replacements,' Haines admitted, 'but it won't be easy. Not at this time of the year.'

'I shouldn't think it will,' retorted Berra crisply, 'considering the effort I put in to ordering everything exactly as I wanted it for my planting plans for their new project. You don't pick up plants such as Strelitzia let alone Gardenia and Bouganvillia from any old nursery anywhere in East Calleshire.'

Half-heartedly Jack Haines muttered something about insurance.

'Mine or yours?' asked Berra on the instant.

'Yours,' said Haines gruffly. 'I've never even insured the orchids. I've lost all of them too.'

Anthony Berra wasn't interested in orchids and made that clear. 'What I'm interested in, Jack, is that greenhouse of yours that had my plants in it and no, I'm not insured.'

'Pity.'

'Actually,' drawled Berra a little unpleasantly, 'since I hadn't actually bought the plants yet I would have thought the loss was entirely yours. Not mine.'

'I grew them especially for you exactly to your precise order, didn't I?' responded Jack Haines, torn between keeping Anthony Berra as a customer and minimising his own loss. 'Especially those citrus trees and the palms, let alone the Mimosa.'

The landscape designer came back on the instant. 'I don't know who left your greenhouse doors open, Jack, and I don't care, but I can assure you it wasn't me.' There was an uneasy pause and then Berra went on in a more mollifying tone, 'It isn't quite as easy as that, anyway. You must know what these particular clients of mine are like. I should think the whole village does.'

Jack Haines had to admit that he did know what the Lingards of Pelling Grange were like and so did everyone else in the locality. 'Not exactly easy people,' he agreed.

'Especially the wife,' added Berra, opening up a little.

'Quite difficult, actually,' conceded the nurseryman. There weren't many people in Pelling who didn't know all about Major Oswald Lingard's new wife, Charmian, and her imperious ways. 'Comes of having the money, I suppose,' went on Haines. The second Mrs Lingard was rumoured to have brought a small fortune to the marriage. The restoration of the old and long neglected gardens was only one of the changes she was making at Pelling Grange. And to its owner, widower and former soldier, Oswald Lingard too.

'She thinks she only has to give an order for it to be carried out,' said the young landscape designer resentfully.

'And pretty pronto too,' added Haines, who knew the lady in question all too well. 'No hanging about with her.'

'She thinks she knows all about landscape gardening too,' muttered Anthony Berra, 'and believe you me she doesn't.'

'He's all right, though,' said Haines fairly. 'Been around in Pelling a long time, the Lingards have. I remember his mother. Nice old lady but hardly a bean to her name.'

'Oh, he's all right,' agreed Berra on the instant, 'although he's no pushover either what with having been in the Army. What his wife's going to say, though, if I can't get the work done on time I can't begin to think. It sounded to me as if she was going to invite half the county to her precious summer garden party just so that she could show them all her improvements to the old place. Not that they didn't need doing,' he added hastily in case the nurseryman should be thinking that he had been

27

making work for himself at the expense of the owners of the Grange. 'The place was falling apart until she came on the scene.'

'No money around until then,' said Jack Haines, making what he hoped were sympathetic noises. Unfortunately the effect of these was somewhat lessened by Mandy Lamb's loudly calling out that his coffee was getting cold. 'Poor as church mice for years, the Lingards,' he added. 'Until now, of course.'

Anthony Berra's mind was still running on. 'You do realise, Jack, don't you, that my client is going to tell all her Calleshire friends that I've let her down. It's not going to do my reputation in the county any good if I do. Or yours,' he added ominously.

'As I told you, Anthony, I've already been on to two or three other suppliers to see if they can make good any deficiencies,' said Haines by way of mitigation. He didn't mention that he'd already had to swallow his pride and approach his three great business rivals for replacements. 'And they're being very helpful.' This was actually stretching a point since Russ Aqueel had not yet returned to the nursery at Pelling after going round them.

'I'm not having any old stuff,' snapped Berra immediately. 'I'll have to go over to the Lingards first to tell them and then I'm coming straight over to you to see for myself. If I put anything at all substandard in that garden it'll all have to come up again and the Lingards won't pay for that. The fact that the lady's loaded doesn't mean she's going to shell out for rubbish, you know. She's not silly.'

'It might just get you through this season, though,' suggested Jack Haines tentatively.

Anthony Berra wasn't listening. 'I'll just have to go back to the drawing board and revise my overall design, that's all, and she won't like that, I can tell you. Not one little bit.'

'I'm sure we can come to some arrangement about the cost of any replacements,' began Jack Haines.

Anthony Berra ignored this *amende honorable*. 'Do you have any idea at all about who could have done all this damage?'

'No,' said Jack Haines quickly.

Much too quickly.

CHAPTER THREE

Jack Haines, tubby and rather more than middle-aged, his complexion an unhealthy shade of red, was still spitting tintacks when the two policemen arrived at his office at the nursery. He barely greeted them before starting on his story. 'My foreman – that's Russ Aqueel, who I told the police about, swears he shut up all the greenhouses before he went off last night like he always does,' he told them heatedly. 'And he says there was no one around that he could see when he locked the main gate and went home.' He turned towards a youngish woman with auburn hair sitting at a desk behind him and said over his shoulder. 'That's right, Mandy, isn't it?'

'Yes, Jack,' she said in studiously uninflected tones, 'that's exactly what Russ says this time.'

'Happened before, has it, then?' asked Detective Constable Crosby chattily.

'No,' said Jack Haines.

'Yes,' said Mandy Lamb in the same breath.

'Which?' demanded Detective Inspector Sloan.

Jack Haines admitted grudgingly 'All right, I suppose it should be "yes". It happened once last autumn but there wasn't anything to speak of in that greenhouse at the time and in any case it wasn't frosty so it didn't really matter.'

'And was there now?' enquired Crosby brightly.

'I'll say,' Haines growled. 'Young orchids in one of them – worth a helluva lot of money; and a load of plants in the other that we were mainly growing especially for a local landscape designer.'

'Is your foreman always the last to leave at the end of the day?' asked Sloan. All policemen knew that workers who stayed around after everyone else had gone home sometimes did so for reasons other than earning Brownie points. If they worked in the office the crime of 'Teeming and Lading' came to mind; in the yard it was usually that of 'stocktaking' of an illicit kind.

'Well, the girls don't hang around after leaving time, I can tell you,' responded Jack Haines warmly. 'Some of them get picked up by their boyfriends and,' he raised his eyes to heaven and added piously, 'who knows who the others get picked up by. I certainly don't know and I don't want to.'

'And the men?' asked Crosby. 'Where do they go?'

'The Crown and Castle pub,' responded Mandy Lamb before her employer could speak. She pursed her lips. 'Every night. You'd think some of them haven't got homes to go to.'

'Greenhouse work is thirsty work,' chanted Jack Haines as if reciting a mantra. 'And hard work too, I give you that. They need to relax a bit after it. Wind down and so forth.'

'Including Russell Aqueel?' asked Crosby. 'Likes his drop, does he?'

The nurseryman nodded whilst his secretary, Mandy Lamb, rolled her eyes expressively.

'So you think some person or persons unknown broke into your grounds last night and opened a greenhouse door? Is that it?' Detective Inspector Sloan, not supplicant gardener now but working police officer, had his notebook prominent in his hand.

'Two doors, actually,' said Haines heavily. 'The two greenhouses furthest from the gate. The orchid one and the one with this year's young plants in.'

'Funny that,' observed Detective Constable Crosby to no one in particular.

'Nothing funny about it,' snapped the nurseryman on the instant, his colour becoming more choleric by the minute. 'It's very serious, especially at this time of the year. It'll put my customers' planting plans back a good bit, I can tell you, and that's only if I can buy in some new stock pretty pronto. It's much too late in the year to start growing any of it again from scratch here.'

'These greenhouses,' began Sloan, himself a greenhouse gardener manqué, 'what exactly was in them?'

'Number one was full of young orchids for any commercial customers who wanted them and number two had Strelitizia, Bouganvillia, Gardenia – that sort of thing – being grown for a posh new Mediterranean garden. Oh, and a lot of baby palms and some citrus trees. You name it, and we were growing on cuttings and raising

seedlings in it for sale to our commercial customers too.'
He groaned aloud. 'I've just thought . . .'

'Yes?' said Sloan.

'Some of those orchids in number one greenhouse are
in our spring catalogue. We must have taken orders for
them from all over the place.' He ran his fingers through
what was left of his hair. 'I can't begin think what I'm
going to do about that.'

'Then there's the rest of that special order from Anthony
Berra for Pelling Grange,' his secretary reminded him. 'All
those plants of his for the Lingards at the Grange were in
there too. Don't forget that.'

'I haven't. I've told him already and he isn't happy.'
Jack Haines groaned again and turned to her. 'Proper
Job's comforter, aren't you, Mandy?'

'Just a realist, Jack,' she said, adding meaningfully,
'and someone round here has to be.'

'A special order?' queried Sloan sharply. The out-of-
the-ordinary was always of interest to the police.

'It's for a local landscape designer,' explained Haines.
'The plants were being grown to order.'

'His order,' supplemented Mandy Lamb. 'Very fussy
about it, he was, too.'

'A bit precious about his reputation, being local and on
the young side still, is Anthony Berra,' conceded Haines,
'but he knows his onions. I'll give him that.'

'At least,' Mandy Lamb reminded him, 'the other
orchids – those that we'd got ready for Enid Osgathorp
to collect yesterday – are safely in the packing shed. The
black Phalaenopsis, the single Oncidium and those big
Cymbidiums – oh, and the two Dracula orchids . . .'

'Don't let her catch you calling her Enid,' said Jack Haines, momentarily diverted. 'She's Miss Osgathorp to you like she is to everyone else in Pelling and you'd better not forget it.'

He wasn't quite correct in what he said. To the police Miss Osgathorp was simply Enid Maude Osgathorp, aged 65, missing person, but Sloan did not say so.

'She seems to have forgotten to collect them anyway,' retorted Mandy pertly. 'She'd arranged to pick them up yesterday for some demonstration she was supposed to be giving somewhere tomorrow evening but she didn't turn up for them.'

Detective Constable Crosby looked around and asked with interest, 'Who are your nearest business rivals?'

'Rivals?' Jack Haines stiffened. 'I don't know that I've got . . .'

'All businesses have competitors,' said Crosby laconically, 'like all God's chillum got rhythm. Fact of life.'

Haines paused. 'Well, I suppose my nearest ones would be Staple St James Nurseries over towards Cullingoak and then there's always the Leanaig Brothers' place and the Berebury Garden Centre. I've heard that Bob Steele there has just started to go in for orchids himself.'

'And Marilyn,' added the girl behind him swiftly. 'Mustn't forget our Marilyn, must we?'

'Marilyn?' queried Detective Inspector Sloan.

'Just another grower,' said Jack Haines, stiffening, 'that's all.'

'Got another name, has she?' asked Crosby.

'Trades as Capstan Purlieu Plants,' said Jack Haines briefly, nothing mellow about him now, 'but I don't think any competitor would stoop to something like sabotage.'

'Except at Show time,' put in Mandy Lamb softly in the background.

'Showing's different,' said Jack Haines quickly. 'We're all rivals then.'

'No holds barred,' agreed Sloan, who knew all about Flower Shows from long experience. His own roses hadn't collected a prize at the Berebury Horticultural Society Summer Show yet but he lived in hope. He said, 'What about Girdler's place over Luston way? They've got a big nursery there.' Sloan, a keen gardener himself, knew that.

Haines sniffed. 'Joe Girdler's trying to breed the best rose in Christendom and good luck to him.'

'Right.' Actually Sloan was into roses himself but he didn't say so.

'Otherwise,' insisted the nurseryman, 'it's a pretty friendly trade.'

As befitted a man who had been in the Police Force all his working life, Detective Inspector Sloan took this last statement with a grain of salt, believing as he did that there was no such thing as a friendly trade. 'What about the other greenhouse? What did you say was in there?'

'Number one?'

'Yes.'

'Young orchids. And they're all dead. Every blooming one of them . . .'

'Except that they're not going to bloom,' murmured Crosby, sotto voce.

'God knows what they were worth,' said Haines, who hadn't heard him.

'This special order,' said Sloan. 'Was that for orchids too?'

Jack Haines shook his head. 'No, it's for this landscape designer I told you about. Name of Anthony Berra. He's got the contract for doing up a big old garden over the other side of Pelling on the way to Larking village and Berebury, like I said. It's been neglected for years.'

'Pelling Grange,' supplied Mandy Lamb, studying the fingernails on her left hand. 'Like I said, too.'

'Has he got enemies?' asked Crosby.

'I couldn't say, I'm sure,' said Haines stiffly.

'Have you got enemies?' asked Sloan.

'No,' said Jack Haines flatly.

'All God's children got enemies,' chanted Crosby almost under his breath, 'like they've got rhythm.'

'And Anthony Berra wasn't best pleased, I can tell you, Inspector,' went on Jack Haines, reverting to his own worries, 'when I told him what's happened to all his plants.'

'Very upset, I should say,' offered Mandy Lamb from the side-lines.

'I'd better have some names,' said Detective Inspector Sloan, tugging his notebook out of his pocket.

'He's called Anthony Berra,' said Jack Haines. 'His plants are . . . were . . . for one of those fashionable Mediterranean gardens that he's creating for Oswald Lingard over at the Grange in Pelling.'

'And Mrs Lingard,' put in Mandy. 'Mustn't forget her.'

'Why not?' asked Crosby curiously.

'She's the one with the money,' said the secretary simply.

'And Marilyn?' prompted Sloan.

'Marilyn Potts,' gritted Jack Haines between clenched teeth.

'She's an orchid specialist,' put in Mandy Lamb helpfully.

Jack Haines glared at her.

'One half of Capstan Purlieu Plants,' said Mandy, transferring her studies from the fingernails of her left hand to those on her right hand. 'The other half is Anna Sutherland.' She did not amplify this.

'I think,' said Detective Inspector Sloan, snapping his notebook shut, 'that before we go any further we'd better take a look at these greenhouses of yours. And then I'd like to have a word with your foreman.'

Jack Haines jerked his shoulder. 'I've sent him into town on an errand.'

'You have, have you?' said Sloan, making a mental note.

'In theory,' began Jack Haines, 'the last fingerprints on the door handles should be Russ's . . .'

'In practice,' Sloan interrupted him, suppressing his irritation, 'they may well belong to someone else.' Policemen, like doctors, didn't like being told what to do. All the same he would get Crosby to take any fingerprints off the door handles while they were at Pelling. It didn't seem a serious enough case to get a Scenes of Crime Officer out all this way, not with the economic climate being what it was. He snapped his notebook shut. 'My constable will soon be able to tell us that. Come along now, Crosby.'

The two greenhouses presented a sorry sight. In one,

serried pots of infant orchid cuttings had been burnt by frost and were clearly beyond aid. In the other, tender young plants had collapsed, their leaves now drooped over their potting compost like so many dying swans. Detective Inspector Sloan led the way inside, noting that the heating of the orchid house was not on. Above the pipes was a mist-maker from which little bursts of spray should have been emerging but weren't.

'No sign of forced entry, sir,' remarked Crosby, peering round. He started to apply his fingerprint gear to the door handle. 'The door hasn't been damaged at all.'

'No,' agreed Sloan, absently, his gaze still on the frosted orchids. They weren't his favourite plants but no true gardener could fail to be moved by the sight of so much wanton destruction.

'And there's no key in sight,' said the constable.

'It wasn't locked,' growled Jack Haines at his elbow. 'We've never had this sort of trouble before.'

Sloan nodded, unsurprised. In his experience very few stable doors ever got locked until after the horse had bolted.

'Now that we're alone,' said Jack Haines, nevertheless looking over his shoulder, 'there's something else you guys need to know.'

'Go on.'

He pointed to a device on one of the windows. 'I've got a frost alarm system rigged up in here. It's connected to a thermostat and should have rung in my bedroom and woken me when the temperature fell.'

'And it didn't?' said Crosby.

'It didn't,' Haines said heavily.

'Or you had been drugged,' suggested the constable brightly.

'No,' said Detective Inspector Sloan, going over and peering at a bimetallic strip. 'It had been disabled.' There wasn't a greenhouse in his own garden yet but that hadn't stopped him from studying the possibilities against the day when there would be. And then he would have such a thermostat in it. 'You can see that's it's been broken.'

'That must mean,' concluded Haines uneasily, 'that whoever left these two doors open knew what he was doing.'

'Or she,' said Crosby inevitably.

'An ordinary thief,' said Haines, carefully avoiding sexism, 'wouldn't have known what it was.'

Sloan was just about to make a proper examination of the other greenhouse when his personal radio spluttered to life.

'That you, Sloan?' boomed a distant voice from Berebury. 'Leeyes here. There's just been a call in from a Marilyn Potts over at Capstan Purlieu complaining about dead orchids. She's talking about sabotage . . . you'd better get over there as soon as you can.'

CHAPTER FOUR

Marilyn Potts surveyed a greenhouse that had once been full of thriving young orchids and now was nothing more than a home for the blackened stubs of dead plants fit only for the compost heap.

'All my chicks and the dam,' she moaned. 'Ruined. Every last one of them. Now I know how that Scottish chap felt. In *Macbeth*.'

'Macduff,' supplied the friend standing beside her.

'Anna,' Marilyn pleaded, turning in her direction, 'tell me it wasn't you who left the door open. Please.'

'Don't be silly,' snapped Anna Sutherland. 'Of course it wasn't. Besides, if it had been me who'd forgotten to shut the door I would have told you. You should know me well enough by now to know that.'

Marilyn jerked her head in tacit acknowledgement of this. Anna was invariably nothing if not forthright.

'Then who did?' she demanded. 'It certainly wasn't me.'

'I don't know. How could I?'

'There's only the two of us here,' Marilyn said tonelessly.

'You don't have to tell me that,' responded Anna Sutherland tersely. The nursery at Capstan Purlieu Plants was run by the two hard-working women and nobody else.

Marilyn made her way slowly up the greenhouse, looking to the right and left, and shaking her head in disbelief. 'Beyond aid – every last one.' She turned, her face stricken, and said 'And the dam – all the stock plants too.'

'Our seed corn, you might say,' agreed Anna bleakly.

'And I'm supposed to be speaking to the Staple St James Horticultural Society on orchids tomorrow evening, remember? Standing in for Enid,' wailed Marilyn Potts. 'How can I possibly do that now? Just talking about orchids will upset me.'

Anna Sutherland was bracing. 'Of course you can. Besides, they've already put a notice in this week's Berebury Gazette saying that old Enid's been delayed on her travels and that you're giving the talk instead. Take some slides or something – they oughtn't to mind too much. After all, you're doing them a favour and at short notice into the bargain.'

Marilyn shook her head. 'No, I needn't do that. Their secretary's quite sure Enid will have ordered some orchids for the evening and she's ringing round to find out where. Enid just hasn't come back from one of her famous trips.'

'It's all very well for some,' remarked Anna. 'I wish I could go abroad at the drop of a hat like she does.'

'She is retired now,' murmured her friend absently, still regarding her plants with a doleful face. She stroked one now as if the touch of a human hand could restore it to life. 'I guess old Doctor Heddon left her something when he died.'

'Where was it this time?' asked Anna as much to divert her friend as anything.

'The next-door neighbour wasn't sure – she couldn't decide from her note whether it was Carmarthen or Carinthia.'

'I thought it was only doctors who couldn't write clearly,' remarked Anna acidly, 'not their receptionists.'

Marilyn wasn't listening. 'I don't think that there's a single orchid left alive in the whole greenhouse.'

'Then I'll turn the heating and the humidifier off,' murmured Anna, pointing to equipment that were meant to keep the temperature of the greenhouse high and its atmosphere moist.

'You're always so practical,' complained Marilyn. 'Have you no soul?'

'You can see yourself that they're all dead,' said Anna, pointing to the plants on the staging. 'And not even you, Marilyn, can bring the dead back to life.'

'I know that,' said Marilyn with dignity, 'but don't you have any feelings?'

'Heating costs money,' retorted Anna, 'and from the looks of things we're going to need every penny we've got to get going again.'

'Get going again?' Marilyn stared at her. 'You must be mad. We can't catch up this year even if we started again now.'

'And if we don't get going again this year,' pointed out her friend, 'we've still got to live, haven't we?'

'I don't know that I want to,' said Marilyn, picking up a pot and staring moodily at the collapsed plant lying on the potting mixture.

'A few dead plants are not a good reason to give up living,' said her friend.

'A few dead plants?' shrieked Marilyn. 'How can you say that when every last one of this year's orchids that we've slaved over since they were potted is done for?'

'Some you win, some you lose, in this line. We've always known that,' said Anna calmly, 'and I must say it looks as if we've lost this time.'

'A greenhouse full of dead plants is a very good reason to give up trying to make a living from horticulture,' sighed Marilyn. She raised her head suddenly, turning an unhappy face in Anna Sutherland's direction as another thought struck her. 'You don't think, Anna, that someone somewhere is trying to tell us something, do you?'

Anna paused, her hand suspended over the heating switches. 'A business rival, you mean?' she said cautiously.

Marilyn shook her head. 'No, not one of them.'

'Well, Bob Steele is trying to get started with orchids and Jack Haines over at Pelling reckons to sell three times as many young orchids as we do even though his aren't half as good as ours,' said Anna.

'We can't be any threat to him, surely,' said Marilyn. 'He's big business by our standards.'

Anna shrugged her shoulders. 'Who knows how his mind works?'

'He mostly only goes in for the commercial market,' Marilyn said. 'And most of his domestic customers don't know what they're doing in the first place. They kill them quickly and then come back for more.' She grimaced. 'That's business. His sort of business, of course, not ours.'

Anna frowned. 'Anyway he sells so many other plants that I shouldn't have thought our orchids were any threat to his business. His catalogue is crammed full of all sorts of plants besides orchids.'

'What you mean is that he's not a specialist like we are.' Capstan Purlieu Plants concentrated on a few choice items for really knowledgeable gardeners. Actually they liked to think of their customers as plantsmen and plantswomen or even enthusiasts rather than mere gardeners.

'I mean that he's more of a knowing "nothing about everything" man while we're knowing "everything about nothing" women,' said Anna Sutherland eloquently. 'So who else wouldn't want us to succeed then?' she asked.

A little silence fell between the two women and it took a moment or two for Marilyn Potts to put a worry into words. 'Norman?'

'He wouldn't surely,' said her friend expressionlessly.

Norman Potts was – had been once, anyway – Marilyn's husband and their divorce had been notably spectacular in its acrimony.

'He would,' declared Norman's former wife vehemently. 'You don't know the half of what he would do.'

'And I don't want to,' said Anna Sutherland crisply. 'I'm your business partner, remember? Not your therapist.'

'If it was him,' hissed Marilyn, 'he's going to regret

it when the police get to him, let alone my solicitors.'

'Besides,' went on Anna, 'I'm a spinster, remember? As far as I'm concerned the secrets of the bedroom are meant to be secret. And stay that way,' she added for good measure. 'I don't need to know what else he could get up to.'

'You're a good friend, Anna, that's what, and I shall never forget that.'

'Talking of the police,' remarked Anna, lifting her head, 'they're arriving now. Look, they're at the gate.'

'Where did you say Capstan Purlieu Plants were, sir?' Detective Constable Crosby had asked Sloan while they were on their way.

'Keep going,' commanded Sloan tersely, his eyes glued to a large scale map of East Calleshire. He couldn't see the police car's sat-nav from the passenger seat and wasn't sure if Crosby bothered to listen to it. 'In about half a mile you should come to a little bridge over a stream and then you follow the right-hand lane until you get to the nursery.'

'Only if we don't meet anything coming the other way,' muttered Crosby. Single-track roads seriously cramped his driving style. 'I don't know how their customers ever find them.'

Lurking somewhere at the back of Sloan's mind was a saying that if you built a better mousetrap the world would beat a path to your door. Instead he pointed out that if someone had damaged the greenhouse at Capstan Purlieu then they at least had found their way there to do it. 'In the dark, too, probably,' he said.

'No one out here to see you in daylight,' countered Crosby, 'except sheep.'

'Where there's sheep there's a shepherd,' said Sloan, less bothered by the high hedges and narrow lanes of deepest Calleshire than the constable. 'Ah, I see a sign.'

A hand-painted wooden board rested on the road verge propped up against a tree. There was an arrow pointing ahead and the words 'Capstan Purlieu Plants' painted beside it in freehand. As the police car drew up in front of the nursery two women emerged from a cottage nearby to greet them. Crosby muttered 'Dr Livingstone and Mr Stanley, I presume,' but under his breath.

'Anna Sutherland,' said a tall, rather gaunt figure with her hair severely scraped back into a bun.

'Marilyn Potts,' said a shorter, plumper woman, standing slightly behind her, curly hair flopping about just above her shoulders. Both were dressed in workman-like trousers and grubby shirts.

'I hear you've had some trouble out here, ladies,' began Sloan formally.

'If by trouble you mean that we've lost half our livelihood for the foreseeable future,' said Anna Sutherland tautly, 'then yes, we've had trouble.'

'That's one way of describing the loss of a greenhouse full of valuable orchids,' supplemented Marilyn Potts, tears beginning to well up in her eyes.

'Trouble in spades then,' muttered Crosby, pleased with the gardening metaphor.

'Trouble with damage to some plants, I believe,' soldiered on Sloan, ignoring him.

'Trouble with all the young orchids growing in our

47

greenhouse,' said Marilyn Potts more precisely. She led the way to their greenhouse and pointed. 'As you can see for yourselves, every single one of them is dead.'

'Big trouble,' concluded Crosby, surveying the scene.

'Someone opened the greenhouse door last night . . .' began Marilyn.

'And left it open,' said Anna Sutherland.

'And then the frost got at them.' The tears in Marilyn Potts' eyes looked perilously near to streaming out as she fondled the remains of what had once been a living plant. She sniffed and the tears receded a little.

'Some person or persons unknown,' contributed Anna Sutherland, echoing, had she known it, Sloan's earlier sentiment. 'In other words, Inspector,' she said with emphasis, 'not either of us.'

'Definitely not either of us,' said Marilyn Potts, still sniffing. 'We would never have done a thing like that. Not in a hundred years.'

'I'm sure you wouldn't,' said Detective Inspector Sloan, although experienced policeman that he was, he was not sure of anything at this stage. It was too early to say. He scanned the greenhouse. 'Do you happen to have a thermostat in here to warn you of frost?'

'Too expensive,' said Anna Sutherland.

Marilyn Potts waved a hand towards the land at the side of their cottage. 'The hardy plants out there are all right. I've checked that nothing's happened to them.'

'Yet,' said her friend mordantly.

Detective Inspector Sloan took out his notebook and got down to business: police business. 'Can you quantify your loss?'

'A year's work,' said Marilyn Potts tremulously.

'That's if you don't count anything we may have to pay out to get going again,' said Anna Sutherland. 'Such as restocking.'

'Tell me,' said Sloan, 'do either of you have any thoughts on who might have left your greenhouse door open?'

'Caused criminal damage you mean,' said Anna Sutherland trenchantly.

'The perpetrator,' suggested Detective Crosby helpfully. It was word that had cropped up in his training that he didn't often have a chance to use.

There was an awkward little silence which Sloan, experienced policeman that he was, did nothing to break. After a moment or two Marilyn Potts said with almost palpable reluctance, 'It might just have been Norman.'

'Norman?' he said.

'My husband – my former husband – that is. Norman Potts.' She gave another little sniff and said, 'We parted brass rags.'

'Big time,' contributed Anna Sutherland.

'He wasn't happy about splitting the money after the divorce, you see,' explained Norman's former wife. 'He thought he should have had more of the final settlement than he did.'

Anna Sutherland gave a little snort. 'Wanted to reduce Marilyn to total penury, I expect.'

This, Detective Inspector Sloan, happily married man, knew all too well was quite often the main object of some ex-husbands and often more important to them than securing funds for themselves. He had no doubt that a forensic psychiatrist could explain this – but then, as anyone who had ever sat in a court of law could tell you – forensic psychiatrists could always explain everything.

'So that I would come crawling back, I suppose,' said Marilyn Potts. She gave a defiant shake of her head. 'But I'm not going to do that even if I starve.'

'Where does he live?' asked Detective Constable Crosby militantly.

'He used to live in Almstone when we were together but where he is now, I couldn't say for sure,' said Marilyn distantly. 'I don't know exactly where but I had heard it was over in Berebury near to a pub called The Railway Tavern.'

'That figures,' murmured Anna Sutherland enigmatically, turning to shift a large crate of plants to one side. She lifted this with great ease.

Detective Inspector Sloan made a note and asked, 'Would he have known Jack Haines' nursery over at Pelling by any chance?'

'I'll say, Inspector, very well indeed,' she said without hesitation. 'In fact, I know Norman went there when he was first trying to find me. I guess he thought I might be back there working for Jack at the time because he knew I was fond of orchids and Jack grows them too.'

'At least Jack Haines had the grace to warn her that Norman had been over to him at Pelling to ask him if he knew where Marilyn was,' interposed Anna Sutherland, hefting another crate and putting it on the staging. 'That was something.'

'But Jack Haines didn't tell him where you were, I hope,' said Detective Constable Crosby involuntarily. In his capacity as a young police officer he had abruptly been exposed to the world of domestic violence and, still a bachelor himself, he hadn't liked what he had seen of it.

Marilyn Potts gave a wan smile. 'No, not Jack Haines. He would never have done a thing like that, I'm sure.'

'Get real, Marilyn,' said Anna Sutherland. 'Norman could easily have found out where you were all the same. He might be a right menace but he isn't stupid.'

'There are always ways and means of finding someone,' contributed Crosby obscurely, a policeman only just beginning to find out about some of the sticky slug-like trails left by human beings on the surface of the planet.

Detective Inspector Sloan, who had been considering writing his report under the heading of 'Criminal Damage', decided that this remit might not be quite wide enough. 'Harassment' might well come into it as well: it was still too soon to say. He made a note of the fact that Norman Potts knew Jack Haines too. Two greenhouses of frosted orchids couldn't be a coincidence. Not on the same night.

Anna Sutherland said, 'There's no hiding place good enough for a battered wife these days.'

Sloan was a methodical man and so he ignored this and dutifully carried on. 'Is there anyone else whom you may have reason to believe bears either of you any ill-will?'

'You mean except Norman?' asked Norman's former wife.

'I do,' said Sloan, quite relaxed. Norman Potts might or might not be able to find Marilyn Potts but he had no doubt at all that, should they want to, the police could find the aforementioned Norman quite quickly.

'Not that we know of,' Anna Sutherland answered his question sturdily. 'Either of us.'

All that Detective Inspector Sloan knew was that that reply wasn't going to be good enough for Police Superintendent Leeyes. The superintendent's default setting was a toxic mixture of disbelief and irascibility.

CHAPTER FIVE

Anthony Berra's approach to his clients, the Lingards at Pelling Grange, was a sophisticated blend of regret and optimism. Fortunately it had been Oswald Lingard who had answered his ring at the front door.

'I thought I'd better come over as soon as I could, Major,' said the landscape designer, 'because I must warn you that there's been a bit of a problem with the plants that were being brought on for the new Mediterranean garden.' Berra hastened to explain about the open doors of the greenhouses at the nursery.

'Sabotage, do you think?' asked the major. His wife had wrought many changes at Pelling Grange but even she hadn't managed to prise Oswald Lingard out of his old tweed jacket. Patches of leather guarded the elbows but there had been nothing stopping the cuffs from fraying at the edges. 'Wilful damage and all that?'

'Could be,' admitted Anthony Berra, twisting his lips wryly. 'Too soon to say.'

'Lot of it about these days, you know, old chap. My apples are always getting stolen. Last year the blighters even pinched half my strawberries.'

'I think it's most likely to be someone with a grudge against Jack Haines,' replied Anthony Berra. He decided against going on to suggest that the strawberry thieves were more likely to have been of an avian rather than human nature.

He himself was dressed rather more carefully than his client although not much better. He didn't suppose for a moment that Oswald Lingard would notice – let alone care – how he, Anthony Berra, dressed but Charmian Lingard certainly would. It was part of the landscape designer's credo that people with money always knew about clothes and of necessity he tried to work with people who had money – hopefully quite a lot of it – so he always paid attention to what he wore and when.

'All of Jack Haines' staff, Major,' he said, 'are pretty certain that the gates to the nursery were properly locked up last night but you never can tell.'

'And employees being what they are they're not going to tell anyone if it wasn't,' concluded Lingard realistically, his time in the Army having left its mark on him in more ways than one. 'So where does this leave us, Berra? My wife will be coming back any minute now and she's sure to want to know.'

'I do have a plan . . .' began Berra.

Oswald Lingard wasn't listening. 'The restoration of the old garden here at the Grange means a lot to Charmian, you know. Very keen on it and all that.'

'At least the medieval herb garden is working well,' put in Berra. 'That's coming along nicely.'

'And then there's this big shindig she's planning. A lot of people'll be coming to that.' Lingard hunched his shoulders and gave a little chuckle. 'Bound to be. They'll all want to see what she's making of the place. And me.'

'Naturally,' agreed Anthony Berra smoothly, omitting any mention of the effect on the garden of his own work. Clients always wanted to think the good ideas had been their own. It was something he encouraged.

'After all,' went on the major reflectively, 'this garden has been pretty nearly derelict since before my great-grandfather's day. It was all right up until then, of course. Gardeners were two a penny until 1914.'

'One man to the acre then,' said the landscape designer. 'Those were the days.'

'We had four of them here until the Kaiser's war.' Lingard tapped his knee. 'And I couldn't do a darn thing myself when I got home – this bit of me hasn't been right since Helmand.'

'Oh, I understand that all right, Major,' responded Berra without hesitation, 'and as I say I've been giving that Mediterranean garden quite a lot of thought since Haines rang me. You remember that statue that Mrs Lingard brought home from Italy . . .'

'I thought she told you to call her Charmian?' interrupted Oswald Lingard.

'So she did,' murmured Berra. 'Now about the statue . . .' There had been no suggestion, though, that he called the major 'Oswald'.

'Rather jolly, I thought it,' said Lingard simply. 'I

55

know you yourself weren't very taken with it at the time, though.'

'It was just that I had trouble fitting it into my original design,' said Berra with perfect truth, the statue in question being of over-generous proportions and doubtful workmanship, 'but I've been thinking that now we're going to be without the plants that I'd planned to put in there, it could go in the bed to good effect. I'd got the ground all prepared in any case while you were away in Italy.'

Oswald Lingard gave a grunt. 'I'm sure that Charmian'll be pleased to have Flora, Goddess of something or other . . .'

'Bounty,' supplied Berra, 'bountiful' describing the statue's ample lines very well. 'And Jack Haines should be able to whistle up something colourful in the way of summer plants to fill the ground for this year and then next year we can put in the ones I had originally planned.'

'So it'll still look all right for the garden party, then?' The major sounded anxious. 'Charmian has set her heart on that being a success.'

'It will indeed, I promise you.' Berra gave what he hoped was a winning smile. 'Then, as I say, next year we can go for what I had organised in the first place.'

'You chaps will keep on talking about next year,' complained the major. 'You're as bad as that woman who was always saying that you should have come to see the garden last week when it was at its best or waited until next week when it would be even better.'

'Ruth Draper,' said Anthony Berra, who had heard this many times before.

It was at this juncture that Charmian Lingard swept in, a copybook picture of a lady gardener as found in the best fashion magazines: straw hat artfully tied on with a colourful scarf, elegant dress unsullied by soil and shoes that had never left the garden paths. She had that untroubled appearance of well-being only accomplished by a life totally untouched by money or any other worries. This was underlined by a chocolate-box complexion, designer clothes and excellent grooming.

'Did I hear Ruth Draper's name?' she said as she came in. She was carrying a wooden trug on which reposed a sheaf of greenery already half arranged for vases in the house. 'I'm not interested in last week or next week, Anthony. You know that. It's this week I want the garden right for. And every week, too, of course, but especially for the party.'

Berra smiled dutifully. 'And so it shall be, Charmian.'

She frowned. 'What are you doing here, anyway, Anthony? I thought you were going to be over at the admiral's today.'

'I'm going there as soon as I can.' He told her what had happened over at Jack Haines' nursery, spelling out the loss of the plants he had had grown there.

Charmian Lingard took this in her stride, difficulties always having been obstacles somebody else ironed out. 'Your problem, Anthony, not mine, but don't forget I'll be inviting your future in-laws and they'll be bound to want to see what you've done here.'

Anthony Berra was engaged to be married to the daughter of the Bishop of Calleshire. 'I know they will,' he said ruefully. 'But you'll be pleased that now I think we could fit Flora herself in the new garden after all . . .'

'I knew you'd come round to that in the end,' she said complacently, dumping the trug on the hall table. 'She'll look just right there with the peacocks on the wall behind her.'

Oswald Lingard grinned. 'I'm not sure what the old monks would have thought of her though, Berra, are you?' Pelling Grange had once been attached to a monastery despoiled by Henry VIII and occasional traces of the outline of the original garden had surfaced from time to time while the landscape designer had been at work. 'Or the Bishop.'

Berra smiled politely and pressed on.

'And I'll put some strongly coloured plants in the bed round her as a temporary measure for this year. I think a really good Centranthus ruber would look quite well against the grey of the sculpture . . .'

Charmian Lingard led the way into the drawing-room. 'Why not roses?' she asked as Anthony Berra had known she would.

'. . . and Cheiranthus cherie with deep red flowers and grey foliage. The one called "Blood Red" . . . '

'Why don't you people ever like roses?' persisted Charmian Lingard.

'Black spot.' Berra swept on persuasively, 'And there's a really striking Centaurea dealbata I'd like to try there. It's got deep pink flowers and a lightish green leaf.'

'I think roses would look even better,' said Charmian Lingard, a touch of steel creeping into her voice.

Anthony Berra, recognising this, gave in gracefully. 'Then, Charmian, I'll try some roses but they won't like the lime in the soil. We should go for varieties with good colours all the same, to lighten the stone of the statue. Now, I'll just need to take some measurements of Flora before I go so that we can get the dimensions of her plinth in proper proportion . . .'

'Flora among the flowers,' murmured Charmian Lingard sweetly. 'That sounds just right. Admiral Catterick hasn't got any statues in the Park, has he?'

'Not yet,' Anthony Berra grinned, reading her mind without difficulty. 'And,' he added, prompted by an eldritch shriek from the garden wall, 'he hasn't got any peacocks either.'

She screwed up her face in a child-like pout. 'He's got that sunken garden, though.'

'I don't think, Charmian,' said Anthony Berra gently, 'that the admiral feels in any way challenged by the work you're having done here. The Park is a very old-established garden with a character all of its own.'

'But ours was a monastery garden and you can't get any older than that.'

'True,' he said diplomatically, refraining from mentioning the Hanging Gardens of Babylon besides those of Persia and China and other plantings in antiquity, 'but I can't imagine the admiral minding that. Besides, I'm just keeping the Park ticking over for him now. Its glory days are over – and so are his too, come to that. He's an old man and not a well one these days.'

'I want him to come to the party all the same,' said Charmian Lingard, 'and see what I've done here.'

'I'm sure he will,' lied Anthony Berra.

* * *

Watched at a distance by both Anna Sutherland and Marilyn Potts, Detective Inspector Sloan and Detective Constable Crosby returned to their car parked outside Capstan Purlieu Plants.

'Now, Crosby, we need to get straight back to Pelling,' said Sloan briskly, 'and start enquiries about this Enid Osgathorp.'

'I don't know that I can remember the way backwards,' said the constable moodily. He had been hoping to drive back to the police station and its canteen.

'If, Crosby, baby elvers can find their way four thousand miles back to the Sargasso Sea without a route map, I think you should be able to manage it.'

He sighed. 'Yes, sir.'

Detective Inspector Sloan toyed with the idea of saying that the elvers then grew up to be adult eels but decided against drawing the parallel. He said instead, 'It makes sense to go back to that other nursery too while we're about it and have a word with Jack Haines about this Norman Potts. It'll save another journey.' Superintendent Leeyes had left him in no doubt that economy was the watchword at the police station these days even though 'Waste not, want not' was not usually a police mantra. Pleasing his superior officer, though, was high on Sloan's agenda all the while his assessment was pending. 'You can take the foreman's fingerprints while you're about it.'

'But there weren't any fingerprints on the door handles,' said Crosby, adding reproachfully, 'I did tell you that, sir. They had been wiped clean.'

'There is no need for that particular piece of information

to be disclosed at this stage of the investigation,' said Sloan, realising that he sounded stuffy even to himself. 'It is a basic principle of policing to give nothing away. Who knows what and who doesn't can be useful knowledge in an investigation.'

'Sorry, sir.' The constable sounded crestfallen. 'But we can ask Jack Haines why he didn't mention this character Norman Potts to us before, can't we?' said Crosby feelingly. 'He ought to have done.'

'Exactly,' said Sloan, who had already made a mental note of the fact. 'So just tell Control where we're going, will you?'

The constable applied himself to his personal radio while Sloan strapped himself in the car with a quiet sigh. Greenhouse doors left open and elderly ladies who had gone walkabout weren't quite the level of policing that he felt really came within the remit of the head of the Criminal Investigation Department of 'F' Division of the Calleshire County Constabulary, small though it was, and it rankled. On the other hand, what with his appraisal coming up so soon, this was no time to say so to anyone, least of all Superintendent Leeyes.

It was Crosby, though, who vocalised the sentiment. 'Who do they think we are?' he demanded indignantly. 'Maids of all work?'

'Maids of all police work,' rejoined the detective inspector crisply. 'Now get going, Crosby.'

Canonry Cottage at Pelling was in the middle of the village, the uncut grass in its front garden giving a clear sign to the world of the continued absence of its owner.

'Miss Osgathorp always lets me know when she'll be

61

coming back,' said her neighbour, a large woman in a flowery apron. It had been she who had rung the police. 'Because of getting in the milk and the bread for her.'

'So when . . .' began Sloan.

'That's just it, Inspector,' said the woman. 'This time she hasn't either done that or come back anyway.'

'Ah . . .' said Sloan, the thought idly running through his mind that large flowers on the apron would have suited the woman better than the tiny little ones that were there. Daisies, he thought they were. Poppies would have been better. Big, blowsy ones. 'What about her mobile phone? Have you got the number of that?'

'She wouldn't have one of them, Inspector. Said she'd spent all her working life answering the telephone for the doctor and she wasn't going to do any more telephoning than she had to.'

'No word then?' asked Crosby, already bored.

The woman shook her head. 'Not even a postcard and it's been three weeks since she went now. It's just not like Miss Osgathorp.' She pointed towards her fireplace. 'You can see that I've got a lovely row of postcards from her on the mantelpiece over there. Come from all over the place, they have.'

'Where had she been going?' asked Sloan.

The woman reached into the pocket of her apron, produced an old envelope and proffered it to the two policemen. On it was a word that began with the letters 'Carmarthen' and then trailed off into an almost illegible scribble, finishing with the signature 'Enid Osgathorp'. 'Search me. Mind you,' she added fairly, 'she doesn't always tell me where she's going, me not being someone to go about much. Proper traveller she's been since the old doctor died.' She sniffed. 'I daresay he left her something.'

'The old doctor?' queried Sloan.

The woman looked surprised that he needed to ask. 'Doctor Heddon, of course. Everyone knew him. Was our doctor out here at Pelling for years and Miss Osgathorp was his secretary and receptionist all the time he was here. Knew everyone, both of them.'

Sloan paused for a moment, seeking a tactful way to put his next question. He decided there wasn't one. 'Did she leave you a key to her house?'

The woman shook her head, unoffended. 'No. I was glad about that. She used to say "Norah, you don't want to be worried about my little old cottage. If it burns down, it burns down, and if burglars get in they won't find all that much there to take and I'm not leaving a key with anyone else either".'

Detective Inspector Sloan forbore to say that that aspect of theft hadn't deterred a lot of housebreakers he had known. He didn't mention either the feeling of outrage left behind by intruders, often worse than any loss of valuables. Instead he dispatched Crosby to take a look round the outside of the cottage next door.

The woman was still going on about her neighbour. 'Miss Osgathorp always said what you had to concentrate on when you got to her age was not being a nuisance to anyone so she wasn't going to be, not no-how. She was always one for spending her money on going places, not on buying trinkets that she didn't need. And that she certainly did, officer. Travel, I mean. If it wasn't one country, it was another. Mostly ones with flowers.'

Sloan opened his notebook. 'Can you remember exactly when it was she went away?'

'Oh, yes,' said the woman called Norah very readily. 'It was the day after poor Mrs Beddowes done herself in.' She jerked her head in the general direction of the policeman. 'I expect you knew all about that what with you being in the police. The rector's wife.'

Detective Inspector Sloan didn't: this was partly because suicides weren't usually within his remit – PC York, the Coroner's Officer, usually dealt with the fall-out from those – but also because it was about three weeks ago that he, Christopher Dennis Sloan, family man, had taken some overdue annual leave. 'And when exactly did that happen?' he asked.

'That's just it, Inspector,' said the woman. 'Three weeks come last Friday. Balance of her mind disturbed, they said, though why she should do a thing like that, I can't think. Nice husband and three lovely children. She left a note,' Norah added lugubriously, 'but they didn't read it out at the inquest.'

'Miss Osgathorp,' prompted Sloan gently.

'Oh, she never stays away anywhere as long as this as a rule. She's her own woman, not like some,' here the woman sighed and let her gaze settle momentarily on a pair of indisputably male boots in the corner of the room, 'and so I suppose she can do just what she likes. Nothing to stop her.'

Sloan nodded. It was a sentiment with which the Force's Family Support Officer would have been the first to agree.

The neighbour was still going on. 'I wouldn't have thought nothing of it at first only this secretary of the Horticultural Society over at Staple St James rang me up because she couldn't get no answer from Miss Osgathorp's telephone. Seems she'd promised to go over there tomorrow night and talk to them about the orchids of somewhere or other. Indonesia, I think it could have been. Or Crete.'

'It could have been Crete,' agreed Christopher Sloan, the gardener in him momentarily taking over from the policeman. It was one of the places he meant to visit one day. 'I'm told the flowers there in the spring are something to write home about.'

'Never mind her not writing home, officer,' responded the woman with vigour. 'It's her not coming home that's beginning to worry me. It's just not like Miss Osgathorp to forget about giving a talk. Set a lot of store by that sort of thing, she did.'

'Did you see the going of her?' asked Sloan, hoping that Crosby would have had the sense to peer in a window or two next door while he was about it. Breaking into houses without demonstrable cause went down very badly with his superior officers and the Force's auditors, to say nothing of the press.

'Oh, yes. She went off like she always does,' said the woman called Norah. 'To catch a bus to Berebury and then a train to wherever she's going.'

'Did you actually see her go?' Sloan asked, possibilities such as a decaying corpse with a broken leg in an empty house coming into his mind.

'Oh, yes, I did that. I was just popping down to the

butcher's when I saw her go off towards the bus stop round the corner in time for the ten to ten bus on the Friday morning. With her suitcase. One of those with wheels that you can pull behind you. Besides,' she said, as if this clinched the matter, 'she waved to me as she walked down the road. And then that young Anthony Berra came by in his car. You know, the gardener man. He's going to marry the bishop's daughter in the summer. He pulled up when he spotted her and gave her a lift.'

Detective Inspector Sloan snapped his notebook shut at this. 'Then you'll let us know when she comes back, won't you? I expect she's just extended her holiday. Must like it where she is but I expect she'll be back in touch soon.'

Looking back later, he was the first to admit that this was one of the least good predictions of his career.

Not at the time knowing this, he set off to collect Crosby and met that worthy as he was coming back down the path of Canonry Cottage. 'Everything all right over there, Crosby?'

The constable shook his head and sounded puzzled. 'I can't quite make it out, sir. There looks to have been a bit of a break-in at the back of the cottage – there's a broken window to the larder with quite a lot of glass about and a bit of blood. All the other doors and windows are secure but someone's been in there through the front door as well but with a key. No doubt about it.'

'How do you know?' asked Sloan, suddenly alert.

'Come and take a look through the letter box, sir.'

Crosby led the way back up the path to the front door of Canonry Cottage and carefully pushed open the flap of the letter box with a pencil. 'See?'

Sloan bent down and took a look for himself. He saw what the constable meant. Letters that had been pushed through the letter box by the postman and landed on the doormat had been swept back as the door had been opened and stayed where they had then lain when the door had been closed again.

'Someone's been in this way, sir, I'm sure, and then come back out again.'

'With a key,' agreed Sloan.

The two detectives reached the same conclusions at the same time although they expressed them differently.

'Not a professional at the front,' decided Detective Inspector Sloan.

'An amateur at the back,' reasoned Detective Constable Crosby. 'Glass everywhere and blood on a sharp bit.'

There was, though, complete unison in what they said next.

'This'll need a search warrant, sir,' said Crosby.

'And Forensics,' said Sloan.

Superintendent Leeyes took a little persuading. 'A search warrant?' he barked. 'On what grounds?'

'A missing person whose house has been entered in her absence, twice,' Sloan said. 'Once with a key,' he added fairly. 'And once without.'

'So?'

'A key which she told a neighbour she hadn't left with anyone else.'

Leeyes grunted. 'That all you want?'

'A check of all the hotels and boarding houses in Carmarthenshire for an Enid Osgathorp would be a help, sir. She's retired and,' he said as an afterthought, 'as far as we know, travelling alone.'

The superintendent added something else. 'And presumably under that name.'

It was something else, agreed Sloan, which they would have to consider.

CHAPTER SIX

'More coffee, Jack?' Mandy Lamb hovered near the kettle, concerned about the unusual immobility of her employer. Jack Haines had sat, motionless, at his desk ever since the two policemen had left his office.

'What's that?' he jerked himself out of his reverie. 'Oh, no thanks.'

She pointed to a stack of letters. 'What about the post?'

He waved a hand. 'You see to it, Mandy.'

'Two whole greenhouses gone are going to set us back quite a bit,' she mused presently.

'You can say that again,' he said, a tiny bit more animated.

'It's bad, this loss, isn't it?'

'Very bad.' He continued to sit quite still, shoulders hunched.

'But it's not only the money, is it?' said Mandy perceptively, automatically herself turning to the kettle on the counter in the corner. Jack Haines was a widower and, although Mandy was years younger than he was, she often found herself in the same position of sympathetic listener and maker of comfortable responses as many a wife.

'No,' he roused himself to answer her, 'although that's bad enough.'

Since he would not do so, Mandy Lamb voiced a name herself. 'Norman Potts?'

'No, not Norman,' he said roughly. 'Norman knows exactly where he stands with me all right. Always has ever since the beginning. Nothing's changed there.'

'You surely don't mean that it's Bob Steele who's worrying you?'

Jack Haines, impatiently pushing aside a pile of old seed catalogues, inclined his head into something approaching a nod. 'Sort of.'

'But the Berebury Garden Centre isn't really into orchids,' pointed out Mandy. 'They only do common or garden stuff.'

'I don't know what they're into,' Haines growled. 'Or up to. But I hope it's not what I think.'

'Sabotage?' said Mandy Lamb and frowned. 'You can't mean that, Jack.'

'Bob Steele came round the other day to see if we could spare him a dozen trays of Polemonium Jacob's Ladder for a customer. Said he was clean out.'

'I know. I saw him,' she said. 'Russ loaded them up for him. He paid for them all right – trade, of course.'

'That wasn't it.' Jack Haines took a deep breath. 'It's that I happened to drive past his place myself a bit earlier on that morning and could see quite clearly that he'd got hundreds of them on sale that day so he can't have needed any more.'

'Same variety?' Mandy Lamb might not know a great deal about plants but she did know that varieties mattered.

'Same variety,' he said. Mandy wrinkled her nose and since once again Jack Haines seemed unwilling to voice his suspicions, she said, 'So the Berebury Garden Centre is spying on us, is it?'

'I'd rather call it a fishing expedition myself,' said Haines.

She shook her head at him affectionately. 'You never did like calling a spade a spade, did you, Jack?'

'How do I know what to call it?' her employer demanded. 'Malicious damage, perhaps?'

'You don't think . . .'

'I don't know what to think but I do know that I saw Russ over there one day when I hadn't sent him.' He had begun to say something more when they were interrupted by the arrival of another visitor.

Minutes later Jack Haines was exhibiting rather more resolve than he had been doing with his secretary, but this time it was with an automatic well-mannered response to a customer. It was Benedict Feakins who had put his head round the office door. 'Got a minute, Jack?' he asked.

'Of course.' Jack Haines got to his feet, now every inch the helpful nurseryman. 'Come for your plants?'

'Not exactly,' said Benedict awkwardly. 'Well, in a way . . .'

'I'm afraid we've had some trouble overnight. Some of your plants got damaged, but some are all right,' began

Haines then, taking a second look at the man's bent back, he said, 'But you're not all right, are you? I can see that.'

'Too much digging, that's what did it,' the other man admitted. 'I was just getting the ground ready for all these shrubs you've got for me. It's getting late in the year for them as it is.'

The nurseryman gave him an indulgent smile. 'Weekend gardeners get a lot of back problems. They're not used to stoop labour.'

'Too right,' agreed Feakins fervently.

'Now your father, he had everything at the right height with his cacti.'

'His cacti are what I wanted to ask you about, Jack.'

'Don't overwater,' said Jack Haines immediately. 'A great mistake.'

'It's not that. It's that I – we – were wondering if you'd take them back in part exchange for my order. Mary doesn't like them and neither do I.'

The deliberate pause that followed was part of the commercial interplay that was innate in the nurseryman. 'I might,' Haines said slowly. 'What's the problem?'

Benedict Feakins flushed. 'You see I may have to keep you waiting for a bit before I can pay you for all the plants I ordered. It's lovely having Dad's house but the upkeep's proving a bit more than I bargained for and with a baby on the way . . .'

'I get you,' said Haines. 'Tell you what – you bring your dad's cacti in and I'll have a look at them for you.'

'Great. It would be good to get rid of them. To a good home, of course,' he added hastily lest Jack Haines happened to be as fond of them as his father had been.

The nurseryman looked at Benedict Feakins and grinned. 'You're not a chip off the old block, then . . .'

To Jack Haines' surprise Benedict Feakins stiffened, his face turning a pasty shade of white. 'No harm in a man's not liking cacti, is there?' he said dully.

'None,' said Haines hastily. 'It's just that your dad was so keen on them, that's all, and you don't seem to be.'

'I can't imagine that it's an inherited characteristic,' Benedict Feakins said stiffly.

'My father couldn't stand lilies,' volunteered Haines at once, 'and I love them. That right, Mandy, isn't it?'

'You do, it's only the cat that doesn't,' said Mandy Lamb tactfully. 'They're dangerous to cats, lilies. They really upset them.'

'Well, cacti really upset me as much as lilies do cats,' said Benedict Feakins more firmly. 'See what you can do about them, Jack, there's a good chap. There must be somebody out there who loves them more than I do.'

It was to the Park at Pelling that Anthony Berra headed when he left Jack Haines' nursery. He was going to see another client who had lost plants – Admiral Waldo Catterick this time. As he steered his car through the decaying entrance gates, he cast a professional eye over the grounds. This was a very different garden from that of Oswald and Charmian Lingard at the Grange. Theirs had once been monastic; this garden was that of a small manor with eighteenth-century grandeur superimposed on its original layout.

It had always seemed to him that whoever had lived here in the Park's glory days had not so much been anxious to keep up with the Joneses as having been making it quite clear that they considered themselves to be the top dogs of the neighbourhood themselves. It still showed in the ghosts of a parterre and carefully sited trees cleverly leading the eye towards a distant perspective. An old pergola, one side hornbeam, one side pleached lime, led to a sunken garden, all very overgrown.

Whoever the grandees of the past had been, they had long gone and only old Admiral Waldo Catterick lived here now. Elderly and arthritic, his horticultural demands were very different from those of the ambitious Charmian Lingard. The landscape designer was prepared to bet that the admiral never even got as far as the sunken garden these days.

Fortunately the house had escaped the worst excesses of the Baroque epoch and it sat squarely as it had always done in a sheltered fold in the land. Anthony Berra metaphorically shrugged his shoulders, only too aware that while a neglected house will stand for years, a neglected garden less than a decade. The admiral wasn't going to last for a decade. No way. Not now. Idly, he wondered who would live there when the old boy had gone and whether they would take an interest in the garden then. A widower for years, the man had no children that Berra knew of although he had heard that there had been a baby who had died.

He brought his car to a stop outside the front door and apologised for being later than he had planned, explaining that he had had to see someone else first. 'Did you get my message that I was very busy, Admiral? And would get here as soon as I could?'

'Signal received,' said the admiral, adding genially, 'You can't make headway in a heavy sea, my boy. I know that.' Elderly and arthritic the old sailor might be but he was still spritely.

'I'm afraid there was a bit of problem over at Jack Haines' nursery overnight,' began Berra, coughing. 'I've just been there to see the damage.'

The admiral regarded him with a pair of bright blue eyes. 'A bit of a problem, eh? That's what they said about the battle of Jutland too. Afterwards, of course.'

'Vandalism,' said Berra, who didn't know what he was talking about.

'Worse things happen at sea,' said the old sailor philosophically.

'I'm sure, but it's a confounded nuisance all the same,' said Berra. 'All those exotic plants I'd got lined up for you are thoroughly frosted and quite useless now. The shrubs are all right, though.' He coughed again.

'What you need for that cough, Berra, is to go sea. Take it from me, a dose of sea air clears the tubes.'

'Haven't time,' he said. 'Not in the spring.'

The admiral said, 'And I didn't waste my time while I was waiting for you.'

'No?' asked Berra warily. He and his client had very different views on what should happen in the garden at the Park.

'I've been thinking about scrapping those shrubs you got Haines to put by for me.'

Anthony Berra sighed. 'They're really very labour-saving, Admiral, and we did agree that low maintenance was what was needed here at the Park these days.'

'Can't wait for shrubs to settle in at my time of life,' he said with a touch of his quarter-deck manner of old. 'I'll be dead before they come into flower.'

'But, Admiral . . .'

'So I'm going to get you to order an extra load of bedding plants which I can enjoy from my sitting-room window this summer.'

Anthony Berra sighed again. 'You haven't been taking advice from Miss Osgathorp, have you? It's the sort of thing she would say. She might know about orchids but she doesn't know all her gardening onions.'

'Certainly not,' said the old man crisply. 'That woman's a downright menace.'

'In what way?' asked Berra curiously.

'Always poking her nose into matters that are no concern of hers,' said the admiral stiffly.

'I thought all old ladies were like that,' said Anthony Berra lightly. 'Especially the unmarried ones.'

'Doesn't understand the meaning of the Hippocratic Oath, either,' pronounced the admiral robustly.

Berra protested. 'But she wasn't the doctor.'

'More's the pity.'

'What do you mean?'

'Then I could have sued her.'

'Whatever for?'

'Dereliction of duty,' said the old man, sometime martinet.

Anthony Berra stared at him, wide-eyed, but the admiral said nothing more.

The two women who comprised Capstan Purlieu Plants' total workforce could not have been more different in temperament as well as in appearance. Anna Sutherland, spare and sturdy, was the total opposite of the shorter, chubbier Marilyn Potts. She was also clear-sighted and uncompromising. Marilyn Potts on the other hand seemed capable of confusing any issue to the point of complete incomprehensibility to herself and everyone else.

Except Anna.

'It's no good your hanging about here, Marilyn, mooning over every single one of your dead plants,' said Anna Sutherland implacably. 'You've got to go over and collect those orchids from Jack Haines whether you like it not.'

'I don't like it,' said Marilyn Potts mulishly.

'There's no sentiment in business. You should know that by now. You need those orchids for your demonstration tomorrow night and,' she added grimly, 'we need your fee for speaking. You've been told by the Society's secretary exactly where Enid Osgathorp had arranged for the orchids to be ready for her talk and all you've got to do now is go over to Pelling and collect them.'

'But from Jack Haines,' she protested weakly.

'He can't eat you,' said Anna.

'I don't know what Norman might have said to him when he went there looking for me.'

'What Norman might have said about you to Jack Haines or anyone else doesn't matter any more,' said Anna. 'Never did anyway,' she added under her breath.

'Norman used to say such nice things to me once upon a time,' said Marilyn, now near to tears again.

'Once upon a time is how all fairy tales begin,' said Anna Sutherland tartly. 'They usually end differently.'

'And now I suppose all his sweet nothings are like all my orchids. Dead and dying, the lot of them. Frosted.'

'The brothers Grimm didn't write much about flowers in their fairy tales,' Anna reminded her. 'Just Jack and the Beanstalk.'

'That was written by someone else,' objected Marilyn.

'I don't care who it was written by,' retorted Anna, 'you've still got to get yourself over to Jack Haines' place and pick up those orchids before tomorrow night.'

'He doesn't know yet that I'm standing in for old Enid.'

'Then you'll have to tell him, won't you?'

'Shall I ring him and let him know it's me who's going to be picking them up so that he can get them ready? And then I shan't have to hang around his place.'

Anna Sutherland gave an unladylike snort. 'Those orchids will be all ready and waiting for you when you get there, Marilyn, don't you worry. Enid would have had his guts for garters if they weren't and he knows she would – just as well as we do. I expect he's as frightened of her as everyone else.'

'Except you, Anna,' said Marilyn Potts, 'except you.' She looked up and caught a curious look on her friend's face. 'You're not afraid of anyone, are you?'

Anna's face relaxed. 'Not of anything in trousers, anyway.'

'Just as well,' said her friend drily, 'because there's one of them coming up the path now.'

Anna Sutherland looked over Marilyn's shoulder at the approaching figure. 'I wonder what our Anthony wants today?'

'Plants, I hope, and plenty of them,' said Marilyn vigorously.

It was indeed plants that the landscape designer was after. Anthony Berra arrived waving a list. 'Just checking if you've got any of these,' he said after punctiliously greeting them both.

'Not if they're orchids,' said Marilyn bitterly. 'We've lost the lot.'

'Not you too?' Berra launched into a graphic description of Jack Haines' losses.

'How very odd,' said Anna Sutherland. She frowned. 'Has some nutter got something against orchids, I wonder? Or him and us, perhaps?'

Marilyn Potts stayed silent while Berra went on, 'It also means I've lost all the plants Jack was growing for me for the Lingards as well.' The landscape designer grimaced. 'And you know what Charmian Lingard's like.'

'More money than sense, that woman,' pronounced Anna.

'Thinks money will buy anything,' chimed in Marilyn. She sniffed. 'Well, all I can say is that she hasn't lived long enough yet to learn that it won't.'

The sniffing became more pronounced and with tears welling up in Marilyn's eyes, Anthony Berra hurled himself into the conversation. 'Well, it seems that it's bad luck all round then.'

'Perhaps it isn't just bad luck,' said Anna Sutherland slowly.

'Well, it certainly isn't a coincidence,' agreed Berra. 'It can't be. Not two nurseries of orchids in one night. It makes you wonder what it could be that you and Jack have in common – besides growing orchids, that is.'

'Norman Potts,' said Norman's erstwhile wife, taking a deep breath. 'That's what.'

'Of course, Jack's stepson!' he whistled. 'I'd never thought of him,' he confessed. 'Ought to have done, I suppose, seeing he used to live and work there when Jack's wife was alive.'

'My once-upon-a-time husband,' responded Marilyn, whose mind seemed still bound up with fairy tales.

'But why should he or anyone else want to attack orchids?' asked Berra, looking mystified. 'I can't imagine any reason myself but then I'm not a psychologist.'

'If you ask me,' said Anna, 'reason doesn't come into it.'

'Is he pathological about them or something, then?'

'The only thing Norman Potts is pathological about is Marilyn here,' declared Anna Sutherland astringently.

'What about Jack Haines then?' asked Berra, still puzzled. 'Norman can't be pathological about Jack's orchids too, surely?'

'Can't he just?' said Anna. 'He always was anti-Jack after Jack married Norman's mother and he hasn't changed that I know of.'

'All I know is that Norman went over to Pelling a week or so back to see Jack Haines,' said Marilyn Potts. 'To try to find out where I lived.'

'It sounds as if he might have succeeded,' observed Anthony Berra, 'if he's the one who's dished your orchids. And Jack's.'

'Well, I haven't tried to find him,' added Marilyn acidly. 'I'd be quite happy if I never set eyes on him ever again.'

'Are you likely to?' asked Berra. 'I mean, is he local these days?'

'Last heard of living in Berebury,' she said, 'somewhere near a pub called The Railway Tavern.'

'Living off his ill-gotten gains, I daresay,' observed Anna Sutherland.

'She means half of our worldly possessions,' explained Marilyn. 'His and mine.'

'Immoral earnings,' said her friend Anna Sutherland trenchantly.

'Yes, of course,' murmured Anthony, a little embarrassed. He started to hand over the list of plants he had brought with him.

Anna plucked it from his fingers and scanned it quickly. 'Cercis canadensis – yes, we've got that; Photinia Red Robin – yes; Cotinus Royal Purple – lots of that; Lonicera etrusca – sorry sold out . . .'

'You got a customer on lime soil, then, Anthony?' said Marilyn.

'Too right, I have,' said Anthony Berra.

'We can't do you any magic potion for neutralising it. You'll have to go to Jack Haines or Bob Steele for that,' put in Marilyn, grinning.

'I know, I know,' he said good-humouredly. 'What you're saying is that Capstan Purlieu is a nursery not a plant centre. I haven't forgotten. Now, what about a good Abutilon, Anna?'

'We've got plenty. Take your pick. We've got a good line in lilies if you're interested?'

He wrinkled his nose. 'I don't like the scent much.'

'Remove the stamen, remove the smell,' said Anna wryly. 'I see you want a Cornus controversa Variegata too.'

'That's the Wedding Cake Tree . . .' began Marilyn, looking again as if she was about to cry.

'I hear you're getting married soon, Anthony,' Anna Sutherland interrupted her hastily.

He nodded. 'In the autumn. In the Minster over at Calleford by the bride's father.'

Anna, looking solemn, said, 'Don't let the girl have any Aegopodium podagraria in her bouquet or you'll never hear the last of it.'

'Anna,' said Anthony, throwing up his hands, 'you've got me there. Explain.'

'Bishop's weed,' cackled Anna.

CHAPTER SEVEN

It was at much the same time that morning when the solicitor Simon Puckle welcomed Benedict and Mary Feakins to his office in Berebury. That the solicitor was sitting behind a desk as he did so and not in an easy chair alongside his clients or even sitting beside them at a round table was thought by the junior members of the firm of Puckle, Puckle and Nunnery, solicitors, to be old-fashioned – even perhaps the making of a statement. That the desk had once belonged to Simon's grandfather only contributed to this image of antiquity.

At this moment, though, Simon Puckle was more concerned about Benedict Feakins' bad back than worrying about his own self-image.

'I'm all right, really,' said Benedict, nevertheless screwing up his face in pain.

'Sure?' asked Simon Puckle as his client lowered himself

into a chair with great caution. 'We could always do this on another day.'

'No,' said Feakins with unexpected vehemence. 'We need everything wound up today, don't we, Mary?'

His wife nodded her head at this, her mind elsewhere. There had been a promise of coffee when they arrived and – her morning sickness having receded – she was now quite hungry. There might be biscuits with the coffee . . .

'Just so,' said the solicitor. 'Now, as you know, probate has already been finalised – which was when you were able to take up residence in your late father's house at Pelling.'

'That means that everything is hunky-dory, doesn't it?' said Benedict Feakins. He essayed an uncertain laugh. 'No last minute snags or anything like that?'

Simon Puckle said, 'Certainly not.'

'Copper-bottomed at Lloyds and all that?' persisted Feakins.

'I assure you that everything is quite in order.' The solicitor was not prepared to state in so many words that the firm Puckle, Puckle and Nunnery were not in the habit of finding last minute snags in their work. Instead he made the point more subtly by moving swiftly on. 'Now we come to the peripheral matters, particularly the transfer of such securities as were held in your late father's name to yours. This, of course, will take time.'

'Everything always seems to take time,' complained Feakins wearily. 'The law's delays and all that. Shakespeare was dead right there.'

Simon Puckle did not rise to this either. 'There is also

the important point that the liability for the insurance of the property is now your responsibility rather than that of the executors and,' he added sternly, 'there can be no delay about that.'

'Are we talking big money?' asked Benedict Feakins warily. 'About the insurance, I mean?'

Simon Puckle glanced down at the contents of the file in front of him. 'Nothing inordinate.'

'I'm a bit strapped for cash at the moment, that's all,' admitted Feakins. 'Moving expenses and all that. But I expect I could raise a loan.'

'Perhaps an overdraft would be better,' suggested the solicitor mildly.

'We've reached our limit,' interrupted Mary Feakins. 'The bank won't let us have any more,' she explained naively. 'We went there first this morning.'

'I see.' Simon Puckle gave the young couple a long hard look. 'It is in my opinion a little early to be thinking of raising money against the property if that is what you had in mind and,' here he raised his eyebrows, 'if I may say so, a little unwise at this stage.'

Benedict Feakins was saved from answering this by the arrival of the solicitor's secretary with a tray of coffee. Mary Feakins gazed hungrily at a plate of digestive biscuits and half-rose in its direction.

'Ah, thank you, Miss Fennel,' said Simon Puckle pleasantly, as she poured out the coffee and handed it round. 'Perhaps you would be kind enough to stay as we shall need you as a witness to Mr Feakins putting his signature on these papers.'

'Of course, Mr Puckle,' she murmured, following the

coffee with an offer of biscuits all round. Mary Feakins took two.

'Now,' said Simon Puckle to his clients, 'do either of you have any other questions?'

'How long will it be before we – that is, I – can sell any of these assets?' said Benedict Feakins, his coffee untouched.

'When you have title to them,' said Simon Puckle crisply.

'And when will that be?' persisted Benedict.

'I think the correct answer,' said the solicitor, 'is that it will be in the fullness of bureaucratic time.'

Benedict Feakins groaned but whether this was from pain or disappointment at his answer Simon Puckle was unable to tell.

After his clients had left his office the solicitor sat at his desk thinking for a minute or two then he rang for his secretary. 'Would you please see if the manager of the Calleshire and Counties Bank is free to have lunch with me today, Miss Fennel?'

'The police are back, Jack,' announced Mandy Lamb unceremoniously as she ushered Detective Inspector Sloan and Detective Constable Crosby into the office.

'Come along in, Inspector,' said Jack Haines heartily. He pushed his chair back and came forward to greet them with every sign of pleasure.

It was Sloan's experience that a visit from the police was only ever welcomed by the victims of an offence. Villains seldom greeted him with the enthusiasm that met their return to Jack Haines' nursery at Pelling. Since the nurseryman and his other visitor were facing each other like a pair of warring dogs, it was obvious, too, that he and Crosby had arrived at a most opportune moment.

'And meet Mr Anthony Berra,' went on Haines, stepping back and ushering the two policemen into chairs. 'He's lost a load of plants too.'

'Only in a manner of speaking,' murmured Anthony Berra coolly. 'It's my clients who will be the losers in the long run. And Jack here, of course.'

'So,' hastened on the nurseryman, 'we're both very keen for you to find out who broke in and opened the greenhouse doors.'

'And why,' added Berra pithily. 'That's what I would like to know.'

'Are you two the only losers here?' asked Detective Inspector Sloan. 'No other victims?'

'I had stuff in there that I was planning to use in the gardens of Admiral Catterick but mostly it was for my clients, the Lingards,' said Berra, giving a little cough.

'And for young Benedict Feakins,' put in Haines.

Anthony Berra pulled a face. 'No, not for him any longer, Jack, I'm sorry to say. He says he's broke and can't afford me any longer.'

'It happens,' said Haines shrugging his shoulders. 'There are some other orchids in the packing shed awaiting collection by a Miss Osgathorp so they're safe enough and the other greenhouses and the hardy plants are all right. I've just checked them myself. As far as I'm concerned the biggest loss is the young orchids.'

'And as far as I'm concerned nearly half of my stuff for

this season was in that one greenhouse,' stressed Berra. 'The remainder is in one of the other greenhouses whose doors weren't left open . . .'

'Now, Anthony . . .' his voice died away as Jack Haines began a protest at this but thought better of it at the last minute.

'There was nothing at all of mine in the orchid one,' said Berra. He cast an enquiring glance in Jack Haines' direction. 'That's so, Jack, isn't it?'

Haines nodded.

Berra gave a twisted smile. 'And so there being "No Orchids for Miss Blandish" is not my problem.'

'You could say that, I suppose,' agreed Haines sourly.

'There were no orchids for our Mrs Lingard at the Grange, either,' said Berra lightly, 'since she wasn't going to have any orchids anyway.' He turned to the policemen. 'She's my client, you know, Inspector. The plants in number two greenhouse were mainly for her – their – garden. But not the orchids, thank goodness.'

Detective Constable Crosby suddenly stirred himself and asked the landscape designer if he'd got any professional rivals. Anthony Berra looked startled. 'Er . . . no,' he spluttered between coughs, 'well, none that I know of anyway.'

'Lucky you,' remarked the constable sardonically.

'I suppose that for the record I should say that there was a big London firm that also put in for the contract to restore the garden at Pelling Grange,' the landscape architect admitted, 'but seeing as I lived in the village anyway the Lingards awarded it to me.' He gave a boyish laugh. 'I suppose I came a bit less expensive too.'

'And lived on the spot,' added Haines generously. 'I'm sure that helps.'

'Also the Lingards know my future in-laws,' admitted Berra sheepishly, 'and I daresay that helps as well.'

'Quite so,' said Detective Inspector Sloan sedately. If there was one thing the police force did not usually suffer from it was nepotism. Most of the policemen whom he knew steered their sons and daughters away from serving in it as energetically as they could. And any such favours dispensed by the police could lead to a prison sentence.

For the policeman.

'It's not what you know, it's who you know,' chanted Crosby under his breath.

'Mustn't forget old Admiral Catterick at the Park,' put in Jack Haines. 'He's one of your clients too, isn't he, Anthony?'

'He is indeed,' agreed Anthony Berra warmly. 'He's a grand old boy. Been at sea all his life and doesn't know the first thing about gardens.'

'Leaves it all to you then, does he?' asked Crosby, an innocent expression on his face.

Berra said, 'Not quite, but I've been trying to get him to go over to labour-saving plants and so I'm mostly planting low-maintenance shrubs there. Unfortunately he's lost quite a lot of the more interesting plants that Jack here was bringing on for him too. There were some more in another greenhouse – one which doesn't appear to have had its doors left open either,' he added pointedly.

'Number three,' said Mandy Lamb before her employer could respond.

'This Miss Osgathorp you mentioned . . .' Sloan hoped

he was dropping this name into their talk with the same delicacy as a fisherman landing a dry fly on a trout stream. He wasn't sure if he had done.

'Fierce old biddy who gives talks,' responded Jack Haines immediately. 'Quite sound on orchids, actually.'

'Knows her stuff, Inspector,' agreed Berra. 'Bit of a battle-axe, though.'

'Well, she was the Dragon at the Gate for years and years, wasn't she?' put in Mandy Lamb from her desk at the front of the office.

'Come again?' said Crosby, looking meaningfully at a jar of coffee.

'She was Doctor Heddon's receptionist,' explained Mandy. 'Protecting the doctor from the patients.'

'I thought these days it was the patients who had to be protected from the doctor,' muttered Crosby, sotto voce, a few famous medical murders at the back of his mind.

'Last time I saw her,' said Berra ruefully, 'she told me exactly what I should be doing in the garden at the Grange. Thought I ought to be having a fernery there.'

'She is something of a pteridophile,' opined Jack Haines. 'She says ferns can manage without her while she's on her travels.'

'But I ask you, a nineteenth-century fernery in an old monastery garden!' Berra gave a short laugh. 'I can't see Charmian – Mrs Lingard, that is – wanting a fernery in her garden.'

'When exactly would that have been, sir?' asked Sloan. 'I mean, when did you last see Miss Osgathorp? Not Mrs Lingard.'

Anthony Berra frowned. 'It's a while since – it must

have been three or four weeks ago. Can't remember precisely when. I gave her a lift to the railway station. She was waiting at the bus stop but I was going into Berebury anyway and I picked her up and dropped her off at the sandwich shop two or three doors away from the station so she could buy something for the journey.'

'Going off on one of her famous trips, I suppose,' grunted Jack Haines.

'She did say where,' admitted Berra, 'but I can't remember where it was now. Not abroad, anyway. I do remember that much.'

With a fine show of indirection Detective Inspector Sloan took out his notebook and said, 'If you remember, Jack, we had promised to come back to interview your foreman . . .'

'I've told Russ,' interrupted Mandy Lamb. 'He's on his way over from the packing shed this minute.'

Anthony Berra stirred and said to Jack Haines that it was high time he was on his way and that he would pick up the plinth he wanted from the yard before he went over to see the admiral. He gave a valedictory wave of his hand to them all as he left whilst Detective Constable Crosby edged his way towards a corner of the office where there was a kettle and a row of mugs standing beside the coffee jar. He stood in front of these like a dog awaiting its dinner.

Jack Haines looked up as the door opened again. 'Ah, here's my foreman now,' he said. He turned to the newcomer. 'Good, I'm glad you've turned up, Russ. The police want to talk to you.'

'Any time,' said the man, shrugging his shoulders. He looked across at the two policemen and jerked his head in the general direction of the greenhouses. 'About this massacre, I suppose? Terrible, isn't it? There was weeks of work there – we'll never catch up, will we, boss? Not this season, anyway.'

Jack Haines shook his head and said sadly, 'No way, Russ. No way. Not now.'

'We need to know when you left here last night,' said Sloan to the foreman. 'It could be important.'

'Same time as usual,' said Russ Aqueel, shrugging his shoulders again. 'Must have been about half five. The others had knocked off prompt at five as normal but I came over to the office and signed off some timesheets for her ladysh . . . for Mandy here.'

Mandy Lamb tossed her head and gave a disdainful sniff in the background but said nothing.

'Then,' went on the foreman, 'I checked all the greenhouse doors and,' he added belligerently, 'I can tell you before you ask that they were all closed when I left. Every last one.'

'Sure, Russ,' put in Jack Haines uneasily.

'And number one properly watered and heated,' insisted the foreman, 'and steamy as it should be for the orchids. I checked the humidity in there before I locked the main gate and left.'

'In that case, sir,' said Sloan to the foreman, 'you won't have any objection to having your fingerprints taken by my constable here.'

The foreman thrust a grimy paw towards Crosby. 'Be my guest, mate.'

'After you've washed your hands if you don't mind,' said that worthy.

'There's a tap out the back,' said the man, turning. 'I'll be back in a minute.'

Detective Inspector Sloan sat back, saying casually to Jack Haines as if by way of conversation, 'You don't happen to know a man called Norman Potts, do you?'

The nurseryman visibly stiffened. 'Of course I know him, Inspector. He's my stepson,' he said between gritted teeth.

'Coffee?' said Mandy Lamb into the silence.

'I thought you'd never ask,' said Detective Constable Crosby.

'I had hoped I'd seen the last of him when his mother died,' growled Haines. 'But no such luck. He sued me for more of her estate than she'd left him. And lost.' He took a deep breath and asked, 'What's he been up to now?'

'Nothing that I know of,' said Sloan blandly. 'Should I?'

'Harassment, for starters,' said Haines. 'Came here wanting me to tell him where his wife – his ex-wife, that is – was.'

'And?'

'I told him to get lost.'

'And did he?' enquired Crosby with interest.

'Haven't seen him since,' growled Haines. 'Or wanted to, come to that. Like I said, I had hoped I'd seen the last of him. He's nothing but trouble as far as I'm concerned. And to his ex-wife too, from all accounts.'

'Tell me,' invited Sloan.

CHAPTER EIGHT

Detective Inspector Sloan had barely settled back at his own desk at Berebury Police Station before he was summoned to Superintendent Leeyes' office.

'Have you got anything else to add to this peculiar shopping list of yours, Sloan?' asked his superior officer testily.

'Not just yet, sir, thank you.' The reported iniquities of Norman Potts as a husband and stepson had slid easily off Jack Haines' tongue. They comprised a catalogue of domestic violence and included a threat heard by Haines to take revenge on a woman – and the legal profession – whom Potts swore to Jack Haines had stripped him of half his worldly wealth by way of a divorce.

Perhaps, noted Sloan, Norman Potts had already taken revenge too, on a nurseryman who had refused to play ball with a disgruntled stepson. The policeman didn't know that.

Not yet.

And Jack Haines certainly wasn't saying anything about that.

Not yet, either.

Sloan gave the superintendent an edited version of Norman Potts' reputation as represented by his stepfather and his former wife.

Leeyes grunted.

The detective inspector glanced down at his notebook. 'So, sir, I've put out a general call for this Norman Potts as a witness in connection with damage caused at the two nurseries.'

'In connection with,' Superintendent Leeyes rolled the phrase round his tongue appreciatively. 'I like it. Non-committal, and better than that old chestnut about helping the police with their enquiries.'

'Yes, sir.' In his time, Sloan been assaulted by men said to be helping the police with their enquiries and it hadn't been of any help at all.

'The press don't like anything non-committal,' said the superintendent with some satisfaction. 'By the way, Sloan, did I say that I've put you down for your personal development discussion for Friday morning?'

'Right, sir. Thank you, sir.' He swallowed. 'I'll make a note of that. And in the meantime,' Sloan plunged on, 'Crosby is checking on the other local nurseries to see if they've had any trouble too. Although,' he added realistically, 'I would have thought we'd have heard by now if they had.'

'Perhaps there's an orchid-hater at large,' suggested the superintendent. 'Can't stand 'em myself.'

'And in the matter of the MISSPER . . .' began Sloan. He wasn't very fond of orchids himself either but didn't think this was the moment to say so.

'I don't like Missing Persons cases, either,' trumpeted Leeyes immediately. 'Never have. In my experience they're neither fish, flesh nor good red herring. If you find them alive and kicking nobody gives you any credit for it. Worse than that, if they didn't want to be found in the first place, you get all the blame and if you find them dead, then you get all the blame too.'

'Up to a point, sir.' He coughed. 'There are one or two matters to be noted about Enid Osgathorp's absence, though. I think she is unlikely to have extended her holiday voluntarily since she had arranged to collect some orchids for a demonstration she had agreed to give tomorrow evening. They're still waiting for her to pick up at Jack Haines' place.'

Leeyes sniffed. 'They weren't caught up in the general orchid destruction then?'

'No.'

'I wonder why not?' he mused.

'I couldn't say, sir. Not at this stage.'

'And this battered wife . . .'

'We don't know that she was actually battered . . .' protested Sloan.

'Emotionally battered, then,' said Leeyes, who didn't normally admit to believing in the existence of the condition.

'Marilyn Potts,' said Sloan, 'was quite guarded about

him.' He hoped his personal development interview with the superintendent would be less challenging than this one.

'Do I understand that she's the one who is going to give this talk on orchids instead of the missing person?'

'That's what I was told, sir.'

'So you've haven't got very far, have you?'

'Not yet, sir,' said Sloan, biting down hard on any response at risk of jeopardising the aforementioned personal development interview.

The superintendent reached forward into his in-tray for a piece of paper. 'Well, you'll be pleased to hear that you've got your search warrant. You'd better go and have another look at Canonry Cottage before anyone else gets in there and muddies the waters.'

Mary Feakins reluctantly made the effort to heave herself out of her chair at the kitchen table of The Hollies where she had been taking a little rest between times. Then she walked towards the sink belatedly to begin washing up the breakfast dishes. She hadn't been able to face doing them earlier, bending over being a sure invitation to nausea. Today her routine domestic activities had been disturbed not only by the bout of morning sickness that had come on first thing but by their visits to the plant nursery and their lawyer in Berebury.

Until she reached the kitchen sink the only thoughts in her mind had been an imaginary confrontation with her doctor in which she was challenging him in the matter of morning sickness and his promises that hyperemesis gravida would not in the nature of things last for much longer.

She stood at the sink for a moment or two, hesitating while wondering whether bending over it now would still bring about another wave of sickness. There was a window above the sink and she allowed her glance to stray outside and into the back garden while she steadied herself against the working surface and tried to suppress the rising feeling of sickness. What she could see there was an unexpected pyramid of white smoke that suddenly billowed out into a cloud that obscured her view from the window. Just as quickly the smoke dispersed and she was able to take a second look and saw that it was rising from a burning pile of rubbish. Beside it was the figure of her husband who appeared to be furiously piling more and more things on the bonfire.

The washing up abandoned, she opened the back door and sailed across the garden towards the bonfire. 'Benedict Feakins, what on earth do you think you're doing out here?'

'Just having a simple bonfire,' he said, poking something under a pile of leaves. 'Nothing more, nothing less.'

'But look at what you're putting on it.' She frowned. 'That looks like a hairbrush to me.'

'It is,' he said, his back still bent almost double.

'And surely that's a toothbrush, isn't it?'

'Yes. It's only some of Dad's old things, that's all.' Benedict kept his head down and muttered, 'I cleared out his bedroom this morning. Everything there reminded me of him too much.'

She stared at him and then said in a softer tone, 'I didn't think you minded losing him so much as that.'

'Well, I did,' he mumbled, trying to straighten up, 'and that's all there is to it.'

'Sorry.' Mary Feakins stepped back a pace.

'I'm getting rid of all Dad's clothes too,' he said, a rising note in his voice. 'I just can't stand seeing all his things everywhere. They're going to the charity shop first thing tomorrow morning.'

'I understand,' she said, all womanly sympathy now.

'I can't explain the feeling,' he said in a choked voice. 'It came over me like a tidal wave yesterday and made me feel quite wretched.'

'There's lots of things that can't be explained,' said his wife cheerfully. 'Like my pica gravidarum.' From quite early on in her pregnancy, Mary Feakins had developed a marked predilection for cold herring. 'The doctor tells me that it's quite common.'

'Your craving fetishes are quite different, Mary,' he said seriously. 'This isn't like eating coal. It's more like . . . oh, I don't know that I can put it into words.'

'Don't even try,' she said kindly. 'Look here, I'll go back indoors and let you get on with it.'

'Bless you,' he said and obviously meant it.

Mary was bent over the sink again and was lowering some dirty plates into it when she was struck by a sudden thought. Wiping her soapy hands on a towel, she left the sink and went into their sitting room. Standing on the sofa table there was a studio photograph of her late father-in-law set in a silver frame. Lifting it carefully, she carried it out of the room and upstairs. Then she laid it safely under some spare sheets inside the linen cupboard. Benedict Feakins never opened the doors of the linen cupboard.

She was back at the kitchen sink in no time at all. Minutes later, a new and different thought in her mind now, she went back to the sitting room. The first time she had been concentrating on the photograph of her father-in-law but now she was looking for something that wasn't there but had been yesterday.

The urn containing Benedict's father's cremated ashes which were awaiting burial in Pelling churchyard was missing.

Detective Constable Crosby came into Detective Inspector Sloan's office and laid his notebook down on the desk. 'I've done the rounds of the other nurseries, sir, like you said. Seen the lot of them and none of them have had their greenhouse doors left open last night or at any other time. Joe Girdler hasn't got any greenhouses, anyway. Only roses. Rows and rows of them. Out of doors.'

'Him, I know,' said Sloan, quondam rosarian.

'The Leanaig brothers have got lots of greenhouses but no orchids and nothing at all happened at their place last night,' said Crosby. He suddenly realised that he needed to consult his notebook again and reached across Sloan's desk to retrieve it. 'Excuse me, sir.' He flicked over a page or two. 'Staple St James Nurseries only do hardy plants and the Berebury Garden Centre has greenhouses galore although only one with orchids in. They say they had no trouble last night but . . .' He fell silent.

'But?' prompted Sloan. In the last analysis a policeman relied on his sense of smell – that indefinable feeling that things weren't what they should be – a feeling that couldn't be put into words and some held couldn't be taught. It was something he was waiting to see if Detective Constable Crosby had.

'But their head honcho, Bob Steele, wasn't happy with the police coming there.' He wrinkled his nose. 'I could tell. He was edgy. Demanded to know why we'd come to see him before I could get a word in. Not a happy bunny.'

'Did you ask him if he knew Norman Potts?' Perhaps, after all, Crosby was developing that sense of smell. Aggressive interviewees always had an agenda of their own. Idly, Sloan wondered what it could be with Bob Steele.

The constable nodded. 'I did, like you said, sir. He told me he'd heard the name, that's all. He was quite cagey about it.'

'Or Capstan Purlieu Plants?'

'He knew them all right. Real specialists, he called the two women. Didn't sound as if he particularly liked them, though, or was bothered about them as competitors.' Crosby scratched his head. 'Called 'em small fry.'

'And Jack Haines and his nursery at Pelling?' said Sloan, deciding that it didn't sound as if the great gardening Goliath that was the Berebury Garden Centre was all that worried about the little David of the gardening world that was Capstan Purlieu Plants either. 'What did he say about him?'

'Bob Steele said he knew him too. He went a bit quiet when I started asking him a bit more about Jack Haines and he clammed up straightaway. He said he didn't know all that much more about either Haines or his nursery except in the way of trade.'

'And Enid Osgathorp?'

'Said he'd never heard of her but that there were a lot of old lady gardeners about, gardening being the new sex, and he couldn't be expected to know them all or t'other from which, could he?'

Detective Inspector Sloan lifted a sheet of paper off his desk. 'I can tell you that there is someone who has heard of her, Crosby. The receptionist at a hotel in the wilds of Carmarthenshire. She got in touch with us after getting our general request. She says they had been expecting a Miss Enid Osgathorp of Pelling to arrive there three weeks ago. She'd made the booking about a couple of months ago for a fortnight's stay, full board, earlier this month. She never showed up at their hotel, though.' Sloan read out from the piece of paper. 'The Meadgrove Park Country House Hotel.'

'Sounds posh, sir.'

'It's not bad,' said Sloan warmly, quoting from the paper in front of him. 'Five star, set in ten acres of landscape, extensive gardens, notable cuisine, fine wines and good fishing. You name it and it seems the Meadgrove Park Country House Hotel would appear to have it.'

'Does herself well, then, this Miss Osgathorp, when she's not at home,' concluded Crosby, whose landlady was notable for her cheese-paring.

'It would have set her back a good bit more than your average bed and breakfast,' agreed Detective Inspector Sloan. Holidays in the Sloan household usually had to be traded against the redecoration of the sitting room or saving for the long overdue replacement of the family car.

Crosby frowned. 'There was nothing very grand about that bungalow of hers in Pelling, though, was there, sir?

Looked very ordinary from the outside to me.' He sniffed. 'And on the small side too.'

'Perhaps,' said Sloan, rising to his feet, 'we shall find it very different from the inside. Let's go and see for ourselves now we've got the search warrant.'

Canonry Cottage, though, was as ordinary on the inside as it had been on the outside. It was furnished in the simple, spare style that had been popular forty years before and was – save for a light scattering of dust on the flat surfaces equating to three weeks without dusting – very neat and clean. Such ornaments as there were could only be described as tourist trophies – and that kindly.

The two policemen had entered with care aided by a set of keys only allowed out of the police station on a very secure basis, the distinction between master keys and skeleton ones being only a semantic one. They noted again the postal delivery that had been pushed back over the hall carpet when the door had been opened before. Sloan peered down at a postmark. 'Someone didn't come in here until almost a week after the missing person is said to have left,' he said, straightening up again, frowning. 'That's very odd.'

Detective Constable Crosby screwed up his face in thought. 'Then whoever came in had plenty of time, didn't they, sir, if they thought they had another week before she was due back home?'

'Or if they knew she wasn't ever coming back,' said Sloan softly. 'Had you thought about that, Crosby?'

'But . . .'

'That is, if she ever went away and they knew that too,'

said Sloan soberly. 'Remember Crosby, in police work all eventualities always have to be considered.'

'But two people saw her leave,' objected the constable. 'The woman next door and that gardener guy.'

'Two people said they saw her leave,' Sloan reminded him, 'which is something quite different. Better make quite sure she's not upstairs, Crosby.'

'Yes, sir,' said Crosby stolidly, dutifully peeling off and doing as he was bid.

'And watch where you're standing when you come back,' called Sloan after him. 'We know someone's been in and out of here through that back window as well as the front door and we need to take some carpet prints.'

'Yes, sir,' repeated Crosby. After a moment he said 'Why didn't that one go out of the front door instead?'

'Because, Crosby, the front door has a mortice lock. Presumably the missing person locked it behind her when she left and took the key with her.'

'But someone else came in and out with it,' said the constable, 'didn't they, sir?'

'It looks very much like it,' said Sloan, liking the situation less and less. 'Now, get upstairs, Crosby.'

Detective Inspector Sloan, himself sticking to the outer edges of the carpet, made first for a little bureau in the corner of the sitting room. It was unlocked. Donning rubber gloves and prising its lid open without leaving his own fingerprints on the wooden flap, he examined its contents carefully. Inside were a series of pigeon-holes and a little drawer. This drawer, too, was unlocked. It contained a few photographs of a child – one of which had 'Me at four' written on the back – and a locket. This had a lock of hair in it. The words 'Little Lucy Locket' welled into Sloan's mind from his sister's infancy – before he started to make notes.

'Anything there, sir?' asked Crosby, bringing Sloan's attention back to the matter in hand. 'Nothing to speak of upstairs except that I would say someone's had a good rummage through the wardrobe, everything else being neat and that a bit topsy-turvy. If that's where she kept her gin, it's gone.'

'Nothing out of the ordinary here, either,' said Sloan, replacing bundles of carefully tied domestic accounts in their pigeon holes one by one, 'except that I think someone's been looking for a secret drawer in here. Someone who didn't know about secret drawers in desks.'

Detective Constable Crosby, who obviously didn't know anything about them either, leant over Sloan's shoulder for a better look. 'Made a bit of a mess of the wood, didn't he, sir?' he observed. 'All those scratches . . .'

'Whoever it was brought a screwdriver with him – I expect he thought the bureau might be locked – but it didn't get him anywhere because I should say this bit of modern furniture hasn't got a secret compartment of any sort. They don't make 'em liked they used to,' said Sloan and stopped. He would have to be more careful about expressing that sort of sentiment, afraid that he was beginning to sound like the superintendent.

'So, sir,' said Crosby, screwing up his forehead into a prodigious frown, 'that means that someone's been in here just looking for something not someone.' His expression brightened. 'Unless the old lady's been abducted.'

'And perhaps not finding anything,' announced Sloan presently, after leafing through the last of the contents of the pigeonholes, 'although I should say that they – whoever they are – have probably been all through this bureau. There's nothing but receipted household bills and plant stuff in here, though some of the bundles have been put back upside down. Oh, and there are a couple of receipts for deposits for two pricey foreign holidays this summer. Very pricey indeed.'

'Some people have all the luck,' said the constable, who was saving up to go to the motor-racing at Spa-Francorchamps.

'We don't know, though, whether the intruders had any luck or not,' mused Detective Inspector Sloan, moving away from the bureau. 'They might well have found what they were looking for and taken it away. Either of them.'

'Or both,' said Crosby.

Sloan nodded absently as he paused at a framed photograph on the mantelshelf. It was of a group on a platform where a clergyman was presenting a bouquet and an envelope to a dumpy late middle-aged woman who was holding out one hand to receive them and shaking the clergyman's hand with the other. The words 'Happy Retirement, Miss Osgathorp' could be picked out on a banner at the back of the platform.

'Get on with circulating copies of the picture of this woman getting the presentation, Crosby,' commanded Sloan, picking up the photograph, 'and chase the railway people for a sight of their CCTV record of people entering Berebury station the day she was meant to be catching a train there now we've got a picture to go on.'

'When exactly would that have been, sir?' the constable asked, searching for a pen. 'Do we know?'

'We do. Norah, the woman next door, told us, remember? It was the day after Mrs Beddowes, the rector's wife, committed suicide. You can find that out quite easily.' Sloan paused and took another look at the man in the clerical collar in the photograph making the presentation. 'And that presumably is Mr Beddowes, the rector, widower of the deceased. We might have a word with him in due course. And with that landscape designer fellow – Anthony Berra – again. He seems to have been the last person to see Enid Osgathorp alive.'

'So far,' said Crosby lugubriously.

CHAPTER NINE

'Not much luck with those replacements, boss,' said Russ Aqueel, his foreman, leading Jack Haines out to the truck standing in the yard. 'A bit of this and that, that's all. Nothing like enough to replace what's been lost, though.' He shrugged his shoulders. 'As for keeping it all quiet, it's a laugh. The Leanaig boys guessed something was up straightaway when they saw what it was we were looking for and the people at Staple St James had heard already over the grapevine . . .'

'Some grapevine,' commented Haines richly.

'So I told Bob Steele at the Berebury Garden Centre anyway.' He studied his employer's face. 'I hope that's OK?'

'It's OK, Russ,' said Jack Haines quietly. 'I reckoned word would get around pretty quickly.'

'Bound to,' said the foreman, pausing.

'It's not every day that someone sabotages a firm's working stock, is it, Russ?' said Haines, giving the man a very straight look.

'Definitely not,' said Russ.

'The plants we were wanting . . .' prompted Haines.

'Bob Steele at the Berebury Garden Centre didn't have anything we wanted.'

'I didn't think he would have,' said Haines almost to himself. 'Not him.'

'But he did say that he had run out of Erysimum Bowles Mauve and if we had any to spare could I drop them over to him,' said the foreman.

'Sure,' said Haines dully.

Russ shot him a quizzical glance before going on. 'The Leanaig boys had quite a bit that would do for us and so did Staple St James Nurseries but both of them only had some of the things we lost – not all of them.'

Haines sighed. 'That figures. Anthony Berra was very precise. That's part of the problem.'

'I'd call him a right fusspot myself,' muttered the foreman.

'But none of them has had any trouble themselves, have they?' asked Haines quickly.

'Not that they said or I saw,' replied the foreman. 'I guess that it's just us.'

That it wasn't just Jack Haines who had had trouble overnight was not borne in upon him until Marilyn Potts arrived at his nursery.

Jack Haines had made his way back to his office deep in thought. He had only just sat down and Mandy Lamb had only just automatically put the kettle on when she looked out of the window and suddenly said, 'Here comes trouble . . .'

'There can't be any more trouble,' said Jack Haines, staying where he was.

'Have a look for yourself,' said his secretary.

He lumbered to his feet and went to the window. 'I don't believe it. Not her. I thought we'd seen the last of her.'

'Well, you haven't,' said Mandy Lamb, not without a certain relish.

'What does she want, do you suppose?'

'Half your worldly wealth, I expect,' she said pertly. 'That was what Norman wanted, wasn't it?'

'You don't have to tell me that,' he said, turning back to his chair. 'And it's not quite true anyway – what he wanted was all of his mother's worldly wealth, not half of mine.'

'Hello, Jack,' Marilyn Potts said cautiously, putting her head half way round the office door.

'Long time, no see,' said Jack Haines.

'I suppose I'd better throw my hat in first,' she grimaced, 'and see what happens to it.'

'No need for that,' he said gruffly. 'That's unless you've brought that no-good ex-husband of yours with you.'

'God forbid,' responded Marilyn Potts explosively. 'I've had enough trouble with Norman to last me a lifetime, thank you.'

'Me too,' grunted Jack.

'No, I've come to pick up Enid Osgathorp's orchids – I'm standing in for her at a talk she was supposed to be giving over at Staple St James tomorrow night because she seems to have gone walkabout.'

'So what's happened to our Miss Osgathorp, then?' asked Jack.

'No one knows. She'll turn up sooner or later I expect like the proverbial bad penny. She won't be happy when she hears what's happened to all my infant orchids, that's for sure . . . they're all dead and she reckons she's a bit of an orchid fancier.'

'Yours too?' Jack Haines' eyebrows shot up. 'God Almighty.'

Marilyn Potts launched into a histrionic account of the devastation at the nursery at Capstan Purlieu.

'Every last orchid,' declared Marilyn bitterly. 'There was the devil of a frost last night.'

'Don't I know it,' said Haines savagely. He peered at her closely. 'But let me ask you something else, Marilyn. Do you know Bob Steele at the Berebury Garden Centre?'

'Don't be silly, Jack. Of course, I do.'

'Has he been over to your place recently?'

She frowned. 'I think Anna said that he'd called round to pick up some Aeschymanthus a couple of weeks back. Said he'd run out of Mona Lisa.' She looked at him suspiciously. 'Why do you ask?'

'Nothing. I just wondered.'

'You lie, Jack.'

'I suppose I do,' he admitted. 'You see rumour has it that Bob Steele has plans to go in for orchids himself.'

'Rumours aren't everything.'

'He made an excuse to come over here to pick up some stock he didn't need.'

'He might have really wanted the Aeschymanthus from us,' she said doubtfully.

'He might,' agreed Haines, 'but I wondered if he was really casing the joints – yours and mine.'

'Whatever for?'

'Seeing how he could undermine the opposition, perhaps.'

Her voice rose to a high doh. 'Are you suggesting Bob Steele targeted our orchids?'

'He could have done . . .'

Marilyn Potts took a deep breath and drew herself up to her full height. 'I know you won't want to do anything of the sort but let's face it, Jack, the only person we know who hates both of us enough to wreak real damage on the pair of us is Norman Potts.' She swallowed. 'And you know that as well as I do so don't pretend that you don't because it won't wash.'

'If we look sharp,' said Detective Inspector Sloan, clambering into the police car, 'we might just be able to see those other two customers of Jack Haines who've lost their plants before we get back to the station.' He latched his seat belt into place, adding 'And that, I must remind you, Crosby, doesn't amount to a licence to kill.'

'No, sir. Of course not, sir.' The constable sounded injured.

'The Park at Pelling first,' decided Sloan. 'We'll see what the Navy has to say.'

The Navy in the person of Rear Admiral Waldo Catterick, R.N., retired, and as bald as a billiard ball, thought that there was altogether too much vandalism about everywhere these days and had the policemen seen the graffiti on the cricket pavilion?

'Not yet,' said Sloan ambiguously.

'Deplorable. Don't know what the world is coming to. Come along in anyway.'

'We're checking up on some unexplained losses at Jack Haines' nursery, including yours,' explained Sloan as they followed him down a corridor, the old gentleman's right leg giving an odd involuntary little kick forward as he walked. 'And out at Capstan Purlieu too.'

Sitting the two policemen down in a small morning room overlooking a lawn, the admiral leant forward and asked what exactly he could do for them.

Detective Inspector Sloan regarded the wizened face opposite him, made to seem smaller and older somehow by a nose so depressed as not to have a bridge. 'We're trying to make sure, sir, that there isn't anyone out there with a grudge against gardeners in general or any of Jack Haines' or Capstan Purlieu's customers in particular and I have been given to understand you are one of them.'

The admiral took the question seriously and said in a curiously high-pitched voice, 'None that I am aware of but as you will know yourself, Inspector, if you've ever been in command, you're bound to have upset somebody at some time or other. You can't run a tight ship without doing that.'

'Put him in the scuppers until he's sober,' chanted Crosby under his breath.

'Comes with the job,' said the admiral, who did not appear to have heard this.

It came with the police job too. Detective Inspector Sloan had upset a good many bad men in his time and said so.

114

'You're not in the Service to make friends,' barked Waldo Catterick in his best quarter-deck manner, 'although of course you do. Old shipmates and all that.' He looked up with a distinctly rheumy eye at the photographs of ships' companies that adorned the walls of the room. 'Most of them are dead now.'

You weren't in the police force to make friends either, thought Sloan to himself. On the contrary, often enough, it was in the nature of police work that enemies always outnumbered friends. 'We're also,' the detective inspector went on almost conversationally, 'looking into the disappearance of an old lady from the village. A Miss Enid Osgathorp. Do you know her?'

The admiral stiffened perceptibly, his back suddenly becoming ramrod straight. 'She used to work at the doctor's,' he said frostily, in tones that would have paralysed the lower deck, 'and that's all I can tell you about the woman.'

His body language, though, was saying something quite different to the police inspector, a man perforce experienced in these matters. Whether it was all he could say or not, the admiral refused to be drawn any further on Enid Maude Osgathorp. Perhaps, thought Sloan, a boyhood reader of Bulldog Drummond and similar clubland heroes, it wasn't done then to mention a lady's name in the Wardroom any more than it was in an Army Mess. He couldn't begin to think what today's young women would make of that.

Detective Inspector Sloan came away from Pelling Park with the uneasy feeling that he had missed something. Oddly enough he was sure it was nothing to do with the missing person but try as he might he couldn't put his finger on what it was that was eluding him.

'I expect he got them to walk the plank as well,' said Crosby as they left the Park.

'There's one thing for sure,' said Sloan, 'and that's that our missing person is not the flavour of the month. I think, Crosby, this is something we should be looking into. I wonder why the admiral didn't like her.' He tucked the fact away in the back of his mind for further consideration.

It was Mary Feakins who answered the doorbell at The Hollies, more puzzled than alarmed by a visit from the police. 'Benedict? Yes, he's here. He's off work with a bad back just now.' She led the way through to the kitchen where her husband was sitting uncomfortably wedged in a Windsor chair, his back cushioned against a hot-water bottle.

If his wife had been calm enough as Detective Inspector Sloan and Detective Constable Crosby arrived, Benedict Feakins certainly wasn't. He started to struggle to his feet. 'Police?' he echoed. 'What? Why?'

'Routine enquiry, sir,' said Sloan comfortably.

Feakins subsided back into his chair. 'What about?'

'I understand you had some plants being grown for you by Jack Haines,' said Sloan.

'Yes,' he agreed warily. 'But I changed my mind about them and I told Jack I didn't want them any more. To be quite honest . . .'

'Always a good idea,' said Crosby under his breath.

'I didn't think I – that is, we – could afford them after all.'

'Mortgage trouble, sir?' said Detective Inspector Sloan sympathetically. The state of their mortgage was a monthly topic with his wife in his own home.

Benedict Feakins shook his head. 'No, not that. I inherited this house when my father died but even so we're finding the upkeep's quite a struggle. I did tell Jack Haines that I'd still have the shrubs I'd ordered, though, and he seemed to be all right with that.'

'For the border in the front garden,' explained Mary Feakins. 'It was digging that up to get ready for them that did for Benedict's back.'

'We saw he'd been at it in the way in,' remarked Crosby conversationally. 'Didn't get very far, did you, sir?'

'I had to give after a bit,' admitted Benedict Feakins. 'I did too much at one go. I've been bent like a hoop ever since.'

'Easily done,' said Sloan, who grew roses because a policeman could tend them in small pockets of time and leave them at short notice when summoned to attend to malfeasance anywhere in 'F' Division. 'I see you've just had a bonfire too,' he remarked, looking out of the kitchen window and observing wisps of smoke rising at the bottom of garden. 'Back not too bad for that, then, sir?'

Feakins flushed and mumbled something about having some things to burn.

Mary Feakins cast her husband a sympathetic wifely look and then said, 'Inspector, I must explain that my husband was getting rid of some personal things of his late father's. He's only just lost him and he was finding it very distressing to have them still around and reminding him of his recent loss so he decided to get rid of them.'

'Quite so,' said Detective Inspector Sloan. He rose as if to leave, something every policeman knew caused the person being interviewed to lower their guard. 'Well, since we don't at this time know why Jack Haines' greenhouses were damaged, we're just checking that none of his customers with plants in them had any personal enemies.'

The expression on Benedict Feakins' face was one of comic relief. 'Inspector,' he said solemnly, 'you can put me down as a latter-day Kim.'

'Sir?'

'Kipling's Little Friend of All the World.'

'Really, sir?' said Sloan. He'd always found that author's poem 'If' set an impossible standard of male behaviour and – worse – made a man feel a failure if he didn't measure up to it.

Crosby merely looked sceptical.

Benedict Feakins turned to his wife. 'That's right, darling, isn't it?'

'I don't think we're very popular with the butcher, the baker and the candlestick-maker just now,' she said obliquely.

Benedict turned back to the two policemen. 'As I said, we're finding living here a bit expensive, Inspector, that's all.'

Sloan nodded. 'Thank you, sir. We'll be on our way, then. Come along, Crosby.' He made another move to leave, paused and then he said casually, 'By the way, we're also quite concerned about someone who's gone missing from Pelling. An Enid Osgathorp. Did you know her?'

There was another change in the man's demeanour. He

sank back in his chair and seemed somehow diminished. 'Oh, yes, Inspector,' Benedict replied in a hollow voice. 'I knew her all right. She's been around in Pelling a long time. She worked at the doctor's.'

'Miss Osgathorp?' said Mary Feakins, coming to life suddenly. 'Wasn't she that odd old woman who came to see you one evening a while ago, Benedict?' She wrinkled her nose. 'I didn't really like her.'

Her husband moistened his lips and essayed a weak smile. 'Yes, that's her.'

'When would that have been exactly, sir?' asked Sloan.

'Oh, weeks ago now, Inspector,' he said.

'Don't you remember, darling?' interjected Mary Feakins eagerly. 'It was just before she went away.' She turned to the two policemen. 'She said she was going off on holiday somewhere the next morning and needed to see Benedict before she left. Quite insistent, she was.'

Her husband gave her a look of such great malevolence that she had never seen on his face before. It quite frightened her and she recoiled as if she had been stung.

'Really, sir?' said Sloan, seeing this look too, and turning back. 'Can you tell us anything more?'

'What do you mean?' he asked.

'Like why she came to see you, sir.'

He flushed. 'She came to remind me of something, that's all. And I hadn't forgotten anyway.'

A rapid change of subject was just another of the techniques that his old Station Sergeant had taught Sloan about questioning. He said now, 'Would you happen to know a Norman Potts by any chance, sir?'

Feakins looked blank. 'No. Why?'

119

'Another routine enquiry, sir,' said that officer blandly. 'That's all. Thank you, sir. We'll be off now.'

Crosby paused on their way out of the garden at The Hollies and looked at the newly dug earth. 'Long enough for a grave,' he observed, 'but not wide enough or deep enough.'

Detective Inspector Sloan was concentrating on something quite different. 'When we get back, Crosby, remind me to think of a legal way we could get a good look at what's in that bonfire. Remember, Benedict Feakins is someone else who knew that Enid Osgathorp was going to be away.'

'Someone else?' asked Crosby who hadn't been paying attention. 'Oh, yes. That gardener fellow who took her to the station – Anthony Berra.'

'And we really need to find out what it was that young man Feakins was burning on that bonfire, the one he got so agitated about and wasn't in too much pain to build.'

'He wasn't all that happy when his wife started talking about Enid Osgathorp either,' contributed Crosby. 'I could see that.'

'So,' said Sloan, 'we're just going to seem to drive away and lie up out of sight of the house and keep an eye on what our Benedict Feakins does next.'

What Benedict Feakins did next was to hobble out of his house at speed into the back garden and rake over the embers of the bonfire very vigorously indeed.

CHAPTER TEN

The Reverend Tobias Beddowes, rector of Pelling, received the two policemen in his study at the rectory there with nothing beyond a courteous greeting and a hasty warning not to fall over a bicycle aslant in the hall. The room was untidy to the point of disorder, the clergyman having to remove piles of books and papers from both chairs before the others could sit down.

'I apologise for the muddle,' he said, looking helplessly round the room, 'but I'm on my own with the two younger children now and things aren't getting done.'

'We were sorry to hear about the loss of your wife,' said Detective Inspector Sloan formally, grasping a conversational nettle ducked by most of his parishioners.

The rector shook his head. 'A very sad business. My elder daughter will be back soon, though, and that will help. She's very good. She'll see to things.'

'Been away, has she?' asked Crosby insouciantly.

'Honeymoon,' explained Tobias Beddowes briefly. 'Naturally, she and her husband couldn't get away straightaway after the wedding ceremony.'

'Naturally?' echoed Crosby as his superior officer stirred uneasily.

'Naturally there had to be an inquest,' sighed Beddowes. 'My dear wife . . . she died just before the wedding, you see. It was all too much for her, you know. The arrangements and the expense and all that just got on top of her.' He took a deep breath and said, 'Now, what was it you wanted to see me about, gentlemen?'

'It's a photograph,' said Detective Inspector Sloan, handing over the one he had abstracted from Canonry Cottage. 'I hope it won't distress you if your wife is on it too.'

The rector scanned the photograph of the presentation to Enid Osgathorp proffered by Detective Inspector Sloan and shook his head. 'No, my wife isn't on this. She didn't come with me that evening.' He lifted his head as if doing so was an effort and asked what it was they wanted him to tell them about the photograph.

'Miss Enid Osgathorp – is that her, shaking your hand?' asked Sloan.

'Yes indeed, Inspector, I can confirm that that is a picture of Enid Osgathorp taken in the village hall when she retired two or three years ago. She gave up work a little early because old Doctor Heddon had died and she didn't want to start afresh with anyone else, which is quite understandable. She had been with him for a very long time.' He went on looking at the photograph. 'Might I ask why you want to know?'

'Enid Osgathorp would appear to be missing from her home,' said Detective Inspector Sloan.

'Really? She does go away a lot of course, you know,' said the clergyman. 'She's become quite a traveller since she retired. I expect she'll be back soon.'

'She hasn't arrived at her destination,' said Sloan.

'Or left word,' added Crosby unnecessarily.

The rector raised his eyebrows. 'I don't think she would have left word anyway. She never said much about where she was going. She was always someone who kept herself to herself. A very private person, you might say.'

Detective Inspector Sloan, experienced policeman that he was, much preferred people who did not keep themselves to themselves. It could make detection more difficult.

'As to why she hasn't arrived,' said the clergyman, 'I'm afraid I can't help you. I think,' he added, smiling faintly, 'it would be fair to describe her as her own woman.'

'That, Crosby,' remarked Sloan as they walked away from the rectory and back to the car, 'usually means that the person they have in mind does what they like when they like.'

'Yes, sir, I'm sure.'

'Right, Crosby, go ahead and get some copies of that picture blown up and see what the sandwich shop has to say.'

'I can guess,' said the constable gloomily, 'that they serve dozens of old ladies every day . . .'

'Or,' Sloan completed the litany for him, 'that they can't remember yesterday, let alone three weeks ago.'

'That's right,' said Crosby.

'Don't forget we've got to find Norman Potts too. We'll try somewhere near the Railway Tavern pub in Berebury, down by the viaduct, first. That's where his wife thought he was living.'

'No, sir, I won't forget. He sounds a right bounder to me and the sooner we've got him, the better.'

'A policeman should not make judgements too early in an investigation,' Sloan reminded him. 'A prejudiced mind,' he added sententiously, 'is no good to an officer, and don't you forget it. Juries don't like it either. And in case you don't know it, they can detect a police prejudice half a mile away.'

'I won't forget, sir.' Crosby's face assumed an expression more commonly found on those of schoolboys reprimanded by their schoolteachers.

'And after we've started to look for the aforementioned Norman Potts, Crosby, you can check up with the bus company about how many tickets they sold on the ten to ten bus from Pelling into Berebury that morning.'

'But Enid Osgathorp didn't catch the bus, sir.'

'So it has been said by Anthony Berra,' pointed out Sloan, 'but we don't have any other witnesses to this yet. But anyone waiting at the bus stop might have seen or spoken to her and perhaps seen her being given a lift. Detection, Crosby, is largely a matter of checking every single thing. Remember that.' Sloan didn't know whether or not his attempts to train the constable in proper procedures would help in his own appraisal or not but there was no harm in trying. Surely Brownie points of any sort would help? On the other hand, on a bad day the superintendent was quite capable of blaming him for not catching Jack the Ripper.

'Yes, sir.'

'And find out how many of those at the bus stop used an old person's bus pass. Any other oldies there would have known Enid Osgathorp for sure.' He paused. 'Come to think of it, the whole village would know her if she had worked for the doctor.'

'Yes, sir.'

'Then, Crosby, you can see how far the railway people have got digging out their CCTV cassettes for us and how long they'll be about it.'

'They'll be semi-fast, I expect, sir.'

'Come again?'

'That's what they call their slow trains,' said Crosby, switching on the car engine.

'What you have to do, Sloan,' said the superintendent crisply 'is to make up your mind exactly what you're trying to do out at Pelling.'

'Yes, sir,' said Sloan, reminding himself that the upside of being back at the police station was the canteen there and he was hungry. The downside did not dare speak its name.

'The "in word" if I remember correctly,' the superintendent added, heavily sarcastic, since the idea that he would remember anything incorrectly was supposed to be thought risible, 'is prioritise. I just call it making up your mind.'

'Yes, sir,' said Sloan cautiously.

'Well?'

'I have. Made up my mind, I mean.' The detective inspector reminded himself to be careful with his choice of words. The superintendent was unpredictable at the best of times. 'The damage to the contents of the greenhouses out there and at Capstan Purlieu has been noted and I have been interviewing all those customers whose plants might have been targeted, but Enid Maude Osgathorp is definitely a missing person and perhaps at risk. Especially as some person or persons unknown would seem to have been in her cottage at some time,' he added carefully, 'and only presumably when she wasn't there.'

'Someone looking for something,' pronounced Leeyes swiftly.

'Or her,' said Sloan soberly.

'Or her,' agreed Leeyes.

'Twice,' said Sloan.

'You're not very clear, Sloan,' complained Leeyes.

'Presumably two people looking for something, sir,' said Sloan. 'But it would seem at different times and perhaps looking for different things. I don't know what. I think that both entries were probably effected after Enid Osgathorp had left but I don't know that either.'

'Ah, you've got a date for that, have you?'

'And her photograph, which we shall now be circulating,' said Sloan. 'We're on our way next to interview the last person known to have seen her and then I want to find out a bit more about a man called Benedict Feakins.'

'Leaving no stone unturned, Sloan, that's what I like to hear. Don't forget those damaged plants in the greenhouses out that way, even so. I don't like the sound of them. Not your run-of-the-mill damage.'

'I won't, sir.' He was tempted to say that that particular

problem could be downgraded since no one was at risk but decided against it. Tackling vandalism was always high on the superintendent's list of police priorities and so he definitely wouldn't want that put on the back-burner. The public probably found vandalism more threatening than the odd missing elderly party: they – and the newspapers – were certainly more vocal about it. 'I've got Crosby seeking the whereabouts of a man with a possible grudge about at least one of the parties concerned and the Scenes of Crime people are going over Canonry Cottage as we speak.'

'You have good reasons for saying all this, I take it?' said the superintendent, adding waspishly, 'Such as evidence.'

'I have, sir. Entry to Enid Osgathorp's cottage was clearly effected by two different methods – a key and a broken window.'

'So what stage are you at?' asked Leeyes, changing tack with disconcerting speed.

'Waiting for a report from the Scenes of Crime people,' Sloan answered automatically – and immediately regretted his speedy response. He should have taken more trouble with it: the superintendent favoured the considered reply. Being a bit late back with him was definitely preferable to an instant response.

'And what else?' his superior officer snapped.

'Replies to our enquiries, sir,' said Sloan, reaching for his notebook, 'including . . .'

'I don't want every last detail, Sloan,' he said testily, changing tack once again. 'Fill me in when you've got something concrete to report. I've got a meeting with the

Assistant Chief Constable about staffing before I can go home.'

Retreating as speedily as he could, Detective Inspector Sloan achieved his own office with relief. Crosby was waiting for him there.

'I've tracked Norman Potts down, sir,' he said. 'It wasn't difficult. He's listed as living just where his wife . . .'

'His ex-wife,' Sloan corrected him.

'Where his ex-wife said he would be, and that garden design bloke you wanted to talk to – the one who gave the missing party a lift into Berebury – he's over at Pelling Grange with his customers there just now . . .'

'I think he prefers to think of them as clients,' murmured Sloan, 'but never mind. Let's tackle him at his place of work first. I'd rather like to take a look at the garden at the Grange myself. It sounds interesting.'

Not only was Anthony Berra at Pelling Grange but his employers were in the garden with him when the two policemen arrived there. He was standing in the middle of a large flower bed that was empty save for a heavy plinth that he was lugging from place to place with some difficulty.

'Further to the right, Anthony,' called out Mrs Lingard, turning to the two visitors and saying plaintively, 'he will go on about the Golden Mean whatever that is.' She slipped effortlessly into hostess role as soon as Sloan explained his and Crosby's presence, while Anthony Berra lowered the plinth back where he had wanted it in the first place.

Charmian Lingard was now dressed in a suit of a mixture of light brown and blue coloured material, the lapels of the jacket of which hung so artfully that even Christopher Dennis Sloan, working husband, realised the whole ensemble was expensively understated. He made a mental note to remember it to describe it in detail to his wife, Margaret, and then just as quickly he made another decision not to. There was something about the fine cloth that bespoke of a different world.

'Anthony here,' Charmian Lingard went on, waving an arm, 'was just explaining his thinking about the new Mediterranean garden he's planting for us. It sounded so interesting. What was it, Anthony? Tall plants at the back, medium in the middle and short plants at the front . . .'

Crosby started to say something under his breath about rocket science.

'After that,' continued Charmian Lingard, who hadn't heard this, 'you have to choose flowers that flourish best in full sun, semi-shade and deep shade. Then flowers for spring, summer and autumn . . . and Buddleia at each end for butterflies.'

'All I really mentioned, Charmian,' protested Berra, 'was that the new Bergenias made good summer and winter foliage.'

She was undeterred and swept on. 'There was something you were saying about colour too, Anthony, wasn't there?'

The landscape designer looked embarrassed. 'Blues and yellows together, Charmian – hot colours massed in big clumps.'

Mrs Lingard said in a proprietary fashion, 'That wasn't all you said, Anthony.'

'This year, next year and five years on,' he said, rolling his eyes, man to man, in Sloan's direction.

'This year, next year, sometime never,' chanted Crosby. 'Cherry stones,' he explained to a bewildered audience. 'You know: tinker, tailor, soldier, sailor.'

'That will do, Crosby,' said Sloan repressively.

Charmian Lingard swept into the conversational void with a charming smile. 'Not, Inspector, that I am a five years ahead woman. It's this year for me, not even next.'

She would have been surprised had she known it how much she slipped down in Detective Inspector Sloan's estimation at this. In his credo, all good gardeners planned ahead. 'Quite so,' he said politely.

'But you say it's Anthony you've come to see, Inspector,' she said, turning to her husband. 'Come along, Oswald.'

'No need for you and the major to go, Charmian,' said Anthony Berra lightly. 'I didn't do it, Inspector, whatever it was, but I'll come quietly.'

'You took a Miss Enid Osgathorp to the station,' said Sloan.

'That's true.' He relaxed. 'So I did. I told you. Was that a crime?'

'Can you tell us again?' asked Sloan.

Charmian Lingard gave a tinkling laugh. 'It doesn't exactly sound like the Third Degree, Inspector.' Her only interaction with the police in life so far had been in the matter of fines for speeding (dealt with by the family solicitor) and parking tickets (paid for by an indulgent father). Her misdemeanours at boarding school had invariably been referred to the headmistress, a prudent woman very conscious of Charmian's family's worldly wealth and social connections. Somehow Charmian's transgressions there had therefore always managed to get left in the pending file. Any stepping over the line at her Swiss Finishing School had gone unrecorded.

'You see, we can't find Miss Osgathorp,' explained Detective Inspector Sloan, keeping his thoughts on the Third Degree to himself.

'Oh, I know her,' said Charmian Lingard, surprised. 'She was the funny old biddy who worked at the doctor's. What do the police want her for? Has she done something wrong?' She raised her eyes dramatically. 'Don't say she's a drug dealer?'

'She's been reported missing,' said Sloan baldly. 'And what we would like to do is to take some DNA material from your car, Mr Berra. With your permission, of course.'

'Sure,' said Berra. He waved an arm. 'It's over there.'

'How would that help,' intervened Charmian Lingard, 'if you haven't found her?' She examined Sloan's face. 'You haven't found her, have you?'

'No, madam. Not yet. We will, of course.'

'And I gave her a lift to the station,' said Anthony Berra to Charmian Lingard, abandoning his spade and leaping back onto the grass. 'And told the police so. She dumped her luggage on the front seat and sat on the back seat behind it. I think,' he said solemnly, 'she may have felt safer there. She has, I may say, always struck me as the archetypal spinster.'

'You can't be too careful if you're a woman on your own,' chanted Crosby sententiously. 'That's what we always teach the ladies.'

'That's what I tell my future intended too,' said Anthony Berra. He grinned. 'Not that she listens, I'm sure.'

'Where did you go after you'd dropped Miss Osgathorp off, sir?' asked Sloan.

The garden designer wrinkled his nose in recollection. 'A bit of shopping and then the bank, I think. Yes, of course, that's why I was going into Berebury that day anyway.'

'That would be the Calleshire and Counties, would it?' asked Crosby. 'On the Parade?'

'It would,' said Berra. 'My worldly wealth, such as it is, is in their hands.'

'Then where on earth did you manage to park?' asked Crosby with genuine professional curiosity.

'You may well ask, constable. In the Bellingham Hotel car park, actually,' said Berra. 'It's about the only free place but if you park there you have to eat there, so I did.'

Detective Constable Crosby nodded knowledgeably. 'That's what the notice in the car park says. "Park here, eat here".'

'So I did both,' said Anthony Berra neatly.

Detective Inspector Sloan raised something else on his agenda. 'Mrs Lingard, we are also looking into the break-in at Jack Haines' nursery. Just for the record, do you know of anyone who would have had a vested interest in the plants being raised for you not being available in time to be planted out properly?'

'I haven't offended anyone here that I am aware of,' she said stiffly, 'and Oswald's first wife is dead, if that's what you're getting at.'

Detective Inspector Sloan denied that it was.

'People can be quite jealous,' she went on with surprising bitterness, 'and of course one never knows with the old guard in any village.'

Sloan wasn't listening. He was concentrating on the meaningful look that Anthony Berra had cast in Oswald Lingard's direction at his wife's last remark. That old soldier, though, was taking good care not meet the other man's eye.

CHAPTER ELEVEN

Detective Inspector Sloan was still sitting in his office when Charlie Marsden, 'F' Division's Chief Scenes of Crime Officer, arrived back at the police station from Canonry Cottage at Pelling. Both Superintendent Leeyes and Detective Constable Crosby had long gone off duty. When Sloan had rung his wife, Margaret, to say he would be late back from work she had pointedly enquired the whereabouts of the other two.

'Gone home,' he admitted. 'Both of them.'

'The man in the middle,' she said, 'that's all you are, Christopher.'

'Someone's got to carry the can for the top and the bottom,' he responded, half-joking.

'Oppressed by those above and depressed by those below, if you ask me,' said his wife.

'So call me Common Man,' he said lightly.

'Have it your own way,' Margaret Sloan said, adding resignedly, 'it's a casserole, anyway.'

Not introspective, he decided that this did describe his state quite well. It described Common Man even better. Charlie Marsden, though, another man late for his supper tonight, could only be described as an enthusiast. Sloan found him cheering to listen to.

'Interesting little trip, Seedy,' reported the Scenes of Crime Officer, one professional to another. 'Challenging too. Gave the boys something to get their teeth into.'

'Tell me more, Charlie,' invited Sloan, leaning forward. 'All we had was a quick look.'

The man pulled up a chair and sat down opposite Sloan. 'You were quite right about there having been two entries. I can confirm that there have also been two quite separate searches in that cottage too, big time. With gloves on. That's what made it so interesting.'

'Big time for what, Charlie?'

'At a guess I should say papers of some sort. No sign of much disturbance in what we call domestic goods except that they've obviously been turned over by someone looking for papers. No ripping of sofas or cushions apart or anything flashy like that as you know . . .'

'Carpets not lifted?'

'Not that we could see but I would say that every single book has been opened and shaken about and then been put back on the shelf quite carefully by one of the intruders. Must have had plenty of time.'

'I think he or she . . .'

'They . . .'

'They probably had as much time as they wanted, Charlie, which is a worry in itself,' he admitted.

'Someone got in there with a key,' agreed Charlie Marsden tacitly.

'But you found no sign of actual theft, did you, any more than we did?'

'Not that we could spot. Nothing all that much worth taking there I should say . . .'

'Unless it's gone already,' put in Sloan automatically. 'We can't be too sure about that.'

'True, but there was nothing to suggest that there might have been great valuables there in the first place. You can always tell, you know.'

Detective Inspector Sloan did know. You only had to step into a house to get the feel for its owners. Just as his friend, Inspector Harpe, from Traffic Division, could tell a lot about the driver from a look at the car, he himself could usually tell what a house owner was like from the garden too. He leant back in his chair. 'So what was your take on the bungalow itself, then, Charlie?'

The SOCO considered this. 'I think it was lived in by one not-so-young but not-really-old party – I mean the place hadn't been grannified, if you know what I mean – no handles in the bath, no walking sticks, no special aids – none of that sort of thing but there was nothing very new there either and hadn't been for years, I should say. A bit on the shabby side but not so you'd notice. Lots of books about foreign parts and gardens. I'd say the owner was into travel – not one of those who devoted themselves to housework or collecting things.' Charlie Marsden knew about the downside of that way of life. His wife collected fine china and the big man was nervous about moving about in his own sitting room.

'There must have been something very valuable to the two people who went in there,' mused Sloan. 'Or that they had reason to believe was valuable, of course.'

'I can tell you a little about both of them,' said Marsden. 'Whoever came in through the pantry window was a bit careless . . .'

'We spotted the blood.'

'Better than that. A few hairs on the broken window. Useful stuff, hair.'

'Bully for you,' he said, metaphorically rubbing his hands. The hair of the dog that bit you had nothing on a single strand of human hair with its follicle still attached for the assistance it could sometimes provide in an investigation.

'His head must have touched the broken glass as he came in.' Charlie Marsden looked justifiably pleased. 'And, of course, we've taken the missing party's DNA from a hairbrush in her bedroom. Routine, these days.'

Sloan nodded. 'Good going, Charlie.'

'Thought you'd be pleased.' Charlie Marsden grinned.

'And I've got some DNA said to be hers from a car in which she was given a lift.' He corrected himself. 'In which she was said to have been given a lift.'

'And that's not all,' went on the Scenes of Crime man.

'Surprise me.'

'He who came through the front door with a key . . .' He paused and shot Sloan a quick glance. 'The male embraces the female and all that guff, you understand.'

'He or she is implied,' agreed Sloan solemnly. The

feminists at the police station were not women to be trifled with.

'He was very careful indeed. Not a single fingerprint or anything else anywhere but he carried out a very thorough search of the place all the same. We couldn't find a safe and presumably neither could either of them. If there had been any locked box then one or other of them took it away with them.'

Detective Inspector Sloan nodded. 'That figures.'

Charlie Marsden said, 'I guess that whoever the intruders were, they both had the same idea about where ladies keep their treasures. Well, their gin, anyway.'

'Back of the wardrobe,' said Sloan promptly.

'Too right. Both had had a rummage round there. No gin, though, but . . .'

'But what?'

'What looked like a very valuable book indeed on orchids. That had been thumbed through too, but with gloves on, of course.' He looked up. 'I think that's about all. It's a missing person case, I think you said?'

'With knobs on, Charlie. So did you find what I asked you to look for?'

'A spare key?' Charlie Marsden shook his head. 'No.'

'That's what's worrying,' said Sloan. 'The neighbour is adamant that she didn't ever leave one with anyone . . .'

'Which could mean,' the Scenes of Crime man finished the sentence for him, 'that whoever went in there with one took it off her.'

'I'm very much afraid so,' said Detective Inspector Sloan soberly. He swept his papers into a drawer and locked it. 'Not that I can do anything more about that tonight but I've got another job for you, Charlie. Just as interesting but different.'

'Surprise me again.'

'I want to know what was in a bonfire lit this morning in the garden of a house in Pelling called The Hollies. The name's Feakins.'

'We'll be round there first thing,' promised Charlie Marsden, making a note.

'Just give me time to get you a search warrant before you go,' said Sloan, 'and for heaven's sake keep a low profile. Make sure that the only pictures that get taken are yours – the last thing we want is the press publishing photographs of an old bonfire. Not at this stage, anyway. I want them to have one of the missing person first.'

'Another search warrant, Sloan?' barked Superintendent Leeyes the next morning. 'Whose house is it for this time?'

'It's not for a house, sir,' Sloan said quickly, the superintendent never being at his best first thing in the morning. 'It's for a bonfire – or rather the remains of one – in a garden belonging to one of the customers of Jack Haines at Pelling. He's one of those who have lost plants at Haines' nursery, which is interesting.'

'Don't say that they've started burning people at the stake out there,' Leeyes said, heavily sarcastic. 'Or that your missing person's gone up in smoke.'

'I don't know what has been burnt,' replied Sloan seriously, 'but there is a man there who was prepared to have a bonfire in spite of being bent double and in great pain from backache. He can hardly stand and yet he got himself out into the garden somehow yesterday afternoon

140

to light it and scuttled back out there again pretty smartly after he thought we'd left.'

'And burn what exactly?'

'That is what we don't know yet, sir. Not until we've got a warrant and had a good look. All we do know is that it was not long after he and his wife got back from seeing their solicitor.'

Superintendent Leeyes, no fan of the Defence Counsel branch of the legal profession, gave a snort. 'You take their advice and they take your money.'

'There is something else,' ploughed on Sloan gamely. 'This man Benedict Feakins also got quite agitated when the name of the missing person was mentioned and as soon as we were out of his sight . . .'

'But not out of yours, I take it, Sloan?'

'No, sir. Crosby drove the car away while I kept watch.'

'And?'

'And Feakins staggered back out into the garden straightway,' said Sloan, 'and started raking about in the remains of the bonfire like a madman.'

'Hm.' Leeyes drummed his fingers on his desktop. 'Anything else to report?'

'We've been checking on other leads, sir.'

'Such as?'

'Crosby has confirmed Anthony Berra's story – he's the last person known to have seen Enid Osgathorp alive. He did visit the Berebury branch of the Calleshire and Counties Bank and he did have lunch at the Bellingham, just as he said he did. We're checking the street CCTV cameras now. No joy from the railway people though – they can't help us at all. No sighting of the missing person on their cameras at all and though she had a pre-booked ticket there is no trace of it having been checked or handed in.'

'And what now?' grunted Leeyes.

'Now, sir, I'm going to check on the recent death of Benedict Feakins' father,' said Sloan, 'just to be on the safe side, and then have another word with the old admiral. He made no secret of not liking the missing person but he wouldn't say why.'

PC Edward York, the Coroner's Officer, was very much a family man. Grey-haired and distinctly on the elderly side for a police constable, he had the bedside manner of an old-fashioned family doctor. Exuding muted sympathy, he attended to the bereaved with a skill honed over the years on the losses suffered by other people.

He was rather more forthright in the presence of Detective Inspector Sloan and Detective Constable Crosby. 'Feakins, did you say? Oh, yes, he came my way all right. An old boy who was found dead in his greenhouse out at Pelling not all that long ago?'

'That's him,' said Sloan.

'Usual thing – milk not taken in, newspapers piled up,' said York. 'Always a great help. I think it was the postman who went looking around the place for him the next morning and found him on the greenhouse floor.'

'Nice way to go,' remarked Crosby, who was only now getting used to seeing the bodies of people who hadn't gone in a nice way.

'Natural causes?' asked Sloan.

'Oh, yes,' said the Coroner's Officer immediately. 'Post-mortem but no inquest. Heart packed up, if I remember rightly. All quite straightforward – from my point of view, anyway. Family very upset, naturally, but they lived away. The usual story – the parent didn't want to be a nuisance and the younger generation didn't want to seem overly concerned because the old man was so keen on keeping his independence for as long as he could.'

'A common problem,' nodded Sloan. His own mother wasn't frail yet but would be one day and perhaps would be like that too.

PC York said, 'The son told us that a regular telephone call every Sunday evening was about all that his father would agree to.'

'Solomon Grundy died on Saturday, buried on Sunday,' remarked Crosby inconsequentially.

Detective Inspector Sloan scribbled a note to himself. 'No sign of the son being overcome by remorse or anything like that?'

The Coroner's Officer, a man experienced in these matters, shook his head. 'His reaction seemed perfectly normal to me or I would have remembered. He was shaken, naturally, but he identified him in the ordinary way.'

'Thanks, Ted,' said Sloan. 'That's been a help.' He shuffled some papers about on his desk until a copy of the photograph of Enid Osgathorp at her retirement presentation surfaced. 'By the way, should this old lady ever come into your view . . .'

'Dead or alive,' interposed Crosby.

Sloan decided to rise above this and carried on. 'Let me know pronto, will you, Ted? She's gone missing.'

PC York regarded the picture with interest. 'Will do. Haven't seen her yet.' He tapped the photograph with his finger. 'I can tell you, though, who the clergyman in this snap is. I saw quite a lot of him not all that long ago. That was at Pelling too. Name of Beddowes.'

'The one whose wife committed suicide,' nodded Sloan. 'Yes, that's him at her retirement presentation handing over something to Enid Osgathorp. We've already seen him.'

'Very unfortunate, that suicide was, what with the daughter's wedding pending at the time.' He frowned. 'I think I heard that they went ahead with the ceremony after the inquest but that it was a very quiet do in the end.'

'Understandable,' said Sloan.

'Lot of gossip out there at the time, of course,' said York, a man used to working with gossip. 'It goes with the territory.'

'Small villages are like that,' opined Sloan.

'It didn't amount to anything,' said York, 'because of course I looked into it. The gossip, I mean.'

'Naturally.' Detective Inspector Sloan, mentor, made a mental note to talk to Crosby sometime about the importance of policemen properly evaluating gossip without spreading it – but not here and not now.

'The daughter blamed herself for wanting a proper wedding reception and honeymoon and all the works but I must say there didn't seem anything very out of the ordinary about their plans to me.' PC York had three married daughters and knew the scenario well. 'Quite the opposite, actually.'

'Didn't want anyone complaining that the Easter

offering was being misspent, I expect,' said Sloan knowledgeably. His mother was a great churchwoman and he knew exactly what was expected of a clergy family: a more stringent economy than that which was practised by the congregation.

'Reception in the church hall, with the parish ladies doing the refreshments,' recounted York. 'And the church flowers rota ladies doing the decorations. Lavender and peonies, I expect.'

Detective Constable Crosby's head came up. 'Not roses all the way?' he said, bachelor that he was.

'Lavender for devotion and peonies for joy and prosperity,' said the Coroner's Officer promptly. 'The language of flowers.'

'Girls come expensive,' said Sloan, who only had a son and was sometimes grateful for this. His wife, Margaret, insisted that this sentiment would only last until the said son was old enough to buy his first motorbike.

PC York was still thinking about the rector's daughter. 'And she could hardly not get married in church anyway, could she? Not with having a clergyman for a father and all that.' The man grinned and said, 'After all, the rector couldn't very well offer the bridegroom a ladder and fifty quid to elope with his daughter, now could he?'

'No,' agreed Sloan. That presumably went for the father of the girl that Anthony Berra was marrying too, especially since her father was a bishop. 'The family insisted to me that she'd been very worried about the cost of the wedding,' he said, casting his mind back to his visit to the Rectory.

PC York stroked his chin. 'She could have been

worried about the expense although I can't imagine why. They'd even got a friend taking the wedding photographs, although I wouldn't advise that myself.'

'Headless bridesmaids,' grinned Crosby.

York pressed on with his narrative. 'You see, the mother had been saving up for it for ages. They showed me her cheque-book. Lots of withdrawals in cash with "Wedding Fund" written on the counterfoil. The only thing is that nobody could find any money stashed away anywhere when she died. Looked everywhere, they did.'

'Perhaps she put it all on a horse,' suggested Crosby jovially. 'Double your money and all that.'

'Were they regular withdrawals?' asked Sloan more pertinently.

'First of the month,' said York. 'Without fail. As the daughter told me afterwards, there should have been enough money there to have had a proper photographer, which, I may tell you from bitter experience, is saying something.'

Sloan tried to remember some of the details of Mrs Beddowes' suicide. 'We were told that there were letters . . .'

PC York nodded. 'There were. I handed them over to old double-barrelled.'

'Mr Locombe-Stableford,' interpreted Sloan, who felt that the decencies should be preserved in the presence of the young.

'Him,' said the Coroner's officer, referring to Her Majesty's Coroner for East Calleshire. 'He didn't read them out at the inquest which is his prerogative. He just said that he was satisfied that the deceased had taken her own life while the balance of her mind was disturbed and gave that as his verdict. That was when the press lost interest.'

'So you don't know what was in the letters then,' ventured Crosby.

The Coroner's Officer cast him a pitying look. ''Course I do, sonny. It was me that unpinned them from her pillow, wasn't it?'

'So what was in them, Ted?' asked Sloan swiftly.

'Said no one was to blame for what she had done then and now but herself and to remember her with compassion no matter what.'

'And what do you suppose she meant by that?' mused Sloan. 'Then and now.'

York shrugged his shoulders. 'Your guess is as good as mine.'

'And what had she done?' asked Crosby curiously.

'Committed suicide,' said York. 'You're not supposed to do it.'

'No,' persisted Crosby, 'I mean what had she done that made her commit suicide?'

The Coroner's Officer shrugged his shoulders. 'Who knows? Disturbed minds aren't easy to read in spite of what the shrinks would have you believe. She'd meant to do it all right, though. She'd travelled over half the county for weeks buying small lots of tablets here, there and everywhere.'

'Determined then,' concluded Crosby.

'The family were still insisting that she'd been worried about the cost of the wedding,' said Sloan, turning his mind back to their own visit to the rectory. Perhaps he should go back and ask if the deceased had known Enid Osgathorp too. He immediately answered his own thought. Of course, she would have done. The rector's wife would have known a lot of people but the doctor's receptionist must have known everyone. And all about them too, probably. Well, everything on their medical records anyway.

'I think,' declared Detective Inspector Sloan obscurely, 'what we are dealing with now are live doubts rather than dead certainties – but this may change.'

CHAPTER TWELVE

Mandy Lamb was usually able to cajole Jack Haines back into his usual good humour but not this morning. Even a continuous infusion of coffee did nothing to raise his spirits. Her employer still sat, listless and preoccupied, at his desk.

'Russ came in earlier looking for you,' reported Mandy.

Jack Haines sighed. 'I'd better see him then.' He pushed a desk diary aside. 'Mandy, you haven't seen Norman about lately, have you?'

'Not for yonks, Jack, thank goodness.' She pulled a face. 'He's not your most lovable character.'

'Margot was fond of him,' said the nurseryman.

'She was his mother,' pointed out Mandy Lamb.

'He couldn't do anything wrong as far as she was concerned,' sighed Jack Haines. 'Everything was all right until she died.'

'That's mothers for you,' said Mandy Lamb who was still single and childless.

'And I reckon I treated him well enough until he got greedy,' murmured Haines, almost to himself. 'Really greedy.'

'You treated him very well,' she said emphatically. She paused and then added, 'Better than he treated you.'

'Stepchildren usually have chips on their shoulders,' he said. 'Goes with the territory, I suppose.' He sipped at the latest mug of coffee, braced his shoulders and said, 'I suppose I'd better get back to business. What does Anthony Berra want now?'

Mandy scrabbled about among the papers on her desk. 'I've got his list somewhere here. Ah, got it!' She handed over the sheet of paper to him. 'He's on his way over now.'

'I suppose in view of what's happened we'd better pull out all the stops for him.' Jack Haines scrutinised the paper she had given him.

Mandy said, 'He's still got that hacking cough. He doesn't look all that well. I hope he's looking after himself.'

'I think we can do most of these,' said Jack, still looking at the list.

'If not,' she said mischievously, 'we could always ask Bob Steele if he could send us some of them.'

'Over my dead body,' he growled, his face turning an apoplectic shade of crimson. 'I'm not going down on my bended knee to that man for anything. Anything at all. Is that understood?'

'Yes, Jack,' she said sedulously, turning back to her own desk. 'But according to Russ the man's happy enough to come to you for almost anything.'

'That's as maybe,' he said enigmatically. 'And mind

150

what you say about Bob Steele in front of Russ. I'm not happy about him either.'

They were interrupted by the arrival of Anthony Berra. 'I hear the admiral's ordered just what he wants as usual,' he said ruefully.

'He has,' said Haines, adding peaceably, 'He's old, of course.'

'And difficult,' sighed Berra.

'Handling him must be good practice for your dealing with the Bishop, Anthony,' said Mandy Lamb briskly. 'I hear your future father-in-law is no pushover.'

'That's nothing – you haven't met his wife,' groaned Berra. 'I call her Mrs Proudie behind her back. Terror of the diocese from all accounts. By the way, Jack, I've just come from the Berebury Garden Centre and Bob Steele said again he was sorry to hear about your troubles and if there was anything he could do, to let him know.'

'That'll be the day,' muttered Haines, half to himself, his complexion again turning an unhappy shade of red.

'Upset you, has he?' concluded Berra. 'No sentiment in business and all that?'

'You could say something of the sort,' Haines managed through clenched teeth. He waved a list in his hand. 'I'll get Russ to look out these plants you want.'

'Thanks. I'll have them as soon as you can get them – our Charmian will have my guts for garters if anything more goes wrong with her precious Mediterranean garden. I must have been mad to agree to do it for her.' He broke off to cough.

'I hope that's not catching,' said Mandy Lamb pointedly, edging away.

He stared at her and said stiffly, 'Certainly not.' Just as quickly his mood changed and he said, 'I've just thought of a good quote for my new business card that I'd like to run past you.'

'What's that, then?' asked Jack Haines, who didn't believe in advertising.

Anthony Berra said '"A good garden is a painting come to life". What do you think of that, Jack?'

'I think,' said the nurseryman firmly, 'that you should tell them the truth – which is that a garden is hell's half acre with everything in it fighting for survival night and day.'

'Not "A lovesome thing, God wot" then?' put in Mandy Lamb.

'Certainly not,' said Haines.

'A man doesn't bite the hand that feeds him,' said Berra obscurely.

'Coffee, Anthony?' As always when dissention threatened, Mandy Lamb took refuge in her universal remedy.

Jack Haines said, 'A cobbler should stick to his last and you should stick to yours, Anthony. Garden design, not playing with words.'

'I'll remember that,' said the other man slowly, turning to go. 'By the way, Jack,' he asked, 'had you thought of your stepson as a possible orchid killer?'

'Yes,' said Jack Haines shortly. 'I had.'

Detective Constable Crosby stood up when Sloan got back to his office. 'Where to now, sir?'

'Where indeed?' murmured Detective Inspector Sloan.

Nothing with its roots in Pelling seemed to fit: in his book, events so far seemed more Rubik's Cube than jigsaw.

'The canteen?' suggested Crosby hopefully.

'Why not? At this stage, Crosby, it's as good as anywhere else.'

The canteen at the police station served an all-day breakfast. The meal could not be further from the 'five-a-day' mantra of the healthy eating brigade. Sloan regarded the bacon, eggs, sausage, mushrooms, tomatoes, baked beans and fried potatoes with enthusiasm, only wondering in passing whether the fried mushrooms, tomatoes and beans could be deemed as three of his 'five-a-day' allotment of healthy fruit and vegetables. He decided not.

'I brought some toast as well,' said Crosby. 'I hope that's all right.'

'Good thinking,' said Sloan. When later in the day his wife Margaret enquired whether he had eaten at work, he could admit with some truth that he'd had some toast. It was not the whole truth, of course, which was important. He reminded himself that not saying anything was a form of lying. But the whole truth at Pelling was something that was beginning to bother him because he seemed to be no nearer to it today. Or to establishing whether the absence of the missing Enid Maude Osgathorp, whose home had been broken into twice, had any connection with frost-damaged plants at Pelling and Capstan Purlieu.

'There's only one thing we really know about Enid Osgathorp,' he mused aloud, 'apart from the two break-ins at her house and that we know she's been missing for over three weeks.'

Detective Constable Crosby, having been brought up

not talk when his mouth was full, for a wonder remained silent.

'That's that she wasn't the flavour of the month,' carried on Sloan, demolishing a sausage. 'There is a certain absence of warmth whenever her name is mentioned although Anthony Berra sounded quite neutral when he told us he had given her a lift into Berebury.'

'That reminds me, sir,' said Crosby, when he had swallowed and regained the power of speech. He parked a piece of toast on his plate while he reached for his notebook. 'I checked on that. I found two old ladies who had also been waiting at the bus stop that day. They remembered him stopping and picking her up.'

'But not them?' said Sloan. 'He didn't give them a lift too?'

'Just her.'

'Perhaps they didn't like her either,' said Sloan idly.

'That man Benedict Feakins sure didn't have any nice feelings about her,' Crosby said. 'He looked like a frightened rabbit when her name cropped up.'

'And the admiral actually admitted he didn't like her,' said Sloan. There was something at the back of his mind niggling him about the admiral – something from way back that he felt he was missing but he couldn't think what it was.

'So that lets him out of anything that's been going on,' decided Crosby, attacking a rasher of bacon.

There would be a moment, resolved Sloan, when he would have to explain the concept of double bluff to the constable but, the man's attention now being centred on the bacon, this didn't seem to be it. Instead he said, 'All the same, Crosby, I think we'll have another word with him later.'

'Don't forget, sir, we haven't traced the husband of one of those women at Capstan Purlieu yet,' said Crosby. 'Norman Potts.'

'That's true, although we don't know where he fits in the picture – or even if he does. Perhaps we'd better get on with that too.'

'Nobody liked him either – at least, not his stepfather or his ex-wife,' said Crosby.

Someone had once listed the reasons for murdering people: gain, conviction, elimination, the lust of killing, revenge, jealousy . . . Not being liked didn't seem to be one of them. The absence of war from the list had struck Sloan as strange at the time he first read it but that was presumably different. Those intent on making war had always said so throughout history, hadn't they?

'More toast, sir?' Crosby, hovering, interrupted his train of thought.

Without thinking, Sloan's hand stretched out for it. He said absently, 'There's really only one thing about Enid Osgathorp that we do know for certain and that's that she knew everyone in Pelling by virtue of her occupation as keeper of their medical records.'

'And those two women out at Capstan Purlieu as well,' pointed out Crosby. 'She knew them too, because one of them is standing in for her at that talk she was supposed to be giving tonight.'

'She must have known the rector's wife, anyway,' concluded Sloan, 'talking of whom it would be interesting to know where she had stashed her wedding fund money. Not in the bank, anyway, because she'd taken the money out of the bank each month, not put it in there.'

'And she couldn't have put it anywhere in the house,' concluded Crosby, 'because the husband and children would have found it by now if she had.'

'True.'

'Perhaps it got stolen?' suggested the constable.

'Then we would have heard about it,' said Sloan, qualifying this immediately by adding, 'unless someone in the family had nicked it. We mightn't have been told in that case, families being what they are. Unlikely, though, I admit.' Struck by a sudden thought, he said, 'If the question of probate has come up, we could always check with the family's solicitor to see if he's found it. Otherwise, Crosby, we might have to consider that Mrs Beddowes had been giving the money to someone else . . .'

'What on earth for?' asked the constable, who was now tackling the bacon.

'What, indeed?' said Detective Inspector Sloan rhetorically, 'but in my book, regular cash payments out of someone's bank account over a long period about which nobody else knows anything spells only one thing.'

'What's that, then?' asked Crosby.

'Blackmail,' pronounced Sloan succinctly, 'especially if it's followed by suicide, so I think we'll see if we can track down all that money of Mrs Ann Beddowes' next. Whether we are dealing with a suicide followed by a murder is something else that has to be considered.'

Crosby chewed his toast for a moment and then

said, 'Ann Beddowes couldn't have murdered Enid Osgathorp . . .'

'No, Crosby,' he agreed, letting out an exasperated sigh. 'She couldn't because she was already dead before Enid Osgathorp went walkabout. What I'm pretty sure about now is that someone else has done, though, and that one of the break-ins to her house was carried out by that someone else looking for the evidence that led to the blackmail.'

CHAPTER THIRTEEN

'Back again, Anthony? You're earlier than usual this morning.' Charmian Lingard appeared in the grounds of the Grange at Pelling as if by magic as the garden designer was working there. She was wearing trousers so well-cut that they shouted as having come from a London couturier. They were of a light brown check, the outfit being topped by a plain cream blouse of expensive simplicity.

'Nothing like as soon as those poor old monks would have been at their first office when they lived here. They had to get going really early.' Anthony Berra straightened up and leant on his spade. 'I wanted to get Flora's plinth settled in.' He gave the statue an affectionate pat. 'I'm just finishing checking the levels of the base so that I can fix her properly. It's very important to get her standing up straight.'

'I quite agree,' said Charmian Lingard whose own

excellent deportment had been refined at the Swiss Finishing School. 'We can't have her doing a Leaning Tower of Pisa act. Not here.'

'She'd look drunk and that would never do,' agreed Anthony solemnly.

'You're teasing me, Anthony.'

He reverted to business. 'I'm hoping to get everything ready before I go and then I'll have to leave the concrete round the plinth to set. I'm going set off next and do another round of nurseries to see if I can replace some of the plants we've lost . . .'

'You've lost,' she corrected him, a touch of steel in her voice.

'I've lost,' he conceded at once, hiding a grimace. 'I've already been to Jack Haines' place and over to the nursery at Capstan Purlieu . . .'

'I've heard of them. One of them's a bit fierce, isn't she?'

'I wouldn't want to tangle with Anna Sutherland myself,' admitted Anthony Berra, adding hastily, 'very sound on her subject, all the same. But I'll have to try some other places too. And you'll be pleased to hear that I've drawn up a new planting plan.'

'You don't waste much time, do you, Anthony?'

He essayed a smile. 'It's not so much time and tide that wait for no man, Charmian, as the length of time the plants are in the ground that matters.' He added, grinning, 'And we do have a deadline, don't we?'

'You know we do and I know you're teasing me again,' said Charmian Lingard sweetly. 'The garden party. I'm already working on the draft of the invitation to the printers. I'm really just waiting for the proof to come back

160

and then I can give them the go-ahead.' She gave a sigh of great satisfaction. 'It's going to be a great occasion. I do hope I can persuade the admiral to come. He's such a game old chap and I'm sure he'll turn up if he can. Besides, he must know the bishop and his wife.'

'And everyone else who matters in Calleshire,' added Anthony Berra, but under his breath.

'It's a bit like being in church, sir, isn't it?' whispered Detective Constable Crosby. 'Sitting on these hard chairs and being so uncomfortable.'

The two policemen were in the waiting room of the offices of Puckle, Puckle and Nunnery, Solicitors and Notaries Public, of Berebury.

'What you are sitting on, Crosby,' Sloan informed him, 'is what is known as a flea chair.'

The constable jumped to his feet. 'I have never had fleas and I don't want them now.'

'But if you had, Crosby, they wouldn't have jumped off you and onto these wooden chairs because they haven't got cushions on them for the fleas to settle on. You may sit down again.'

Crosby resumed his seat with a certain caution.

'You don't need to worry,' said Sloan kindly. 'They're hall chairs and they're what the hoi polloi were supposed to sit on while they waited for the local nobs to ask them what they wanted.'

'We're not hoi polloi,' objected Crosby. 'We're different. We're sworn police officers.'

'Just so,' agreed Sloan as Miss Fennel appeared and said that Mr Puckle would see them now.

'As you know, Inspector,' said Simon Puckle pleasantly, 'I can't give you any information about any client – not without a court order, that is.'

'We were just wondering,' Sloan said to the solicitor, 'if that applied to the affairs of deceased clients. I understand that death cancels all contracts.'

Simon Puckle frowned. 'Inquest reports, probate records and court judgements are all in the public domain . . .'

'Let alone what they put in the newspapers,' grumbled Crosby who felt he had been misreported after making his first arrest. 'Everyone sees that.'

'That is,' carried on the solicitor urbanely, 'they all become available in the public domain in due course.'

'The law's delays,' murmured Crosby, sotto voce, still put out over the mention of fleas.

'What we are looking for,' explained Sloan, 'is missing money.'

'Theft, you mean?' Simon Puckle's eyebrows went up.

'Not necessarily.'

'In that case you might need a forensic accountant rather than a solicitor.'

'What I want,' said Detective Inspector Sloan in a straightforward manner, 'is to know what the late Mrs Ann Beddowes did with the money that she took out of the bank every month.'

'Nobody else seems to know,' contributed Crosby in an antiphon.

Simon Puckle sat back in his chair and steepled his fingers while he gave the matter some thought. After a moment he said, 'Presently neither do I. Nor indeed does

162

anyone else to whom I have spoken.' He coughed. 'As her executor I have a duty at law to establish the extent of her estate and . . .'

'No joy?' suggested Crosby.

'Not so far,' he temporised. 'And I think I am in a position to tell you also that her family haven't been able to help in this respect. There is no trace of where it went every month although I still have the requirement to establish that it hasn't been salted away somewhere and thus requires to be included in her estate. If it has simply been disbursed by the deceased in any way whatsoever it is not my responsibility as her executor to know on what. In my capacity as her executor I am only concerned with what remained in her estate at the time of her death.'

'And it's not there?' asked Sloan, rising to take his leave. Solicitors, he had been told, unlike policemen, measured their time in minutes.

Simon Puckle shook his head. 'Not to my knowledge, Inspector.'

'Come along then, Crosby,' said Sloan. He paused with his hand on the door, struck by a sudden thought. He thanked the solicitor and then said, 'If you can tell us that perhaps you could tell us something else.'

'Perhaps.' Caution was obviously the watchword with Simon Puckle.

'The late Doctor Heddon of Pelling. Did you act for him?'

The solicitor nodded. 'Our firm were his executors and we duly submitted details of his estate for probate.'

'And these aren't secret?'

'No. Probate was granted in due course.'

'We would like to know how much money he left to Miss Enid Osgathorp. How do we find out?'

Simon Puckle said, 'I can tell you that myself, gentlemen. He didn't leave her anything at all. If I remember rightly – I could check for you if it's important – everything went to a niece of his in Calleford.'

As the two policemen walked back from the solicitors' premises through the streets of Berebury to the police station, Detective Inspector Sloan remarked to his subordinate, 'So that's someone else who didn't like Enid Osgathorp either.'

'Simon Puckle?' said Crosby.

'Doctor Heddon,' said Sloan. 'Enid Osgathorp had worked for him for years and years out there at Pelling but he didn't remember her in his Will.'

'I'll have worked for the Chief Constable for years and years,' said Crosby stoutly, 'but I bet he won't remember me in his Will either.'

For a long moment Sloan toyed with the idea of trying to explain to the constable the concept that he worked for the well-being of the populace as a whole, not that of the superintendent, but just as soon decided against it as being too abstract. Instead he said, 'We know that Enid Osgathorp had a large enough income in her retirement to support a long series of exotic holidays abroad and luxurious ones in this country although she still lived very simply when she was at home.' The fact reminded him that they still hadn't got any further with identifying the blood and hair on the broken glass at the back of her house. He resolved to give this his attention as soon as he could – not that he knew where to begin. All that he could deduce was that whoever it was who had come in through the front door with a key was more likely to have got it from Enid Osgathorp somehow, somewhere, than whoever had come in through the broken window at the back. This could hardly be described even by an optimist as progress on that investigative front.

The police station came into view as they turned the corner. 'My guess,' continued Sloan, 'is that the money to finance her lifestyle came from people such as the late Mrs Ann Beddowes by way of blackmail, which is why the money can't be found, and that is also probably why the poor woman committed suicide.'

'But she was the rector's wife,' protested Crosby.

'That, I am afraid, Crosby, does not automatically convey blamelessness, although,' he added grimly, 'it does make the appearance of blamelessness very important as far as her husband's parishioners were concerned.' His own mother, a great churchwoman, always reminded him that Caesar's wife was a woman above suspicion but even that was something, police officer that he was, that he had always taken with a pinch of salt.

The superintendent greeted his return without enthusiasm. 'The fact that nobody liked the missing person, Sloan, is not evidence.'

'But it may be relevant . . .' began Sloan.

'She sounds to me like that "fat white woman in gloves",' interrupted the superintendent.

'Enid Osgathorp was short and thin,' pointed out Sloan, somewhat mystified and not knowing where this was leading. 'Everyone has said so.'

'"Who walked through the fields missing so much and so much",' quoted Leeyes. 'It's a poem, Sloan.'

'Ah,' said Sloan. That explained it. Once upon a time the superintendent had started to attend a series of lectures on modern verse but had left declaring to all and sundry that poems weren't what they used to be when he was a lad and what had happened to the works of Sir Henry Newbolt? Sloan thought what was more important from a police point of view was whether they too – like the fat white woman in gloves – were missing so much and so much.

And, if so, what.

Answer came there none and Sloan made his way back to his own office. There was a report on his desk awaiting his return. Crosby was waiting for him there too.

The report was from Charlie Marsden, the Division's senior Scenes of Crime guru. He wrote that, as instructed, he had examined the remains of a bonfire in the garden of The Hollies at Pelling, the home of Benedict and Mary Feakins. He had retrieved a half-burnt gentleman's hairbrush and the handle of a toothbrush from the embers, the fire being out but its remains still warm by the time he and his team had got there. He had also found traces of fibres and substances that could have been ivory, horn or bone, and did Detective Inspector Sloan want them sent for forensic examination.

'Not half,' said Crosby when he had read this too.

Charlie Marsden had appended a footnote to the effect that Benedict Feakins had appeared very anxious when he and his men arrived and kept on saying that he had only been burning some items that had belonged

166

to his late father because he found it upsetting to have them around and that wasn't illegal, was it? 'I assured him that it wasn't,' wrote Charlie, 'since under my understanding of English Law a man could do what he liked provided there wasn't a law against it, unlike some benighted countries where you could only do it if the law allowed you.'

'It doesn't sound as if Feakins was cremating Enid Osgathorp,' said Sloan mildly, leaving aside Charlie Marsden's world view. 'It's not something you usually do in full view of the neighbours and he would have had to park the body somewhere out of sight and smell for the best part of three weeks which wouldn't have been easy.'

'Someone's done it somewhere, though,' observed Crosby. 'If she's dead, that is.'

'I asked the bank to let me know if she had made any withdrawals since she went missing,' said Sloan in passing. 'And they haven't so far. The trouble is if she was only using her credit card any purchases wouldn't show up quite yet.' He pulled his notebook towards him. 'What I want to know is why should Feakins need to dispose of anything on a bonfire at a time when any sort of movement gives him so much pain?'

'And why get so twitchy if he hasn't done anything wrong?' Crosby responded. 'That's important.'

'You must always remember, Crosby, that the appearance of guilt does not prove guilt,' said Sloan, an early lesson by his own mentor fixed for ever in his mind. It was something juries need to be reminded of too.

'Yes, sir. I mean no, sir.'

'It looks to me as if he was trying to destroy evidence of his father's DNA,' remarked Sloan thoughtfully.

'I can't think why he should,' said Crosby.

'Neither can I,' said Sloan seriously, 'but if for a moment we suppose that our Miss Osgathorp was blackmailing both him and Mrs Beddowes we ought to be able to find out why.'

'And why he's so frightened now.'

'There's something else you're forgetting, Crosby.'

'Sir?'

'If they are victims, then you can bet your bottom dollar that they're not the only ones.' He pushed the report to one side. 'Our trouble, Crosby, is that we've got a jigsaw with too many pieces and we don't even know if they come from the same puzzle let alone our having a pretty picture to go on.'

'That's makes them too easy,' opined Crosby. 'Anyone can do a jigsaw with a picture.'

'Then,' said Sloan with a touch of asperity, 'you tell me what deliberately frost-damaged plants, a missing woman and one who has taken her own life have in common.'

'If anything,' said Crosby, adding casually, 'Oh, I rang the admiral's house like you said. No point in going out there just now, sir. The woman what does for him said he's just been taken in hospital. He's gone and broken his hip.' He grinned. 'I asked her "Did he fall or was he pushed" and she said it had just broken but he wasn't in any pain. Hard luck for the old boy, though, all the same, isn't it?'

Crosby got no further. Detective Inspector Sloan brought

one of his hands into the palm of the other with a loud smack in what he was later to describe as a light bulb moment. 'That's it!' he exclaimed softly. 'Of course. I should have thought of it before.'

'Thought what, sir?'

'What William Shakespeare told us. He said "Consumptions sow in hollow bones of man".'

'Beg pardon, sir?' said Crosby, even more bewildered.

'The car, Crosby,' Sloan snapped, springing to his feet. 'Now!'

CHAPTER FOURTEEN

'Still no sign of Enid coming back,' said Marilyn Potts over at Captain Purlieu Plants. 'I've just rung her house in case she's got home after all and could give her precious talk herself tonight but there was no reply.'

'She's probably stuck on a donkey in Petra,' said Anna Sutherland.

'Not Petra,' said Marilyn. 'She's been there. Not enough flowers for her in Jordan, anyway. Now, if you'd said she was marooned on a mountain in Anatolia, that would be more likely.'

'It wouldn't surprise me,' said Anna darkly, 'if she was one of those vandals who pinch rare seeds while they're there.'

'Wrong time of the year for seeds,' said Marilyn ambivalently.

'Rare plants, then. Have trowel, will travel. Don't

you remember that unusual cyclamen she brought back last year from above the tree-line somewhere in Turkey?'

'I don't know if Customs look in sponge bags,' said Marilyn doubtfully, 'but I wouldn't put it past them.'

'And I wouldn't put it past Enid to try to smuggle something interesting back here and then ask us to grow it on for her. Goodness knows why she doesn't have a greenhouse of her own.'

'Greenhouses,' declared Marilyn, 'need watching. And don't we know it,' she added mournfully.

'Our Enid never misses a trick,' said Anna. 'Not never.'

Marilyn Potts gave a great sigh. 'And now I must make a few notes for the Staple St James people tonight.'

'You don't need any notes, my girl. You could talk about orchids standing on your head. And all evening too.'

'But not necessarily the ones we've got in the shed for tonight. Enid must have ordered those six special ones from Jack Haines for a reason. I'll have to try to work out why.'

Anna Sutherland gave one of her high cackles. 'Don't you start on the language of flowers.'

'Why ever not?' Marilyn giggled. 'If it came to that, I could always send Norman a bouquet of lobelia.'

'Malevolence,' interpreted Anna. 'Good thinking.'

'Mock orange . . .'

'Deceit,' said Anna.

'And bilberry,' said Marilyn.

'Can't remember,' admitted Anna.

'Treachery.'

'Just the job,' concluded her friend. 'That's him – malevolent, deceitful and treacherous. And don't we know it.'

'Do get a move on, Crosby,' urged Detective Inspector Sloan.

'Yes, sir. Of course, sir.' Crosby had followed Sloan at a dog trot out to the police station's car park and into their police car. 'Where to, sir?' he asked as he started the car's engine.

'Berebury Hospital and don't hang about.'

Had it not been for the set look on his superior officer's face, Detective Constable Crosby might have been inclined to retort that he never hung about when at the wheel but one glance at the expression on Sloan's countenance was enough to ensure that he stayed silent as the car ate up the distance between the police station and the hospital. At one point he was tempted to ask what the hurry was all about but he held his tongue. After a few minutes he was rewarded with a terse explanation.

'What I want to do, Crosby,' said Sloan, 'is to get to the hospital before they put the admiral under.'

'I see, sir.' The constable pressed his foot down on the accelerator a little more firmly.

'They'll be giving him an anaesthetic any minute now so they can set his leg and I must talk to him first.'

'I'm sure, sir,' said Crosby. He made a token pause at a roundabout, cutting in neatly ahead of a sports car to the manifest surprise of its young driver.

'And I'm sure of something else,' murmured Sloan,

more to himself than to Crosby. 'But I need to know for certain.'

Detective Constable Crosby waited until more of the road had slipped by and then ventured a question. 'Is it important, sir? I mean, seeing the admiral now.'

'Anaesthetics can do funny things to the memory and also,' he added caustically, 'can be a gift to the defence.'

'Am I being a bit slow, sir?' Crosby asked humbly.

Detective Inspector Sloan essayed a small smile. 'I think that in the motoring sense, Crosby, that would be a first but we're not talking fast cars now, are we?'

'No, sir.'

'And you're not being slow. If anyone's been slow it's me. It's the admiral's leg that's broken for no reason and without pain that's made me remember.'

'Remember what, sir?' Crosby caused the police car to round a blind bend with impeccable respect for any cars that might have been oncoming and straightened the vehicle up at just the right moment afterwards.

'Timon of Athens.'

'A Greek gentleman would that be, sir?'

'No, Crosby, just a character in a play.'

'But with hollow bones, I think you said.'

'He was a man with many friends. Too many friends,' Sloan said ambiguously, as some more of the play came back to him. It had been a youthful schoolmaster who had seen fit to bring it to the attention of a group of pubescent boys in a lesson called 'Relationships' but really to do with the facts of life: the dangerous ones. English literature had had nothing to do with it; sexually transmitted diseases everything.

'You can't have too many friends, surely,' objected Crosby, who found it difficult to make them, based as he was in modest lodgings.

'It depends on the friends,' said Sloan dryly.

'In Athens, were they, these friends?'

'What? Oh, no, just in this play by William Shakespeare called *Timon of Athens*.'

Detective Constable Crosby promptly returned his whole attention to the steering wheel, while Detective Inspector Sloan went back in his mind to when he first heard that bit of the play read out. It was the shape of the admiral's nose that should have told him in the beginning. What was that quote? 'Down with the nose, down with it flat, take the bridge quite away.' The admiral's nose had had no bridge.

'Which door, sir?' asked Crosby, swinging the car through the hospital entrance gates with a flourish and bringing it to a standstill in a bay marked 'Ambulances Only'.

'This will do,' said Sloan, leaving the constable to find out for himself whether the authority of a policeman on duty ranked higher than that of an ambulance man with a patient on board. Once inside the hospital, though, and presented with a long direction board, Sloan wasn't sure where to go next. As far as he was concerned it was a toss-up between 'Orthopaedic' and 'Geriatric' wards.

Opting for the orthopaedic ward, he was met at its portals to his relief by a woman in nursing uniform. In Sloan's experience people in uniform had the weight of authority behind them and as a rule knew what they were doing. This one admitted to having a patient called Waldo

Catterick in her care and certainly knew what she was doing.

This was refusing to let him onto her ward. 'Until visiting time,' she said flatly, 'and then only if the patient is feeling like visitors.'

'It is important that I see him before he is operated on,' said Sloan. 'Very.'

'It is important that he has his premedication before then,' she countered, adding in an acidulated tone that mocked his own, 'very.'

'Really important,' he pleaded.

This she showed no sign of responding to.

'Please, sister,' he said.

'I really cannot have a patient disturbed at a time like this,' she said austerely, the majesty of the nursing profession meeting the majesty of the law head on.

He tried another approach. 'Not even if it's a matter of life or death?'

The distinction between the two was obviously less important in the medical world than the police one since it cut no ice with a ward sister accustomed to daily matters of life or death. She said, 'It is important that the patient goes to the operating theatre in a calm state of mind and,' here she gave a minimal smile, 'I cannot imagine that a visit from the police could be other than unsettling.'

It wasn't, thought Sloan, so much a case of irresistible force meeting immoveable object as of Greek meeting Greek. He decided on a different – and definitely duplicitous – ploy. 'I could always arrest him,' he said to the ward sister, even though he wasn't sure that he could.

He made to take a pair of handcuffs out of his pocket. 'Neither you nor anyone else, sister, can stop me doing that in the performance of my duty as a police officer.'

'All right then,' she conceded, yielding very reluctantly, the majesty of the law prevailing over the Florence Nightingale ethos at last. 'I'll give you a minute or two with the patient. No longer, mind. And don't upset him.'

It was all he needed.

Admiral Waldo Catterick was lying on the bed, a pale blue flowered hospital operation gown giving the old sailor an oddly feminine appearance and one quite at odds with his grey beard.

'There's something I need to know about Miss Enid Osgathorp,' said Sloan without prevarication.

A pair of china blue eyes stared back at him. 'A nasty piece of work,' responded the admiral without hesitation.

Sloan pulled up a chair and sat down beside his bed. 'Tell me why. I need to know.'

The old man gave him a shrewd look. 'Will it stay between you and me?'

'I'll do my best but I can't make any promises.' There were other, higher, authorities than his and truth – the whole truth – came into their reckonings well ahead of such trifles as personal privacy, career and reputation.

The beard lifted and fell, signifying its owner's understanding of this. 'She tried to blackmail me about having had what we called one of the venerable diseases,' he said. 'Oh, not directly but I knew quite clearly what she meant.'

'They were old in history,' offered Sloan. This much he did know. And he knew too, that judgements were for the courts, not the police. And perhaps – who knows? – to Saint Peter.

'Oh, they're treatable now but it wasn't so easy in my day, Inspector. You're too young to remember.' He shifted slightly in the stiff hospital bed and then went on, 'I caught a dose of the clap out east when I was a young man and it's on my medical record. And,' he added dryly, pointing to his broken leg, 'you might say that I'm now paying the wages of sin.'

The young schoolteacher had skirted round most of these in his talk on relationships but Sloan could see some of them embodied in the patient before him now.

'That was enough for the Osgathorp woman, of course,' he said. 'She knew, all right, and could prove it.' He sighed. 'Every nice girl loves a sailor. That was the trouble.'

Detective Inspector Sloan tacitly agreed with him. 'And now, Admiral, she's been missing for three weeks, which is our problem.'

'She'll turn up,' said Waldo Catterick. He echoed an old hymn. 'Jesus can't possibly want her for a sunbeam.' Something approaching a grin crossed his weather-beaten face. 'You're too young to remember that expression too.'

'I should have worked out where the woman was getting her information from before,' said Sloan, concentrating on the job in hand.

'It shouldn't surprise you in my case,' said Catterick frankly. 'All admirals have been midshipmen once upon a time, you know, just as all bishops have been curates in their day.'

'What did you do about it?' asked Sloan, leaving aside this nugget of conventional wisdom.

'Took the tablets.'

'I mean, about Miss Osgathorp.'

He gave a high laugh just as a nurse approached with a tray with a hypodermic needle on it. 'Like the Duke of Wellington, I told her to publish and be damned.'

'But she didn't,' said Sloan, eyeing the nurse and getting to his feet to go.

'Of course not, Inspector. Then everyone would have known what she was up to with everyone else's medical records at her fingertips, wouldn't they? It would have quite spoilt her little game and I counted on that.' The blue eyes twinkled. 'I was right too.'

'But you didn't tell us that she had attempted to blackmail you so that we could have done something about it,' pointed out Sloan astringently.

'Then everyone would have known, wouldn't they?' said the old man simply.

'Just a little prick,' said the nurse, advancing with her hypodermic syringe at the ready.

Sloan left hastily before the admiral could catch his eye.

CHAPTER FIFTEEN

'So every single patient on the doctor's list at Pelling could have been being blackmailed by this woman?' barked Superintendent Leeyes back at the police station. 'Is that what you're trying to tell me, Sloan? And not very clearly, if I may so.'

'Theoretically, sir, but actually it would only be worth her while . . .'

'If it was her, remember,' intervened the superintendent. Only the prospect of the Annual Assessment and his Personal Development Discussion coming up very soon stopped Sloan from quoting Erasmus in the matter of going where the evidence led – another kernel of wisdom brought to his attention by his philosophical old Station Sergeant. Instead he went on, 'Quite so, sir. That being so, obviously there would only be any point in her trying it on with those who knew or had reason to believe that there was something discreditable on their medical records.'

'But we don't know who they are, do we? That it?'

'We don't know yet, sir,' said Sloan patiently. 'And we have no idea how many there are of them either.' He'd been running over in his mind his own medical history, hoping that it didn't have anything in it worse than acne. Mind you, as he remembered, that had seemed very shameful at the time. Prompted by this thought, he went on, 'And we don't know at this stage exactly what medical information there could have been on their records that made them vulnerable to blackmail.'

'Plenty, I daresay, human beings being what they are,' said Leeyes, a natural cynic if ever there was one.

Detective Inspector Sloan, experienced police professional that he was, could only agree. He didn't need a statistician to tell him that quite a large percentage of the population had something to hide. He knew that already.

The superintendent drummed his fingers on his desk. 'But that woman, Enid Osgathorp, would have known all about their little medical foibles by virtue of having access to their records. That's what you're telling me as well, isn't it?'

'If it was her, sir,' he said, tongue in cheek.

'I take your point,' said the superintendent loftily.

'And I'm very much afraid that at least two people weren't like the admiral and didn't refuse to play ball.' He was tempted to add that it took two to tango but thought better of it.

'And therefore presumably paid the price of silence instead?' said Leeyes.

'Just so, sir. Two people who didn't tell her to publish

and be damned, anyway.' There had been something engagingly straightforward about the old sea-dog at Pelling. Sloan hoped the operation on his hip was going well.

'Two, you said?'

'The SOCO reported that there are signs of two separate break-ins at Enid Osgathorp's house after she'd left it.'

'Looking to see if she had evidence of their weaknesses there,' concluded Leeyes, who was wont to equate illness with culpability – and always with failure. 'And finding it, do you suppose?'

'I don't think that there would have been any evidence there to find,' said Sloan, who had been thinking about this. 'She didn't need evidence. Such that there was would have been on their medical records anyway or Enid Osgathorp wouldn't have known about it. Presumably the records – hard copy or computer – were safe enough from anyone else.' He hoped that this was true. The records were in government hands, which, he thought realistically, wasn't by any means the same thing as being safe from prying eyes. 'The victims would have only needed to be sure that she was aware of their medical histories. They wouldn't have needed proof because they, too, knew it would be there – written on their records.'

'And they themselves naturally knew them, as well, of course,' said the superintendent, stroking his chin, a sure sign that he was thinking too. 'So there wouldn't have been any question that she hadn't got her facts right.'

'Exactly, sir.' Sloan coughed. 'There is, though, the

possibility that they wanted to be sure that there was nothing in her house that led directly to them.'

Leeyes shuffled some papers about on his desk. 'And are you telling me that one of the people who broke in has killed her?'

'All that we know for certain,' Sloan said steadily, 'is that she's been missing for three weeks now and that we can't as yet trace her whereabouts. Of course we now also know that some person or persons unknown would seem to have a motive for silencing her.'

'Do you have anyone else in your sights, Sloan? Besides the two unknown breakers and enterers of her cottage, I mean?'

'Not the vicar's wife, anyway,' he said. 'She was dead before Enid Osgathorp is said to have left – did leave – but I'm fairly sure she had been one of her victims.'

'Wonder what she'd been up to?' Leeyes asked, with something approaching a grin. 'Mrs Beddowes, I mean.'

'I couldn't say, I'm sure, sir,' said Sloan austerely. He paused and then said, 'Benedict Feakins is still up to something but I don't know what.'

'Then find out,' commanded Leeyes automatically.

'He seems to be short of money, which could be accounted for by blackmail, and he shied away like a frightened pony when Enid Osgathorp's name was mentioned. But he doesn't strike me as having the bottle to do away with a kitten, let alone an elderly party, although,' he added fairly, 'desperate men can be driven to take desperate actions.'

'He was one of those who lost plants at Jack Haines' nursery too, wasn't he?' mused Leeyes. 'So, you said, did

184

that old admiral. What you need to be looking for, Sloan, like Charles Darwin, is the missing link.'

'Sir?'

'The one between the missing party and all those dead orchids.'

'There may not be one.' Charles Darwin had known there was a missing link before he started looking for it. Sloan did not.

The superintendent swept on. 'There was someone else too, whose plants were damaged . . .'

'A couple called Lingard,' supplied Sloan. 'No sign of any financial pressure there but there wouldn't be anyway.'

'Why not?'

'The wife's got money so it wouldn't easily show up if she'd been shelling out to the Osgathorp woman.'

Leeyes thought about this for a moment. 'What about those two women at the nursery at Capstan Purlieu? Where do they come in?'

'They lost plants all right, although they didn't seem to have been growing them for specific customers so we couldn't explore that aspect further. I would have said there was no money there for a blackmailer anyway, besides which they're blaming a disaffected husband. I'm going to interview him as soon as we can locate him.'

Superintendent grunted. 'Anyone else?'

'The nurseryman Jack Haines – he lost plants too, of course; quite a lot of them, including a greenhouse full of orchids. He seems to have got something on his mind but I don't know exactly what. It could be blackmail too.'

'Sounds as if someone doesn't like him either,'

commented Leeyes. 'Wilful damage to those greenhouses must have a reason.'

'Yes, but we don't know what it is. Any more than we know why the orchids at Capstan Purlieu were trashed. Anthony Berra says he doesn't know either why his plants should have suffered – we're seeing him again next. Haines' stepson, who is also the former husband of one of the women at Capstan Purlieu, is the only one in the frame for the greenhouse jobs so far. But as I said we haven't caught up with him yet.'

'It's about time you did,' said Leeyes. 'And found out if the missing person had any connection with him or Jack Haines.' He bared his teeth at something approaching a smile at an impeding witticism. 'We can't have anyone leading us up the garden path, can we?'

'No, sir,' said Sloan, taking this as his leave to depart.

'We're going back to Pelling next, Crosby,' announced Detective Inspector Sloan to the waiting constable, 'to have another chat with the last person admitting to having seen Enid Osgathorp alive.'

'So far,' said Crosby elliptically.

They found Anthony Berra in the garden at Pelling Grange. The Lingards were out but he was still working on the new border. 'I'm just getting the frost tolerant plants in,' he said, kicking some soil off his spade. 'This business at Jack Haines' greenhouses has really knocked my planting plans back.'

'I'll bet,' said Crosby, who didn't know his crocus from his Crocosmia. 'Big job you've got on here,' he added, looking up and down the long bare stretch of ground.

'Too right, I have,' said Berra.

'Just a few questions, sir,' said Sloan.

'Fire away.'

'There were three women waiting at the bus stop but you only picked up Enid Osgathorp.'

Anthony Berra wrinkled his brow. 'You didn't know our famous Miss Osgathorp, did you, Inspector? It looked to me as if the other two did because they stepped back when she got into my car. It seemed that they weren't too keen to join her.'

'Not popular?' So far, Anthony Berra would appear to have been one of the few people not to have openly criticised the missing woman.

'To put it kindly, Inspector, I think the power of being the gateway to the doctor sometimes went to her head.'

'Power corrupts,' observed Crosby. He started to say something in that connection about his superintendent until quelled by a fierce look from Sloan.

Berra threw him an amused glance. 'So they say,' he murmured.

'But she knew you well enough to get into your car?' persisted Sloan.

'She knew my bad chest even better,' the young man said wryly. 'And that my cough isn't infectious, which everyone else seems to have difficulty in believing.'

'Can we just run over what happened next?' said Sloan. 'You said you went to the bank and had lunch at the Bellingham. What else did you do?'

'What I always do when I go into Berebury – trawl through all the charity shops.' He grinned. 'I collect old gardening artefacts and that's where you find them – if you're lucky. I picked up a Victorian dibber there once and my collection's never looked back. You'd be surprised at what turns up in those sorts of shops.'

Detective Inspector Sloan, a policeman and thinking like one, made a mental note that these days while most High Street shops had automatic tills which recorded the time and nature of all transactions, your average charity shop was staffed by elderly and probably unobservant volunteers. He was about to ask for more details of Berra's shopping trip when his personal phone rang.

It was the Division's Chief Scenes of Crime Officer Charlie Marsden, sounding quite excited. 'I've just heard back from Forensics about those items we collected from the Feakins' at The Hollies. Guess what else was in the remains of that bonfire?'

'Surprise me, Charlie,' said Sloan.

'I bet I will,' chortled Marsden. 'Fasten your seat belt.'

'Go on.'

'Cremated ashes. Forensics weren't quite sure but they thought it was a full set, so to speak.'

CHAPTER SIXTEEN

'The Hollies, Crosby,' ordered Sloan, speedily taking his leave from the Grange. 'We are about to hold what I am told the Army call an interview without coffee with Benedict Feakins.'

They found the man again sitting huddled motionless in his chair in the kitchen at his home.

'He didn't sleep at all last night so I took him to the doctor this morning,' explained Mary Feakins as she ushered the two policemen into the room. 'He advised him to keep moving but Benedict says that's still too painful.' She raised her voice slightly. 'You've got visitors, Benedict.'

Benedict Feakins started to struggle to his feet and then fell back into his chair, the colour in his face draining away. 'What is it now?' he asked running his tongue over patently dry lips.

'Your bonfire,' said Sloan.

'What about it?'

'What exactly were you burning on it?'

'You should know,' he retorted with a flare of anger. 'Your people came and took all the embers away. God knows why.'

'Tell me,' ordered Sloan peremptorily.

'As I said yesterday, just old things.'

'Such as?'

'A hairbrush.'

'Whose?'

'My father's – my late father's.'

'Why?'

'I didn't want to use it myself.'

'What else?'

'His toothbrushes.'

'You're sure they were his?'

Benedict Feakins looked at him blankly. 'Of course I am and I certainly wasn't going to use them myself.'

'What was wrong with using your waste bin?'

'Nothing, but I was having a bonfire anyway.'

'In your condition?'

'I've already told you that I just couldn't stand having Dad's things around. That's all.'

'There were traces of fabric in the bonfire,' said Sloan, taking out his notebook and making as if he was looking up a page.

'So?'

'I'm told there is evidence that you had been burning clothes as well,' carried on Sloan.

Detective Constable Crosby stirred. 'You can't argue with laboratories.'

He was ignored by both men.

Feakins' jaw jutted out. 'Old underclothes that couldn't very well go to the charity shops. No harm in that, is there?'

'Got a guilt complex about your father dying alone, have you?' That, Sloan knew, was unfair.

'No,' Feakins protested in anguish. 'Well, yes, I suppose I might have. Something like that, anyway,' he added, latching on to the suggestion with suspicious speed.

'And how, Mr Feakins,' said Sloan sternly, 'do you account for the presence on that bonfire of cremated ashes?'

The man mumbled something about them being his father's and wanting to be rid of them too.

Detective Inspector Sloan suddenly switched his questioning away from the bonfire. 'When did you last see Enid Osgathorp?'

He started. 'Exactly when I told you I did. Just before she went away.'

'How often did you usually see her?'

'From time to time,' he said uneasily.

'Why?'

'She knew Dad and she used to call round to see how I was getting on.'

'Did you go to her house?'

'I have been there.'

'Why?'

Feakins became more flustered. 'She liked talking gardening. Old ladies do.'

'True,' said Sloan, leaning forward. It was at this point that his notebook tumbled off his lap and onto the quarry tiles on the floor. It slithered in Feakins' direction. The man automatically looked down and as he did so Sloan took a look at his scalp. 'Nasty cut you've had there,' he said. 'How did you do that?'

'It's nothing,' he said, raising his hand to brush his hair back.

'I suggest you did it on the window you broke while effecting an entry to Miss Osgathorp's cottage after she left for one of her trips.'

'No,' he shouted. 'No, I didn't. It wasn't me.'

There was a muffled sound behind him. Sloan spun round and was just in time to catch Mary Feakins as she fainted and fell towards the floor.

'And so, sir,' Sloan reported to Superintendent Leeyes the next morning, 'I sent for the doctor for Mrs Feakins and arranged for her husband to report here to be interviewed under caution. He's not going anywhere – he can only hobble as it is. He said he'll be bringing his solicitor but Simon Puckle is in court this morning so it'll be this afternoon.'

'Sentencing in the Corrigenda case,' said Leeyes knowledgeably. 'The leader of the gang should get twelve years for fraud.'

Detective Inspector Sloan was not interested in that case, beyond being glad that they'd got another villain nailed. He'd learnt long ago not to take on problems that weren't his. 'So, sir, I'm going to take the opportunity of checking up on Norman Potts while I've got the time.'

The less salubrious end of the market town of Berebury was seafaring writ large in the history of the largely rural county of Calleshire: old seafaring, that is, the river having silted up in an earlier century. Its level had long ago become too low even for the barges that had once plied their trade between the town and the coast. Its dwellings, though, had been designed in response to the activities of the pressgang. This was in an age when a prison sentence had been viewed as a desirable alternative to service in the Royal Navy.

The cottages there had been built beside narrow lanes leading to a veritable rabbit warren of twisting alleys and blind corners, all designed to thwart those seeking to kidnap men to crew naval ships. These avenues of escape lay between cottages huddled cheek by jowl with each other with only an apology for a garden. Here and there dwellings had been upgraded, window-boxes and double-glazing added and old doors replaced with shiny new ones, but the general effect was still of dilapidated antiquity.

The coming of the railway had brought navvies to build bridges and carve tunnels and they had succeeded the old seamen in the little dwellings. The most individual building in the vicinity in which the two policemen found themselves was the public house called the Railway Tavern. It was on a corner of the main street and was slightly different in appearance from the other buildings by virtue of having coloured glass windows and old saloon doors. The last known address of Norman Potts in Ship Street was only a few doors away and the two policemen found it easily enough. There was no sign of gentrification about the outside of his house; indeed it had a generally neglected look about it.

Detective Constable Crosby gave the front door what he always thought of as an official knock. When this did not produce any response he knocked again, but louder this time.

'Perhaps,' suggested Sloan mildly, 'the man's out at work.'

'Or lying low,' said Crosby militantly.

'Go round the back and see,' ordered Sloan, 'while I have a word in the pub. Then with a bit of luck we can clear up the orchid business and get on with finding out exactly what happened to Enid Osgathorp.'

'Yes, sir.' The constable disappeared down an alleyway further down the road and Sloan took himself to the Railway Tavern.

The landlord was busy attending to his beer machines when Detective Inspector Sloan entered the saloon bar. 'We're not really open yet,' he began, his voice dying away as Sloan reached for his warrant card and showed it to him. He examined this before saying, 'Licensing hours are different now, you know, Inspector.'

'We're looking for a Norman Potts,' began Sloan without preamble.

'Join the club,' responded the landlord unexpectedly. 'Said he'd be in last night to settle up and did he come? No is the short answer. He didn't.'

'What about the night before?' asked Sloan, seeing that was really what lawyers called the material time as far as the opened greenhouse doors were concerned. 'Did you see him out and about then?'

The landlord screwed up his face in thought. 'He was in then quite early but he didn't stay. Slid off before I could have a word with him about what he owes me. Saw me coming over and scarpered, I expect.'

'Got a lot on the slate, has he?'

'And some,' said the landlord, adding briskly, 'although what it's got to do with the police I don't know, I'm sure. Has he been in trouble then?'

Detective Inspector Sloan laid his warrant card flat on the bar counter. 'I'm not sure either that it has anything at all to do with us but we'd like a word with him, that's all.'

'Wanted for questioning,' sniffed the landlord disparagingly. 'That's what that's called by the mealy-mouthed. Can't say that I'm all that surprised.'

'We just wanted a word, that's all,' said Sloan truthfully, the police force being collectors of information not purveyors of it.

'Well, I can tell you for starters that he lives alone and moans a lot,' said the landlord who appeared to be nursing some personal grievance. 'He's got a chip on his shoulder as big as a sack of potatoes.'

'About what?'

The landlord gave the handles of the beer machine a final wipe. 'Stepfather threw him out and then his wife did the same. Can't say I blame either of them. You name it and he's complaining about it. Miserable sod.'

'Like that, is it?' said Sloan. 'What work does he do?'

'None if he can help it, I would say,' said the landlord. 'Officially he's employed by the local authority when it suits them and when they can't get anyone better. Markets and Parks department seeing as he said he used to work in a nursery.'

'That figures,' said Sloan, getting ready to leave.

'Can you tell me something,' said the landlord, 'seeing as you're a copper?'

'Try me.'

'There's a man committed a crime in here the other evening but I don't know what to call it.'

'Go on.'

The landlord pointed to a pair of drab curtains hanging by the window. 'See those?'

'Yes,' said Sloan. 'What about them?'

'And the radiator under the window?'

Detective Inspector Sloan sighed. 'Of course.'

'The other evening one of my customers – he's a plumber – put his hand round the curtain and slid his key into the bleeder valve. Must have loosened it just enough to make it leak a bit.'

'So?'

'So next morning I notice water on the floor and send for him, don't I? The bastard says I've got a leak and charges me a score for repairing it.'

'I'd call that grievous harm to your pride and pocket,' said Sloan briskly. 'Now, tell me if Norman Potts is out and about today.'

The landlord jerked his shoulder in the direction of the man's house. 'He should be in all right – at least I haven't seen him go out this morning.'

Detective Inspector Sloan thanked the publican and made his way back there. Crosby was waiting for him outside the front door looking distinctly uneasy.

'The back door was unlocked, sir, so . . .' his voice faltered and died away.

'So?' said Sloan.

'So I went in . . .'

'You did what, Crosby?' exploded Sloan. 'Don't you know that that's something that you have no right to . . .'

'And he's in there, sir,' interrupted Crosby. 'Norman Potts, I mean – at least I think it's Norman Potts – because it's a bit difficult to tell who anyone is with a face like it is. He's dead, sir. Very.'

CHAPTER SEVENTEEN

Superintendent Leeyes took the news as a personal affront. 'Norman Potts? Hanging? Where?'

'From a beam in his kitchen,' replied Sloan literally. 'They're all quite ancient buildings down by the old harbour and there are lots of beams in them.'

'I don't want an architectural survey, Sloan,' Leeyes bellowed down the telephone from the police station. 'I want to know if it's suicide.'

'Too soon to say, sir, although the rope was lashed over the beam all right,' said Detective Inspector Sloan. 'As I said, it looks like suicide. I can't say for certain at this stage if it is, though, but Doctor Dabbe is due here any minute . . .'

Leeyes grunted. 'I hope he doesn't kill anyone on the way.' Doctor Hector Smithson Dabbe was not only the consultant pathologist to the Berebury Hospital Group but acknowledged to be the fastest driver in the county of Calleshire. He was Crosby's only known hero.

'There is one thing, sir . . .'

'Yes?'

'There are a couple of orchids on the dresser.'

'I hope, Sloan,' said Leeyes loftily, 'that you're not going to start talking about flower power now.'

'There were no other flowers in the house, sir, and there is no garden to speak of here since these are old fishermen's cottages.' He paused, wondering how to put a new thought to the superintendent without damaging his own prospects for promotion for ever. 'There was something, though, that seemed quite purposive about the way the orchids were set out on the sideboard. As if where they were had a meaning . . .' Sloan decided against saying that their position reminded him of the placing of candlesticks on an altar. There were those at the police station, he knew, who had been known to doubt aloud if Superintendent Leeyes had ever stepped inside a church, let alone been christened. Some of them, bitter men, had also been heard to express the conviction that his parents had never been married either.

'Saying it with flowers again, eh?' said Leeyes. 'Is that what you're trying to tell me?'

'Not exactly, sir, but it was mostly orchids that were damaged in both nurseries and the deceased – if he is Norman Potts, as we suppose – is the former husband of one of the growers.'

'Are we talking remorse?' enquired Leeyes. 'Couldn't live with what he'd done – that sort of thing.'

'It's too soon to say, sir.' It was too soon to jump to

any conclusions either but Detective Inspector Sloan was not going to voice that particular thought. Not with his Personal Development Discussion in the offing. 'There does seem also to be some question of his owing money to the publican along the street.'

'Has he got a record? Always worth a look, you know,' pronounced the superintendent magisterially. 'You can't unchequer your history.'

'We're looking into that now,' said Sloan, reminding himself not to sound too defensive or to start talking about any Rehabilitation of the Offender legislation designed to do just this. That always upset the superintendent. As far as he knew in history, blots on the family escutcheon remained there even unto death. Heralds were adamant on this. So was Superintendent Leeyes.

'And find out who benefits from his death while you're about it,' commanded Leeyes. 'Someone must.'

'Of course, sir,' murmured Sloan. That was something he himself always thought of under the heading of 'churchyard luck'. The Assistant Chief Constable, a man with plenty of Greek and even more Latin, always phrased it even more neatly as *cui bono*? It was an aspect of every suspicious death that he, a professional detective, always followed up as a matter of routine.

'Was there a note?' asked the superintendent more mundanely, bringing him back to earth.

'Not that we have found in a superficial examination of the property,' said Sloan with precision. He ventured to say that the cottage did not seem to be one where flowers – especially exotic ones – might ordinarily have been expected to be found.

'Are you trying to tell me, Sloan, that instead of a note the orchids are meant to be a message in themselves?'

'There is a definite connection between the deceased – if the deceased is Norman Potts as we suppose – and both of the nurseries whose doors were left open and the orchids in them killed,' Sloan reminded him. 'That at least we know – with his stepfather and his former wife, neither of whom had a good word to say for him.'

Superintendent Leeyes sniffed. 'Funniest suicide note I've ever heard of, Sloan. Orchids on the sideboard.'

'If it is a message, then it would have the advantage of not having had to be written by hand,' pointed out Detective Inspector Sloan, 'and therefore there is no handwriting to be examined.' It also meant that the orchids could have been put there by anybody – anybody at all – but he did not say so to the superintendent. Instead he made a mental note to have the plant pots photographed exactly where they were and examined for fingerprints or, better still, DNA.

There was a pause while the superintendent digested this. 'I suppose,' he said grudgingly, 'you'd better deal with the whole business before you get back to that missing person inquiry in Pelling and the damaged nurseries there. After all, it's nearly three weeks since the old lady disappeared so it isn't exactly urgent and you say the man Feakins isn't going anywhere.'

'Yes, sir. I had just hoped that we could clear up the matter of the damage to the greenhouses while we were about it before we got back to looking for Enid Osgathorp.' He toyed for a moment with the idea of saying something about the best-laid plans of mice and policemen but he wasn't sure if the superintendent would appreciate the reference especially as it ended with something about aforementioned plans, as the poet had it, being apt to 'gang aft agley'.

'How did he do it?' asked the superintendent.

'It would appear at first sight that he stood on a chair and then kicked it away,' said Detective Inspector Sloan, choosing his words with care.

'Not what the Italians call *Una Bella Morte* then,' said the superintendent, whose attendance at an Italian language class had been brief but explosive even by emotional Italian standards. His view of Omerta had upset teacher and class alike.

'So,' went on Sloan hastily, 'Crosby's just making sure that the distance of the chair from under the body measures up.'

'It would be a help if you could make sure that Crosby measures up too,' said Leeyes tartly. 'I don't know that we'll ever make a copper out of him.'

The rapid approach of a car heralded the arrival of Doctor Dabbe and saved Sloan from having to respond to this. The pathologist stepped briskly inside the cottage, followed by his taciturn assistant, Burns. He took in the grisly scene at a glance. 'I can't tell you anything about the sort of knot, Sloan,' he said, circling the dependent body. 'Not from here and not yet. The neck is too engorged. There are all the superficial signs of death by asphyxiation, though, especially in the face.' He shot the inspector a perceptive glance. 'How did you come to find him?'

'We came here in the course of making some enquiries, doctor,' said Sloan sedately.

'You did, did you? I see.' The pathologist gestured to his assistant who was rootling about in a black bag. 'Burns, are we booted and spurred yet?'

'I'm just getting the gloves out, doctor.'

'Then note the ambient temperature, please.'

As Burns took out a thermometer Sloan ventured to say, 'It would help a lot, doctor, to know the approximate time of death.'

'I daresay that it would,' agreed Doctor Dabbe affably, 'but it's too soon to say. Much too soon. I'll do my best when I've measured the post-mortem lividity and had a good look at him on the table. Rigor mortis seems to have been and gone so we're talking at least sometime last night. That much will have to do you for the time being.'

Detective Inspector Sloan nodded, while Detective Constable Crosby laboriously wrote down some measurements in his notebook. It became obvious to the others that Crosby had not yet mastered the art of doing calculations without the tip of the tongue sticking out of the corner of the mouth.

Sloan voiced something that had been bothering him. 'My constable tells me that the back door was unlocked when he arrived, doctor, and there is no immediate sign of a key.'

'Not my field, Sloan.' The pathologist was still circling the body. 'The actualities of the scene of death are all yours.'

'What I meant, doctor, is that we will be very interested to know if the deceased had a key in his pocket. One would have thought that normally he would have locked the back door before – er – suspending himself.'

'Normally doesn't come into it, Sloan. You should know that. And pathologists can only tell you what the brain looks like after death. Not what's been in it before the subject died. You want a psychiatrist for that.' He shot the policeman a quizzical look. 'If the deceased had been up to no good, which I presume was on the cards since you two are here in the first place, then all I can offer is that old truism that shame asks for punishment.'

'If you ask me this is a very funny way to go about it,' said Crosby, straightening up and indicating the deceased.

'And tell you both also that – as Shakespeare put it so well – "there's no art to find the mind's construction in the face",' the pathologist took another look at the hanged man and went on thoughtfully, 'especially when its oxygen supply has been cut off by a rope.'

'Applied by himself or someone else,' pointed out Detective Inspector Sloan, taking a close look at several scratches on the beam.

'I don't see how anyone else could have got him up there,' objected Crosby. He had taken up a position over by the sideboard, about as far away as he could from the dead man.

'There are ways and means,' contributed the pathologist obscurely.

'Surely he must have stood on the chair with the rope round his neck and then kicked the chair away,' persisted the constable.

Doctor Dabbe glanced up at the beam. 'All anyone else

had to do was toss the rope over the beam and haul away. That right, Sloan?'

'That's right, doctor.'

'But then he'd have to have been dead first,' said the constable.

'Or unconscious,' voiced Sloan.

'Exactly,' said Doctor Dabbe. 'Now, Burns, pass me an oximeter. We must get on . . .'

The four men already packed inside Norman Potts' old fisherman's cottage in Berebury were soon interrupted by the arrival of the Force's two forensic photographers, Williams and Dyson. Set about with equipment, the pair could be heard clattering down the narrow lane as they approached the cottage. Crosby admitted them and, with the addition of two more men, the room suddenly became very crowded.

''Ullo, 'ullo,' said Williams, the senior of the pair, looking round, 'what have we here?'

'That's my line,' objected Crosby indignantly. 'You've pinched it.'

Sloan sighed.

'What we seem to have,' explained Doctor Dabbe precisely, 'is a simple suicide. What we actually have may well not be.'

'Go on, doctor,' said Sloan, his notebook at the ready.

'Well, if I was a Scotsman,' said the pathologist, 'I would say that "I hae ma doots". Take a look at his mouth.'

'For why, doc?' asked Crosby insouciantly.

Sloan winced. That this was no way for a detective

constable to address a consultant forensic pathologist during the course of a case went without saying. He started to apologise but Doctor Dabbe cut him short.

'That's all right, Sloan,' Doctor Dabbe said amiably. 'No need to stand on ceremony. Not where crime is concerned.'

'Crime?' pounced Sloan. 'Here?'

'The skin doesn't look normal, especially round the mouth and eyes,' said the pathologist absently, still studying the hanging man and in no way put out by the constable's comment.

Detective Inspector Sloan said crisply to Williams, 'I'd like some photographs of the face, please.' Dyson was already setting up an arc lamp at the other side of the room.

'Say cheese,' said Williams, approaching the hanging man with his camera.

Sloan took a deep breath. He was about to bring all and sundry to order when he changed his mind and said nothing. His old mentor when he was a rooky constable – that highly experienced Station Sergeant – had more than once lectured him on the importance of levity in the face of tragedies: only other people's tragedies, that is, not your own. It was sometimes, he would say, better than various other ways of not coping, including kicking the cat, taking it out on the children and having nightmares. Detective Inspector Sloan was the first to admit that the dead man here was not a pretty sight and he therefore kept his peace.

Doctor Dabbe, at least, remained totally professional. 'There are burn marks on the face and you can see evidence of lachrymation which has coursed down the cheeks prior to death.'

'Tear gas,' concluded Sloan immediately, his mind starting to run along quite new lines. The atmosphere in the room changed suddenly when he murmured softly, 'It's not called Captive Spray for nothing, is it?'

'It is more than a possibility, Sloan. I might be able to confirm it at the autopsy,' said the pathologist. 'Tear gas can sometimes leave traces in the body after death.'

'If you do find . . .' began Sloan, a possible whole new scenario begin to flood into his mind while the phrase 'assisted suicide' took on a whole new meaning.

'And I'll check up on the knot too,' promised Doctor Dabbe. 'I daresay we'll find it the usual Hangman's . . .'

'Send the rabbit round the tree and then down the hole, up and round again. Twice,' chanted Crosby. 'Then send the knot up the line.'

'Thank you, Crosby,' said Sloan stonily. 'We all know how to make a Hangman's Knot.' Now he came to think of it, perhaps not everybody did, but it was beginning to look as if there had been someone about who not only knew how to tie a hangman's knot, but how to use CS gas. He motioned the photographers to record the upturned chair lying on the floor near the dangling man and the beam over which the body had been suspended.

'He was quite a small man,' Sloan said, unconsciously thinking aloud, 'so he wouldn't have been too heavy to haul up.'

'We'll be weighing him, won't we, Burns?' promised the pathologist.

The ever-silent Burns nodded.

'Render him temporarily unconscious, put the rope round his neck, throw the other end over the beam and heave away,' suggested Sloan.

'Could be done,' agreed the pathologist.

'Crosby,' ordered Sloan, 'measure the height of the seat of the chair from the floor – without touching it, mind you.'

'Yes, sir.' The constable bent over it and extended a metal tape.

'Now measure the height of the body from the floor,' ordered Sloan.

'Bingo,' said Crosby.

'By which I take it you mean they are the same,' said Sloan frostily.

'Yes, sir. Sorry, sir.'

'And then, Crosby, you can rustle up the Scenes of Crime people.'

'Charlie Marsden and his Merry Men,' said Detective Constable Crosby. 'Will do. I'll ask for a few portlies too, to guard the back lane.'

'And after that, Crosby,' said Sloan, rising above this slur on the uniformed branch, 'you can go round and chat up the landlord at the Railway Tavern before he finds out what's happened. We'll need to set up an incident room and I'll alert Tod Morton that we'll be needing a hearse when we're done with the body here. I'll be in touch with the Coroner myself.'

Doctor Dabbe said so would he. 'When I've done the post-mortem,' he added. 'And examined the hands properly to see if he put up a fight.'

'And what I will want to know, among other things,' said the detective inspector, 'is whether or not the deceased knew whoever came in . . .'

'Always presuming that someone did,' pointed out the pathologist. 'Remember it's too soon to say for sure, Sloan.'

'Friend or foe,' said Crosby, looking round. 'That's what we want to know, isn't it?'

'Whichever way you look at it,' observed Williams, the photographer, 'it can't have been a friend. Not if he ended up swinging like this.'

CHAPTER EIGHTEEN

Detective Constable Crosby slid into the saloon bar of the Railway Tavern as instructed after the manner born. The landlord stopped polishing glasses and asked him what he was having.

With a fine show of ignorance, Crosby asked him what the local brew was.

'Stranger in these parts, then?' The landlord waved his hand in a gesture designed to take in the whole area.

'Sort of,' said Crosby obliquely. 'I've just come over from Pelling.'

'Try our best bitter.'

'Will do,' said the constable, temporarily putting to the back of his mind all he had been told about not drinking on duty. He waited until it had been drawn and he had taken a first sip. He nodded appreciatively and then jerked his shoulder in the direction of Norman Potts' house.

'What's going on down the road? There's a load of police cars outside one of the houses there.'

'Where?' The landlord shot to the door and looked out. 'Well, I'll be blowed. That's Norman Potts' house. What's he been and gone and done now, I wonder?'

'What does he usually do?' asked Crosby, taking another sip.

'Make trouble,' said the landlord briefly. 'Big trouble, usually.'

'Bit of low life, is he?'

The landlord shook his head. 'No, not that, but he'll pick a fight with anyone over anything, if he can. Combative, if you ask me. Or do I mean aggressive?'

'What about?' asked Crosby, burying his face in his glass of beer.

'Money and family,' said the landlord. 'In that order. He owes me. Had to throw him out last week but he still came back. Wanted to borrow some more to tide him over.' He snorted. 'At least, that's what he said. Me, I think it's the gee gees.'

'Some wives,' advanced Detective Constable Crosby, bachelor, trying to sound wise, 'will spend every penny a man's got.'

'It's not that,' said the landlord. 'He had a wife but she took off. Or threw him out. I don't know which. Don't blame her myself. He must have been a real pain to have around. No, it's horses with him.' He paused and then said after some thought, 'Not that they're any more reliable than women.'

'They don't answer back,' observed Crosby.

'No more they do,' agreed the landlord. A smile split

212

his features. 'And some of them are faster. Only some of them, mind you. The ones you don't put money on.'

Crosby grinned appreciatively and said he'd have another half. 'Got a lot on the slate, has he?'

'Too much,' said the landlord grimly. 'Said he was working on something new out in the country and would pay me back soon but if you ask me, he wasn't working on anything.'

'Not up and about?'

'Not up at all, I should say. Lazy beggar except on race days.'

'And when he did work was it anything to do with flowers?'

The landlord gave Crosby a curious look. 'Funny you should say that. Do you know him, then?'

'No,' said the constable truthfully.

'He was always going on about his stepfather doing him out of his share of a nursery. I wouldn't have thought he'd know one end of a daisy from the other myself. Not until he starts pushing them up.'

Resisting the considerable temptation to say that that was just what the late – and apparently unlamented – Norman Potts would be doing quite soon, Crosby drank up and took his leave.

In his day Detective Inspector C.D. Sloan, like all policemen, had done his time as a breaker of bad news. Sometimes it was as the unhappy herald of sudden death after a road traffic accident, sometimes as the deliverer of an unwelcome arrest warrant. Only very occasionally did the harbinger bear intelligence that the recipient was pleased to hear. The finding of a live lost child was one of them although the tracing of an aged demented relative who had gone walkabout usually only occasioned modified rapture.

Thus responses normally ran the gamut from grief to joy and Sloan had gradually become inured to them all. What he hadn't experienced before, though, was such an equivocal reception to the information given.

'Norman dead?' echoed a bewildered Marilyn Potts when the two policemen arrived at Capstan Purlieu Plants with the news. 'Are you sure?'

'Quite sure, madam,' said Sloan steadily.

'Tell us more,' said Anna Sutherland, standing protectively behind her friend. 'Where, for instance?'

'At his home in Berebury,' said Sloan, telling the truth but not the whole truth.

'What on earth from?' asked Marilyn.

'That we don't know for certain,' said Sloan even more truthfully.

'But he wasn't even old,' protested Marilyn.

'That we don't know either,' said Sloan. The age of the asphyxiated man hanging from a beam in a cottage had not been easy to assess from his face. 'Not for sure.'

'So you're just telling me that he's dead, are you?' said Marilyn Potts truculently. 'Is that all?'

'Why are you telling her this anyway?' intervened Anna Sutherland brusquely. 'He and Marilyn were divorced. She told you that yesterday. Good grief man, you haven't come here to ask her to identify him, have you?'

'Not at this stage,' said Sloan cautiously. Mortuary technicians could work wonders but it took time.

214

Marilyn Potts began a low keening.

'What's it got to do with Marilyn now in any case?' demanded Anna Sutherland only just short of belligerently.

Sloan took refuge in police-speak. 'There are certain anomalies surrounding the death.'

'What does that mean?' demanded Anna roughly.

'That there are some enquiries still to be made about the deceased . . .' began Sloan. These days the duty of candour was enjoined upon the medical profession but not, thank goodness, on the police.

Yet.

'The deceased . . .' Marilyn Potts choked on the word. 'It's poor Norman who you're talking about, remember . . .'

'What enquiries?' asked Anna Sutherland.

'The provenance of some orchids is one of them,' said Sloan.

Marilyn Potts stared at him. 'Orchids? Are you joking, Inspector?'

'Certainly not, madam. I am quite serious. I understand you were at Staple St James giving a talk on the subject yesterday evening.'

'What about it?'

Detective Inspector Sloan, all policeman now, turned to Anna Sutherland and said, 'And you, madam? Where were you?'

'She was with me,' said Marilyn Potts quickly before her friend could speak.

Anna Sutherland said quite calmly, 'I was with Marilyn in the sense that I drove her over to Staple St James but I stayed in the car outside the hall while she spoke.'

'Why?' asked Crosby.

The older woman replied, 'You probably don't understand, constable, but it's quite difficult to deliver a lecture when there's someone you know well in the audience.'

Detective Inspector Sloan didn't need telling that. His wife, Margaret, knew it too. There had been that trying time when he had been lured into giving a talk to her Tuesday evening club, when to his relief she had fled to the kitchen. He hoped the ladies had forgotten the occasion but he hadn't. He asked the two women at Capstan Purlieu instead, 'Have you any other orchids here apart from the damaged ones we saw yesterday?'

Anna Sutherland muttered, 'The dead ones, you mean,' under her breath.

'Of course I have,' said Marilyn with dignity. 'I brought some back from Staple St James last night after I had given my talk.' She waved a hand. 'They're in one of the sheds over there.'

'With the door closed,' said Anna Sutherland drily.

'I'm keeping them for Enid Osgathorp,' said Marilyn. 'She's bound to ask for them when she gets back.'

'Bound to,' contributed Anna Sutherland. 'No flies on old Enid. If she's paid for them, then they're hers.'

Detective Inspector Sloan said that he would like to see them.

'No problem.' Marilyn Potts led the way to a shed behind the cottage and flung the door open. 'Here we are, Inspector. Six orchids. All different. They're Enid Osgathorp's by rights, you understand.'

Detective Inspector Sloan, who wasn't sure that he understood anything at this point, nodded.

As they entered the shed, Sloan pulled his mobile phone out of his pocket and summoned up a photograph of the two orchids on the sideboard in Norman Potts' house. He compared them with those in the shed. Neither bore any strong resemblance to those standing on the decking in front of him. 'These orchids,' he said, 'which you presumably collected from Jack Haines for your talk last night . . .' If he remembered rightly their provenance had cropped up when he was over there yesterday.

'That's right,' sniffed Marilyn Potts. 'I did.'

'How many did you take with you last night to your talk?' he asked.

'Six,' she said, 'and I brought six back.'

Sloan ran his eye along the row. There were four orchids there.

'I'm sure I brought them all back,' she began, looking more worried than ever. She turned to her friend. 'Didn't I, Anna?'

'You did,' said Anna Sutherland, staring at the four orchids. 'I helped you carry them in.'

Detective Constable Crosby looked up and said brightly. 'She counted them all out but she didn't count them all back.'

'Oh, yes, she did,' Anna Sutherland contradicted him flatly. 'Six of them.' She pointed to the photograph in Sloan's hand. 'I saw them too – including two Dracula orchids just like those.'

'Dracula was a vampire, wasn't he?' remarked Crosby to nobody in particular.

'Yes,' said Anna Sutherland. 'A blood-sucker.'

217

'I brought six orchids back with me,' insisted Marilyn, looking troubled. 'I know I did. You'll back me up on that, won't you, Anna?'

'Oh, yes,' she said, adding enigmatically, 'but we're both heavy sleepers.'

The police car had scarcely faded from view at Capstan Purlieu Nursery before Marilyn Potts turned to her friend Anna Sutherland and started to speak. She seemed to be having some difficulty in forming her words.

'Anna . . . .'

'What is it?'

'Last night.'

'What about last night?'

'When we were over at Staple St James . . .'

'What about it?' said the older woman discouragingly.

'You wouldn't come into the Hall when I was speaking.'

'You know how my being in the audience puts you off. You're always saying so. I must say I myself don't understand why you feel that way but . . .' she opened her hands expressively, 'there you are.'

'No,' said Marilyn.

'No what?'

'No, you weren't there.' Marilyn flushed and went on awkwardly, 'I came out, you see. Someone in the audience wanted one of our plant lists and I'd forgotten to take them into the hall with me so I said I'd get one for him from the car.' Her voice trailed off and she said miserably, 'And you weren't there.'

'No more I was,' agreed Anna Sutherland easily. 'I'd gone for a bit of a potter round, that's all.'

'I thought we were saving petrol now we're so broke.'

'I didn't go far.'

'You took your time about it then.'

'How do you know?'

'I came out again later on and you still weren't there.'

'I was there when you were ready to come home and that's all that matters.'

'No,' said her friend, looking troubled. 'No, it isn't, Anna.'

CHAPTER NINETEEN

'Four orchids and not six?' exploded Superintendent Leeyes, sounding tetchy. 'Is this a criminal case or a flower show, Sloan? What on earth is going on at Capstan Purlieu and in Berebury too, for that matter? First blackmail and now a doubtful death.'

'I don't know exactly, sir,' admitted Sloan, 'but Norman Potts had connections over there.'

'And what about that old party missing from Pelling? Is she connected with of all these floral shenanigans too? Or the death here in Berebury? And where does her blackmailing come in?'

'I don't know that either,' said Sloan, spelling out what he did know about Enid Maude Osgathorp's connections with events to date.

'Was she blackmailing Norman Potts too?' the superintendent enquired with interest. 'He presumably once lived at Pelling since he's Jack Haines' stepson and so she would have known his medical history too.'

'We're already looking into that, sir. The deceased was certainly said to be short of money,' said Sloan. 'At least the landlord of the Railway Tavern told us he was.'

'I wonder what unmentionable lurgy he had been suffering from?' mused the superintendent. 'That's if the missing person was blackmailing him too.'

'I couldn't say, I'm sure, sir,' said Sloan astringently. What he himself really wanted to know was what exactly had been wrong with Benedict Feakins that could account for behaviour bordering on the bizarre.

'There you are, then,' said Leeyes ambiguously.

'We have reason to believe that the six orchids were Enid Osgathorp's in the first place,' he began carefully. 'Ordered by the missing person from Jack Haines . . .'

'Whose nursery was broken into the night before and orchids damaged,' the superintendent reminded him. 'And who also has connections with Norman Potts.'

'But used in a demonstration by someone else because the woman wasn't around to give it herself . . .'

'Not around for reasons which we don't know,' interrupted Leeyes, 'but have reason to suspect.'

'We don't know that yet,' put in Sloan swiftly – and promptly wished he hadn't. It was the sort of rejoinder that his superior officer didn't like and with his Personal Development Discussion pending . . . He belatedly added 'sir', by way of amelioration.

'And it would seem two of the same orchids were probably used by some joker after that,' finished Leeyes for him. 'That's what you're trying to tell me, isn't it?'

Joker wasn't a word Sloan would have used. There had been nothing at all funny about the figure of the man hanging in his kitchen in one of the less attractive neighbourhoods of Berebury. 'We have no way of proving yet that they are the same orchids, of course, but it would seem to be the case. Especially since they were of a variety called Dracula, a name with all its connotations with blood-sucking.'

'Blackmail,' said Leeyes bleakly.

'We're checking on the fingerprints of the two ladies at Capstan Purlieu and those on the pots the orchids at Berebury are in.'

'Is someone saying it with flowers?' asked Leeyes, demonstrating that advertising had reached an unlikely audience.

'That I can't say, sir, not at this stage,' said Sloan regretfully, 'but I think the variety and the gesture must have a meaning. I just don't know what it is.'

'Then find out,' ordered the superintendent grandly. 'And while you're about it, you'd better find that missing person too. Since they were her orchids in the first place she might be able to throw some light on the whole business – if she's still alive, that is. Blackmail is a very dangerous undertaking.'

'We've put out a general alert for her but there hasn't been any response so far. She had a pre-booked return railway ticket for that journey to Wales but it hasn't been handed in there or anywhere else on the route. The Transport Police have been showing her photograph to passengers on the Berebury to London trains.'

'Give 'em something to do,' growled Leeyes at his most

curmudgeonly. He didn't like other police of any sort on his patch.

'But no one remembers seeing her that morning.' Sloan hadn't been surprised at that. His own mother frequently said that grey-haired old ladies were as good as invisible to the general public.

Leeyes grunted. 'And you still don't know whether the deceased here at Berebury was murdered or took his own life.'

'Not yet, sir. A post-mortem is being arranged. We're waiting to be told the time at attend.'

The superintendent sniffed. 'Medical evidence isn't everything.'

Detective Inspector Sloan was the first to agree with him. His own doctor was being quite equivocal about a persistent rash on Sloan's left leg; hesitant about giving him a diagnosis, the physician had merely prescribed a succession of ointments to no avail. Subconsciously reminded of the itch, Sloan now rubbed one leg against the other.

'But let me know what he finds,' said his superior officer.

'We are also very aware,' persisted Sloan, 'that there are connections between the deceased at Berebury, Jack Haines at Pelling and Marilyn Potts at Capstan Purlieu – if not with Enid Osgathorp. We're going back to see Haines at Pelling next.'

Leeyes waved a hand. 'Put it all in your report, Sloan.'

'And then we propose to check up once again on everyone whose plants were damaged by the frost in the greenhouses just in case there is a link somewhere along the line with whoever turned off that greenhouse thermostat. Someone might have wanted to damage a particular customer's plants rather than just Jack Haines' business generally.' He had Benedict Feakins in mind but he didn't say so.

'A scattergun approach, you mean?' Leeyes grunted again. 'Odd way of carrying on, if you ask me.'

'Some of the dead plants,' ploughed on Sloan, 'were for the old admiral and some others for that young couple in the village who had the bonfire as well as those we already know about for the Lingards and Anthony Berra, their garden designer.'

'What does one of those do?' enquired Leeyes with interest. 'Some sort of glorified gardener, is he?'

'A garden designer is,' said Sloan unkindly, 'in my opinion something between an architect and a cookery presenter.'

'Takes all sorts, I suppose,' said Leeyes.

'And to be on the safe side, sir, we'll be checking up on Haines' competitors in the nursery business.'

'That's what I like to see, Sloan,' said the superintendent, unconsciously using a horticultural metaphor, 'you leaving no stone unturned.'

Mandy Lamb had reached the office at the nursery at her usual time that morning but there had been no sign of Jack Haines there when she arrived. It wasn't long though before Russ Aqueel came in looking for him.

'Boss not about then?' the foreman said.

'If he is, he's not here. As you can see,' she added pointedly.

'Well, he's not outside either or I wouldn't have come in here looking for him, would I?'

'Probably not,' said the secretary ambiguously. Rather late in the day she asked if there was anything that she could do for the foreman.

'Bob Steele's been in asking if he could pick up some Penstemon Blueberry Fudge if he came over for them.'

'Again?' Mandy Lamb raised her eyebrows.

'Again,' said Russ.

'Trade, of course,' she said.

'Naturally.'

Mandy Lamb sighed. 'I expect, knowing him as we do, that Jack would say yes.'

'That's what I thought.' He turned. 'I'll get back to Bob and tell him.'

Just then the telephone in the office rang and as Mandy picked it up the foreman slipped away. She listened carefully and then said in the impersonal tones of the perfect secretary, 'I'll tell Mr Haines when he comes in.'

It was another half an hour before Jack Haines arrived at the office. 'Sorry to be so late, I slept in,' he said, flopping wearily into the chair at his desk.

'You don't look as if you've slept at all,' said Mandy, making for the kettle. 'And you've cut yourself shaving.'

He brushed a hand over his jowl and stared bemusedly at the blood on it. 'Any messages?'

'The police are on their way.'

'What for this time?' He didn't sound particularly interested.

'They didn't say.'

He turned over his post in a desultory way. 'Anything else?'

'Anthony Berra's coming in to pick up his new plants for the Lingards.' She indicated a couple of crates on the floor. 'And Benedict Feakins said he was going to bring his cacti in this morning for you to look at but he hasn't turned up yet.'

Jack Haines grunted.

She went on, 'As the admiral's still in hospital Russ hasn't brought the load of bedding plants he ordered inside. It's going to upset our Anthony anyway. He's trying to wean him off them.'

'Tough.'

'And Russ says Bob Steele wants some more plants from us.'

'He does, does he?' It wasn't clear who Jack Haines meant by this.

'But Russ thought you would agree and so he's gone to ring him.'

'Oh, he has, has he?' It was quite clear that the nurseryman meant the foreman this time. He accepted the coffee gratefully. 'I've got a helluva headache.'

'I can see that,' she said, noting the black shadows under his eyes. 'You look like you've had a night on the tiles.'

'Only in a manner of speaking.' He gulped his coffee down.

'Not under them anyway,' she concluded neatly. 'You need some sticking plaster on that cut, by the way.'

'What I actually need is some more coffee before the police arrive.'

Mandy Lamb looked up as a car drew up outside the window. 'Too late. They're here.'

'I understand,' stated Detective Inspector Sloan, with some formality, 'from what you told my constable and myself earlier that you know a man called Norman Potts.'

Jack Haines said, 'I do. Only too well.'

'Do you mind telling me when you last saw him?' Detective Inspector Sloan, a man well-versed in the many pitfalls associated with dealing with potentially injured parties as opposed to suspects, kept his questioning as low-key as possible.

The nurseryman shrugged his shoulders. 'Weeks ago. Like I told you. He came round to see if I could tell him where his former wife was. I told him to push off. Why do you want to know? What's he done now?'

Sloan was not deflected. 'Why should he have come here looking for her?'

'I trained her,' said Haines briefly. 'It's where she first met him and he thought I might know where she was.'

'And did you?'

'Yes.'

'Did you tell him?'

'No.'

Sloan nodded and made a note. Unexpanded responses were only one stage removed from the proverbial 'No Comment' and usually about as helpful. Sloan's eyes, gardener that he was, strayed in the direction of the two crates in the corner of the room. The plants looked top-notch – he spotted evergreen shrubs and some roses. They would be ready for planting – in fact the roses would be better for being in the ground by now. 'Tell me, this Norman Potts – would he have had any reason for damaging your plants?' With an effort he took his eyes off the crates, both full to overflowing, and brought his attention back to what Jack Haines was saying.

'No, but he probably thought he had.'

Sloan nodded. 'Quite so.'

'Matrimonial causes,' put in Crosby without quite knowing what the phrase meant.

'I'll say,' said Haines.

Deliberately lowering the temperature of the interview still further, Detective Inspector Sloan pointed to the plants. 'Someone's got some good stuff coming their way.'

'They have indeed,' said Haines, sounding cheerful for the first time, the nurseryman in him rising to the fore. 'They're for the Lingards – some replacements for what was lost in the break-in. We had a bit of trouble getting hold of some of them but I don't think we've done too badly in the circumstances.'

Sloan walked over and read some of the labels aloud. 'Abelia, Philadelphus, Ribes, Syringa, Cistus, Osmanthus . . .' He stood for a moment, something stirring at the back of his mind. He waited for a moment for it to surface and when it didn't he turned a label over on one of the plants. 'Here's one I don't know – Japanese Bitter Orange.'

'Can you eat it?' asked Crosby.

'Not if you've got any sense,' growled Jack Haines, 'but it does well in lime.'

Detective Inspector Sloan, still looking at the plants, asked absently, 'And Marilyn Potts at Capstan Purlieu?

Would Norman Potts have had anything against her?'

'I imagine he thought so.' Haines sounded almost indifferent, certainly not alarmed. 'Norman was like that.'

'Interesting lot of plants you've got there,' Sloan said, producing a photograph of the two orchids found at the house in Berebury and asking Jack Haines if he recognised them.

The nurseryman held it in his hands and said, 'Orchid Dracula andreettae. I sell quite a few.' He handed the photograph back to Sloan who folded it away carefully in his notebook. 'Want some?'

Sloan shook his head and then asked casually as if it was of no consequence, 'Last night, sir, do you mind telling me where you went after work?'

'Home,' said Jack Haines.

'Home alone?' intervened Detective Constable Crosby involuntarily.

'My wife died some years ago,' said Haines with dignity.

'Thank you, sir,' said Detective Inspector Sloan as if totally satisfied by this and getting up to go. He saw no point in revealing at this stage that Traffic Division's number recognition system had noted that Jack Haines' car had been recorded stationed outside Berebury Garden Centre for some time before travelling back to Pelling in the early hours of the morning.

That nugget of information could wait.

CHAPTER TWENTY

Inspector Harpe had been quite adamant on the matter. Two members of Traffic Division had spotted a car parked outside the grounds of the Berebury Garden Centre in the early hours of the morning with the driver sitting at the wheel. They had seen it again an hour or so later, still there.

'You're quite sure, aren't you, Harry?' asked Sloan, back at the police station again.

'I'm not, but they are,' responded Inspector Harpe promptly. He was known throughout the Calleshire Force as Happy Harry on account of his never having been seen to smile. He on his part maintained that there had never been anything in Traffic Division to make him smile. 'They couldn't think what an old codger like him was doing out and about at that hour of the night so they kept an eye . . .'

'He's a bit past "taking without owner's consent", a

man of that age,' agreed Sloan, glad that stolen cars didn't come within his own remit.

'Twocking's a young man's crime,' agreed Harpe, experienced in the matter. 'Even so my boys fed the number of his car through our trusty number recognition system and decided he was the registered holder all right and properly insured.'

'But you don't know what he was doing out at the time?'

'Sorry, Seedy.' Harpe shrugged his shoulders. 'You know how it is. The man's driving was OK, he wasn't speeding, he wasn't even on a mobile phone which makes a change from some of the young ladies we come across. They had no reason to suppose he was drunk in charge so they couldn't very well breathalyse him. His car seemed to be all right too, so my lads couldn't think of anything to stop him for.' The inspector sounded faintly regretful.

'Where exactly was he when they saw him?'

'Sitting outside the place. That's all.'

'Got any times?'

'Is that important?'

'It might be,' said Detective Inspector Sloan, adding fairly, 'on the other hand it might not.'

Inspector Harpe has just given them to him when Sloan's telephone rang. He listened for a moment and then said 'Sorry, Harry, go to go. A post-mortem . . .'

Detective Constable Crosby did not like attending post-mortem examinations. This was made manifest by his seeking the furthest point in the mortuary at which he could stand and still be nominally part of the proceedings.

Detective Inspector Sloan did not exactly relish having to be present at post-mortems either but took good care not to allow this fact to be evident to Doctor Dabbe or the pathologist's reserved assistant, Burns.

The doctor welcomed them to his domain as if the place was his home. Perhaps it was a good as his home, thought Sloan, some men being more married to their work than others. A vision of his own wife, Margaret, in their own home rose unbidden into his mind. He banished it as he realised that Doctor Dabbe was talking to him.

'We've done his blood picture for you, Sloan,' said Doctor Dabbe, adding somewhat unscientifically, 'Alcohol levels pretty well ringing the bell at the top. He must have been as drunk as a monkey.'

'What about drugs?' As far as Sloan knew monkeys had more sense than to get drunk.

Doctor Dabbe shook his head. 'No evidence of anything else found as yet. We'll be doing more tests, of course.'

'According to the pub landlord,' said Sloan, 'the deceased hadn't been in the Railway Tavern last night but there was a great heap of empty cans out the back.'

'They should have been recycled,' observed Crosby censoriously.

The pathologist spoke some numbers into the microphone that dangled above the post-mortem table at mouth height, adding in an aside to the two policemen, 'He's more than a bit underweight which compounds the effect of alcohol.'

Sloan regarded the body on the post-mortem slab. 'He was quite a small man in the first place.'

Doctor Dabbe pinched a fold of the dead man's skin

between his gloved fingers and said with professional dispassion, 'Undernourished too, but not dehyrated.'

'Heavy drinkers don't eat well,' said Sloan.

'They don't usually eat at all,' said the pathologist, peering round the puny body. 'I'll be surprised if we don't find that he's got an enlarged liver too.'

'Quite so,' said Detective Inspector Sloan, who would have liked a little less of the 'we' in these particular surroundings.

There was a slight movement at the edge of the laboratory indicating that Detective Constable Crosby had put two and two together. 'A small, unwell man who was as high as a kite wouldn't have been able to put up much of a fight if someone came into his house late at night,' he said.

'A very drunk man of any size wouldn't have been up to tying a rope over a beam and tying a noose round his neck of the right length, let alone clambering up on a chair and then kicking it out of the way,' pointed out Sloan. 'That's right, isn't it, doctor? We're not talking suicide here, are we?'

'Not like that poor lady over at Pelling,' remarked Crosby brightly.

Doctor Dabbe looked up. 'Oh, you mean the rector's wife? Oh, no, no doubt about that one. Open and shut.'

That wasn't a simile Sloan liked in the mortuary but anything that had happened in Pelling interested him just now and so he asked, 'Had she been treated for depression or didn't that come out?'

'It did and she hadn't,' said Dabbe pithily. 'At least she hadn't consulted her general practitioner because he was called to the inquest.'

Sloan searched in the recesses of his mind for a name. 'Doctor Heddon?'

'No, not him. He'd died by then. A new fellow. I forget his name. Pity she didn't go and see him rather than taking an overdose.' Dabbe looked solemn. 'Did you know that some early Christians used to feel that illness was sent by God and it was impious to attempt to cure it? Now they blame the doctors for not being able to cure everything.'

Detective Inspector Sloan, policeman to the last, took a deep breath and said, 'I didn't know that.' The parallel that crime might equally have come from the Devil shouldn't in his view stop a law officer from trying to prevent it or trying to bring the culprit to justice.

'Perhaps she was one of those,' said Doctor Dabbe. 'Not,' he added judiciously, 'that you could do much about disease in those days so it probably didn't matter anyway.'

'How exactly did she do it?' asked Sloan. One thing he did know was that suicides tended to follow a pattern. Copycat, like some crimes. And sometimes catching.

'Overdose of paracetamol,' said the pathologist succinctly.

Detective Constable Crosby chanted softly to himself, 'Why are there no aspirins in the jungle? Because the "parrots eat 'em all".'

Sloan elected not to hear this.

So did Doctor Dabbe, who said 'Paracetamol makes for the liver like a homing pigeon.'

'The Coroner brought in a verdict of suicide anyway,' said Sloan.

'Don't talk to me about Coroners,' said the pathologist.

'Delusions of grandeur, most of them,' said Crosby.

'What they say goes,' said Sloan, who wasn't sure if that was the same thing.

'What they say gets reported in the press without the benefit of correction,' said Doctor Dabbe ineluctably. He turned back and resumed addressing the microphone hanging above the deceased. 'Macroscopic examination also shows burns on the face, lips and mouth consistent with the use of a control spray at close quarters. Further superficial signs include bruised fists and an appendix scar.'

Detective Inspector Sloan knew all about bruised fists in heavy drinkers, the pugnacious ones, that is.

Doctor Dabbe said, 'My man, Burns, has got all the photographs of the knot that we need but I can't tell you much more about it at this stage.' The pathologist reached for something approximating to a saw while Crosby looked away.

Sloan asked, 'If he didn't tie it himself could someone standing behind him do it the same way without that showing?'

'I'm afraid so. No help there but there's no doubt about the facial burns. Or about the death being by suspension.'

Why this sounded better than hanging Sloan didn't know.

CHAPTER TWENTY-ONE

'The pathologist,' began Sloan, reporting back, duty bound, from the mortuary to Superintendent Leeyes, 'has advised me, sir, that he is minded to say that in his opinion the late Norman Potts did not take his own life.'

'Then find out who did take it, Sloan,' said Leeyes in his usual peremptory manner, adding for good measure 'And why.'

'The "how" might be a little easier to discover than the "who",' ventured Sloan more than a little tentatively. 'Or even than the "why".'

'Means, motive and opportunity,' the superintendent chanted the three essential constituents of crime perpetrated by the sane as if it was a mantra, which perhaps it was.

'A rope, a beam and bit of know-how might do for the means,' said Sloan, putting the old phrase 'a rag, a bone and a hank of hair' firmly to the back of his mind, although now he came to think of it a hank of hair – well not so much a hank as just a hair or so – had turned up at the break-in of Enid Osgathorp's cottage. He mustn't forget that. Or the blood on the glass of the broken pantry window. He mustn't forget Benedict Feakins' interview either. He shot a surreptitious glance at his watch. 'As for motive, sir, it's a bit too soon to say. It would appear that the deceased was a less than ideal husband and stepson but whether he was the one who destroyed their orchids and therefore either his former wife or his stepfather . . .'

'Or both,' said Leeyes, a man capable of complicating any situation.

'Or both,' said Sloan compliantly, 'took their revenge in a tit-for-tat way . . .'

'This isn't playground stuff surely, Sloan.'

'No, sir, I'm aware that sounds highly unlikely.'

'But you never can tell,' agreed Leeyes. 'There was that woman who could have been done in for a hatpin.' The superintendent's encounter with the dramatic works of George Bernard Shaw had foundered very early.

'Quite so, sir,' said Sloan, hastening on, 'As for opportunity, no one seems to have seen or heard anything near his house down by the railway here.'

'Two orchids scarcely amount to Birnam Wood coming to Dunsinane,' said Leeyes.

'Beg pardon, sir?'

'Macbeth,' said the superintendent vaguely.

'According to Doctor Dabbe,' said Sloan, making for firmer ground, 'the death took place either side of midnight last night.'

'The bewitching hour,' grunted Leeyes. 'At least

Cinderella got the time right. You knew where you were with her, timewise.'

'The doctor won't say further than that at this stage,' said Sloan stolidly. There was a school of thought that held that both nursery rhymes and fairy stories were rooted in crime, citing Little Red Riding Hood and the Babes in the Wood, but this was no time to be advancing the theory.

'Doctor Dabbe never will say,' grumbled Leeyes. 'He's too fly.'

'And we don't know at this stage either whether time was of the essence.' There would be someone in the background whom he hoped was already establishing a timeline of events and alibis for him to work on later.

'It doesn't take us any nearer the "who" anyway,' said Leeyes unhelpfully.

'No, sir,' agreed Sloan.

'Well, don't hang about, Sloan.'

'No, sir,' he said, making for the door.

The superintendent stopped him when his hand was on the door handle. 'I did say that your Personal Development Discussion was on Friday morning, didn't I?'

'You did, sir,' said Detective Inspector Sloan, adding in an even voice. 'I hadn't forgotten.'

It was later when Sloan saw the superintendent again. 'I don't know which is worse,' said Leeyes morosely.

'Sir?' Sloan was surprised. Admissions of doubt from his superior officer were few and far between.

'Blackmail or murder.'

Detective Inspector Sloan didn't know either. Blackmail, he thought, because there were sometimes – only rarely, of course – extenuating circumstances for murder, such as when the murderer was driven to commit it by the victim. That happened. Mercy killings came to mind too. He said, 'We seem to have both, sir.'

Leeyes sniffed. 'Blackmail is the worst, I think. Not that it's in the Ten Commandments.'

'A nasty mixture of power and greed,' said Sloan, surprised. The superintendent usually only quoted the criminal law, not the moral one.

'What we don't seem to have, Sloan, is another body. That is if someone's done for your lady blackmailer.'

'What we do seem to have, sir, in Norman Potts,' he advanced tentatively, 'is a victim of unlawful killing. He may or may not have any connection with either the missing person or blackmail but would seem to be involved somehow with orchids.' So, he thought, were Jack Haines and the two ladies at Capstan Purlieu but he didn't know how or why.

Yet.

'Would seem, Sloan?' echoed Leeyes derisively. 'Surely when two blooms of the same variety, said to have been supplied by one nursery and missing from another, are found sitting on the deceased's sideboard after he's been murdered it's more than just chance?'

'It's subject to proof,' murmured Sloan. He wasn't at all sure how he was going to bring that about, one plant of a species being very much the same as another – as presumably nature intended.

'And the aforementioned blooms known,' added

Leeyes for good measure, 'to have been the property of the missing woman.'

That too was subject to proof but Sloan thought it prudent not to say so.

'And of a variety named after a bloodsucker,' sniffed Leeyes. 'You'd noticed that, I take it, Sloan?'

'Yes, sir.' Sloan went on to murmur vaguely that horticulture did seem to come into things somehow but he wasn't sure quite how.

Superintendent Leeyes, no gardener, responded with something that would have greatly upset Capability Brown.

'Quite so, sir,' said Sloan hastily. 'In the meantime the Scenes of Crime team are going over the deceased's house and I am about to question Benedict Feakins under caution to see if I can get any further with him.'

Simon Puckle of Puckle, Puckle and Nunnery, who was sitting beside Benedict Feakins in the interview room at Berebury Police Station, was presenting a very different side of his work to the three other men there. Gone altogether was the professional family solicitor solemnly advising a client on probate matters. Gone too was the urbane man of the law and public citizen demonstrating helpfulness in response to a legitimate police inquiry. In its place was something more akin to a she-wolf protecting her young.

'My client,' he began formally, 'has duly attended here for interview under caution in response to the written request delivered to him under the Police and Criminal Evidence Act of 1984.'

'I didn't need to come,' said Benedict Feakins, sounding sulky. He pointed to his legal adviser. 'But he said I ought to.'

'Quite so,' said Detective Inspector Sloan, administering the caution without delay.

'What I advised my client,' murmured the solicitor, choosing his words with care, 'was that he was not obliged to accept the police's invitation to attend . . .'

'Some invitation!' echoed Feakins scornfully.

'But,' continued the solicitor smoothly, 'I also advised him that if he did not attend as requested, his refusal to do so could be brought to the court's attention at the time of any sentencing.'

'Sentencing for what?' howled Feakins, starting to leap up in his chair and then falling back in pain from his back.

'For whatever you'd done,' said Detective Constable Crosby in the manner of one spelling things out to the young.

'I haven't done anything,' protested Feakins. 'You're just setting me up.'

'On the contrary,' said Sloan stiffly, 'we are primarily interested in establishing further lines of enquiry in matters that have arisen in the village of Pelling.' In the opinion of Detective Inspector Sloan what Benedict Feakins needed was a nursemaid, not a solicitor.

'Why didn't you call it a summons in the first place if that's what it is?' exploded Benedict Feakins.

'Because it isn't,' repeated Detective Inspector Sloan austerely.

'I must explain to you, Mr Feakins,' said Simon Puckle, turning to his client, 'that had you been served with a summons you wouldn't be being questioned any further.'

Unsure what this meant, Benedict Feakins sat back looking mutinous.

Detective Inspector Sloan took the lead. 'It is an interview under the caution I have just read you. It is an occasion to give you the opportunity to comment on some matters that have been brought to our attention.'

'Such as?' challenged Feakins in spite of an admonitory look from Simon Puckle.

'I do think, Inspector,' intervened the solicitor, 'that it would be a help if you could possibly be a little more specific.'

'That's right,' said Feakins, sitting back and folding his arms across his chest.

'Such as exactly what you had put on your bonfire,' said Sloan.

'I've told you already,' said Feakins. 'All my father's old things.'

'Including some cremated ashes,' said Sloan. 'You didn't tell us about them.'

'Why should I have done?' Feakins came back quickly. 'It's not a crime what I did with them. They've got to go somewhere, haven't they?'

Simon Puckle bent towards Benedict Feakins and said something under his breath to his client.

'All right then,' said that young man ungraciously, 'but I don't see why I should say anything.'

'Because we have grounds for suspicion that an offence has been committed,' Sloan proceeded patiently.

'Over a bonfire?' said Benedict Feakins, while Simon Puckle leant forward attentively.

'Over a breaking and entering at Canonry Cottage, Pelling, at an unknown date,' said Detective Inspector Sloan in a steely voice. He pulled a sheet of paper towards him and went on, 'During which it is alleged that you scratched your head on some broken glass on a window, the property of Enid Maude Osgathorp, leaving traces of blood and hair on it.'

There were two quite different responses in the interview room to this. One was from Simon Puckle who said something sharp to his client but inaudible to the two policemen. The other was from Benedict Feakins himself. 'I didn't . . .' he began and then fell quite silent.

And would say no more.

Not even when Detective Inspector Sloan advised him that his silence would be deemed to be a refusal to answer questions and recorded as such; and definitely not after Detective Constable Crosby had remarked in conversational tones that he had always understood that silence constituted consent.

'Not in this instance,' said Simon Puckle suavely. 'I can if you wish quote the precedents.'

It was only after the detective constable had been rebuked for making the comment and told he was out of order by Detective Inspector Sloan that a faint smile crossed Feakins' face. Simon Puckle merely shook his head sadly, but at what it was quite impossible to say.

The atmosphere at Capstan Purlieu Plants was still somewhat strained but it had been considerably relieved by the arrival there of Anthony Berra. Declaring himself in search of even more plants, he looked from one to the other of the two women at the nursery before saying, 'What's up, Marilyn? Is there something wrong, Anna?'

'No,' said Anna Sutherland. She shrugged her shoulders. 'Well, yes, I suppose, in a way.'

'Yes, there is,' said Marilyn Potts tearfully. 'It's Norman.'

'Your Norman?' asked Berra, giving a cough.

'He's not her Norman any more,' insisted Anna. 'Hasn't been for ages.'

'What about him?' persisted Berra.

'He's dead,' gulped Marilyn.

Anthony Berra sat down on a bench. 'What's happened? Tell me.'

'We don't know,' said Anna. 'The police have been round but they wouldn't tell us anything much.'

'Except that he was dead,' wailed Marilyn, aping police-speak and adding in a solemn voice, 'in circumstances that have still to be established.'

'Whatever that might mean,' said her friend.

Anthony Berra looked blankly from one to the other. 'But he wasn't an old man.'

'And he isn't going to be one now,' said Anna Sutherland grimly. 'And you won't be either, Anthony, unless you get something done about that cough of yours.'

'Come on, Marilyn,' urged the landscape designer, ignoring this. 'For heaven's sake, fill me in.'

'I can't,' she said. 'I don't know anything more.'

'Yes, you do,' her friend Anna contradicted her. 'Some person or persons unknown nicked some of Enid's orchids from our shed after we got back from Staple St James last night.'

'She won't like that,' said Anthony Berra immediately. 'Enid's always very particular about anything that's hers.'

'You can say that again,' said Anna.

'But why would anyone want to steal two of her orchids?' he asked, clearly puzzled.

'Search me,' said Anna. 'But the police were looking for whoever did it all right.'

'And what – if anything – has that got to do with Norman dying?' frowned Berra. 'I don't get it.'

'The police didn't say,' said Anna in a detached manner. 'In fact they didn't say very much at all.'

'We don't even know where they are – the missing orchids, I mean,' put in Marilyn. 'They didn't tell us that either.'

'Or Norman, come to that,' said Anna. 'We don't know where he is either.'

'Except that he's dead,' said Marilyn, showing signs of bursting into tears.

Anthony Berra asked hurriedly, 'What about Jack Haines? Does he know about Norman?'

Anna Sutherland shrugged her shoulders again. 'I couldn't say but I expect the police have been to see him too.'

'They have,' said Marilyn tremulously. 'I rang him and he's as puzzled as we are. Jack wondered if he'd committed suicide from remorse.'

'Could be, I suppose,' commented Berra, 'if he was the one who opened Jack's greenhouse doors.'

'And ours,' pointed out Anna vigorously.

'All the same it seems going a bit far,' said Berra. 'Suicide, I mean.'

'He always was a bit unbalanced,' said Anna.

'I hope Jack has told Russ Aqueel too,' said Marilyn. 'He and Norman were pretty thick when Norman lived and worked at the nursery.'

'So they were,' said Anthony Berra slowly. 'I'd quite forgotten that connection.'

'So I expect he knows, all right, by now,' said Anna.

'Bad news travels fast,' said Berra sententiously, getting to his feet. 'And I'll have to get going too. I've got to get back to the Lingards at the Grange and do some watering.'

Anna Sutherland gave something approaching a chortle. 'Can't very well ask your lady employer to do it for you, can you? Not her.'

'Not likely,' said Anthony Berra. 'She might get her feet wet and I daren't begin to think what her shoes cost. They're Italian jobs.'

CHAPTER TWENTY-TWO

Mary Feakins took one look at her husband's face as he hobbled out of the police station at Berebury and made for their car. She waited while he parted from Simon Puckle – apparently without saying very much – and then she hurried round to open the front passenger door and help him in. As he lowered himself with great care onto the car seat she asked breathlessly, 'Well, how did it go?'

'I think the police believe I've made away with Enid Osgathorp,' he said hollowly.

'Never!'

'Apparently she's been missing for over three weeks now. At least, that's what they told me.'

'Don't be silly, Benedict. Why on earth would you want to do a thing like that?'

Her husband seemed to sink between his own shoulders. 'They say they found some blood and hairs on a broken window at her cottage and want to test them against mine. Simon Puckle said I should agree to samples being taken from me as it would look bad if I didn't.'

'But you hardly know the woman,' she protested, the real import of what he'd said not yet registering in her mind.

'She knows me though,' he said elliptically. 'Well, the family, anyway.'

'What exactly does that mean?'

'I can't tell you,' he said miserably.

Her eyes widened. 'You mean you really did break into her cottage, Benedict? I don't believe it! Are you mad? Didn't you think that she might have been in there and that it would have frightened her?'

'They say I knew she wasn't there. Don't you remember she told us she was going away? And anyway it wouldn't have frightened her,' he added bitterly. 'Nothing would.'

'But whatever for?' she asked, still bewildered.

'I was looking for something she said she had.'

'Something of yours? Why should she have anything of yours?' She swung the car out onto the road to Pelling, hardly paying any attention to other road users. 'And why should you have gone looking for it, anyway?'

'Not of mine. Dad's.' He pushed his foot down hard on the floor of the car as if braking. 'Watch it, Mary. You'll hit something in a minute if you're not careful.'

'Your father's?' she said, taking her eyes off the road to stare at him.

He nodded speechlessly, keeping looking straight ahead and not meeting her eye.

She tightened her hands on the steering wheel until the

knuckles whitened. 'I don't understand anything, Benedict. Anything at all. And whatever it is, you haven't told me.' Her voice sunk to a whisper. 'Don't you remember? We promised not to have any secrets from each other.' Even if her husband didn't realise it, Mary Feakins knew that they had just crossed the Rubicon in their marriage. It was borne in on her too, that she didn't like being on the other side of that particular river.

Benedict Feakins had other things on his mind altogether. 'Apparently they've got me recorded on one of those street cameras in Berebury High Street too.'

'What about it? You often go in there.'

'It was on the day Enid Osgathorp disappeared not far from the station. They say I was photographed coming out of the ironmongers two doors away from the station with a spade.'

'That's the one you bought for digging the border,' she said promptly. 'Oh, God . . . they don't think that you . . .'

'I don't know what the police think,' he said shakily. 'They don't ever say, but I know they wouldn't stop asking me questions. Like whether I'd been a patient of Doctor Heddon's. Well, of course I hadn't because the old boy had died before we came to live in Pelling.' He frowned in recollection. 'The inspector seemed to lay off a bit after that.'

'That's something, anyway.'

'But it's not all.'

'Go on.'

'They asked if I'd got anything left of Dad's. Anything at all. And I said I hadn't. They didn't like that for one minute, I can tell you.'

'Benedict,' she was the one looking straight ahead now and not meeting his eye, 'there is one thing in the house left of his.'

'What's that?' he shot at her. 'Tell me.'

'His photograph. The one of him in the silver frame that was in the sitting room. I put it somewhere safe before you could put it on the bonfire.'

To her surprise he greeted this with a hollow laugh and a shaking of his head. 'You don't understand a single thing that this is about, do you, Mary?'

'No,' she said bluntly. 'I don't.'

'That photograph's not my father's.'

'Don't be silly, Benedict. Of course, it is. I knew him, remember?'

'It's only a picture of him.'

'That's what I just said.'

'But it's not his in the sense I'm talking about, which is a very different thing.'

Mary Feakins sighed. 'I still don't understand, Benedict.'

'And I can't explain,' he said unhappily.

Police Superintendent Leeyes was more sympathetic about Benedict Feakins having kept silent than Sloan had expected. 'Happened to me once,' he said gruffly. 'I kicked up rough about the interviewee not speaking and got told pretty sharpish that the solicitor can tell his client to keep schtum if the interviewing officer hasn't disclosed enough about the nature of the case against the suspect for the legal-eagle to advise him properly. Or her,' he added belatedly. He didn't like female solicitors or, come to that, female criminals.

'The trouble, sir, is that we don't know quite enough about it ourselves to disclose very much more,' admitted Sloan. 'Besides, I didn't want to show my hand too soon.'

'But you say two separate entries have been made to that property at Pelling and the old party hasn't been seen since,' rumbled Leeyes.

'Yes, sir.'

The superintendent shot a suspicious look in Sloan's direction. 'You're not holding off because she might have been up to no good, are you?'

'No, sir.' This was true. Somewhere at the back of his mind the line about 'Theirs not to reason why . . .' surfaced. He knew what his job was and he would do it; crime was a hydra-headed monster and he knew too that a policeman should not select which parts of it to tackle. A crime was – and remained – a crime.

'The missing person must be somewhere,' rumbled on Leeyes. 'Dead or alive. Not that you can dig up half Calleshire to look for her.'

'No, sir. We have good reason to believe that she was a blackmailer, though,' said Sloan. 'I've got a reliable witness whom she tried it on but who wouldn't play ball.'

'But presumably no actual proof,' pointed out the superintendent, a genius for finding the weakness in a case. 'You can't prove a negative, you know.'

'Yes, sir, I remember you saying,' said Sloan. This, he knew, was a legacy from some evening class or other that the superintendent had graced. Had it been Philosophy? Or was it Logic, a class abandoned by the superintendent over a difference of opinion with the lecturer about the nature of Occam's Razor? He couldn't remember and went on hurriedly, 'I have high hopes that Admiral Catterick will be prepared to testify to this. But we still don't know whose ashes were on that bonfire of Benedict Feakins – and as far as I can see we have no means of finding out since DNA doesn't survive cremation.' He put wild thoughts of Enid Osgathorp having been cremated under a false name out of his mind as being quite impractical, the clerical work involved in certifying death being what it was.

'We may never know short of this fellow Feakins telling you,' said Leeyes.

'And being truthful about it,' said Sloan, making for the sanctuary of his own office as soon as he could. There was a pile of reports waiting for him there. So was Detective Constable Crosby.

The first was a message from the forensic pathologist, Doctor Dabbe, stating that as a result of further tests he could now confirm the presence in the body said to be that of Norman Potts, deceased, of a substance consistent with its having come from a so far unidentified variety of control spray. Sloan tossed the report over to Detective Constable Crosby.

'Bit wordy, isn't he?' said Crosby.

'You may say he's dotting the *i*'s and crossing the *t*'s, all right,' agreed Sloan, 'but remember what he says has got to stand up in court. Mind you,' he added, 'he's quite possibly proving murder on the way but by whom and why we don't know.'

'Yet,' said Crosby optimistically.

Sloan ignored this touching faith in their ability to find a murderer and picked up the next message. It was from

Inspector Harpe of Traffic Division. None of his squad had spotted a small runabout truck registered in the joint names of Anna Sutherland and Marilyn Potts of Capstan Purlieu Plants in or around Ship Street in Berebury the night before.

Or, indeed, anywhere else.

'Not that there's any reason why either of them would want Norman Potts knocked off,' said Crosby when he too read this.

'No reason that we know of,' Sloan corrected him, 'but it very much looks as if those orchids came from their shed.'

'And from Jack Haines' place before that,' said Crosby.

'Much, Crosby, as I dislike being manipulated,' Sloan said acidly, 'I can see that someone, somewhere, is behaving as if they wanted us to make the connection – and with Dracula – but exactly why escapes me for the moment. Anyone could have picked those flowers up from that shed after the two women got back from that precious lecture of theirs. It wasn't even locked.'

'Which lecture Marilyn Potts was delivering instead of Enid Osgathorp,' Crosby reminded him.

'I know, I know,' said Sloan, picking up the third report. It was from the police constable whose beat included Pelling and several other villages out that way. As requested he had kept a watchful eye on Russ Aqueel, foreman at Jack Haines' nursery. But at a distance.

'A bit of a drinker,' ran the text, 'and not too discreet. Keeps dropping hints in the pub that he might be getting a better job soon. Visits the Berebury Garden Centre a lot, usually taking trays of plants over there. Insists to all and sundry that he doesn't know who left the greenhouse doors open but that it wasn't him. His mates aren't so sure.'

Sloan tossed the paper over to Crosby. 'If Bob Steele at the Berebury Garden Centre is thinking of making a bid for Jack Haines' place then lowering its value would certainly help,' he said. 'And a fall in its value must definitely have happened big time after he lost two greenhouses full of plants – especially at this time of the year. With or without the assistance of Russ Aqueel, who may or may not have been promised a better job by him.'

'Steele could have been aiming at making Jack Haines bankrupt instead,' offered Crosby. 'Keep the price down a treat that would. He could buy at a fire sale.'

'Or even just destroying all those baby orchids so he could sell his own instead,' mused Sloan. 'A shortage could then be met from the Berebury Garden Centre, not Haines' nursery. That would explain the trouble at Capstan Purlieu as well. Even so, we'd better see this man Steele and have another word with the foreman at Pelling.'

'Turf wars, I bet,' pronounced Crosby. 'Fits with garden centres, doesn't it? They sell turves, don't they?'

Detective Inspector Sloan ignored this and replaced the last of the message sheets on his desk. 'That it, then?'

'In a manner of speaking, sir.' The constable was toying with yet another piece of paper, reading and re-reading it. 'There's one here that I don't understand.'

'From Forensics?' Sloan hazarded a guess. They were a section that tended to speak in tongues of their own devising.

'No, sir. It's from Admiral Catterick's daily woman

at the Park. She rang to say that she's heard from the hospital that the admiral has answered Gabriel's call. Who's Gabriel, sir?'

'An archangel, Crosby,' said Sloan, well-brought up son of a churchwoman.

'An archangel?' Crosby sounded mystified.

'I'm very much afraid,' said Sloan slowly, 'it's her way of saying that Waldo Catterick has been transferred to Ward 13 at the hospital.'

The detective constable looked quite blank. 'So?'

'Ward 13 is a euphemism for the hospital's mortuary,' said Sloan sadly. 'It sounds better if the patients overhear the porters being sent for.'

Crosby's face cleared as unconsciously he used yet another euphemism. 'Oh, he's popped his clogs, then. Bad luck.'

'It's bad luck for us all. Our operation and his. His must have been too much for him.' Sloan paused and added thoughtfully, 'Especially in his state of health.'

CHAPTER TWENTY-THREE

'Right, Crosby, we need to get going out to Pelling to interview Jack Haines again now we know a bit more background.' Detective Inspector Sloan was just shovelling some papers into his briefcase when the Coroner's Officer, PC Edward York, put his head round the office door. 'And then get back to Norman Potts' house,' said Sloan.

'Got a minute, Inspector?' York asked.

'Have a heart, Ted,' pleaded Sloan. 'I've only just got back from reporting to the old man on the outcome of conducting an interview under caution to do with a missing person.' He didn't suppose for one moment that the Coroner's Officer was interested in missing persons. Not until they had been found dead, that is. 'And you know that I can't even begin to write my own report for the Coroner on the Potts' case until the doctor's done his. I haven't had a full report from Charlie Marsden yet, either. The SOCOs are still at the house.'

'I can see you're busy,' said the other officer calmly.

'Yes,' put in Crosby importantly, 'besides we think we're into murder.'

The Coroner's Officer said, 'Oh, really? No, I don't need anything more about Norman Potts. Not just yet, anyway. The Coroner'll only be taking formal evidence of identification when the inquest comes up, which won't be for a bit.'

'And that'll be adjourned while further enquiries are made,' chanted Crosby in mocking tones.

'That's right. To give you guys time to get on with finding out who did it,' rejoined York amiably. 'No, it's not him I've come about.'

'Who, then?' asked Sloan in tones that he hoped implied he didn't have all day.

'The rector of Pelling's been in touch.' As Coroner's Officer, Edward York was quite used to being seen as the friendly face of the constabulary and approached as such.

'Mr Beddowes?' Sloan's head came up and he turned to his constable. 'That reminds me, Crosby. We need a photograph of Norman Potts so that we can see if any of the street cameras picked him up in Berebury as well as the others the day Enid Osgathorp disappeared. See to it.' He turned back to the Coroner's Officer and explained. 'We caught the rector on CCTV in Berebury that day too. What does he want now?'

Edward York carried on, 'He thought he ought to tell somebody about a letter that's come to the rectory and being a clergyman he wanted to do the right thing.'

Sloan forbore to remark that he had known a number of men of the cloth who had done the wrong thing, clerical errors not being unknown to the Force. 'Tell us what exactly, Ted?'

'He's had a letter – or more accurately, a letter came addressed to his late wife – which naturally he opened. It was from the Calleshire Adoption Support Agency over at Calleford.'

'Ah,' breathed Sloan, light beginning to dawn.

'The agency said it was providing intermediary services for an unnamed male applicant of theirs. They were asking on his behalf for Mrs Ann Beddowes' consent to tell them her name and address and for permission for the person concerned to make contact.'

'Bit difficult that, seeing she's dead now,' remarked Crosby.

'That explains a lot,' Sloan let out a long breath. It probably explained why the rector's wife hadn't been at the presentation ceremony on her retirement to Enid Osgathorp too.

'Like what?' asked Crosby, clearly mystified.

'Like why she committed suicide, I expect,' said York, adding sapiently, 'A permanent solution to a temporary problem, that's what suicide is.'

'Like why she was being blackmailed,' said Sloan grimly.

'Apparently,' York continued on his current theme, 'the system is that at any time after its eighteenth birthday an adopted child can attempt to get in touch with its birth mother through the Adoption Agency. They can only go ahead, of course, if they know who she is and has previously agreed to it.'

'What if she hasn't?' asked Crosby.

'I think,' frowned York, 'the applicant can be given some sort of info – whether the birth mother's in good health . . .'

'But not good wealth, I hope,' said Detective Inspector Sloan, policeman first and last and all the time.

'News of general well-being I think is as far as it goes,' said York. 'But not her name or her whereabouts. They can pass on some relevant information, though, such as details about a hereditary disease or an inheritance.'

'Circumstances alter cases,' observed Sloan dryly.

'Some you win, some you lose,' said Crosby.

'But it doesn't work the other way round, does it?' asked Sloan, rapidly reaching a conclusion. 'Not vice versa?'

'The birth mother can ask but the child doesn't have to respond,' said the Coroner's Officer. 'If the child doesn't want it, there's no way round. All she can do then is deposit her name and address with the adoption people, leaving the initiative to make contact entirely with the son or daughter.'

'Fair's fair,' said Crosby.

'And that's only after they've been given professional assistance and counselling,' said York, adding wisely, 'They could be opening a can of worms all round.'

'If you've made your bed, you've got to lie on it,' said Crosby with all the assurance of the young and inexperienced.

Detective Inspector Sloan asked the Coroner's Officer

what the rector had had to say about the contents of the letter, if anything.

'Oh, yes, he said something all right,' replied York promptly. 'It was a quotation. He sounded very sad and said "Thy Mother's son! Like enough, and thy Father's shadow". He told me it was from something Shakespeare wrote but I wouldn't know about that myself.'

'If we look smart about it, Crosby,' said Detective Inspector Sloan, taking a swift look at his watch, 'we could interview Bob Steele before we go back to the crime scene.' Clearing away the undergrowth as you go along was one of the superintendent's great maxims. 'It'll give Charlie Marsden time to give the place a going-over.'

Nothing loth, Crosby turned the police car in the direction of the Berebury Garden Centre.

'We should probably have done it before,' said Sloan. 'There's something going on there but I don't know what. Norman Potts or Russ Aqueel might have known more about it than we do and taken action accordingly.'

'Or Jack Haines might have done,' said Crosby. The Berebury Garden Centre was on the outskirts of the market town and there were no open roads on the way, just winding streets with Anglo-Saxon origins. He negotiated these with virtuous attention to all the road signage. It was only when Sloan spotted a Traffic patrol car hidden up behind a school that he realised why.

Bob Steele received the two detectives civilly and without any apparent anxiety. 'Jack Haines? But I've already told you I know him. What's up now?'

'We are making enquiries into another matter that's cropped up.'

'Another matter . . .' The man caught sight of Sloan's face and said, 'I see, and you aren't going to tell me what it is. That right?'

'If you would just answer our questions, sir, it would be very helpful.'

'I'm sure,' said the other man roughly. 'Go ahead.'

'Russ Aqueel, the foreman at Jack Haines' nursery, would appear to be a frequent visitor here.'

Bob Steele visibly relaxed. 'That's no secret. If I run out of plants I buy them from old Jack. If Jack wants anything from me I do the same and Russ brings them over. Custom of the trade. We all help each other.'

If Bob Steele heard the little snort that escaped Crosby at this he gave no sign of having done so.

'I pay him on the nail, Inspector,' went on Steele, 'if that's what's worrying you. Ask that secretary of his over there – Mandy somebody. She wouldn't let anyone get away without.' He sniffed. 'Proper watchdog, she is.'

'And when exactly,' asked Sloan, 'did you last see Jack himself?'

Steele's eyes narrowed. 'Ah, so this is what this is all about. Well, if you must know I spotted his car outside here pretty late last night. As you're detectives I expect you'll have worked out that I live on the premises.'

'We were not unaware of the fact, sir,' said Sloan, whose mother had taught him that politeness could be as sharp-edged a weapon as any knife. 'What was Jack Haines doing?'

'Besides sitting in his car,' put in Crosby.

'Waiting for Russ Aqueel to come out of my house I expect.'

'And what was Russ Aqueel doing in there?' asked Sloan patiently.

Bob Steele spread out his hands in a gesture that included two thumbs-up. 'Promising me he was going to hand in his notice to Jack Haines next Friday and agreeing to come to work for me instead. If you must know we were having a drink on it. Or three,' he added after a moment's thought. 'Russ can put them away, all right.'

'Thus,' said Sloan regretfully, reporting back to Superintendent Leeyes when he'd checked everything out, 'apparently giving all three of them an alibi for Norman Potts' death last night.'

'That's if the pathologist's got the estimated time of death right,' said Leeyes, a last ditch man by nature.

'There's one thing the doctors have got right, sir,' said Sloan, a sheet of paper still in his hand. 'Benedict Feakins' blood group has been confirmed by the haematologist. It matches the specimen on the window at Canonry Cottage. We'll be charging him with breaking and entering.'

Detective Inspector Sloan, head of the Criminal Investigation Department of 'F' Division, was at a loss to explain why he was not gripped by this information.

'And they're in the process of seeing if they can confirm his DNA from some hair they collected from the scene,' he added, equally unexcited by this.

As Anthony Berra's car disappeared down the road from Capstan Purlieu Plants nursery, Marilyn Potts took a deep breath and announced to her friend that she was going over to Pelling to see Jack Haines. 'I want to talk to him, Anna.'

'He may not want to talk to you,' responded Anna Sutherland trenchantly. 'He never did. Well, at least not since you married Norman and then started your matrimonial causes action or whatever it is they call it these days.'

'Divorce proceedings,' she said pithily, adding, 'but this is different.'

'Of course,' suggested Anna thoughtfully, 'we mustn't forget that Jack may know more than we do.'

'And what exactly is that supposed to mean?' demanded Marilyn.

'Those orchids you used last night came from his place the other day.'

'But, Anna, the police didn't say anything about where the ones they had had come from.'

'Cagey, weren't they?' said her friend pleasantly.

'You don't think that Jack had anything to do with Norman's death, do you? Not Jack, surely.'

Anna shook her head. 'Frankly, I wouldn't have thought he was up to anything as strenuous as killing Norman, not with his figure. Too much tummy.'

Marilyn stared at her. 'Who said anything about Norman being killed? The police only said that he had been found dead.'

The other woman shrugged her shoulders. 'Stands to reason, doesn't it? Me, I couldn't see Norman killing himself. Not no way. He was a man with an eye for the main chance if anyone was.'

'He certainly looked after number one first,' admitted Marilyn sadly. 'Even after we were married.'

'Well, all I can say is that if someone has killed him then he didn't look after himself well enough, number one or not.' She stood up. 'Now I must get on with some potting up. Besides, I've got a phone call to make. I've got a lot to do today.'

Jack Haines barely looked up when Marilyn Potts came into his office. 'Back again, Marilyn.'

'Like the proverbial bad penny, I keep turning up.' Uninvited, she pulled a chair up and sank into it.

'What is it this time?' he asked.

'Call it curiosity.'

'Dangerous thing, curiosity,' said Haines.

Mandy Lamb slid a couple of mugs of coffee before them and remarked, 'It killed the cat too. Sugar?'

'What's to do with Enid's orchids, Jack, and come to that, what's to do with Enid?' Marilyn Potts waved away the sugar. 'There's been no sign of her for weeks. She should have been back before now.'

'Search me. I don't know that either.'

'Nobody tells him anything,' said Mandy Lamb ironically.

'Look here, Marilyn,' said Jack Haines, stirred by this, 'we don't know that there is anything to tell.'

'Oh, yes, we do,' she said with unusual firmness.

'Speak for yourself, my girl.'

Marilyn Potts took a deep breath. 'Two of Enid's orchids were taken from our shed last night after we got back from my talk and they've been found by the police somewhere but they won't say where. They had a photograph of them.'

'Two Dracula,' said Haines. 'The police have been here too.'

'Checking,' contributed Mandy Lamb from the sidelines, 'like they do.'

Marilyn Potts sighed. 'I don't know what's going on, Jack, but I know I don't like it.'

'Me neither,' he said, 'but I can't think what either of us can do about it.'

Marilyn Potts sat in her chair, twisting her hands together. 'Why should it be two Dracula that were taken?'

Mandy Lamb leant over the table that the other two were sitting at and remarked that Count Dracula was a vampire. 'Vlad the Impaler, they called him.'

Jack Haines shrugged his shoulders. 'For heaven's sake, Mandy, it's only the name of an orchid – that's all.'

'A bloodsucker,' the secretary persisted. 'Perhaps Norman Potts was a blackmailer and someone was trying to tell you something about him.'

'Two orchids . . .' said Marilyn, frowning suddenly.

Jack Haines stirred irritably. 'For God's sake, Marilyn, stop going on about them.'

She pushed her chair back and got to her feet, struggling to wrest her mobile phone from her pocket. 'I must ring Anna. It's important. Very important.'

CHAPTER TWENTY-FOUR

Although the photographers had long left Norman Potts' house in downtown Berebury, Charlie Marsden and his team of Scenes of Crime experts were still examining the place when the two policemen arrived back there.

'We've done a preliminary search, Inspector,' said Charlie Marsden as the two detectives stepped inside the door. 'Not a lot of real interest,' he jerked a finger in the direction of the sideboard, 'unless you count those floral offerings over there.'

'We're looking for a true artist in crime here, Charlie, remember.' It was something that Sloan was only just beginning properly to appreciate himself. The choice seemed wide enough. He cast his mind back to Anna Sutherland, effortlessly humping heavy loads about at their nursery. She could have hauled the body of an unconscious Norman Potts over a beam easily enough –

and she hadn't liked his treatment of Marilyn, her friend. Benedict Feakins, bad back or not, was young and had the strength. So also did Russ Aqueel, although where he came into the equation was what the mathematicians called an unknown factor. Bob Steele of the Berebury Garden Centre, who had insisted he didn't know Enid Osgathorp, would certainly have known Norman Potts and Norman Potts might have had some legal leverage on Jack Haines' business through his late mother's estate, thus thwarting Bob Steele's ambitions. It was something he would have to look into.

'We've checked the plant pots with the orchids in, Inspector.' Charlie Marsden interrupted Sloan's thoughts.

'And?'

'No joy. Handled with gloves on. By the way, you might like to know that we got some DNA off a bit of a toothbrush that wasn't completely burnt on that chap Feakins' bonfire over at Pelling. The report's on its way.'

'Bully for you,' responded Sloan absently.

Marsden sniffed. 'Can't imagine why he didn't want us to find it.'

'Neither can I, Charlie, but that'll have to wait.' Sloan put the information at the back of his mind for the time being. It wasn't by any means the only thing that he couldn't explain. What he really wanted to know was where those dead orchids came in – well, not only the orchids – all the plants that had been destroyed by frost. As a keen gardener, he, Christopher Dennis Sloan, could blame Jack Frost for a lot; as a policeman, he, Detective Inspector C.D. Sloan, still couldn't see where a low temperature in March came into the picture. What he could see, though, was that there was undoubtedly a scheme of things in the background. And it was this scheme that was so puzzling.

It was easy to see who had lost out in it, not least Norman Potts, but there didn't seem to be an obvious answer to the opposite question beloved by detectives of 'Who benefits?'

'What's that, Charlie?' he asked, suddenly conscious that the Scenes of Crime Officer had gone on speaking to him.

'Bit bizarre in a place like this, if you ask me, those orchids,' said Marsden. He waved an arm in a disparaging gesture at an unlovely and uncared for domestic interior.

'Lacks a woman's touch,' agreed Sloan in an unconscious tribute to his wife, Margaret, as he mentally compared his own early bachelor surroundings with his present home comforts.

Charlie Marsden grinned. 'No signs of a lady here at all. First thing we checked. No signs of much else either really.'

'Cupboard bare?' suggested Crosby.

'The deceased doesn't seem to have gone in for eating much at all,' said the Scenes of Crime Officer. 'There's the odd tin of baked beans and half a loaf but that's about it.'

'"A Little Bit of Bread and No Cheese",' chanted Crosby.

The other two men stared at him.

'Birdsong,' stammered the constable, abashed. 'The yellowhammer. We did it at school.'

'The only sort of birdsong that I know about,' said Charlie Marsden heavily, 'is called Twitter.'

Detective Inspector Sloan ignored them both while he

gave some thought to the possibility of Norman Potts' meagre lifestyle being the end result of blackmail rather than alcohol or slow horses. This man too must at some stage in his life have been – when he had lived there with his mother – on the medical list of the late Doctor Heddon of Pelling and thus any weakness that he might have had surely been known to Enid Osgathorp. Although Doctor Dabbe hadn't mentioned discovering any unmentionable disease at the man's post-mortem, he would have to check back with the pathologist. Sloan sighed. He should have thought of that before but at this moment he felt like a juggler struggling to keep one ball too many in the air.

And therefore risking dropping the lot.

Was the near-squalor of these tawdry surroundings really down to the demon drink, a penchant for slow horses, or had Norman Potts too been subjected to blackmail? Sloan turned to Charlie Marsden. 'Any money in the house?'

'Not a lot,' said the worthy. 'The odd note in a teapot, that's all.'

'All of a pattern,' murmured Sloan, although it was another pattern he was trying to visualise – one that took in a still unexplained entry into Canonry Cottage with a key, a unloved missing person, the blackmailing of more than one poor soul, the probable suicide of one of them, the odd, naive behaviour of a maker of bonfires, inexplicable goings-on in the horticultural trade and, cast into the mixture for good measure, the destruction of hundreds of infant orchids.

To say nothing of the murder here of a man whom it appeared nobody liked much either. As soon as Norman

Potts' face could be made recognisable he would get on with having the CCTV records scanned for him on the day Enid Osgathorp was last seen in Berebury.

If she had been, that is. That was something else that had to be considered too.

The river, that swift carrier of bodies down to the sea, wasn't very far from the house where they were now. A body could have easily been slipped out unnoticed into the estuary on a dark night on the ebb of a spring tide, unnoticed by anyone – anyone that is except possibly Norman Potts. A watery burial would at least explain the absence of a body – and if he had observed it, perhaps the subsequent death of Norman Potts. That was if he hadn't carried it out himself. Sloan didn't know.

Not yet.

And where on earth did all those orchids come in – well, not only the orchids – all the plants that had been destroyed by frost? At least some of the plants for Anthony Berra's clients, the Lingards, were already in the way of being replaced, well not so much replaced as substitutes found. Idly he wondered why the substitutes meant for the Lingards' garden at Pelling Grange that he had seen in Jack Haines' office had been so different from the ones he'd been told had been destroyed by frost. Sloan stiffened as he realised that they'd changed from being lime-hating plants to lime-lovers . . . His pulse quickened: all detectives had been well schooled in one of the important functions of lime.

Charlie Marsden started to draw his attention to something else he'd found in the house but Sloan wasn't listening. Something that the superintendent had said had swum into his mind, something about the police not being able to dig up half Calleshire. He'd agreed that they couldn't, but it came to him that there was someone who could dig up at least some of the county without arousing suspicion.

'Not now, Charlie,' he said. He was trying to remember something that Crosby had said too. What had it been? Something about making your bed and lying on it – that was it. He breathed out very slowly, a picture of great villainy suddenly becoming very clear to him.

Before he could even begin to think this through and take action, the telephone in his pocket started to pulsate against his thigh. It was Superintendent Leeyes. 'That you, Sloan?' he barked. 'I'm told there's a woman called Marilyn Potts who's been on the line screaming that we should get over to Capstan Purlieu Plants urgently. She says she can't reach her friend on her mobile and she's frightened for her. I don't see why myself,' he harrumphed, 'that that constitutes a police emergency.'

'I do, sir,' said Sloan grimly. 'Now.' He cut the superintendent off without ceremony and turned. 'Come along, Crosby. We need our time.'

As it was the two policemen got out to Capstan Purlieu Plants only just in time to stop Anthony Berra from strangling Anna Sutherland.

CHAPTER TWENTY-FIVE

'I guessed it had to be Anthony,' said Anna Sutherland, anger and shock fighting for supremacy in her voice, leaving it reduced to a quaver. She was still shaking slightly. 'It was when he obviously knew that it was two orchids that were missing that I thought it must be him. It had to be. You see, we hadn't told him how many and I suddenly remembered that.' The woman had the grace to look a bit sheepish. 'I do know I shouldn't have rung him but I did.'

'No, you shouldn't,' exploded Marilyn Potts, who had just arrived hotfoot from Pelling. 'He might have killed you too.'

'He very nearly did,' said her friend hoarsely, fingering her bruised throat. She looked awkwardly at Sloan and said, 'I should be thanking you.'

'You'll have to unfriend him now,' put in Detective Constable Crosby, a recent convert to online connections.

Marilyn Potts had just realised something else. She looked enquiringly at Sloan and said, 'Are you saying Anthony killed poor Norman, then?'

For one moment it looked as if Anna Sutherland was going to bridle at the mention of 'poor Norman' but then she must have thought better of it because she sank back in her chair instead and held her peace.

'We think he must have done,' said Sloan, although Crosby had so far devoted all his energies to arresting Anthony Berra on a charge of the attempted murder of Anna Sutherland and hadn't had time to think of anything else at all. The constable had warned the handcuffed man that further charges might be preferred but he only got a cough in response.

'Why?' demanded Marilyn. 'Why on earth Norman, I mean? He hadn't done anything wrong, had he?'

Anna Sutherland had now recovered sufficiently to snort at this.

'Not that we know of,' said Sloan cautiously.

Anna Sutherland suddenly looked up and gave Sloan a very intelligent glance indeed. 'And what,' she said in a voice still croaky, 'about Enid Osgathorp?'

'We think we now know exactly where to look for her,' he temporised before turning away. 'Come along, Crosby, we're going there next.'

'And I need a stiff drink,' announced Anna Sutherland. 'Whatever you say, Marilyn, I am going back to the King's Arms at Staple St James,' here she cast a meaningful look in the direction of her friend and went on, 'where I am not unknown.'

*   *   *

Charmian Lingard, who until now had thought her social skills equal to any occasion, discovered for the first time in her sheltered life that they weren't. 'You want to dig up the Mediterranean garden?' she echoed as a squad of police officers in workmen's overalls turned up on her doorstep. 'Anthony won't like it.'

'And remove the statue,' supplemented Sloan.

'But it's all planted up,' she protested, 'in time for the flowers to be ready for the garden party.'

Oswald Lingard took in the scenario more quickly and limped forward and took his wife's arm. 'I think you'd better come indoors, my dear,' he said, leading her away.

Detective Inspector Sloan thought he heard her still protesting about Anthony's plants as she left the garden but his mind was elsewhere. 'Start here,' he ordered the men with spades. 'And go carefully.'

Their leader waved at the statue of the goddess Flora presiding over the long border. 'What do you want doing with the lady, sir?'

'That lady I want taking away. The other one I want finding,' said Detective Inspector Sloan. 'Carefully. Oh, I'll be wanting some soil samples too, although I think I know what you'll find. A lot of lime.'

CHAPTER TWENTY-SIX

Mary Feakins had helped her husband out of their car and back into the kitchen at The Hollies, settling him back in what he insisted was the only chair in the house that he found comfortable. Then she went upstairs to the airing cupboard and retrieved the photograph of her father-in-law. She set it down on the kitchen table in front of her husband and said in a tone that brooked no refusal, 'Tell me why this photograph doesn't matter and all your father's other belongings did.'

Benedict Feakins passed a hand in front of his face as if he was clearing away something from his mind. 'You won't understand.'

'Try me.'

'It's that awful woman.' He struggled to speak her name. 'Miss Osgathorp.'

'What about her?'

'She said I wasn't who I thought I was.'

'Don't be silly. You're Benedict Feakins.'

'You don't understand, Mary,' he said earnestly. 'She said I wasn't.'

'But she didn't know you. She can't have done. We've only just come to live in Pelling and she'd never seen you before.'

'She knew Dad.'

Mary Feakins frowned. 'Go on.'

'She said she knew from his medical record that Dad was impotent. She said Dad had had mumps when he was a lad and that he was unable to have children because of that. She told me that therefore he couldn't possibly have had me.'

Mary Feakins bounced back, light dawning. 'And I suppose she wanted some money to keep quiet about it?'

'I had such a lot to lose,' he said dejectedly. 'This house, you perhaps . . .'

That roused her. 'Me?' she said on a rising note of indignation. 'What about that bit in the marriage service about for better or worse, or weren't you listening at the time?'

'I didn't hear any of it,' he confessed simply. 'I was looking at you.'

'Oh, Benedict, you're hopeless.' She was struck by something else. 'So this is why we're so skint and can't pay the bills. You've been giving her money.'

He stared at the floor. 'She was quite remorseless.'

'And I suppose it never occurred to you to go to the police? Blackmail's a serious crime, you know.'

He hung his head. 'I just wanted us to be happy here.

If I wasn't Dad's son, then I had no claim on this place. Besides . . .'

'Besides what?'

'There's young Benedict . . .'

'Benedict the Third,' she reminded him meaningfully.

'I didn't want him to grow up not knowing who he was either.'

Mary Feakins sighed. 'And I suppose it never occurred to you to demand some proof from the woman?'

He looked really uncomfortable at that. 'No, but I did try to find it.'

'So you did break into her cottage, then?'

Shamefaced, he confessed to this. 'I wasn't a very good burglar and I couldn't find anything there anyway.'

She shook her head. 'You took all this nonsense from someone you ought to have known you couldn't trust? And at face value?'

He wouldn't meet her eye. 'She was very convincing. Well, plausible, anyway. How was I to know whether it was true or false?'

Mary Feakins sat up, another thought crowding into her mind. 'You realise that would have meant your mother had been playing around before you were born?'

'Yes,' he said, his despair evident. 'Mind you, she was very beautiful when she was young. I did check that I hadn't been adopted, though. And I hadn't,' he added.

'So,' she deduced logically, 'you set about systematically destroying everything that might have had your father's DNA on it so that whatever it was that this woman was alleging couldn't be proved. Hence the bonfire.'

'That's right.'

Mary Feakins abruptly got to her feet and went upstairs again. Her husband could hear her moving about in their bedroom above. She came downstairs carrying a mirror. Placing it on the table she commanded him to turn his head to the left.

'Why?'

'Do it,' she said in a tone he hadn't heard her use to him before.

Obediently, he moved his head as instructed. As he did so she brought the photograph of his father alongside the mirror. She smiled at his expression. 'You silly fool, Benedict, you're too gullible for words but I love you. Where else do you think you got that nose?'

'I love you too,' he said humbly. 'I should have told you all this before.'

'So you should,' she said briskly, 'and now the woman has gone missing. No wonder the police are suspicious. Anyone would have been.'

'I don't care what happens to her as long as she stays away.'

'But the police care,' she said, exasperated. 'They have to. It's what they're for. Hasn't it dawned on you that that's why they've been after you? After all, they must know that you've been behaving pretty suspiciously.'

He was almost indignant. 'I didn't kill her, Mary.'

'Then,' she said, 'I suggest you ring that detective inspector and tell him what you have been doing and why.'

He hesitated. 'Are you sure?'

'If you don't,' she said implacably, conscious of having crossed yet another river in the marriage process, 'I will. Here's the phone.'

Minutes later he put it down and said to her, 'They say that Detective Inspector Sloan is very busy just now. They promised he'd get back to me.'

Detective Inspector Sloan was indeed very busy. He was back at the police station in Berebury, dictating to Detective Constable Crosby the first of the charges to be preferred against Anthony Berra. 'The assault on Anna Sutherland for starters,' he said, 'but warn him that further charges are to be preferred in due course.'

'Like killing the Osgathorp woman?'

'Just like that, Crosby. And Norman Potts too. Those Dracula orchids were a nice touch to divert blackmail – otherwise blood-sucking – in Potts' direction and away from the major blackmailer. A very clever move.'

Mention of blood stirred Crosby. 'You're quite sure, sir, aren't you, that he's not infectious?'

Anthony Berra had not gone quietly but had proved no match for two trained police officers.

'Quite sure, Crosby. His doctor assures me that although Berra is HIV Positive you are not at risk. Berra's marriage would have been, though,' Sloan added, 'if his future wife or her family had ever found out about his having AIDS.'

'That woman'd got him over a barrel, hadn't she, sir?'

'I'm afraid so and he knew it. Now, Crosby, what I want you to do next is to search the accused's house for the key to Canonry Cottage. I think you'll find it there while I've got to report to Superintendent Leeyes.'

'No doubt about the identification, then?' asked Leeyes when Sloan arrived.

'None, sir. The body is that of the missing person, Enid Maude Osgathorp, all right. Her luggage was buried in the flower bed there with her and her handbag too. Her name's on both of them.' While the woman's luggage and handbag had withstood three weeks under the soil quite well, her body was not a pretty sight, the insect world being no respecter of persons – especially dead ones.

Leeyes grunted.

'Berra made the commonest of mistakes and buried her in quicklime,' carried on Sloan. 'Murderers will do it.'

'The amateurs, anyway,' said Leeyes grandly. 'They read too much crime fiction.'

Sloan agreed. 'They all think that it destroys bodies. And slaked lime's even worse,' he added. 'It's only got to rain . . .'

'So you reckon she never got as far as Berebury that day?' said Leeyes.

Sloan had been thinking about this. 'I think Berra gives her a lift – he almost certainly knew her holiday plans . . .'

'That fool of a bonfire boy did,' interjected Leeyes, 'so I expect Berra did too.'

'Feakins was talking his way into being a prime suspect,' admitted Sloan, 'but he's off the hook now.' He took a deep breath and went back to talking about Anthony Berra. 'So he picks her up at the bus stop, quietens her with a few doses of control spray if she gets difficult while he drives her to the Grange. The Lingards are in Italy and so he's been able to prepare the ground in the long border in his own time . . .'

'If you mean dig a hole, Sloan, say so.'

'Yes, sir. He kills her there . . .'

'Weapon?'

'Edge of a spade, probably. Doctor Dabbe is nearly sure but he won't commit himself until he's had a really good look at the post-mortem.'

'Par for the course,' said Leeyes, a weekend golfer. 'He never will commit himself if he doesn't have to and leopards don't change their spots.'

Sloan ploughed on. 'If she screams the peacocks there'll get all the blame. He covers the body with quicklime and then soil and hightails it over to Berebury as quickly as he can.'

The superintendent flipped over an earlier report. 'He says here that he visited a few charity shops there first . . .'

'Which don't have automated timed tills,' Sloan reminded him. 'So we couldn't check on his timing until he got to the bank and cashed a cheque. Then he ends up having lunch at the Bellingham Hotel. We did check on that.'

'Busy, busy,' said Leeyes.

'That's right, sir, but he's still got a lot to do. He doesn't dare plant any of the lime-hating plants he'd got on order from Jack Haines because they'll die if he does and that wouldn't do. Besides, the ground would have needed time to settle and he needs to be able to smooth it out and delay the planting without anyone commenting. Well, not anyone – Mrs Charmian Lingard, to be precise.'

'Ah,' exclaimed Superintendent Leeyes, light dawning, 'so he breaks in and causes mayhem at Haines' nursery. Clever.'

'Exactly so, sir. By killing all the orchids there and all those over at Capstan Purlieu as well, he muddies the waters nicely. Everyone thinks the damage is all to do with the orchids – not what's in the other greenhouse.'

'You can get away with a lot as collateral damage,' pronounced Leeyes, sometime soldier.

'He loses all the plants he doesn't want and at the same time gets a chance to order new . . .'

'And different ones,' concluded Leeyes smartly.

'Precisely so, sir. Plants that do well in lime.'

'So where does Norman Potts come in?'

'I reckon,' said Sloan, 'that he caught sight of Berra driving into Berebury without a passenger in his vehicle. Don't forget that they would have known each other from Haines' nursery and Potts was living in Berebury. It was the only real risk Berra took but we're a long way from Pelling here and the chances were pretty slim that he would have been seen by anyone who knew him before he got to the railway station. I expect he actually stopped outside that sandwich shop for a moment or two to add a little local colour to his story.'

'Verisimilitude is the word you want,' declared Leeyes.

'Thank you, sir,' said Sloan humbly. 'I think it was just bad luck for both of them – Berra and Potts – that Potts spotted him. I daresay the silly fellow tried a little blackmail on his own account.'

'Dicing with death if you ask me,' said Leeyes. 'The biter bit.'

'Very unwise, I'd say.'

'It's what we call evidence of system, Sloan,' said the superintendent loftily. 'Especially when you've got means, motive and opportunity like Berra had.'

'A dangerous thing to do, anyway,' said Sloan. As

far as he was concerned, if there was evidence of system anywhere it had been in the behaviour of Enid Maude Osgathorp. He wondered how many other people in Pelling there were who would sleep more soundly tonight knowing that a blackmailer had literally gone to ground.

For ever.

They would never know.

Not now.

'Sorry, sir, I didn't quite catch that.' He realised that the superintendent had been speaking to him.

Leeyes sounded tetchy. 'I said you haven't forgotten your annual assessment and Personal Development Discussion on Friday morning, have you, Sloan?'